THE MOVEMENT OF SHOWING

SUNY series in Contemporary French Thought

David Pettigrew and François Raffoul, editors

THE MOVEMENT OF SHOWING

*Indirect Method, Critique, and Responsibility
in Derrida, Hegel, and Heidegger*

JOHAN DE JONG

Published by State University of New York Press, Albany

© 2020 State University of New York

All rights reserved

No part of this book may be used or reproduced in any manner whatsoever without written permission. No part of this book may be stored in a retrieval system or transmitted in any form or by any means including electronic, electrostatic, magnetic tape, mechanical, photocopying, recording, or otherwise without the prior permission in writing of the publisher.

For information, contact State University of New York Press, Albany, NY
www.sunypress.edu

Library of Congress Cataloging-in-Publication Data

Names: Jong, Johan de, 1982– author.
Title: The movement of showing : indirect method, critique, and
  responsibility in Derrida, Hegel, and Heidegger / Johan de Jong.
Description: Albany : State University of New York Press, [2019] | Series:
  SUNY series in contemporary French thought | Includes bibliographical
  references and index.
Identifiers: LCCN 2018048804 | ISBN 9781438476094 (hardcover) |
  ISBN 9781438476087 (pbk.) | ISBN 9781438476100 (ebook) Subjects: LCSH:
Methodology. | Continental philosophy. | Thought and thinking. |
  Derrida, Jacques. | Hegel, Georg Wilhelm Friedrich, 1770–1831. | Heidegger,
  Martin, 1889–1976.
Classification: LCC BD241 .J66 2019 | DDC 101—dc23
LC record available at https://lccn.loc.gov/2018048804

10 9 8 7 6 5 4 3 2 1

Foor mim

Without discrete parody, without writing strategy, without difference or spreading of pens/feathers [*écart de plumes*], without style, therefore, the grand one, the reversal would amount to the same in the noisy declaration of the antithesis. Hence the heterogeneity of the text.

—Jacques Derrida (*Spurs: Nietzsche's Styles*)

The sole interest of reason is to sublate such rigidified antitheses.

—Georg Wilhelm Friedrich Hegel (*The Difference between Fichte's and Schelling's System of Philosophy*)

The point is not to listen to a series of propositions, but rather to follow the movement of showing.

—Martin Heidegger ("Time and Being")

CONTENTS

Acknowledgments   xi

Abbreviations   xiii

Introduction   xix

PART I
SOURCES OF DERRIDA'S INDIRECTNESS: LANGUAGE, METAPHYSICS, CRITIQUE

Chapter 1
Why There Can Be No Derridean Theory of Language   3
    "This Incompetence of Science . . ." *Of Grammatology*'s
       Opening Complication   4
    Language: The "Effacement of All its Limits"   11
    What a Derridean "Theory" Would "Oppose": The
       "Traditional Determination" of Writing   14
    What a Derridean "Theory" Would "Oppose" to the
       Traditional Determination: What Is "Generalized" Writing?   19
    Why "Retain the Old Name"? Toward "Acts of Writing"
    Conclusion   24

Chapter 2
The Inextricability of Metaphysics   31
    The "Structural Figure": Demarcation, Opposition, Hierarchy,
       Presence   33

The "Historical Totality": Epoch, History, the Future, and
  Beyond   41
Overcoming Philosophy's Self-Overcoming   45
Conclusion   48

Chapter 3
The Question of Justification and the Law of Resemblance:
Empiricism—Skepticism—Critique   51
  Empiricism: Deconstruction and Method   52
  Skepticism: Deconstruction and Self-Contradiction   62
  Critique: Deconstruction and Vulnerability   71
  Conclusion   80

PART II
MOVEMENT AND OPPOSITION: FROM HEGEL TO DERRIDA

Chapter 4
Hegel's Movement of the Concept and the Limits of the
Understanding   85
  The Origins of Hegelian "Movement" and the Critique of
    the Understanding   87
  What Exceeds Reflection Is Its Own Movement   92
  The Affirmation of Limits in Hegel's Response to Kant   97
  The *Difference* Essay and the Need for/of Philosophy   100
  Hegel's Early Problem of Philosophical Exposition: Skepticism
    and the Necessity of Self-Contradiction   104
  The Problem of Speculative Exposition in the *Phenomenology
    of Spirit*   108
  The Speculative Proposition   115
  Conclusion   119

Chapter 5
Derrida's "Textual Maneuvers": Exceeding the Opposition to
Hegelianism *Contributions*   123
  Situating Hegel in Derrida's Development   125
  "Tympan": The Limits of Philosophy and the Need to
    Write Otherwise   127
  "Hors Livre" and the Multitude of Derrida's Hegels   139
  Conclusion   150

PART III
HEIDEGGER:
THE PRESERVATION OF CONCEALMENT

Chapter 6
The Transition to Transitional Thinking: From *Being and Time* to the *Contributions* — 155
  The Movement of Showing of Itself by Itself: the Circularity of *Being and Time* — 158
  The Complication of "Being-in" and the Opening of *Being and Time* — 166
  Introduction to the "Transitional Thinking" of the *Contributions to Philosophy (Of the Event)* — 171
  The "Cessation of all Overcoming" — 176
  What Turns? From *Being and Time* to the *Contributions* — 180
  Conclusion — 183

Chapter 7
Reticence and Exposition: Heidegger's *Contributions to Philosophy (Of the Event)* — 185
  Style and Systematicity: The Conjuncture of the *Contributions* — 185
  The *Contributions*' "Reflection" on its Own Language: *Denkerisches Sagen* and the Limits of Representation — 191
  Do the *Contributions* Preserve or Overcome the Failure to Say Beyng? — 195
  Bearing Silence, Withdrawal, and Λήθη in the *Parmenides*-Lectures — 198
  Reticence and Sheltering in "On the Essence of Truth" — 202
  The Philosophical Necessity to be Unassertive: *Stimmung* and its Distinction from *Erlebnis* — 208
  Conclusion — 216

PART IV
OF DERRIDA'S HEIDEGGERS:
STYLE, AFFIRMATION, RESPONSIBILITY

Chapter 8
The Question of Style: Heidegger, Nietzsche and the Heterogeneity of the Text — 221

Nietzsche's "Feminine 'Operation'" 222
Does Heidegger Reduce the Plurality of Nietzsche's Styles? 226
Derrida's Two Heideggers: *Ereignis* Outside the Hermeneutic Circle 231
Perhaps: "I Have Forgotten My Umbrella" 235
Conclusion 240

Chapter 9
Strategy and Responsibility: Derrida, Heidegger, and the Ethics of Complicity 241
Of Spirit and the Unavoidable 243
Irreducible Complicity and the Desire for Non-Contamination 248
Unprecedented Responsibilities and Affirmation "Before" the Question 253
The Undeconstructible and the Vulnerability of Justice 257
Conclusion 261

Afterword
Philosophical Indirections 263
Indirectness and the Question of Critique 265
Necessity and Motivation: Performativity and Responsibility 267
The Philosophical Tradition 269

Notes 275

Bibliography 315

Index 331

ACKNOWLEDGMENTS

This book is a thoroughly rewritten version of a dissertation that I started working on in 2009. Thanks are due to everyone at the Department of Philosophy of the University of Amsterdam who helped make that project possible. I thank Ruth Sonderegger and Josef Früchtl, without whose efforts on my behalf, and faith in my abilities, this project would not have seen the light of day. I especially thank Kees Jan Brons for many conversations and profound insights. Without his availability and guidance, this text could not have been written. I am grateful to the members of my doctoral committee (Rudi te Velde, Victor Kal, and especially Gert-Jan van der Heiden and Aukje van Rooden) for their critical comments and stimulating conversations. I thank the ASCA for believing in my project and for providing me with the means to carry it out.

My stay in the United States in 2013 would have been impossible without the financial support of the Prins Bernhard Cultuurfonds. I thank David Wood for the extraordinary generosity with which he welcomed me to Nashville and for providing such an intellectually stimulating environment. I am grateful to the participants in the Heidegger seminar at Vanderbilt for our discussions and their friendship, and want to mention in particular Peter Kline, Jessica Polish, Eric Ritter, and Garrett Bredeson for making my stay worthwhile. I have also benefited greatly from many discussions with participants and faculty at three editions of the Collegium Phaenomenologicum in Città di Castello.

The dissertation could not have been reworked into this book without the support of my colleagues at the Departments of Philosophy and of Liberal Arts and Sciences at Utrecht University. I especially wish to thank Paul Ziche and Iris van der Tuin. At SUNY Press, I thank Andrew Kenyon and Chelsea Miller for their patience and assistance, François

Raffoul for his encouragement to submit the manuscript, and two anonymous reviewers for valuable advice that greatly helped improve the text.

Thank you to Herman Adèr, Harry Büller, Fred Thoolen, and Tineke van Roozendaal for so generously providing what were essentially lavish versions of the sine qua non that is the writer's cabin (and I thank David for providing an actual one). I am grateful to many others for their assistance, critical comments, inspiring discussion, encouragement, or friendship, including Niels Büller, Wout Cornelissen, Robert Goené, Sara Murawski, Pieter Pekelharing, Jasper Renema, Maurits Romijn, Matthé Scholten, Johannes-Georg Schülein, Joris Spigt, Michal van Zelm, and, in remembrance, Olle Kruyt.

Finally, I thank Janna, for everything, and I thank my parents, Dirk and Hiltje, for their unconditional support. I am deeply saddened that my biggest fan was not given the time to witness the completion of this book. I cherish, as an enduring motivation, the memory of her unwavering love and pride.

ABBREVIATIONS

Only the most frequently cited works have been abbreviated and are listed here. A full overview is found in the bibliography. If in the text two page numbers are given, separated by a slash (e.g., 12/34), the first always refers to the German or French original and the second to the English translation.

FREQUENTLY CITED WORKS BY JACQUES DERRIDA

D   *Dissemination.* Translated by Barbara Johnson. London and New York: Continuum, 2004. Translation of *La dissémination.* Paris: Seuil, 1972.

"E"   "Envoi." In *Psyche: Inventions of the Other, Volume I,* edited by Peggy Kamuf and Elizabeth G. Rottenberg, 94–128. Stanford: Stanford University Press, 2007.

"EW"   "'Eating Well,' or the Calculation of the Subject." In *Points . . . , Interviews, 1974–1994,* translated by Peggy Kamuf et al., edited by Elisabeth Weber, 255–87. Stanford: Stanford University Press, 1995.

"FL"   "Force of Law: The 'Mystical Foundation of Authority.'" In *Acts of Religion,* edited by Gil Anidjar, 228–98. London and New York: Routledge, 2002.

G   *Of Grammatology.* Translated by Gayatri Chakravorty Spivak. 2nd ed. Baltimore: Johns Hopkins University Press, 1997. Translation of *De la grammatologie.* Paris: Minuit, 1967.

LI	*Limited Inc.* Translated by Samuel Weber and Jeffrey Mehlman, edited by Gerald Graff. Evanston: Northwestern University Press, 1988.
MP	*Margins of Philosophy.* Translated by Alan Bass. Chicago: University of Chicago Press, 1982. Translation of *Marges: de la philosophie.* Paris: Minuit, 1972.
N	*Negotiations: Interventions and Interviews, 1971–2001.* Translated and edited by Elizabeth G. Rottenberg. Stanford: Stanford University Press, 2002.
"OR"	"On Responsibility." *PLI—Warwick Journal of Philosophy* 6 (1997): 19–36.
"ORH"	"On Reading Heidegger: An Outline of Remarks to the Essex Colloquium." *Research in Phenomenology* 17, no. 1 (1987): 171–85.
OS	*Of Spirit: Heidegger and the Question.* Translated by Geoffrey Bennington and Rachel Bowlby. Chicago: University of Chicago Press, 1991. Translation of *De l'esprit: Heidegger et la question.* Paris: Galilée, 1987.
"P"	"Passions: 'An Oblique Offering.'" In *Derrida: A Critical Reader,* edited by David Wood, 5–35. Oxford: Blackwell, 1992.
PC	*The Post Card: From Socrates to Freud and Beyond.* Translated by Alan Bass. Chicago: University of Chicago Press, 1987.
Pos	*Positions.* Translated by Alan Bass. Chicago: University of Chicago Press, 1981. Translation of *Positions.* Paris: Minuit, 1972.
QBH	*Heidegger: The Question of Being and History.* Edited by Thomas Dutoit. With the assistance of Marguerite Derrida. Translated by Geoffrey Bennington. Chicago: University of Chicago Press, 2016.
Sp	*Spurs: Nietzsche's Styles / Éperons: Les styles de Nietzsche.* Translated by Barbara Harlow. Chicago: University of Chicago Press, 1979.
"Uni"	"The University Without Condition." In *Without Alibi,* translated and edited by Peggy Kamuf, 202–37. Stanford: Stanford University Press, 2002. Translation of *L'université sans condition.* Paris: Galilée, 2001.
VP	*Voice and Phenomenon: Introduction to the Problem of the Sign in Husserl's Phenomenology.* Translated by Leonard Lawlor. Evanston:

Northwestern University Press, 2011. Translation of *La voix et le phénomène*. Paris: Presses Universitaires de France, 1967.

WD *Writing and Difference*. Translated, with an introduction and additional notes, by Alan Bass. London and New York: Routledge, 2005. Translation of *L'écriture et la différence*. Paris: Seuil, 1967.

FREQUENTLY CITED WORKS BY G. W. F. HEGEL

"Diff" *The Difference between Fichte's and Schelling's System of Philosophy*. Translated by H. S. Harris and Walter Cerf. Albany: State University of New York Press, 1977. Translation of "Differenz des Fichte'schen und Schelling'schen Systems der Philosophie." In *Werke in zwanzig Bänden*. Theorie-Werkausgabe. Band 2, 9–138. Frankfurt am Main: Suhrkamp, 1970.

PH *Phenomenology of Spirit*. Translated by Arnold V. Miller. Oxford: Oxford University Press, 1977. Translation of *Phänomenologie des Geistes*. *Werke in zwanzig Bänden*. Theorie-Werkausgabe. Band 3. Frankfurt am Main: Suhrkamp, 1970.

"Skept" "On the Relationship of Skepticism to Philosophy, Exposition of Its Different Modifications and Comparison of the Latest Form with the Ancient One." In *Between Kant and Hegel: Texts in the Development of Post-Kantian Idealism*, translated by H. S. Harris, edited by George di Giovanni and H. S. Harris, 311–62. Indianapolis: Hackett Publishing Company, 2000. Translation of "Verhältnis des Skeptizismus zur Philosophie. Darstellung seiner verschiedenen Modifikationen und Vergleichung des neuesten mit dem alten." In *Werke in zwanzig Bänden*. Theorie-Werkausgabe. Band 2, 213–72. Frankfurt am Main: Suhrkamp, 1970.

SL *The Science of Logic*. Translated and edited by George di Giovanni. Cambridge: Cambridge University Press, 2010. Translation of *Die Wissenschaft der Logik*. *Werke in zwanzig Bänden*. Theorie-Werkausgabe. Bands 5 and 6. Frankfurt am Main: Suhrkamp, 1970.

"Sys" "Fragment of a System." In *On Christianity. Early Theological Writings*, translated by T. M. Knox. With an Introduction and Fragments translated by Richard Kroner, 309–20. New York:

Harper & Brothers, 1961. Translation of "Systemfragment von 1800." In *Werke in zwanzig Bänden. Theorie-Werkausgabe. Band 1*, 419–27. Frankfurt am Main: Suhrkamp, 1970.

FREQUENTLY CITED WORKS BY MARTIN HEIDEGGER

BT   *Being and Time*. Translated by Joan Stambaugh, edited by Dennis J. Schmidt. Albany: State University of New York Press, 2010. Translation of *Sein und Zeit*. Tübingen: Max Niemeyer Verlag, 2006.

CP   *Contributions to Philosophy (of the Event)*. Translated by Richard Rojcewicz and Daniela Vallega-Neu. Bloomington: Indiana University Press, 2012. Translation of *Beiträge zur Philosophie (Vom Ereignis)*. GA 65. Frankfurt am Main: Vittorio Klostermann, 1989.

"ET"   "On the Essence of Truth." In *Pathmarks*, edited by William McNeill, translated by John Sallis, 136–54. Cambridge: Cambridge University Press, 1998. Translation of "Vom Wesen der Wahrheit." In *Wegmarken*. GA 9, 177–202. Frankfurt am Main: Vittorio Klostermann, 1976.

"LH"   "Letter on 'Humanism.'" In *Pathmarks*, edited by William McNeill, translated by Frank A. Capuzzi, 239–76. Cambridge: Cambridge University Press, 1998. Translation of "Brief über den Humanismus." In *Wegmarken*. GA 9, 327–28. Frankfurt am Main: Vittorio Klostermann, 1976.

NI   *Nietzsche Volumes I and II: The Will to Power as Art, The Eternal Recurrence of the Same*. Translated and edited by David Farrell Krell. New York: Harper Collins, 1991. Translation of *Nietzsche I*. 3rd ed. Stuttgart: Verlag Günther Neske, 1998.

Par   *Parmenides*. Translated by Andre Schuwer and Richard Rojcewicz. Bloomington: Indiana University Press, 1992. Translation of *Parmenides*. GA 54. Frankfurt am Main: Vittorio Klostermann, 1992.

PR   *The Principle of Reason*. Translated by Reginald Lilly. Bloomington: Indiana University Press, 1991. Translation of *Der Satz vom Grund*. GA 10. Frankfurt am Main: Vittorio Klostermann, 1997.

"TB" "Time and Being." In *On Time and Being*, translated by Joan Stambaugh. New York: Harper & Row, 1972. Translation of "Zeit und Sein." In *Zur Sache des Denkens,* 1–26. Tübingen: Max Niemeyer Verlag, 1969.

INTRODUCTION

Hegel, Heidegger, and Derrida consistently characterize their thought in terms of a development, movement, or pathway, rather than in terms of positions, propositions, or conclusions. To do philosophy is not (at least not primarily, exclusively, or ultimately) to take up a standpoint or one side in a debate, but it is to engage in a different kind of showing. This showing involves texts that function on different levels, often complicating or contradicting on one level the conclusions drawn on another.

"Movement" (and its modifications: path, track, development, *Weg, Bewegung, parcours, mouvement*) is the metaphor of choice to which all three resorted when pointing out how their work exceeds the claims or conclusions found within it. Examples of this abound. For Hegel, the need for philosophy arises every time determinate, fixed positions—that are necessarily one-sided and incomplete—are posited as absolutes. This deprives them of their vitality, and *opposing* this fixation only exacerbates the problem. Instead, what exceeds the oppositions of reflection is their "own movement," and the task of philosophy becomes tracing the immanent self-development or the "movement of the concept" [*Bewegung des Begriffs*]. The motto that Heidegger appended to the collected edition of his works is: "ways—not works" [*Wege—nicht Werke*]. He considered the propositional form an "obstacle" for what he called a "philosophical saying," the concern of which is "neither to describe nor to explain, neither to promulgate nor to teach" (CP 4/6). Therefore, at the start of his 1962 lecture "Time and Being," Heidegger gives "a little hint" to his audience: their task is "not to listen to a series of propositions," but rather to hear the "movement of showing" [*Gang des Zeigens*] in those propositions, and to follow that movement ("TB" 2/2). And in *Of Grammatology*, Derrida writes that if his text were "abandoned to the simple content of its conclusions," it would be indistinguishable from a merely "precritical" text. What exceeds those conclusions (yet is somehow still legible through them) is a "pathway" [*parcours*] that traverses the text and "must leave a track" there (G 90/61). Indeed, deconstruction itself is "not a constative statement" but, as Derrida writes in numerous places, "something like a movement" ("OR" 27).

Two main questions guide the investigations in this book. The first is how we should understand such a form of thought that refuses to identify with the claims or conclusions it produces. What does movement mean? What is the sense of this indirect approach, and what necessitates it? The second main question concerns the possibility of critique. Hegel, Heidegger and Derrida attempted to complicate (and show that thinking or philosophy should not be reduced to) what can be *posited* in a theoretical *position*, what can be contained in a *proposition*, or what can be determined or decided through *opposition* (pro or contra, yes or no). I stress this in this way, not just to note the conceptual solidarity between these words, but also because my concern is with a certain model of critique and of relating to the philosophical tradition. This is a model of critique as one of competing positions, what Hegel called the type of "commotion" or "bustle" about "truths" in the plural [*Gedränge von Wahrheiten*] that a philosopher should stay away from,[1] or what Heidegger called "going counter" to a philosopher instead of "going to their encounter" [*entgegengehen* or *Dagegenangehen* instead of *begegnen*],[2] or what Adorno has so aptly called "mere standpoint philosophy" [*Standpunktphilosophie*].[3] If the work of Hegel, Heidegger or Derrida may not be reduced to the specific positions found within it, then what does a meaningful critique of their work look like? How, and in what sense of the term critique, can one criticize, or critically engage with, a text that refuses to identify with an unequivocal position, if there is no final position to be judged, opposed or decided upon? What should a critical reader look for, if not the text's conclusions? And how, conversely, are these texts themselves "critical"? How should the critical force be understood of a discourse that so blatantly, to use the words of Foucault, seems to "avoid the grounds on which it could find support"?[4]

These two questions could be reformulated as the general question whether there is something like a necessary indirectness, or a necessary equivocality of philosophical texts or of philosophical method. Is there a necessary self-complication of philosophical discourse? Where, when, at what point? What necessitates, justifies or motivates it? What kind of philosophical exposition could expose such a necessity? Could it do so unequivocally?

What I expected to write, was a book about reflexivity or performativity. That is: about the relation between what is written in philosophical texts and how they are written—combining certain concerns that I had about reflection, performative self-contradiction, justification, knowledge, method, style and language. I expected to critically engage with Derrida's texts, aided by the work of Hegel and Heidegger in the background, exploring their mutual affinities on this point. These affinities seemed to me to have gone too much overlooked in the literature, in favor of explications of differences between the "schools" of dialectics, hermeneutics, and deconstruction—differences which seemed to me often too superficial and oppositional to be meaningful. For the most part, this expectation came true: this is a book about the relation between philosophy's object and its method, about the logical necessities and impossibilities guiding the highly reflexive types of philosophy that attempt to put in question the very concepts and procedures that are unavoidably employed when putting anything in question (the value of truth, the nature of language, the structure of thought, the meaning of questioning, the role of writing, etc.).

What I did not expect, and what I can only now see clearly, is that this book has an overarching ethical concern. I now see that what the final chapters deal with explicitly is in fact a concern throughout. The questions of reflexivity should be read in the light of a question of responsibility. The questions of method to which this book is largely devoted (why do Hegel, Heidegger and Derrida not take themselves to be engaged in the production of conclusions or assertions, of more conventional theoretical treatises, of standpoints with respect to "debates," etc.) can only be answered in light of the question what one considers one's task and one's responsibility as a philosopher to be. Method means: how should one respond? What is the responsible way to proceed? This is a responsibility that is displayed, exhibited, or shown in steps taken or procedures followed, rather than in taking up or defending a position with respect to some ethical or moral dilemma.[5]

My questions about movement originated in a critical engagement with Derrida's texts. If Derrida's position is privileged in the *Architektonik* of this book, it is because it was the question of the possibility of a critique of Derrida's work that gave this study its initial impetus. I soon came to recognize that the very idea of a "critique of Derrida" presents structural difficulties. If there is anything consistent about his writings, then it is their irreducibility to conventional theory or to the unequivocal presentation of a position. It is not that no clear positions or claims can be found in

Derrida's texts—it is that they never seem to be unequivocally endorsed. Rather than embodying the text's final intention, Derrida's claims and conclusions are invariably repeated, reversed, retracted, contradicted, visibly erased, or otherwise implicitly or explicitly complicated. He has recognized the necessity of this undercutting gesture under many names, calling it an "undecidability," a "hesitation," or a "trembling" proper to his writings, a necessary "avoidance" or a need to proceed "obliquely" or "strategically." I refer to this situation of Derrida's writings under the heading of "indirectness."[6] That this indirectness is structural, that it names something of the essence of Derrida's writings, is not contradicted but only affirmed by the fact that Derrida so often explicitly denied that there is an "essence" or unity to his writings at all—by stating, for instance, that there is not "one" deconstruction, that it is "not a method"; that its categories are "not concepts"; that it is "not relativism" (or nihilism, or historicism, or skepticism) and not a "critique" or "criticism" or "analysis"; that it is "not philosophy"; that it is not certain whether deconstruction "exists" or is even "possible," and so on. All of this belongs to that very indirectness. Including the fact that the very term "indirect" is itself also not the adequate, definite, final or right word for what is investigated here—something Derrida continually stressed with regard to all his central categories.[7]

It seemed to me that the major point of contention when it comes to reading and understanding Derrida's work, is this indirect mode of writing. Paradoxically, it is this same charactertistic that his staunchest admirers hail and his fiercest detractors criticize. As I describe in a bit more detail below, *polemics* has, in a variety of ways, made it difficult to investigate the specific kind of undercutting that is a necessary characteristic of Derrida's writings, in a way that would not require one to immediately submit to the oppositionality of being either "Derridean" or "anti-Derridean." Today, there are possibilities for a different type of commentary. My issue has been to ask, without already eyeing either a justification or a refutation of Derrida's work, how such a discourse of movement can be understood and criticized. Answering this question does not, as some may think, itself require indirectness, textual extravagance, or a poeticization of philosophical method (even though these cannot in principle be excluded from the realm of philosophical efficacy). I return to this question of my own method in the Afterword to this book.

If this book focuses on the indirect character of Derrida's writings, then what exactly are we looking at? To which topics, names, or philosophical traditions is it related? It does not seem to constitute a recognizable

Derridean theme (such as hospitality, writing, the gift, responsibility, justice, and so on). Instead, I seem to be making a theme out of Derrida's very way of proceeding. One answer would be to say that we are looking at Derrida's style of writing, but only if that concept is not already determined in its opposition to content, as mere externality or contingent form. It is certainly true that Derrida's indirectness also manifests itself "externally," or on the surface of his writings: it is marked in syntax, in the nonlinear structure of his essays, in his frequent use of hypotheticals and subjunctives, in the printed erasures and in the layout of his writings. But it would be insufficient to focus solely on these "external" aspects of style, or to perform a literary analysis of a certain type, if the question is whether there are reasons that necessitate that style. If the focus is on the entanglement of what Derrida writes with how he writes, then the meaning of Derrida's "indirect style" cannot itself rely on a rigorous distinction between form and content. The same holds if we were to say that this investigation is about Derrida's language (or his "use" of language) or his method (Derrida's tireless insistence that deconstruction is "not a method" is integral to his indirectness).

Though in one sense these questions undeniably concern the topics of language, style, and method, in another sense the issue is what in a certain way exceeds language, or at least a language of a certain direct or propositional type. Whatever "movement" may mean, it at least signifies what apparently cannot be stated or posited unequivocally; what one cannot directly talk "about" or (re)present in the conventional form of a theoretical treatise that provides results or conclusions. The word "exceeds" and the negative language that I employ here (what one "cannot . . .") indicate a concern with *limits*. The indirect approach indeed seems to point to certain limits of what can be talked "about," of what can be represented in the form of a presentation of a determinate thesis, theory, proposition, or conclusion. Perhaps we would have to say that this is an investigation of certain unsurpassable limits. However, that negative language suggests there would be something beyond these limits, something that one could not say, or at least not say directly or head-on; something that would be beyond our grasp: the ineffable or the unknowable.

At first sight, and for many interpreters, this might seem to be in line with some of Derrida's deepest concerns: with disruption, with "alterity," or with the "(wholly) other." These concerns arise in his "broaching" [*entamer*] what he calls the "order of logocentric metaphysics." Derrida's work would then be emancipatory with respect to this tradition and this way of thinking, his work would be directed "towards the outside." That is how, for example, Leonard Lawlor says it when he writes: "Derrida's thought is structured by an exiting movement, a line of flight to the outside. That the outside is a sort of utopian non-place, an 'elsewhere,' in which it is possible to think and live differently, indicates what motivates deconstruction."[8]

This is the thought that I resist in my reading. There is no question that, under the headings of alterity and singularity, Derrida always affirmed the necessity of emancipation.[9] But Derrida is always highly suspicious of the elsewhere,[10] and everything depends on to what extent such a non-place is indeed "utopian," in which precise sense it would be "possible" to think and live "differently," and how that difference is to be conceived. For in one sense of the term, a sense suggested by Lawlor's quote, such an outside is itself the result of a particular binary *representation* of the limit (a boundary or dividing line that opposes a *diesseits* to a *jenseits*, an inside to an outside, or a this-side to a beyond) that is tributary to the very oppositionality and representation that it purports to "exceed."

My claim is that Derrida is well aware of this complication, and one of my central claims in Part I is that alterity cannot be reduced to externality: there cannot be said to simply "be"—or be "possible"—anything outside or *opposed to* the oppositionality of what Derrida calls "logocentric metaphysics."[11] Now, on the one hand, this is hardly news. It is, after all, one of Derrida's best-known adages that "there is no sense in doing without metaphysics in order to shake metaphysics" (*WD* 412/354). But how must we understand that those who approvingly cite this phrase often take *that very insight* to elevate Derrida *above* "mere" metaphysics? What Derrida calls the "de-limitation of metaphysics" is not achieved by taking up a position counter to, above, or at a deeper level than the concerns of the metaphysical tradition he engages (if we can even speak of "achieving" at all in this regard). A consistent application of that insight alone is enough to open up possible dialogues between Hegel, Heidegger, and Derrida that have been absent in the literature.

Instead of positing an unattainable ineffable, it is in and through the movement of these writings that something of these essential limits is shown. This requires reading Derrida's writings as the performative attempt to take into account an irreducible entanglement with, or inextricability from, metaphysics—an entanglement that Derrida identified under such headings as "irreducible contamination" or "complicity" (these are also the concepts that form the basis of Derrida's ethics, which is, I argue, fundamentally an ethics of complicity). This is what we must make sense of: that, in Derrida's words, the excess (whether as trace, supplement, or *différance*), in a certain sense, "*is nothing*"—that "[this] thought has no weight" (G 142/93).[12]

If it is not a matter of escaping to an outside—if, as I intend to show, Derrida's alterity is not simply externality and if deconstruction "works from the inside" (similarly: if Heidegger's philosophical saying is still bound to the representation it exceeds, and if Hegel's "movement" of reflection does not lie *outside* reflection)—then all the weight of explanation falls on how to interpret this "in."

First of all, if the notions of outside or beyond are themselves still oppositional determinations that, as such, undercut the excess of oppositionality they are supposed to signify, then "in" can also no longer simply signify containment within determinable borders. What I am out to show is that this is a thought that Hegel, Derrida, and Heidegger each takes on board in his own way. It can be recognized in the necessary "immanence" of Hegel's movement of the concept, in the inextricability of Derridean "contamination" or "complicity" and the denial of the "outside-text," and in the very special hermeneutical sense that Heidegger gives to "(always already) being-in" (the distinction of *in-sein* from *sein in*).[13]

These senses of "in" are far from identical, but what binds them is an awareness that there is an inextricable relation between *what* is written and *how* it is written. The character of the investigation (its method, its own language, its style, the sequence of its steps) cannot be dissociated from the content that is discussed within it (the nature of its object, or the subject that it speaks "about"). What *exceeds* "metaphysics" (Derrida), "representation" (Heidegger), or a merely subjective "philosophy of reflection" (Hegel) is the movement of or *in* the metaphysical, representation, reflection. Its excess is *implicit*.

If indirectness and movement signify an "implicit excess" or an "entanglement of method and object," then to this subject there does not correspond exclusively a single philosophical discipline, subject matter, or conventionally demarcated tradition. This entanglement takes on many forms, and the awareness of it is as old as philosophy itself. It is part and parcel of all philosophy insofar as philosophy by necessity employs the very procedures, values, or criteria that it sets out to put in question. The terms that come closest to naming this entanglement, and that have been most influential in the literature on Derrida, are perhaps reflexivity (for instance, in Rodolphe Gasché's classic 1986 *The Tain of the Mirror: Derrida and the Philosophy of Reflection*)[14] or performativity.[15] And to the extent that the indirect discourse performatively questions the values that it "itself" employs, there is a convergence between the question of movement and that long tradition of philosophical concern with "self-reflection."[16] In her description of the language that Heidegger employs in his *Contributions to Philosophy (Of the Event)*, Daniela Vallega-Neu has coined another term for this problem of performativity when she calls Heidegger's philosophical saying a "poietic saying."[17] She does this with reference to Heidegger's interpretation of ποίησις as bringing-forth, to denote a language that stands in a productive rather than a representative relation to "what" it says. I am not able to use any of these terms entirely without reservation. Whether we call it performative, reflexive, or poietic (and there are other options: think of the distinction between "gesture and statement" or of Levinas's distinction of the "saying" from the "said" [*le dire et le dit*]), the problem of indirectness and movement is the problem, to put it in Heidegger's terms, that philosophy demands "a conceptuality of its own" and that it fundamentally "belongs to an attempt that requires other forms" (*PR* vii/1). I believe that with this question I am addressing the central point of contention in the discussions about the so-called continental-analytic divide in philosophy,[18] as well as, broader still, about "postmodern" thought in general. These clashes have always been about method and about responsibility, about what procedures one ought to follow in order to think well; what language one ought to use and what steps one ought to take in order to philosophize responsibly.

By now, the interpretive challenges that I face in this book have already been laid out. Does not my emphasis on "in" not stand for the very Hegelian "immanence" that Derrida so vehemently criticized? Does Derrida not explicitly state that deconstruction "affirms the outside" (*D* 42/36)—an emphatic affirmation that does not sound very "indirect" at all, and an affirmation of an "outside" that, for that matter, does not sound very "implicit" either? How to align deconstruction on this point with Hegel and Heidegger? And why does the point of entry into these problems lie in the mode of writing?

This book is divided into four parts. My initial question was how a critique of Derrida's discourse is possible at all, as it so blatantly "avoids the grounds on which it could find support," and this is the subject of Part I. In order to answer that question, it is first necessary to qualify Derrida's indirectness: what exactly does it mean, and what necessitates it? This is the subject of chapters 1 and 2. In chapter 3, I return to the question of the possibility of a critique of deconstruction, and related problems of justification, refutation, skepticism, and method. Part II is about Hegel, before turning to Heidegger in Parts III and IV. Multiple complex interrelations (of influence and interpretation) exist between Hegel, Heidegger, and Derrida, and I am not able to do justice to all of them. The discussion of Hegel and Heidegger not only functions as an exemplification of Derrida's "critical" relation to the tradition, but also shows the way in which Hegel and Heidegger are themselves thinkers of movement, outside the confines of their Derridean interpretation. That is what I start with in both cases: in chapter 4 on Hegel before turning to Derrida's Hegel-interpretation in chapter 5, and in Part III (chapters 6 and 7) on Heidegger before turning my attention to Derrida's reading of Heidegger in Part IV (chapters 8 and 9). I discuss my approach in each of these parts below.

PART I:
DERRIDA, INDIRECTNESS, AND CRITIQUE

Chapter 1 is devoted to showing exactly what is meant by Derrida's indirectness. I start from the opposite point of view: before conceding that a "structural indirectness" pervades Derrida's writings, couldn't one object that there is more than enough that is quite unequivocal in Derrida's texts? Is there not something like a Derridean "theory"? How to justify the focus on movement when Derrida presents us with so many quite unequivocal, direct propositions, and rigorous insights?

As it is commonly held that there is at least a recognizable theory of language to be found in Derrida's texts, especially in his earlier works (the published works up to 1972), my first chapters focus on those. At the center of my approach is a reading of *Of Grammatology*. I show in chapter 1 how that text undercuts the theoretical or scientific status of the theory of language that we seem to be able to find within it. Derrida aims to uncover an "*incompetence* of science" from which the accomplishment of this very uncovering—the text of *Of Grammatology* itself—is not exempt (G 142/93). This means that Derrida's notion of a "generalized arche-writing" cannot be taken to form a rival account to writing's traditional, narrow determination. But then the question becomes: what is the theoretical status of the text, what are its results or insights, and how or to what extent are these results defensible or justified?

Derrida announces that his reflections on the sign and language are not an end in themselves, but that they serve the "de-construction of the greatest totality—the concept of *epistēmē* and logocentric metaphysics" (G 68/46), which is the subject of chapter 2. Because for Derrida the very question of what logocentric metaphysics is entails a performative complication, I first show in a preliminary manner how Derrida uses the concepts of metaphysics and logocentrism under the headings of demarcation, opposition, hierarchy, and presence. The remainder of the section is then devoted to my main interpretive thesis: that alterity is not reducible to externality, which is to say that Derrida's attempt to "write otherwise" is not reducible to a counter-position with respect to metaphysics. That is by no means a revolutionary thesis, but everything depends on the conclusions one draws from it.

The attempt to emphasize a Derridean theory or position on language evolved within a specific type of commentary. It arose in the early 1980s, primarily in the attempt to *defend* Derrida from accusations of the irresponsibility of skepticism, relativism, nihilism, or textual "free play." Those accusations, and the ensuing polemics of defense and refutation, have long determined, and often still determine, the understanding of Derrida's texts and the landscape of commentary. Such refutations usually either distill from Derrida's work a certain thesis and show it to be flawed—thereby negating the very style and strategy (the movement) that is essential to his writing—or they show Derrida to be in contradiction with himself (whether immanently, logically, or performatively), thus eliminating the need to engage with Derrida's texts at all, because they "refute themselves." The question is, of course, what the force of such an objection could possibly be with regard to a work that so emphatically affirms, even blatantly flaunts, its own "self-contradiction."

One of the strategies to defend Derrida against such criticisms consisted in asserting that Derrida *is in fact* very rigorous, and that there are good arguments to be found in Derrida's texts. The supposition here is that the force of Derrida's words and the value of his texts can be felt if these texts can be shown to be *theoretically* strong.[19]

Derrida is no simple relativist, and these attempts to defend his work therefore are no doubt necessary. But there is a risk involved in equating the force of Derrida's writings with theoretical strength. Not only does such a reaction tacitly endorse the presupposed framework of critique (a polemic of positions pro and contra), but it also tends to underemphasize deconstruction's most essential feature: that Derrida's discourse "does not restore confidence," that it "hesitates" for "essential reasons," that it "does not lead to possibilities," and that, in a certain crucial way, the activity of deconstruction "falls prey to its own work" (G 39/24). In this way, polemics (the dynamic of defense and refutation) endorses the very oppositionality that Derrida, through his writings, attempted to exceed. The form of Derrida's indirectness is what makes it exceed a simple relativism, but it is also what distinguishes it from a simply justified position. This *vulnerability* of deconstruction is grounds for neither justification nor refutation. But then what does this mean for the possibility of a critique of Derrida?

In chapter 3, I attempt to answer that question by focusing on three figures related to the question of justification, with which Derrida maintains a structurally ambiguous relation: empiricism, skepticism, and critique. That the movement of showing of Derrida's writing exceeds the positions one finds within it is confirmed by the fact that, on the one hand, Derrida often explicitly distances himself quite categorically from empiricism, skepticism, and critique. He repeatedly does this in the most unequivocal, propositional manner: deconstruction simply "is not" empiricism, skepticism, or critique. On the other hand, Derrida in various ways acknowledges a structural relation between deconstruction and each of these figures. The question of a critique of Derrida, in terms of justification and defense, therefore, has to be: what exactly is the relation between, on the one hand, Derrida's explicit opposition to these figures, and, on the other hand, the explicitly acknowledged structural "resemblance" between deconstruction and empiricism, skepticism, and criticism?

If Derrida is approached as a thinker of movement, and if alterity is not simply externality, then deconstruction's *own* critical force, that is, its relation to the metaphysical tradition, is not simply one of the very oppositionality that the movement of his writings attempts to exceed. This makes it possible to rethink Hegel and Heidegger as thinkers of movement with whom Derrida maintains a structurally ambiguous relation. Therefore, two questions guide Parts III and IV, which are dedicated to Hegel and Heidegger, and Derrida's relation to them: (1) in what sense are Hegel and Heidegger thinkers of movement, and how does the specific form of their "performativity" relate to Derrida's? (2) how does the non-oppositional character of Derrida's relation to metaphysics show itself in his "critique" of Hegel and Heidegger?

PART II:
HEGEL, MOVEMENT, AND OPPOSITION

In the case of Hegel, the main challenge was already outlined above: if Hegel is to be a thinker of *movement*, then he must be understood as affirming the limits of reflection. There are several traditions that stress the importance of limits for Hegel's philosophy. I do not argue for an "originary" negativity (as it is in certain postmodern interpretations), nor is my conception of limits fundamentally a matter of "finitude," specifically finitude of "man" (as it is for the classic existentialist interpretations of Kojève, Hyppolite, or Merleau-Ponty).[20] Instead, I locate the limits in the implicit self-complication of the philosophical exposition: that the excess of the absolute with respect to the determinations of reflection can only be shown in and through an exposition of the movement of those very determinations. One could call that limits of Hegel's "language," but not if that means, as Hyppolite has it, that the dialectic becomes a movement of "sense."[21] Such a determination risks underemphasizing what I take to be the dialectic's most important aspect: that it is essentially an explication of the implicit, the exposition of which is never entirely unproblematic or reducible to positive sense.

I do not intend to present an exhaustive, or even an entirely new, account of Hegel's philosophy. The elements of my reading can already be found scattered across the literature, not least in some of the works of the authors mentioned above. My main intentions are to counter certain prevalent misconceptions about Hegel to which some readers of Derrida are especially prone (a climate I show Derrida's texts to have in part helped shape); to provide a point of entry in reading Hegel for those sympathetic to Derrida's concerns; and to come to a better understanding of the relation between Derrida and Hegel than that of an opposition of philosophical positions.

How does Derrida relate to the Hegel that I sketched above? I discuss his relation to Hegel in chapter 5, and we will see that Derrida differs from the approaches above by maintaining an essential ambiguity with regard to Hegel. The relation is similar in structure to the explicit denial of skepticism, empiricism, and critique: on the one hand, Derrida unequivocally distances himself from a certain Hegel and defines deconstruction in opposition to a "reappropriating dialectics" in which all negativity is reverted back to positivity, and in which every "outside" is reduced to the "immanence of the system." That kind of reading goes squarely against the Hegel that I present in chapter 4. To the extent that this aspect of Derrida's Hegel-interpretation is isolated and absolutized, it has helped misguide a host of twentieth-century readers in their confrontation with Hegel. But Derrida is well aware that Hegel cannot be reduced to this figure of reappropriation, and there is always another Hegel at play in Derrida's texts, one who cannot simply be reduced to a figure of reappropriation. The question then becomes what the place of the oppositions and reversals of these different Hegels is within the broader movement of Derrida's writing. I argue for an understanding of Derrida's relation to Hegel in terms of a departure from Hegel that is enacted more than it is posited, by supplementing his oppositions to Hegel with what Derrida calls certain "textual maneuvers" (*MP* vii–viii/xv).

PARTS III AND IV: HEIDEGGER, PERFORMATIVITY, AND RESPONSIBILITY

The publication in 1989 of Heidegger's 1936/38 *Contributions to Philosophy (Of the Event)* and the works in its wake[22] has profoundly changed the way we understand Heidegger's development, philosophy, and authorship. It has sparked renewed interest in a host of themes from Heidegger's later works. Of these themes, no doubt the one that stands out most is the theme of language.[23] Heidegger writes: "Here the speaking is not something over and against what is to be said but is this latter itself as the essential occurrence of beyng" [. . . *hier ist das Sagen nicht im Gegenüber zu dem zu Sagenden, sondern ist dieses selbst als die Wesung des Seyns*] (*CP* 4/6).

With that, the *Contributions* is an exemplary text with which to qualify the specific form of performativity, the entanglement of method and object in Heidegger's work. The limits of the propositional no longer lie, like they did for Hegel, in a necessary "one-sidedness" of any given determination, but in a "destruction of the genuine relation to words" that characterizes our time. "In" now no longer stands for Hegelian immanence. Instead, the very form of the problem of entanglement changes. It now takes the shape of the question: how to question the limits of what one is always already essentially caught up or involved in, in such a way that it is—at least partly and at worst completely—hidden, concealed, or withdrawn? I argue that for Heidegger the "failure" of representational language is not to be (nor can it be) fully overcome, but that the required poietic saying consists in a different "attunement" [*Stimmung*] *to* the (re)presentational language of metaphysics. It is an attempt to recognize and preserve a certain necessary failure-to-say with respect to the question of being, which is why Heidegger calls it a saying that "effects the highest thoughtful reticence" [*Welches Sagen leistet die höchste denkerische Erschweigung?*] (*CP* 13/13). Part III is devoted to unpacking what this means. Chapter 6 consists largely of a reading of *Being and Time*. I show how that text—though it is often considered one of Heidegger's methodologically more conservative texts—is constituted by an indirectness and a performative complexity that centers around Heidegger's special hermeneutical notion of "being-in." What I show is that it is not only with the later works that performativity and language become essential. Against the idea of a fundamental turning in Heidegger's thought around 1930, I argue for a continuity of concern from *Being and Time* to the *Contributions*. I then devote chapter 7 to Heidegger's later texts, centering around a reading of Heidegger's *Contributions*, in order to interpret Heidegger's indirectness by looking at the *Contributions*' style and Heidegger's ideas about a new philosophical language or "saying" constituted by withdrawal, reticence, silence, and attunement. I show that Heidegger's search for a new language is not, as Derrida sometimes objected, the search for a language that finally gets it right, but for one that recognizes and preserves a certain failure to say the truth of being.

Then, in Part IV, I look at what this means for Derrida's relation to Heidegger. At first, it is possible to recognize the same structure in Derrida's relation to Heidegger that I articulated with respect to Hegel in chapter 5 (as well as that of deconstruction's relation to empiricism, skepticism, and critique from chapter 3). Again, it is a matter of several Heideggers that are at work in Derrida's texts: the one who according to Derrida works within the "hermeneutical circle," which Derrida interprets as fundamentally a project aiming for the fullness of *meaning* (one is "caught" in the "confines" of that circle), and another Heidegger, whom Derrida locates around the central figure of the *Contributions*: that of *Ereignis*. Derrida distinguishes the two and fails to fully grasp their inner connection, as I show it in Part III. Still, it is important that Derrida does not straightforwardly choose between these Heideggers. Rather, in his texts he moves from the one to the other, while also enacting a departure from Heidegger through a "textual intervention." One text that brings this out well is Derrida's masterful 1978 essay *Spurs: Nietzsche's Styles*. (Because of these textual interventions, and because the need for indirection is intimately related to the need for a "plurality of styles," Nietzsche's thought is a recurring feature throughout this book.)

No philosopher has had a greater impact on Derrida's writing than Heidegger. Can we equate Derrida's mode of ambiguity with respect to Heidegger to that of his oppositional entanglement with Hegel? In chapter 9, I show how in *Of Spirit* we seem to encounter a different kind of critical relation. There Derrida addresses concerns that seem to be systematically *avoided* or underrepresented in Heidegger's work (such as gender, politics, race, heritage, animality, or the body). By taking Derrida's indirectness as our frame of reference, it becomes possible to show why that avoidance cannot be simply countered or reversed. At stake is to question whether a thought of "irreducible complicity" can aim for a *presentation*, a *making-present* of what Heidegger avoided, or whether there is something like a necessary avoidance. The ambiguity of Derrida's critique of Heidegger is exemplified by his diagnosis of what he calls the "privilege of the question" in Heidegger. In the very impossibility to question that privilege, Derrida identifies an excess of the horizon of Heidegger's question of being that nevertheless cannot be understood to go "beyond" or "deeper"; an unquestioned privilege "before" the question that, because the privilege is only *affirmed* in questioning it, is not simply before. It is an affirmation at work *in* all questioning; a commitment that is not the commitment to any definite principle. It is on this thought that Derrida bases a new concept of responsibility.

Derrida's concept of responsibility leads to questions that exceed the scope of the present investigation. I do not aim to give an exhaustive account of that concept and the texts in which Derrida presents it. What necessitates Derrida's indirectness lies in the strictures of reflexivity as I bring them out in Derrida's works on language, metaphysics, and the way he relates to Hegel and Heidegger. These strictures make up the, if you will, structural or theoretical part of the philosophical sense of Derrida's indirect approach. It is with this new concept of responsibility that we explicitly move toward more normative or ethical considerations.

Two central thoughts are often associated with the question of an ethics of deconstruction. The first is that there was something like an ethical turn in Derrida's work, which would have taken place in the second half of the 1980s. The second is, especially because this turn coincides with a certain engagement with the work of Levinas, that the ethics of deconstruction revolves around the concept of the "other" and a responsibility "to the other." What I want to show is that one can identify an ethical turn superficially at most, and that the relation of deconstruction to responsibility lies precisely in the mode of writing. Second, I show that the question of the "other" is liable to misinterpretation because, like the "outside," it risks interpretations of the kind of oppositionality that Derrida's indirectness is out to exceed. Instead, Derrida's affirmative responsibility lies in the indirect way of writing as it attempts to account for the various strictures that any critique (or emancipation, resistance, or protest) is involved in when questioning a norm to which one cannot simply oppose oneself, or from which one cannot simply extricate oneself. More than the "other," I argue that it is the thought of an "irreducible complicity" that guides Derrida's concept of responsibility. This ethics of complicity is the ethical expression of the structures of entanglement worked out in the earlier parts of this book.

The attempt to affirmatively assume this responsibility is the most positive sense of what motivates deconstruction. This is the point where Derrida is furthest removed from the kind of destructive or merely negative discourse, indeed from the kind of theoretical irresponsibility, that he has so often been accused of taking up. The perspective of movement enables me to show that this affirmation is not the positivity of an ethical position, but that the enactment of Derrida's indirect movement is for him the form of an affirmative philosophical commitment and the way to produce the least irresponsible response. For him, to engage in the deconstructive mode of writing, or to enact or engage in that kind of movement of showing, *is* what it means to respond responsibly.

PART I

SOURCES OF DERRIDA'S INDIRECTNESS

Language, Metaphysics, Critique

CHAPTER 1

WHY THERE CAN BE NO DERRIDEAN THEORY OF LANGUAGE

> . . . whatever one thinks under that name, the problem of language has no doubt never been one problem among others.
>
> —Derrida (*Of Grammatology*)

In what precise sense can Derrida's writings be characterized as "indirect"? In effect, this means asking why Derrida writes in the way that he writes. Those familiar with his works might immediately object to the implication that Derrida has a (that is to say: one, identifiable) way of writing at all. But Derrida's consistent insistence that there is no such thing (e.g., no "method" or no "one" deconstruction) is an important part of the very indirectness that structurally characterizes his writings. So the first question is what I mean by indirect here, and the second is what the sense of that indirectness is or why Derrida writes in this way. Why does Derrida conceive of his texts in terms of a "movement" rather than as the presentation of a position?

In order to show this, I start with the opposite assumption: are there not many "direct" texts by Derrida? Is there not a lot of rather unambiguous Derridean theory? It is commonly held that if there is such a theory, it is primarily a theory of the sign, of meaning, or of writing—in short: of language—and that the core of this theory can be found in Derrida's relatively early works. That is why I focus here on a reading of *Of Grammatology*.

In this first chapter, I show how the possibility of direct, theoretical presentation is complicated at the outset by the very nature of the project of *Of Grammatology*. By direct presentation, I mean taking up a position on language; to write in such a way as to produce unequivocal claims or conclusions "about" language. I show this through a close reading of its preface, exergue, and opening pages. *Of Grammatology*'s indirectness—the complication of the form of its presentation—is essentially tied to its main theme. The main form of that complication is this: on the one hand, what I call this "entanglement" of form and content, or of method and object, leads in a certain sense to a new account of language and writing (of what Derrida calls a "generalized" writing that would "comprehend" language). On the other hand, however, the main characteristic of that Derridean account (as it is formed by the notions of "arche-writing" [*archi-écriture*] and "[originary] trace") is precisely the impossibility of developing a rigorous "account" of it at all. In other words, I argue that this supposed account of language itself suffers from the very "incompetence of science" that it sets out to expose. At this point, the discussion of language and writing is no longer an end in itself. For Derrida, it rather provides a privileged access to his main problem: to complicate what he calls "logocentric metaphysics," which is the subject of chapter 2.

"THIS INCOMPETENCE OF SCIENCE..." OF GRAMMATOLOGY'S OPENING COMPLICATION

Starting to read *Of Grammatology* from the beginning, one encounters a short *avertissement* (a preface or foreword, but also a warning) that precedes two main parts, the first of which is, in turn, preceded by an "exergue."

Because our present interest is in the "theoretical" status of the work, the opening lines of the cautionary foreword seem to point us in the direction of the first part. It reads: "The first part of this book, 'Writing before the Letter,' sketches in broad outlines a theoretical matrix. It indicates certain significant historical moments, and proposes certain critical concepts" (G 7/lxxxix). Part two, on the other hand, is said to "put to the test" these concepts proposed in part one. What seems to be a rather conventional distinction between "theory" and its "application" is, however, immediately undone. Because this would make part two the "example," but, according to Derrida, "strictly speaking" [*en toute rigueur*], that notion—and here the reader receives his first warning—is "not acceptable" [*irrecevable*], and it is retained only "for convenience" [*par commodité*] (G 7/lxxxix).

Already a certain indirectness presents itself. Part of the book contains an example, but what the book proves is that this notion is unacceptable.

How is it "convenient" to retain an "unacceptable" concept? What kind of investigation allows itself the use of such concepts, and why?

There are easy ways to do away with such questions. One way would be to explain this peculiar opening by pointing to the history of the essay. We know that *Of Grammatology* was not originally conceived as a single project. What we now know under that title is the conjunction and revision of, first, a two-part essay in *Critique* from 1965–66 and, second, of material from a seminar on Rousseau at the École normale supérieure.[1] One could also refer to Derrida's own admission that the essay is "made up of two heterogeneous passages, put together somewhat artificially."[2]

This would amount to saying that these opening lines are not that significant and not to be taken too literally. Or it would be like saying that *Of Grammatology* is only contingently a title for what is in fact not one thing, which would amount to saying that there are no strict reasons why these essays are joined together in a single volume. But Derrida goes on to contend that he has argued "patiently and at length" for not only the "choice" but also the "necessity" of his "examples" (G 7/lxxxix). Moreover, *Of Grammatology* is far from the only text of Derrida's that begins with such a complication, with the introduction of an unacceptable concept, and with a distinction introduced and then in another gesture immediately retracted. A great many of Derrida's earlier texts open with that structure,[3] and one of the decisive motifs of these texts is their "moving on" from distinctions, concepts, or propositions that they state are unacceptable.[4] This begs the questions: what necessitates that gesture (the introduction of the unacceptable and the act of moving on from it), and what authorizes it?

I answer that these considerations are not just matters of circumstance. It is essential to the content of the project of *Of Grammatology* that it is not essentially one project. Its fractured nature is intrinsically connected to one of the essay's main intentions, which is to put in question the model of the book.[5] The book, for Derrida, is no mere model among others, but represents the very form of exposition that implicitly underlies or constitutes Western science and metaphysics. To its central characteristics belong the ideas of a self-contained whole or totality, within determinable borders, with a clearly distinguishable beginning and end, so that it is possible to rigorously distinguish external "form," "style," or manner of carrying out from its internal "content" or from the matter at hand (the subject or object of investigation).

To an extent, such a questioning of the book undercuts itself in its very articulation. If the book is what *Of Grammatology* wants to put in question, then this must have consequences for that investigation itself. I say "consequences" for lack of a better word here: a consequence usually follows the antecedent, but the exposition of *Of Grammatology* is not complicated *after* it successfully achieves some result that would *then* complicate matters. This complication is, for Derrida, neither conditional nor hypothetical. The specific form of this complication is Heideggerian: to be "always already in" what is being put in question. It is therefore fundamentally unclear at the start whether *Of Grammatology* itself will be able to form a self-contained totality, whether its proper beginning is rigorously determinable, whether its exposition can be "complete," and especially whether its content and its method (i.e., what it says and how it says it) can be rigorously discerned. Can there be a complete exposition of the necessary incompleteness of the book? Derrida calls this a "logic of incompleteness."[6]

For these reasons, Derrida indicates in the famous "Question of Method" (the significance of which is already starting to show itself) that the main concern of his essay revolves around problems of "outlining" [*découpage*]. That is: the essay concerns a certain inability to rigorously distinguish or to determine at all, to the extent that determination entails delineating what something is, that is: drawing a line that distinguishes where a matter begins and where it ends; distinguishing its inside from its outside or its essence from its accidents. Derrida speaks in this context of "contamination," of "overflowing" [*débordement*], or of the "effacement of (all of) its limits" [*effacement de (toutes) ses limites*], and I sometimes refer to this in terms of an "entanglement" of method and object.

It is in this entanglement, in the way the essay's subject matter interferes with the possibility of its presentation, way of proceeding, or unfolding, that the sources of Derrida's indirectness must be sought. The very relation between the method of the investigation and its content is itself a theme for that investigation.[7] This is affirmed when Derrida goes on to call the example that may not be called an example a "reading" [*une lecture*], of which he writes (and here comes the second warning) that it will be merely sketched or outlined. That is: it will be incomplete, not only for its limited text-selection, but because *through this reading* Derrida sets out to *produce the problems of critical reading* [*nous tentons de produire [. . .] des problèmes de lecture critique*]. Perhaps that is the most assured description of the work so far: it will be a production of problems. It is this production of the problems *of* reading *by means of* a reading that constitutes the "unacceptable" value of "exemplarity." So the title of *Of*

Grammatology's first chapter—"The end of the book and the beginning of writing"—therefore announces (1) that a certain notion of "writing" will be employed to challenge the idea of the book, as well as (2) that the very act of such challenging, and the concept of writing employed in it, are themselves problematic; that these notions carry with them an implicit complication. This complication makes it necessary for Derrida to maintain equally that "there is no end of the book and no beginning of writing" and that "writing can no more begin [...] than the book can end" (*Pos* 23/14).

For now, let us take from the preface of *Of Grammatology* that it does not introduce an unambiguous position, but instead focuses on a reflexive complication that is constitutive of the essay; the co-complication or mutual implication of, on the one hand, its subject (or its object or content; what it is "about") and, on the other hand, its method or its mode of investigation.

If we look beyond the preface, we see that the essay again stutters before truly starting (as is already indicated by its title: "Writing before the letter" [*l'écriture avant la lettre*]), this time not by way of a warning, but by way of an *exergue* (an "outwork"). The exergue announces above all the auto-complication of what is to come. What it introduces, however, are the recognizable elements of what is commonly taken to be Derrida's "theory."

The exergue is composed of three statements on writing (a scribe, a passage from Rousseau's *Essai sur l'origine des langues,* and one from Hegel's *Encyclopedia*) and a short interpretation of what these passages "should focus attention on." In the course of that interpretation, Derrida sets up what at first glance may seem to be a collection of assured propositions concerning the entire project of *Of Grammatology*. It is possible to at least identify the following: Derrida points to (1) the existence of a "metaphysics of phonetic writing" that he calls "logocentrism" and that, "for enigmatic yet essential reasons," is said (2) to "command in one and the same order" the concept of writing, the history of metaphysics, and the concept of science, because (3) "the concept of science, or of the scientificity of science has always been determined as logic." Also: (4) that metaphysics "has always assigned the origin of truth to logos" and has as such always been (5) "the debasement of writing." Last, (6) that what Derrida calls "the phoneticization of writing" must "dissimulate its own history as it is produced" (G 11/3).

These are all very complex statements. For now, I focus only on their status as theoretical assertions. On the one hand, they seem to be posited as the elements of a general theory, encompassing nothing less than the identification of the origin of truth and that which commands the determinations of writing, science, and the history of metaphysics. At the heart of Derrida's "theory" lies *writing*; the preface already announced that it is through a certain concept of writing that the model of the book and its logocentric or metaphysical order are challenged. As such, the science that would have to establish all of this (writing's relation to the scientificity of science and to metaphysics) would be a science of writing: a *grammatology*.

Yet the exergue is consciously set up in such a way as to repeatedly announce "not only" all of the above ("*pas seulement . . . ni seulement*"—effectively turning it into a buildup to something else) but "above all":

> I would like to suggest *above all* that, however fecund and necessary the undertaking might be, and even if, given the most favorable hypothesis, it did overcome all technical and epistemological obstacles as well as all the theological and metaphysical impediments that have limited it hitherto, such a science of writing runs the risk of never being established as such and with that name. Of never being able to define the unity of its project or its object. Of not being able either to write its discourse on method or to describe the limits of its field. (G 13–14/4, emphasis mine, JdJ)

The themes introduced here (determination of writing, scientificity of science; metaphysical determination of the origin of truth as logos; writing's "self-dissimulation," etc.) do not form claims that combine into a "theory." Rather, they form the unestablishable elements of a science not to be. Grammatology—the very science that would have to justify all this, establish it rigorously, or produce these insights securely—that very science itself runs the risk of never being established. It is not complicated in merely one aspect, but it is complicated in its *name*, in its *project*, in its *object*, in its *method*, in the *limits of its field*. It is the idea of a science thoroughly complicated, complicated throughout. And this is said to be so "for essential reasons":

> For essential reasons: [. . .] The idea of science and the idea of writing—therefore also of the science of writing—is meaningful for us only in terms of an origin and within a world to which

a certain concept of the sign (later I shall call it *the* concept of sign) and a certain concept of the relationships between speech and writing, have *already* been assigned. (G 14/4)

If Derrida is right, then the very idea of a science of writing, the question of "what writing is," itself already presupposes a determination of the very concept of the sign and of the relation between speech and writing (Derrida stresses: "[. . .] have *already been* assigned"). It is the very positing of that question, its very form or character, that Derrida will show to "have already assigned" this determination. This determination, in fact, is said to command the very idea of science (and, indeed, the history of metaphysics and the determination of truth). The science of writing would put in question a meaning of writing or a determination of that meaning that is itself said to be constitutive of the very idea of science and, thus, of the very question that institutes that science: "what is writing?"

It is here that the complication of a grammatology comes into focus, and the stakes involved in a meditation on it become clear: it would amount to scientifically putting in question the very idea of science, of scientificity and its possibilities. If it were a theory, it would be one of the limits of the possibility of theory. It would put in question the values of metaphysics, logic, truth, science, and writing—values that simultaneously seem to be necessary for any putting-in-question to be possible at all. Derrida puts it like this: a science of writing would have to reflexively "produce its own dislocation and itself proclaim its limits" (G 14/4).

Derrida has always been very clear on this point. *De la grammatologie* ("Of" grammatology) is a meditation on the nature and possibilities of a grammatology—it is not that science carried out. One of the most succinct formulations of the complicated nature of the work is Derrida's remark that, rather than being a presentation or a theory "of" or "about" grammatology, *Of Grammatology* is "the title of a question." What question? According to Derrida, it is a question about "the necessity of a science of writing [. . .]; but also a question about the limits of this science" [*la nécessité d'une science de l'écriture [. . .]; mais question aussi sur les limites de cette science*] (*Pos* 22/13). He writes that *Of Grammatology* is neither a "defense" of that science nor an "illustration" of it. Rather, it is the meditation on what a general science of writing would amount to; what its demands would be or what it would entail. The work shows such a meditation to reveal that those demands do not lead to a realizable science, but that they point to the very limits of theory, science, or philosophy.

This complication thus operates on two levels: grammatology is the idea of a science that questions writing, yet, as science, it simultaneously already presupposes a specific determination of writing. And *Of Grammatology* itself is "about" that science, setting out to challenge this very "aboutness"; the limits of scientificity or the possibility of the rigorous distinction between method and object that is requisite for the presentation of any theory. It is in that sense that *Of Grammatology* is itself indirect: it does not proceed to a solution but aims to show the aporetic character of that question. The indirectness of this approach—which, in contrast to proceeding toward an answer, is rather like a step back—consists in the reflexive awareness that this showing itself cannot lay claim to any (prior) theoretical or scientific legitimacy. For the complication to arise, Derrida must insist on the "already": phonocentric writing is not merely something one must presuppose *in* the carrying out of a science of writing; it is a determination that must *have already been* assigned. This must have *already happened*, so to speak. Insofar as this is a presupposition, it is not presupposed *in* or *with*, but a determination "already assigned" *before* any idea of a science of writing can make sense to us. This temporalization of the conditions of possibility is a Heideggerian motif, as is a certain spatialization of the notion of objectivity. Derrida's approach requires both. For Heidegger, as I show in more detail in Part III, "always already in" [*immer schon in*] is the central category of his ontological hermeneutics. Derrida consistently takes over Heidegger's conception of the conceptual solidarity between the object [*Gegenstand*] as it can be posited and/or (re)presented [*Stellen, Darstellen, Vorstellen*], that is, spoken "about" [*über*] in contrast to the "object" of philosophy that is precisely never simply an "object," but what one is essentially (always already, *immer schon, toujours déjà*) "in." The question then becomes: how does one *thematize* what one is irreducibly in, and for that reason does not let itself be objectified, which for Heidegger always means presented or represented, put "before oneself" [*Vor-stellung*] as a describable "object," that is, something that stands over against [*Gegen-stand*]; describable, that is, from a so-called neutral standpoint? How would or could such an investigation *begin*, except by *already* presupposing what is at stake? This is the "hermeneutical situation" in which *Dasein* finds itself in *Being and Time*, and only through a hermeneutical effort can Dasein find its proper way "into" this "circle." In it, Heidegger also recognized Derrida's "incompetence of science."[8] It is also the general form of the complication as it guides Derrida's writing generally and the opening of *Of Grammatology* specifically. It is what complicates the "end" and "beginning" of writing ("*L'écriture avant la lettre*") and the famous remarks in the "Question of Method" that "we must begin wherever we are," to which I come back in detail below.

We have established that the general structure of the complication as it guides the opening of *Of Grammatology* is the Heideggerian problem of the thematization of what one is "always already in" (what is thus always already presupposed in any thematization or questioning). Now, the general term that, for Derrida, best describes this hermeneutical situation of "always already being in," the term that gives rise to or opens up the interpretation of that situation in an exemplary way, is language.

LANGUAGE: THE "EFFACEMENT OF ALL ITS LIMITS"

Of Grammatology is not "about" language in two ways: (1) insofar as language stands for what one is irreducibly "always already in" (including the attempts to put it in question), this complicates the possibility of a determinate concept of "language" that could properly function as an object for or subject of the investigation. Paradoxically, this does not mean that *Of Grammatology* is *not* about language. Quite the contrary: according to Derrida, this very indeterminacy makes language flow over into the "totality" of the "problematic horizon" of "a historico-metaphysical epoch" (G 14/4; a designation I return to at length). But then we are no longer speaking about language as merely one subject among others. (2) Precisely because of this overflowing, interpreting language in a certain sense always involves more than what the supposedly determinable "subject" of language would designate (as just one subject among others). The exergue announces that the questioning of language is not an end in itself: in finding one's way into the problem of language, one necessarily puts in question the very scientificity of science (including the science that is doing the questioning), as well as metaphysics and its history. This is what gives language its privileged position in Derrida's earlier works.[9]

I devote chapter 2 to the question of what exactly this order of logocentric metaphysics is according to Derrida, and to the complication inherent in asking that question. For now it is important to point out that Derrida calls logocentric metaphysics both a "structural figure" and a "historical totality." It is a structural figure to the extent that it describes the general structure of Western rationality or conceptuality, such as it structures our concepts as well as the means with which we (scientifically, metaphysically) question them. It is a "historical" totality because this rationality belongs essentially to the West and its history. More precisely: it is the historical rationality within which the very idea of history—which is no less logocentrically determined—could emerge. For this reason, Derrida sometimes speaks of an "epoch" or "age." Also for this reason, Derrida will speak of "traditional" concepts, conceptions, or oppositions, but because they are as "structural" as they are "historical," they do not simply belong to the past. It is important to signal this from the start: the question is exactly how we must understand Derrida's specifically indirect (and thus not simply negative or oppositional) type of response to so-called "classical oppositions" and, in this chapter specifically, to what he calls the "traditional determination" of writing.

Derrida opens the first chapter of *Of Grammatology* with the statement that "whatever one thinks under that title, the *problem of language* has no doubt never been one problem among others." Derrida clarifies this by looking at language's irreducibility to a determinable object or subject in two essentially related ways, by pointing to two moments of the same gesture that he is out to articulate with respect to language. What is it that distinguishes the "problem of language," not so much from *other problems*, but from *problems among others*? Derrida writes (1) that "everything one tries to exclude" [*arracher*] from language is itself "recaptured in it" *and* (2) that in the same gesture [*parce que du même coup*], language would then itself no longer be "self-assured, contained and *guaranteed*" [*rassuré sur soi, contenu et bordé*] by anything that would "exceed" it (G 15/6). In other words: the very idea of language "itself" would be complicated.

These two moments express something of the general structure of Derrida's approach to language, writing, and metaphysics broadly speaking. The moments are two aspects of the same gesture that I introduced above and that Derrida frequently calls the "effacement of (all) the limits" [*effacement de (toutes) ses limites*] of language, or its "overflowing" [*débordement*]. Because every determination or even every questioning of it is itself essentially "in" language, language is not unequivocally conceivable in terms of interiority and exteriority (inside and outside, what does or does not "belong to" language, what it is and is not, where it "begins and ends"). Because there is no way to rigorously make these distinctions, everything one tries to exclude from language is "recaptured in it." *Of Grammatology*'s central problems thus concern *delineation* or *outlining*, and the central categories of its first part are "inside and outside." Where the first moment states that what was otherwise opposed to language now falls under it, the second complicates matters. It indicates that the same problem of the possibility to delineate language (to draw the dividing line between what belongs to language and what does not, i.e.: what language is and what it is not) complicates the very determinability of language. Language is, in a certain way, indeterminate.

Why "in a certain way"? The indeterminacy of language is often taken to be an important aspect of Derrida's theory of language. The reason why grammatology is the title of a question, however, is that there could never be an unequivocal theory of the indeterminacy of language. Two possible senses of "indeterminacy" converge here. The first leaves description and theory intact. "Indeterminacy" would be a property attributed to language. The idea that language is indeterminate is still a determination of language. The diagnosis of indeterminacy would still be *about* language (this is the source of relativism and its derivations, which are characterized by *positing* indeterminacy. I get back to this in detail in chapter 3). But positing the indeterminacy of language in such a way would still presuppose or leave intact the integrity of language as a determinable subject or object "about" which one can say all these things and it would thus, as a determination of the indeterminable, contradict itself. The other sense is that language lends itself for no such theory, thetic discourse, or positive determination. The indeterminacy of language is then not a statement about language, but the complication of language's resistance to being an object of investigation, the subject of a theory or description.

I said that these two moments show something of the general structure of Derrida's strategy with respect to language and metaphysics more generally. *On the one hand*, there is Derrida's resistance to a simple outside, which corresponds to the first moment: one does not indicate language's limits by opposing something to it (the non-linguistic, the signified, the thing, the referent). Only in this way and in a certain sense, language is absolute. This holds equally for the limits of science, the limits of metaphysics, or the limits of the structural figure and/or historical totality called logocentrism. If they are limited, they are not limited in such a way that something falls outside them, is opposed or opposable to them (the utopia of a "new" language, an "other" metaphysics, a "future" epoch). This motif gets its most famous expression in that "axial proposition" of *Of Grammatology* that there is "no outside-text" [*il n'y a pas de hors-texte*], to which I return later. *On the other hand*, they (language, science, metaphysics, etc.)

are not absolute to the extent that there *are* limits. But these limits don't form the dividing line between what lies inside language or metaphysics and what falls outside it.

On the one hand, this double impossibility—of fashioning for oneself an outside position from which to determine the matter at hand, as well as of determining the matter itself by distinguishing it rigorously from what is outside or opposed to it—could be called a certain *internalization*. The phrase, after all, has become famous: deconstruction "works from the inside" (G 39/24). Here, I indicate preliminarily, questions arise with regard to Hegel as the thinker of the movement of opposition as a "recapturing" of the outside (spirit finding *itself in* the other), and to Heidegger as the hermeneutic thinker of what one is essentially "in."

But on the other hand, if there is no simple outside, there is no simple inside either. Internalization cannot mean containment. This is the second moment: the internality of language, what it is to be in it, cannot be equated with being contained within determinable borders. And here other questions arise, about the "immanence" of the Hegelian movement (that his idealism is "absolute" precisely *not* because it "contains" a totality), as well as Heidegger's famous distinction of *In-sein* from simply "being in."

So what is the general strategy? To explicate the limits of metaphysics without simply opposing something to it. That there is no outside does not mean there are no limits. It means they must be "inner" limits, only there is no unequivocal internality either. Instead, this very equivocality or lack of rigorous determinability *itself* forms the "limit" to which metaphysics must be confronted "from within": it is this necessity-yet-insufficiency of a distinction such as that between the inside and the outside that forms the limit of metaphysics or logocentrism.

WHAT A DERRIDEAN "THEORY" WOULD "OPPOSE": THE "TRADITIONAL DETERMINATION" OF WRITING

If Derrida's claims concerning language and writing do not combine into an unambiguous theory of language, then what is their function within the movement of his texts? What are they supposed to show? Because my interest here is with the status of Derrida's propositions, my aim is not to reconstruct *differently* the claims that are already so well-known about the functioning of the sign and the relation of writing and speech and to presence. My concern is the relation between the statements that Derrida makes and the gesture he performs in making them. This is also Derrida's own concern when, in order to produce the problems of writing, he takes to Ferdinand de Saussure. Derrida states that he will recognize in De Saussure's work a "tension between gesture and statement" [*tension du geste et du propos*] (G 45/30).

There are two positions on Derrida's claims concerning language as writing that seem to me equally insufficient. The first is too negative and holds that with his destabilization of the traditional conception of language, Derrida's position amounts to mere relativism. The second is too positive and holds that Derrida provides or presents a new and positive account of the nature of language, one that better or more adequately corresponds to or describes the nature of language. Both, I want to argue, misunderstand Derrida's gesture. I treat the latter in this chapter and am only truly able to respond to the former in chapter 3.

I can be relatively brief about the basic elements—the statements—of Derrida's reading. Derrida identifies an element common to all traditional linguistics, namely that language is a system of signs in which the sign is a signifier of a signified. What is "traditional" in that conception is the general idea that a sign refers to or represents *something*. It does not matter what it is that is signified by the sign (the world, an intention, an idea, a thing, a thought, "mental content," a "meaning," etc.). A sign can itself refer to another sign, but for it to signify *something*, we must suppose that this chain of significations must end somewhere—at a signified that is not itself a signifier (e.g., the world, the thing, the thought, the experience, etc.). Because such a signified that must ultimately be external to the sign-system (i.e.: not itself a signifier) is thus constitutive for signification, because it constitutes the condition for the possibility of signification, Derrida speaks of a "transcendental signified."

How then, "traditionally," does writing fit in here?

De Saussure assumes a view that Derrida traces back to Aristotle, and that according to Derrida is constitutive of Western thought, that is, of the entire history, epoch, or structural figure of metaphysics. According to De Saussure, "language and writing are two distinct systems of signs; the second *exists for the sole purpose of representing* the first." Derrida quotes Aristotle: "spoken words are the symbols of states of the soul and written words are the symbols of spoken words" (G 21/11).

For Derrida, in this traditional view, writing is both narrow [*étroite*] and derivative [*dérivée*]. Narrow because *foreign to the essence* of language, and derived because merely *representative*. Derivative and representative of what? Derivative and representative of the *voice*:

> [. . .] within this logos [the history of metaphysics and the metaphysical determinations of truth], the original and essential link to the phonē has never been broken. [. . .] As has been more or less implicitly determined, the essence of the phonē would be immediately proximate to that which within "thought" as logos relates to "meaning," produces it, receives it, speaks it, "composes" it. (G 21/11)

As such, the voice, as "producer of the first symbols," has a "relationship of essential and immediate proximity with the mind. [. . .] It signifies 'mental experiences' which themselves reflect or mirror things by natural resemblance" (G 21/11). In contrast to the voice, which is "closest to the signified," writing will always be derivative: because it is a mere representation of the "first" representation in spoken language; "foreign to the essence of language" as mere "signifier of the signifier" instead of signifier of a signified:

> signifier of the first signifier, representation of the self-present voice [*de la voix présente à soi*], of the immediate, natural and direct signification of sense (of the signified, the concept, the ideal object, or what have you). (G 46/30)

Such a writing Derrida therefore calls "phonetic": "[. . .] it will be the outside, the exterior representation of language and of this 'thought-sound.'" The tradition that approaches writing in this way is therefore called "phonocentric."

So the traditional view of language is that its signification is constituted by the signified that it represents. The voice is the model for the immediate signification, the self-presence of the signified in the signifier. In contrast, writing is always merely signifier of the signifier and maintains no essential relation to the signified in the way the voice does. For that reason, writing has traditionally been "debased" or considered to be secondary with respect to the voice.

Now, what the first part of Derrida's reading of De Saussure does ("the outside and the inside," the part that focuses on De Saussure's "stated purpose" and not yet on his "gesture") is to chart all the ways, all the conceptions, all the oppositions within which writing has in this way been debased or regarded as secondary with respect to spoken language. That is: all the ways in which writing is considered outside, or external to the essence (inside) of language. The terms with which this is done include the difference between "natural" and "conventional" signification; natural language and writing as "instrument" or "technique"; the immediacy of the voice and the mediacy or mediation of writing; signifier of a signified as the "essence" of language, this essence itself being the "image" of "reality," "representation" of a "presence" as opposed to writing as mere representation of a representation, "image of an image." To this also belong the differences between "symbol" and "sign"; the "soul" and the "body"; "living" language and the "dead" letter; autonomy and heteronomy; origin and substitution.

So in all these analyses of the hierarchical nature of what Derrida calls these "traditional" oppositions with which we think writing—where is the "indirectness"? Is all of this not quite unequivocal theory? Is it not a clearly outlined and detailed analysis of the history of linguistic theory and the conceptual grid within which writing has always been determined?

Certainly in the diagnosis of the phonocentric character of traditional determinations of writing there is little indirectness. The question is: if that determination is "narrow" and "derivative," do we find in Derrida's work an alternative position, theory, or account that would not be narrow or derivative? Is there a different, expanded, and original determination of writing that Derrida opposes to the phonocentric determination?

The second part of the reading of De Saussure sets out to show how the conceptual grid with which writing is conceived in the *Course in General Linguistics* contains the resources for the conception of a more "general" writing. It is in order to articulate this general writing that Derrida will introduce the well-known critical vocabulary in which we have come to recognize the elements of a Derridean "theory of language": the "(instituted) trace" [*trace (instituée)*], "arche-writing" [*archi-écriture*], and "*différance*." If Derrida has a theory of writing, it is often held to reside in this notion of a "generalized" writing. And it is here that Derrida's *gesture*, the movement of showing in the "claims" he makes, becomes decisive. This is so for at least two reasons.

First of all, Derrida's claim is that the necessity to conceive of a "generalized" writing (as opposed to a narrow and derivative writing) arises from the theoretical framework that De Saussure *himself* employs (the conceptual grid that makes his work an "exemplary" instance of logocentrism). It is this framework *itself* that allows for the articulation or the conception of a different, general writing. According to Derrida, the "intention that institutes general linguistics as a science" itself "remains [. . .] within a contradiction" (G 45/29). This is a contradiction between its "declared purpose" ("saying what goes without saying, the subordination of grammatology, the historico-metaphysical reduction of writing to the rank of an instrument enslaved to a full and originarily spoken language") and "another gesture" (of a general or originary writing, G 39/29). This means that Derrida's claim is that it is not *he* who supplies an alternative account of writing, but that it is De Saussure himself who implicitly goes against his own declared intentions. That is what Derrida so often emphasizes when he writes of deconstruction as working "from the inside"; of the "inhabiting" of texts "in a certain way"; that, as a way of reading, deconstruction "[does] not destroy structures from the outside," but "[operates] necessarily from the inside, borrowing all the strategic and economic resources of subversion from the old structure," and so forth. This should already indicate that a generalized writing cannot be contrasted to writing's traditional determination as being "Derrida's position."

Moreover, second, what Derrida names under the heading of a generalized writing cannot be a rival view opposed to the traditional determination of writing because the very idea of such an expanded writing undercuts itself in its very articulation. And it is to the necessity of this undercutting—of this performative contradiction or implicit self-complication—that Derrida wants to testify above all in the broader movement of his writing. Rather than supplying a better description of the nature of language and writing, Derrida sets out to show an inability to describe, an "incompetence" of science that for Derrida is the incompetence of theory and of philosophy, or of what he calls the "epistēmē." It is here that one must take very seriously Derrida's claim that *Of Grammatology* "does not restore confidence."

But before being able to show just how the idea of a generalized writing complicates itself, we must first understand what it would mean. For that reason I now reconstruct the necessity of such a writing while bracketing its complicated status. So supposing that the idea of a generalized writing *would* be an "alternative account," what would this account consist of? The answer to this question is found in the second part of Derrida's reading of De Saussure, the part on the "gesture" of De Saussure's stated intentions.

WHAT A DERRIDEAN "THEORY" WOULD "OPPOSE" TO THE TRADITIONAL DETERMINATION: WHAT IS "GENERALIZED" WRITING?

The difficulties in the interpretation of Derrida's texts lie not so much in a mischaracterization of his claims or statements, but rather in the (theoretical) status that is accorded to them, or in the nature of their gesture. The statements themselves, which supposedly make up Derrida's theory of language, are quite easily recognizable.

What are the resources within the conceptual grid of De Saussure that "liberate the future" of a "general grammatology"? First of all, this complication already revealed itself in the first part of the reading of De Saussure, to the extent that writing's supposed "exteriority" with respect to the essence of language raises the question: why, if writing must be considered exterior to the essence of language, is it not harmless with respect to that inner logic of language, but rather conceived in several ways and consistently by several authors as a "threat" to that essence? In its most systematic expression, this is Derrida's question:

> Why does a project of *general* linguistics, concerning the *internal system in general of language in general*, outline the limits of its field by excluding, as *exteriority in general*, a *particular* system of writing, however important it might be, even were it to be *in fact* universal? (G 58/39)

Derrida goes on to show in a great variety of ways that this supposedly exterior writing is by no means conceived as therefore harmless, but rather as "dangerous," as "threat," as "crisis," even as "evil," as "sacrilege." He discusses Plato (writing "[condemned] to blindness, wandering and mourning"), De Saussure's complicity with Husserl concerning the determination of empty intuition as a "crisis" ("usurpation": the "danger" of the "violence" with which "writing would substitute itself for its own origin"), and of course Rousseau (on the "tyranny" of writing as the risk of mispronunciation). The exteriority of writing is considered to be a *threat to the stability* of language.

At that point, Derrida traces the first clear mark of a certain "overflowing." If Derrida wants to show that logocentric metaphysics is essentially, constitutively phonocentric, it is because it consists precisely in this consistent exteriorization *of* writing. But that means that writing is not simply exterior to the essence of language, but rather threatens it "from within." The move to exteriorize writing cannot be understood if writing was already harmlessly "external to the essence of language." For Derrida, it also means that a certain complication of maintaining the integrity of the distinction between language's "inside and outside" starts to become visible: in one sense, writing must be wholly external to the essence of language; in another sense of the same gesture, it *cannot* be.

According to Derrida, this would account for the amount of attention De Saussure devotes to writing as well as the important exemplary value he regularly accords it. The idea that writing would *not* be considered to be external to the essence of language gives a new meaning to the instances in which De Saussure states that writing is nevertheless "comparable" to language and that for this reason De Saussure uses writing to "clarify" the structure of language.

This suggestion—that writing must, according to De Saussure's *own* text, at the same time *not* be thought to be external to the essence of language—is implicit in the gesture of two of its main statements: (1) "the thesis of the arbitrariness of the sign" and (2) "the thesis of *difference* as the source of linguistic value." Here Derrida recalls De Saussure's remark that "arbitrary" and "differential" are "correlative qualities" (G 65/44. Cf. 77n18/327n18).

The first thesis complicates, first, the possibility of writing being a "figuration" or "mere image" of language (if all signs are arbitrary, there can be no relation of figuration to the signified), which was constitutive for writing's exteriority, as well as, second, the supposedly immediate, "natural attachment" of signifier and signified in the *voice* from which writing was distinguished. Derrida argues that the thesis of the arbitrariness of the sign ruptures any sense of such attachment. The sign is wholly "unmotivated" (G 65ff./44ff.).

What this means according to Derrida is that one would have to attribute to language *generally* the structure for which writing was traditionally debased and *excluded* from language.

That is also the implication of the second main De Saussurrean statement, the thesis of difference as the source of linguistic value. The constitutive value of difference "contradicts the allegation of a naturally phonic essence of language"[10] (G 77/53).

Thus, there arises the necessity to think a writing that would not be external to the essence of language: a "general" rather than a "narrow" writing. Now one might suppose that, if not simply external, such a writing would then have to be "internal" to the essence of language. That is indeed one of the formulations that Derrida employs to describe such a generalized writing: "It threatened the desire for the living speech from the closest proximity, it breached living speech *from within* and from the very beginning" (G 79/56–57, emphasis mine, JdJ).

However, it is at this point that the movement of Derrida's writing becomes essential. For even given all the necessities to think in the direction of such a writing, it still does not lead to a *better determination* of the nature of language. Derrida states that even though all this "amounts, of course, to reforming the concept of writing," still this "never gives rise to a new 'scientific' concept of writing" (G 79/57). This is what we must come to understand. I start with this "reformation" of the concept of writing before looking at its resistance to "scientificity."

What would it mean to say that writing would be "internal" to the essence of language? This would mean that (all) language would be constituted by the very structure for which writing was considered to be derivative. But what does that amount to? Writing was debased as mere sign of a sign; signifier of a signifier rather than signifier of a signified. One would then have to think such narrow writing in a more general way: "[. . .] writing is not a sign of a sign, except if one says it of all signs, which would be more profoundly true":

> There the signified always already functions as a signifier. The secondarity that it seemed possible to ascribe to writing alone affects all signifieds in general, affects them always already, the moment they *enter the game*. There is not a single signified that escapes, even if recaptured, the play of signifying references that constitute language. The advent of writing is the advent of this play [. . .] (G 16/7)

What does it mean to think this general writing? To think the movement of language as a "play" of signifiers that would not be "arrested" by a signified. In Derrida's words—contamination, overflowing, and effacement of limits: "[. . .] effacing the limit starting from which one had thought to regulate the circulation of signs, drawing along with it all the reassuring signifieds, reducing all the strongholds, all the out-of-bounds shelters that watched over the field of language" (G 16/7). In this way, the "absence of the transcendental signified" signifies the "limitlessness of play."

Now, if we were to "abandon" these statements "to the contents of their conclusions," without thinking through their place within the broader scope of Derrida's movement of showing, then it would be at this point that one would attribute to Derrida a linguistic relativism. That relativism would consist in the *assurance* that the play of significations is arrested *nowhere* by a signified. The play of significations being endless, anything can mean anything whatsoever; and all meaning is unfounded and arbitrary.

But the signified is *transcendental*. That is: *constitutive* for the functioning of the sign. If the very functioning of the sign and language rests for its possibility on such a signified (whether this be the "thing itself," or "context," or "(authorial) intention" or "mental content" or whatever "presence" one would imagine language to refer to or signify, as such determining its "full" meaning), and if we are now asked to think of a general writing that would be a language without such a signified, if we say that "we think only in signs," then indeed this "amounts to ruining the notion of the sign at the very moment when, as in Nietzsche, its exigency is recognized in the absoluteness of its right." It "amounts to destroying the concept of 'sign' and its entire logic" (G 16/7).

It is here that we recognize that Derrida cannot be said to give us a theory of language. What emerges here could never be a theory, could never be a *better determination* of the nature of language. What confronts us here is, according to Derrida, an "overwhelming" that "supervenes at the moment when the extension of the concept of language effaces all its limits" (G 16/7). We already saw this complication at work in the very structure of the question of writing. Now we see that a general writing would destroy the very notion of the sign.

Here Derrida shows himself to be a thinker of movement. It is not that the proposition of language as a "limitless play" cannot be found in Derrida's writings; it is rather that it does not take on the character of an unequivocal assurance. It does not form an endpoint or a conclusion ("Derrida's position"), but rather forms a part of a broader strategy of writing that "does not provide assurances." What holds for a general linguistics holds equally for a general writing: one cannot think its inside and outside in terms of determined linguistic models. But as generalized *writing*, nor can its outside be thought in terms of determined *non*-linguistic models (the transcendental signified as the presence that would arrest the play of meaning). Rather, thinking language as writing implies an "effacement of its limits," which signifies a certain inability to determine, rather than a better determination of, the nature of language. In fact, the very idea of a "nature of language," to the extent that this is conceived as an "internal system," in terms of its "inside and outside," has now become problematic. And it is this "internal system," the *very ability to distinguish* inside from outside (what belongs from what does not belong; essence from accident; nature from culture; beginning from end, etc.), that lies at the heart of what Derrida calls "scientific exigency." This is how the question of writing confronts one with a certain "incompetence of science."

This incompetence is what informs all of Derrida's indirectness, or the movement of his writing. Derrida speaks also of a "hesitation," or of a "trembling" of his writings that is, however, crucially, "not an 'incoherence'" (G 39/24). Here arises a need for Derrida to write what he explicitly recognizes cannot be written. Asking the question of writing means explicating a function of the sign (in a generalized writing) that simultaneously destroys that very concept. It means explicating a writing that can no longer answer to its classical determination—it could not be the object of a science.

This becomes even clearer when we realize that the full implications of this "modification" of the concept of writing exceed that of generalization alone: phonocentric writing was not only a narrow, but also a *derivative* determination of writing. A generalized writing, however, complicates the norm with respect to which a phonocentric writing would be "derived." That norm is *presence,* as the source of linguistic value, represented most fully in the idea of the self-presence in the voice. If that norm is itself problematic (if, in Derrida's words, "'signifier of the signifier' no longer defines accidental doubling and fallen secondarity" but describes "on the contrary the movement of language") then this general writing would constitute language in its "origin" or "archè." For this "originary" writing, Derrida employs the concept of "arche-writing" [*archi-écriture*]: "[. . .] writing itself as the origin of language" (G 64/44). But here, again, one must say what cannot be said because "one can already suspect that an origin whose structure can be expressed as 'signifier of the signifier' conceals and erases itself in its own production."

So where does this leave us? There is a need for a general instead of a narrow writing, but it would "destroy" the concept of the sign altogether. There is a need to think an "originary" instead of a "derived" writing, but that is a contradiction in terms that destroys the very concept of originarity. What is it, then, that the broader movement of *Of Grammatology* is out to show? At this point it is important to adhere to the warnings that one hears often, which have even become something of a slogan, namely that deconstruction does not "rehabilitate writing in the narrow sense" or "reverse the order of dependence" between language and writing (G 79/56). Because there could be no coherent "view" of a general writing that did not simultaneously undercut itself, rather than constructing a "new" writing or call for a rehabilitation of the "old" writing (so that it would *not* be derivative), the articulation of arche-writing in fact shows the very *movement of exteriorization* that is constitutive of the vulgar, colloquial, or narrow writing. It shows metaphysics to be the very movement that attempts to maintain the rigor of the distinctions between inside and outside—a "desire for presence" that manifests itself in the repression of writing. It is not a matter of opposing this metaphysics or opposing something to it, but of recognizing an arche-writing in its very movement of the repression of writing. It shows that writing is derived and determined only by virtue of its exteriorization by metaphysics, and in that sense arche-writing is the "condition" both for the possibility of colloquial writing as well as for the traditional concept of the sign. The same holds for the determination of language as such. In this way, the very movement by which the "internal system" of language (with presence as the source or norm of its signification) and writing are separated from each other would be the very movement that arche-writing is to name. It is not a matter of rehabilitating writing, but of understanding the movement of the "repression"[11] of a certain kind of (phonocentric) writing. Such a repression takes place *as* the "desire for presence." This repression and this desire go hand in hand; they name the same movement, and they name the structure of the movement of logocentrism or of metaphysics. This means we have not arrived at a place beyond metaphysics, but at an explication of its movement. The movement of thought is desire for presence.

But how, then, to account for such a movement in writing? For Derrida this always means: how can it be "marked"? Throughout *Of Grammatology*, Derrida stresses that it cannot simply be a matter of developing a new language (which would then get it right). He stresses the need to "retain the old name" and its "legibility." Instead, to account for this movement, Derrida works toward "acts of writing."

WHY "RETAIN THE OLD NAME"? TOWARD "ACTS OF WRITING"

Derrida insists on calling this movement of arche-writing a "writing." He spends quite some time emphasizing this crucial necessity to "retain the old name." If arche-writing is supposed to account for the very production of the difference between colloquial writing and the norm with respect to which it is regarded as derivative ("language," "full" speech, the auto-affection of the voice, in short: presence), then is this not a totally different structure? Why retain the old name? According to Derrida, he retains the name because arche-writing "essentially communicates" with writing in the colloquial sense. Why? First, the structure of arche-writing is the very structure for which writing has always been "debased": "Not that the word 'writing' has ceased to designate the signifier of the signifier, but it appears, strange as it may seem, that 'signifier of the signifier' no longer defines accidental doubling and fallen secondarity."

But here one might object that it is a characteristic of Derrida's writings not to confine himself to old names, but to make strategic use of neologisms. If there were a "new" account of language, then in *Of Grammatology* its central category would have to be the "(instituted) trace." Is that not simply the name for Derrida's new account?

If arche-writing cannot simply denote a new position on the nature of language, then how does Derrida describe it? He now thinks the movement by which writing is exteriorized and by which it thus turns into colloquial, vulgar, derivative writing *as* the very movement *of* the "dissimulation" of an arche-writing—a movement in virtue of the reassurance and protection of the "internal system" and the integrity of the distinction between inside and outside. This arche-writing then names how difference was reduced in the historical imposition of the colloquial distinction of (phonocentric) language and writing—that is, how writing was repressed. Only arche-writing's "threat from within" can explain the necessity for that repression, and the force of the "desire for presence." Thus, Derrida states that the "derivativeness of writing" was possible "on one condition: that the 'original,' 'natural,' etc. language had never existed, never been intact and untouched by writing, that it itself had always been a writing" (G 79/56). The claim here is that the movement of the desire for presence, the movement of or toward presence, can only be understood as the repression of a difference that threatens "from within." The movement of presence is that movement of difference effacing itself: difference is not external to presence, but presence carries difference within itself: it is its own effacement.

To understand this self-effacing arche-writing as "condition" of all systems of signification, Derrida introduces the notion of the "(instituted) trace," two concepts (institution and trace) that would, for reasons now becoming increasingly clear, have to be "[detached] from the classical discourse from which I necessarily borrow them" (G 68/46). What classical discourse?

The word "institution" colloquially acquires its meaning by virtue of its opposition to nature; if something is instituted, this means it is not natural. The word "trace" is borrowed, according to Derrida, from Nietzsche and Freud. Colloquially, that notion implies the presence of an absence, of something that is not or no longer itself present.

It is the concept of the trace that is said to be "irreducible" to the deconstruction of the metaphysics of presence, which is announced to be the "final intention" of *Of Grammatology* to the extent that it "[makes] enigmatic what one thinks one understands by the words 'proximity,' 'immediacy,' 'presence' (the proximate [*proche*]), the own [*propre*], and the pre- of presence)."

One can see how the trace, as the presence of an absence, could be irreducible within such a project that sets out to show the self-effacement of presence. Nevertheless, Derrida insists that that notion must be detached from the discourse from which it is borrowed. How is Derrida's concept of the trace, like the concepts of writing or of language, reformed?

The colloquial concept of the trace still leaves the present intact as the source of what it signifies. The footprint in the sand does not signify the complete absence of man, but rather his delayed presence. The trace is then the representation of an absent, because past, presence, and it is this past presence that is what the trace ultimately signifies. It leaves intact in an unproblematic fashion the notion of origin and its essential relation to presence. Derrida's instituted trace, however, is introduced to describe the movement by which the distinction of absence from (and its derivation with respect to) presence can be understood. This means that it essentially complicates the possibility of full presence (a presence to which difference is wholly exterior) as well as the notion of origin. The trace "[retains] the other as other in the same." In this way, what Derrida articulates involves stating what undercuts itself or saying what cannot strictly speaking be said. But this negative language only holds when trying to explicate the mutually excluding "positions" that the trace would imply. As Derrida says it, the trace cannot be "interpreted within the classical system of oppositions" (G 68/46). But in a more positive way, one could see this notion of the trace as precisely the expression of the aporetics of presence and absence that the questions of language and signification require. A better way to say that, more in line with Derrida's terminology, would be to say that "trace" "marks" these aporetics. Another way in which Derrida marks the necessity and the impossibility of a concept is through the technique of erasure. Thus, for example, the first part of the reading of De Saussure is called "the inside and the outside" (the distinction that controls De Saussure's "statements" and the "traditional" determination of writing), and the second part of the reading is called "the inside is the outside" (the "overflowing" corresponding to De Saussure's "gesture" that does not let itself be unambiguously articulated, as it exceeds the "metaphysical oppositions"). And another mark would be the inaudible difference between the French ("et" and "est"), like the "a" of différance, that would complicate phono- and logocentrism—the primacy of the voice—not by opposing it or opposing something to it, but through a written mark, or an act of writing:

> Certainly a new conceptualization is to be produced, but it must take into account the fact that conceptualization itself, and by itself alone, can reintroduce what one wants to "criticize." This is why this work cannot be purely "theoretical" or "conceptual" or "discursive," I mean cannot be the work of a discourse entirely regulated by essence, meaning, truth, consciousness, ideality, etc. What I call text is also that which "practically" inscribes and overflows the limits of such a discourse. (*Pos* 81/59)

If there is a "new" writing at work in Derrida's texts, then it is not that of a better account, but rather of a performative and strategic deployment of concepts that prevents any reduction of the text to the presentation of a position. It is important to stress that this *does* lead to a new understanding of language *in a certain sense,* and even one that could perhaps be called "better." I don't doubt that there is a sense in which Derrida would say that, for instance, "experience of the impossible" is in a certain way a much *better* description of a decision than, for example, "the application of a general rule to a specific case." But the way in which such a better description complicates the very idea of a position and even of description as such, how it does not lead to a coherent "account," should be enough to indicate that such a position is not an end in itself for Derrida. And that means that the purport of his writings cannot be reduced to it. Ultimately, the question is what place "taking up a position" or "defending a proposition" should have in doing philosophy or in the attempt to take intellectual responsibility. That is a question to which I return in detail in the final chapters of this book.

So the problem underlying the too positive as well as the too negative reading of Derrida is that they both take him to propose a new determination of writing. But how could one oppose the classical oppositions as such without reintroducing exactly what one is trying to avoid? How could one identify the "proper" character of language or writing outside of or in opposition to the very "logic of identity"? For Derrida, the marks mentioned above and the acts of writing he employs are his attempts to find a language that would be able to account for these complications. This is the precise point at which Derrida is a thinker of movement. This is why Derrida systematically emphasizes that one must "faithfully repeat" the movement of metaphysics "in its *totality*" and in doing so "[*make*] it *insecure* [*l'ébranlant*] in its most assured evidences" (G 107/73). Derrida speaks of "going through" the concept of the arche-trace. In other places, he speaks of the necessity of a certain "track" [*parcours*]. To repeat *and* to make insecure, or, better: to make insecure only *in* or *through* its repetition—a movement of showing in or through sentences and positions that, if left to themselves, will have been merely propositions. It is through such a series of repetitions (not through an "escape" or a position "outside" metaphysics) that one can question metaphysics or make it "tremble." One would therefore be tempted to say: make it tremble "from within," if the very idea of this trembling was not to make unstable the supposed rigor of the distinction between inside and outside.

I end this chapter with a final example. Derrida's movement shows itself well in his treatment of the "transcendental." This is an exemplary concept under erasure, aside from origin, arche, writing, and so forth. Derrida consistently emphasizes the necessity of "going through" the transcendental. The instituted trace, arche-trace, or originary trace must both fulfill a constitutive, transcendental, or originary function as well as signify the very impossibility of such a constitution, put transcendentality in question, and signify the impossibility of a (single) origin. And it is because of this irreducibility to any specific constituted difference that Derrida writes that he "nicknames" this movement the "*pure* movement which produces difference": différance (G 92/62).

According to Derrida, one must "refer" to the transcendentality one puts in question. Because of this double necessity with respect to the transcendental, Derrida's discourse has been dubbed quasi-transcendental, or "ultra-transcendental," as Derrida designates it in *Of Grammatology* (G 90/61). But in the literature, the desire for such designations still betrays a desire to pin down Derrida's position. One sees that the "quasi" here does not have the form of a sort of compromise, but rather the Kierkegaardian hyperbolic sense of the necessity of an impossibility.[12] Thus, Derrida maintains that "the ontological and transcendental problematics must first be seriously *exhausted*," which for Derrida means to "patiently and rigorously [work] through" them: "the critical movement of the Husserlian and Heideggerian questions must be effectively followed to the very end, and their effectiveness and legibility must be conserved" (G 73/50). Derrida is very clear on the necessity for the "legibility" of the metaphysical movements (here: the transcendental and ontological questions in Husserl and Heidegger). Erasure and legibility are equally necessary: without the first, not a single critical step in the direction of the limitations of metaphysics is possible. But without the second, the "ultra-transcendental text will so closely resemble the precritical text as to be indistinguishable from it." Therefore: "[. . .] the value of the transcendental arche must make its necessity felt before letting itself be erased. The concept of arche-trace must comply with both that necessity and that erasure" (G 90/61).

CONCLUSION

I have shown that in *Of Grammatology*, Derrida's concern from the outset is to bring out a certain "incompetence" of science and philosophy from which the discourse that brings it out is not exempt.

It shows itself in the hesitant presentation and essentially ambiguous and provisional character of the distinctions with which Derrida opens his text (theory/example, to "produce the problems" of reading "through a reading," etc.). This incompetence of science is due to the Heideggerian complication of the question: to scientifically put in question the very scientificity of science means to *already* rely on what one wants to put in question. It is that aporetic structure of the question that Derrida attempts to bring out and to which the question of language provides an exemplary mode of access. In the words of Heidegger, it is no longer a matter of avoiding the circularity of this question but of finding the right way into it (BT 315–16/302). As I show later, "circularity" is always a pejorative for Derrida. Instead, he understands this circularity as a "de-limitation" or an overflowing of language into the structures formerly thought to be alien, external, or opposed to it. The most important of these structures is what is colloquially called writing. I have stressed that Derrida's account of arche-writing does not boil down to a theory of language that one could oppose to a traditional view. We do not find two "rival accounts" of writing—one "derived" and one "originary." Rather, Derrida explicates a certain necessary indeterminacy of language at the very heart of the "traditional" view. Even the neologisms, the erasures, and the "acts" of writing, though they certainly function as a liberation, are still not simply a new or better language, but an operation on the "old name" of which the legibility must be retained.

One cannot understand the erasure, or the "performative contradiction" of an arche-writing or of an inside that "is" outside, if one attributes to Derrida the assurance of a theoretical position. It does not matter whether one does this to refute him as an irresponsible relativist (to deprive his work of "legitimacy") or to defend him as a responsible post-metaphysical thinker by attempting to *provide* him with some kind of legitimacy. Neither refutation nor defense is adequate. I return to this question of justification in detail in chapter 3. The movement by which Derrida complicates metaphysics can only be understood if one sees that though he is out to expose the limits of metaphysics, he is not out to oppose anything to it or to free himself from it, both of which would not lead to the limits of metaphysics. As Derrida indicates in his discussion of Husserl: "[. . .] in the deconstruction of the arche, one does not make a choice" in terms of "yes or no."

This structure of the both-and of legibility and erasure, of necessity and impossibility, structures the specific form of indirectness of Derrida's movement of showing and the ambiguity of his "position." The "limits" of the propositional do not let themselves be conceived in terms of "something" that would be "external" to it, which is why the showing of these limits does not result in a "new account" of language. This does not mean that propositions, language, and metaphysics are "unlimited" in the sense of *absolute*. It means that what "exceeds" them is not simply "external" to it or, thereby, simply "internal": it is specific to Derrida's thought that he conceives of these limits precisely *as* both the necessity and the impossibility (this "double bind") of the very distinction between inside and outside.

The meditation on writing is not an end in itself in *Of Grammatology*. It is said to "broach" [*entamer*] the "order" of logocentrism: the meditation on the "Saussurean text" and "in a general way the treatment of the concept of writing [. . .] already give us the assured means of broaching the de-construction of *the greatest totality*—the concept of the *epistēmē* and logocentric metaphysics." That is the focus of the next chapter.

CHAPTER 2

THE INEXTRICABILITY OF METAPHYSICS

> One is never installed within transgression, one never lives elsewhere. [. . .] At the conclusion of a certain work, even the concepts of excess or of transgression can become suspect.
>
> —Derrida (*Positions*)

> It is a trace, and a trace of the erasure of the trace.
> Thereby the text of metaphysics is *comprehended*. Still legible; and to be read. It is not surrounded but rather traversed by its limit, marked in its interior by the multiple furrow of its margin.
>
> —Derrida (*Margins of Philosophy*)

The discussion of language in *Of Grammatology* serves to question what Derrida designates under the heading of "epistēmē." This groups together what he most frequently calls "logocentrism" or "(logocentric) metaphysics," the "scientificity of science," or sometimes just "philosophy." In a chapter devoted to these matters, the first question should obviously be: what exactly *is* logocentric metaphysics? I start by showing that Derrida takes the very form of that question ("what is . . . ?") to be one of metaphysics' main hallmarks. This means that, as in the case of language, the question of what metaphysics is causes a performative or implicit complication that Derrida is out to expose.

Where does this leave us if we want to have some grip on what Derrida means by the term? What he does state quite clearly is that metaphysics stands both for a "structural figure" and a "historical totality"

(G 7/lxxxix). After having first demonstrated the Heideggerian form of the complication, I proceed by describing the general characteristics of what Derrida understands under the structural figure of "logocentric metaphysics." In a list that is not meant to be exhaustive, I gather the main traits of Derrida's use of the term metaphysics under the headings of "demarcation," "opposition," "hierarchy," and "presence." In keeping with the lines set out in chapter 1, I still focus on Derrida's relatively early works, and *Of Grammatology* in particular.

I emphasize with respect to Derrida's relation to metaphysics that alterity cannot be reduced to externality. In a way, that is a thoroughly uncontroversial statement. After all, many have echoed Derrida's famous declaration that "there is no sense in shaking metaphysics without the concepts of metaphysics" (*WD* 412/354). However, I argue that even in doing so, Derrida's work has still too often been presented as a move *away from* or *out of* logocentric metaphysics, or as the attempt to do so. In this view, metaphysics stands for the structural figure or historical totality that we are essentially in. I do not disagree with that, but this "in" is then taken to mean the already familiar and more or less determinable (the "traditional," the oppositional, etc.). That in turn makes Derrida's question of "alterity" (of how to think or write "otherwise") into a question of how we can get *out of* it. I hold, however—analogous to Heidegger's warning that it is not a matter of getting out of the vicious circularity of the question of being, but of getting *into* it in the right way—that alterity does not arise in the movement away from metaphysics but in the movement toward metaphysics, in the very attempt to put it—and with that ourselves—in question.[1] But this means that logocentric metaphysics cannot itself be the rigorously determinable or the already familiar from which we are supposed to free ourselves. Just as the deconstruction of the sign does not lead to "new assurances" concerning the nature of language and writing, so there cannot be found a determined idea or definition of logocentrism in Derrida's works, any more than of what would supposedly lie outside it.

Why is this matter so important for the problem of Derrida's indirectness? Because the decisive insight for the performative complexity of Derrida's writing is that, though he is out to expose the limits of what he calls metaphysics, its oppositionality cannot itself be unequivocally *opposed*; its demarcation cannot simply be contrasted to something outside it; its domination of the very form of the (scientific, philosophical) "question of essence" cannot be simply questioned—without some kind of reaffirmation of what is put in question. And it is the total movement of these strictures that Derrida seeks to expose. The most decisive Derridean idea is not that a certain overcoming of metaphysics should be realized, but that this very overcoming cannot have the form of a movement outside of, or away from, an opposition to metaphysics. For now, I consider the theoretical and performative implications of this insight. But this entanglement or inextricability already foreshadows the thought of an "irreducible complicity" or the "fatal necessity of a *contamination*" (OS 26/10) on which I base my interpretation of Derrida's ethics in chapter 9.

With this, the very idea of a beyond itself comes under erasure. This has very important consequences for how all the basic concepts that seem to imply a beyond—such as "new," "future," or "limit"—are interpreted. I end this chapter with a discussion of these concepts. After having done so, I then am able to consider in detail the consequences of my indirect reading of Derrida for the questions of critique and justification in chapter 3.

THE "STRUCTURAL FIGURE": DEMARCATION, OPPOSITION, HIERARCHY, PRESENCE

It is hard to overstate the importance of "logocentrism" in Derrida's works of the late 1960s, yet it is difficult to find an explicit, rigorous account of exactly what it means.[2] The situation is exacerbated by the fact that Derrida seems to freely use a wide range of related concepts quite interchangeably. Among them are (in *Of Grammatology* alone): "logocentrism" or simply "logos," "science" or "scientificity," "epistēmē," "philosophy," and of course the "metaphysics of presence" or simply "metaphysics." He also associates these concepts with "theory" and with "(theoretical) knowledge." We saw in chapter 1 how the question of the sign points beyond knowledge or to "a knowledge that is not a knowledge at all"; positing the question of writing means to "understand this incompetence of science which is also the incompetence of philosophy, the closure of the epistēmē." In this way, the question of writing points "beyond the field of the epistēmē": arche-writing "cannot and can never be recognized as the *object of a science*" (G 83/57). Thus, the question of writing enables the "de-construction of the greatest totality" that is logocentrism. But what exactly, then, *is* logocentrism? And what, for Derrida, is "metaphysics" or "science" if these terms can apparently be used interchangeably?

What is logocentrism? What is metaphysics? What is science? Much like Heidegger when he introduces the problem of positing the question of being, for Derrida these questions primarily prompt hesitation, a pause or a step back. Positing them complicates the possibility of a progression toward an answer because, according to Derrida, logocentrism *already* "commands" the "question of essence," the very form of the question "what is . . . ?" To interpret that circularity means to recognize that the "what is . . . ?"—what Derrida calls "the (onto-phenomenological) question of essence"—is itself one of the moments of what logocentrism, metaphysics and the scientificity of science is. *Of Grammatology* is a meditation on what is "broached" in positing these questions that *put in question* "the arche-question 'what is . . . ?'" (G 110/75).

Where does this leave us? Though we do not find a definition of metaphysics in Derrida's writings, this does not mean that we cannot, in a more empirical fashion (this is Derrida's solution at several points in *Of Grammatology*[3]), gather the instances in which Derrida employs the term in order to identify what he seems to understand under that heading.

What do we know about logocentric metaphysics? Derrida states that he is out to "[demonstrate] the systematic and historical solidarity of the concepts and gestures of thought that one often believes can be innocently separated" (G 25/14). Logocentrism is an order of "conceptual solidarity." Solidarity of what with what? We know that Derrida states in *Of Grammatology*'s exergue that the "order" of logocentrism "commands" the phonocentric determination of writing, the scientificity of science, and the history of metaphysics. There, just like in the quote above, he stresses that with it he attempts to articulate what is both a "structural figure" and a "historical totality," as well as a "hierarchy and an order of subordination" (MP 392/329).

In what follows, I try to specify this broad notion of logocentric metaphysics by mentioning the most important of those "concepts and gestures of thought" that the notion of logocentrism binds together. I have done this under the headings of *demarcation* (or *delimitation*), *opposition*, *hierarchy*, and *presence*.

Demarcation: Determination through Delimitation (Inside, Outside, Borderline)

For Derrida, the "instituting question" of science and philosophy is "what is . . . ?" Identification of a subject (what something is "about") or object (what something is "directed at") in question is conceived by Derrida as drawing the line that distinguishes the matter's *inside* (what it is, its definition or its essence; what "belongs" to it; where it "begins" and "ends") from its *outside* (what it is not, what does not belong, is not "proper to"; what lies "beyond" the matter or what is opposed to it). This means that to know *what something is* (to *define*, to establish the essence) means to draw the line (the boundary or the border, the limit) between what belongs to the matter (where does it begin?) and what does not (where does it end?).

This corresponds to a certain, specific model of *determination*, which could be called demarcation: to establish "what something is" (the "onto-phenomenological question of essence") by "pinning down" (*de-*) its endpoint, edge, border, or limit (*terminare, terminus*); to draw the line between inside and outside, essence and accident, beginning and end. As Derrida writes in "Otobiographies": "[. . .] this difficulty crops up whenever one seeks to make a *determination*: in order to date an event, of course, but also in order to identify the beginning of a text, the origin of life, or the first movement of a signature. These are all problems of the borderline."[4] This quote makes especially clear that this is a ubiquitous characteristic of conceptuality as such that is at play as soon as any distinction whatsoever is made. Derrida also calls this logic of the borderline the logic of the "internal system" (internality as it depends on the exclusion of what falls outside it) or the logic of totality or of the "field." Therefore, insofar as fields are distinguished from one another, one could call this *demarcation through delimitation*.

Opposition

Logocentrism is the order that maintains the integrity of the borderline. The structural figure through which this is achieved is the figure of *opposition*. The opposition between inside and outside is constitutive for the figure of determination described above. In a way this means that the distinction of inside from outside is privileged—that distinction is the main target of the first part of *Of Grammatology*. Nevertheless, Derrida almost always speaks of "binary oppositions" as such and in general, rather than of a specific opposition. In what may seem like a lack of rigor, he often groups such binary distinctions together (distinction of essence from accident, inside from outside, positive from negative, presence from absence, nature from culture, etc.). Derrida's primary concern is clearly with the general structure of oppositionality as it guides the movement of logocentric determination (the identification through delimitation by means of such binary distinctions, what he also calls the "logic of identity" (e.g., G 90/61; the phrase reappears several times). In this sense, when it comes to his understanding of oppositions, Derrida is more Nietzschean than Hegelian.[5]

In the afterword to *Limited Inc*, Derrida will speak of this structure of oppositionality as the indispensable structure of all conceptuality. There, he calls it a "logic of all or nothing" that is "confounded with the demands of rational logic and of philosophy as a rigorous science." This logic is ubiquitous: "*Every concept* that lays claim to *any rigor whatsoever* implies the alternative of 'all or nothing'" (*LI* 116, my emphasis, JdJ). Its very universality and necessity both demand as well as defy (necessity and impossibility) critical determination:

> [The] discourse that seems problematic to me [. . .] neither can nor should avoid saying: it's serious or nonserious, ironical or nonironical, present or nonpresent [. . .] etc. *To this oppositional logic*, which is necessarily, legitimately, a logic of "all or nothing" and without which the distinction and the limits of a concept would have no chance, *I oppose nothing*, [. . .]; rather I add a supplementary complication that calls for other concepts, for other thoughts beyond the concept and another form of "general theory," or rather another discourse, another "logic" that accounts for the impossibility of concluding such a "general theory." (*LI* 116–117, emphasis mine, JdJ)

With the notions of arche-writing, instituted trace, or différance, we have already seen a number of the "(nick)names" for the logic that accounts for the impossibility of the "general theory." In the course of this chapter, I attempt to develop an account of what this "supplementary complication" stands for.

Hierarchy

According to Derrida, the distinction of essence from accident (of what belongs from what does not belong, of proper from improper) inaugurates the figure (Derrida says the "model") of a *distinction between norm and derivation:* "[. . .] an opposition of metaphysical concepts (speech/writing, presence/absence, etc.) is never the face-to-face of two terms, but a hierarchy and an order of subordination" (*MP* 392/329). The distinction of the nonarbitrary from the arbitrary is the "gesture, which in truth presides over metaphysics" (*G* 50/33). This makes metaphysics a double movement. In a single gesture, (1) what counts as norm—the essence; interiority; original; the present; what is; the natural; and so forth—is inaugurated, as well as (2) what counts as derivative with respect to that norm—the secondary or accidental; the exterior or excluded; the mere image; mere presentation or re-presentation of that which is; the mere medium or instrument; the technics or technique, and so forth. Recognizing the movement of metaphysics means for Derrida to recognize in an apparently neutral determination a distinction that is hierarchical, that is: to recognize in it a manifestation of what Derrida calls "desire." As a "structural figure," desire is not a psychological phenomenon. It is rather a name Derrida uses to describe any conceptual configuration in which a norm is posited or implied. This is why Derrida analyzes the philosophical tradition (following Nietzschean lines) in terms of a *consistent privileging*. As a movement toward a norm, all desire is simultaneously a repression, a movement away from what is mere "derivation" with respect to said norm. Derrida devotes considerable attention in "Freud and the scene of writing" to stressing that the thematics of desire and repression are not primarily Freudian: "[. . .] despite appearances, the deconstruction of logocentrism is not a psychoanalysis of philosophy" (*WD* 293/246). Instead, the problematics of repression and desire function more along lines running from Kierkegaard and Nietzsche through Heidegger: it is not a matter of (therapeutically or otherwise) *making present* what is repressed in metaphysics, but of questioning metaphysics as a consistently privileging movement. Consistent privilege of what? Strictly speaking, precisely the privilege of the "what . . . ?" or of its paradigmatic form: presence.

Presence, Presentation, Representation

If metaphysics is desire, then the primary "object" of that desire is presence. Derrida follows Heidegger in claiming that the determination of being as presence forms the "matrix" of the "history of metaphysics" and of "the West": "It could be shown that all the names related to fundamentals, to principles, or to the center have always designated an invariable presence— *eidos, archē, telos, energeia, ousia* (essence, existence, substance, subject) *alētheia,* transcendentality, consciousness, God, man, and so forth" (*WD* 411/353).

Heidegger never thought of "binary oppositions"—as such—as the hallmark of the history of metaphysics, and he was not concerned with exposing the oppositional character of conceptuality and the problem of what exceeds it. But there is another, more methodological, way in which, not so much *oppositions* (plural: pairs of concepts that one can sum up), but *opposition* plays an important role for Heidegger, and that is in his conception of the object [*Gegen-stand*, to stand opposed to] that is implicit in the determination of being as presence. Here at issue is less the oppositions within or by means of which a matter is conceived, and more the distance one puts between oneself and the matter at hand in order for it to become object. The following Heideggerian notions all correspond to this: the being as present-at-hand [*Vorhanden*] in *Being and Time*; that which is present *as* something in the apophantic sense of the "as" (as determinable or determined identity); that which "stands or lies before," whether that be understood in terms of οὐσία or παρουσια [*ständig Anwesen*] or as ὑποκείμενον (what lies before as the "subject"; as that "about" which one speaks); as *Vor-stellung* (what is before one as *representation*, the knowing re-presentation of something *as* what it is) or as the "object."

In Part IV, I describe in detail how Derrida's determination of the metaphysics of presence is intertwined with Derrida's reading of Heidegger. For now, it is important to stress that, analogous to Heidegger's vicious circle (that it is not a question of avoiding it but of entering into it in the right way), the question for Derrida is not how one gets out of these metaphysical structures. Instead, the complication arises in the attempt to even question metaphysics itself. What could count as a sufficient determination of metaphysics if the latter stands for determination as such (or the "as such" as such)? If determination is the delimitation of inside from outside, then how to determine the inside and outside of determination itself, the inside and outside of inside and outside? The same holds for the hierarchical interrogation of conceptual hierarchy, the opposition to opposition, and so forth. There is an unavoidable "performative contradiction" at play in these attempts. Derrida's claim in deconstructing the inside/outside-distinction is that the very movement of metaphysics itself cannot simply be accounted for with metaphysical (i.e.: demarcating, binary, hierarchical, representative) means. But there is no way to do without these means either. The predicament on which Derrida insists, therefore, does not surface in a flight from metaphysics but in the question of how to interrogate that structure itself—how to determine determination, to write writing, to scientifically question the scientificity of science, or the very form of the question? This does not mean that logocentrism has no limits. It rather means that, as metaphysics designates the system of delimitation as such, its own limits would no longer be conceivable as border or outer edge dividing its inside from its outside. In talking of the "limits of metaphysics," a transformation of the concept of limit is called for. Therefore, the claim that we will have to unpack is that metaphysics "*is not surrounded but rather traversed by its limit*," or, as Derrida puts it elsewhere, "the closure of metaphysics [. . .] would not occur *around* a homogenous and continuous field of metaphysics. Rather, it would fissure the structure and history of metaphysics [. . .]" (*MP* 206n/172n). This transformation of the limit—or this "supplementary complication," of which Derrida stated that it calls for "other thoughts beyond the concept"—now has important consequences for all of the structural figures that are held together by the order of logocentrism as I outlined them above:

Demarcation. The limits of metaphysics cannot have the form of overseeable borders that separate its determinable interior from its exterior. Metaphysics is not determined by drawing a boundary or border separating two fields. Derrida's tireless insistence on the complication of inside and outside as well as beginning and end (e.g., that we have "always already begun," writing "before the letter," etc.) should be understood in light of the question of how to qualify this very *movement of determination itself.* It is the movement of delimitation as it cannot itself simply be delimited that Derrida will come to call the "movement of différance."

Opposition. Deconstructing metaphysics cannot be a matter of opposing metaphysics or of opposing something to it (a new, better, or other order, independent from and outside it). What I have called the entanglement of method and object holds for metaphysics in the same way that it did for language: for Derrida, we are "in" metaphysics in the same way that we are "in" language, lacking a vantage point from which to de-limit or describe it. Derrida's explicit concern (to which all the problems of "overcoming metaphysics" belong) is with, on the one hand, the necessity of a certain conception of "outside" to trace the limits or the "closure" of metaphysics (the "point of a certain exteriority" that Derrida speaks of in *Of Grammatology*'s "Question of Method"), without, on the other hand, simply *opposing* it (placing oneself outside it, opposing to it an *outside*, an end, another metaphysics, a new age, etc.). Derrida's concern with opposition and reversal is to articulate that structural risk: the problem of the unavoidable repetition of the gesture that is constitutive of metaphysics, *in* the very attempt to escape it.

Hierarchy and the Privilege of Presence. Many commentators have emphasized that Derrida is not out to "reverse the hierarchy" or order of dependence of metaphysics. Yet often in the same breath they assert that deconstruction targets an overthrow or transformation of the "existing hierarchy." I would say with Derrida that on this point "alternatives are not so simple." In *Voice and Phenomenon*, Derrida explicitly makes the point that he is not out to diminish the "founding value of presence":

> That [. . .] does not cut into the founding value of presence [*Cela [. . .] n'entame pas la valeur fondatrice de la présence*]. "Founding value of presence" is, moreover, a pleonastic expression. It is only a matter of making the original, non-empirical space of non-foundation appear at the irreducible void from which the security of presence in the metaphysical form of ideality is decided and removed [*de faire apparaître l'espace original et non empirique de non-fondement sur le vide irréductible duquel se décide et s'enlève la sécurité de la présence dans la forme métaphysique de l'idéalité*]. It is within this horizon that we will here interrogate the phenomenological concept of the sign. (VP 5–6/6)

This is one of those prototypical Derridean quotes that is fodder for the skeptics of deconstruction. Because what could possibly be meant by an "original, non-empirical space of non-foundation" that would appear at an "irreducible void"?

First of all, Derrida stresses here that the value of presence is not diminished. Rather, in a gesture inspired by Nietzsche, he is out precisely to show the very *value-character of* presence. So, for instance, in the case of "originary writing" or the "originary trace," we saw that instead of presenting the trace *as originary* (which would be impossible and counter to what the very notion of trace itself expresses), it would be a matter of recognizing the movement of the "concealment of origin," or to understand how such an "origin" (under erasure) "produces itself as self-occultation" (G 69/47). The reason why Derrida distinguishes deconstruction rigorously from a psychoanalysis of philosophy is that the goal cannot be to make present what has been repressed in the history of metaphysics—this movement toward the *presentation* of the repressed would remain wholly or simply complicit with logocentric metaphysics rather than bring it into view. Instead, it is a matter of showing what is repressed *as* repressed, showing the movement of metaphysics itself as a movement that is *oriented*. It is not a matter of "rehabilitating" undecidability or of annulling the repression, but first of acknowledging this movement of repression itself, which is already a task that cannot be undertaken through a simple "presentation." This "incompetence" through which the ineluctable structures of metaphysics are incapable of bringing these very structures themselves into view—this is what for Derrida makes it that presence itself, as the horizon of the very idea of "foundation," is as "original" as it is "founded," or founded only by a "space of non-foundation." That space is described as the moment at which the metaphysical form of ideality is, *in the very same gesture,* both decided and removed (i.e.: the movement by which presence is posited as the norm, and by which this very positing itself is obscured and not itself presentable).

This brings us finally to that other main aspect of logocentrism: that it is not only a systematic, but also a *historical* order of conceptual solidarity. Derrida calls it an "epoch."

THE "HISTORICAL TOTALITY": EPOCH, HISTORY, THE FUTURE, AND BEYOND

That Derrida also conceives logocentric metaphysics as a "historical order" is highly pertinent to the question of his indirectness. For if Derrida's writing were to present an alternative or better account of language, then this would be the "new" account, as opposed to the "old" metaphysical way of thinking. So the question of the historicality of metaphysics is a question of the specific form or type of "criticism" that Derrida engages in. But if I stress that Derrida is not out to oppose anything to logocentrism, then why speak of it in terms of a determined historical period, even one that is "all in all a short enough adventure"? (*G* 18/8). Those latter words are clearly Nietzschean echoes. From the opening of his early, 1873 essay on "truth and lie in an extra-moral sense," to the preface of *Beyond Good and Evil*, Nietzsche consistently emphasized the insignificance of the metaphysical epoch. But does not the very terminology of the epoch imply that there are *other* epochs? And how to reconcile what Derrida says here with what he writes about epochs in his "Letter to a Japanese Friend":

> [. . .] we still have to think through what is happening in our world, in modernity, at the time when deconstruction is becoming a motif, with its word, its privileged themes, its mobile strategy, etc. I have no simple and formalizable response to this question. All my essays are attempts to have it out with this formidable question. They are modest symptoms of it, quite as much as tentative interpretations. I would not even dare to say, following a Heideggerian schema, that we are in an "epoch" of being-in-deconstruction, of a being-in-deconstruction that would manifest or dissimulate itself at one and the same time in other "epochs." This thought of "epochs" and especially that of a gathering of the destiny of being and of the unity of its destination or its dispersions (Schicken, Geschick) will never be very convincing.[6]

What is an epoch? One would think of a period in time, a more or less determinable part or portion of history. If it is the limits of an epoch that the deconstruction of logocentrism tries to explicate, one would think that these limits are such that *other* epochs would lie beyond, before, or after them. This has been a strong tendency in commentary: the idea is that Derrida is showing us a way of doing philosophy that allows us to leave the stifling strictures of traditional thought behind.

Yet the limits of the epoch cannot form the dividing line between "our" time and an "other" time. First, according to Derrida, it is the epoch of logocentrism in which the very concept of history has been produced:

> It is this history (as epoch: epoch not of history but as history) which is closed at the same time as the form of being of the world that is called knowledge. The concept of history is therefore the concept of philosophy and of the epistēmē. [. . .] What exceeds this closure *is nothing*: neither the presence of being, nor meaning, neither history nor philosophy; but another thing which has no name, which announces itself within the thought of this closure and guides our writing here. (G 405/286)

I have no room here to explore how specifically phonocentric writing conditions the concept of history. But we have already seen enough to be able to state that the "(non-)position" from which to judge metaphysics itself can neither be simply beyond nor wholly within it, which means that the "new" writing, the "beyond" of logocentrism, can neither be unproblematically said to "be" nor to be "possible." This is a beyond that announces itself "within" the thought of this closure. The beyond (and the related notions of excess or exceeding, limit and overcoming) must themselves be used "under erasure." This means that the limits of the "age of metaphysics" cannot be thought as the line that divides it from an *other age*: "This would perhaps mean that one does not leave the epoch whose closure one can outline. The movements of belonging or not belonging to the epoch are too subtle, the illusions in that regard are too easy, for us to make a definite judgment" (G 24/12).

Because a new writing (or science or metaphysics) or a new epoch is not conceivable in terms of a possibility without complication, Derrida refers to it under the heading of the "future." In his later work, he will distinguish the "predictable, programmed, scheduled, foreseeable" future [*la future*] from the "totally unpredictable" "to-come" [*l'avenir*].[7] The latter is not a determinable period that may at a certain point become present. In *Of Grammatology*, Derrida states that the future can only be *presented* as "a sort of monstrosity" [*sous l'espèce de la monstruosité*].[8]

The figure of the future first comes up in the early considerations of the paradoxical necessity and impossibility of a new concept of writing—of the "production [by the science of writing] of its own dislocation." It is found in the quasi-revolutionary rhetoric, which at first glance seems to support the idea that Derrida does in fact present a new account of writing, or that a grammatology might at some point become possible: Derrida writes of "signs of liberation all over the world," of the possibility after "several millennia" to finally "proclaim the limits" of the predetermination of the sign, of the "world of the future [. . .] beyond the closure of knowledge" (G 14/4). Such formulations might lead one to think that it is the dawn of a new age, that there would be a place to go beyond "knowledge," beyond the old concepts and categories; a place that, though difficult to achieve, is now becoming a reality. But Derrida stresses that he uses the concept of the future in the sense of "that which breaks absolutely with constituted normality" (G 14/5). The future, that is, what can be *presented* only as a "monstrosity," is not the *external*, but the unpresentable. It would go against Derrida's sense of the term if the future were thought as the becoming-present of what is still absent. That conception of the future would be simply metaphysical in Derrida's sense of that term. The future does not just transcend what we colloquially call the present, but everything that lets itself be presented; for Derrida it signifies what complicates presentability or (re)presentation as such.

This is why the figure of the future returns at the end of *Of Grammatology*'s third chapter when Derrida returns to the question of the possibility of a scientific grammatology:

> The constitution of a science or a philosophy of writing is a necessary and difficult task. But, a *thought* of the trace, of differance or of reserve, having arrived at these limits and repeating them ceaselessly, must also point beyond the field of the epistēmē. Outside of the economic and strategic reference to the name that Heidegger justifies himself in giving to an analogous but not identical transgression of all philosophemes, *thought* is here for me a perfectly neutral name, the blank part of the text, the necessarily indeterminate index of a future epoch of differance. *In a certain sense, "thought" means nothing.* Like all openings, this index belongs within a past epoch by the face that is open to view. This thought has no weight. It is, in the play of the system, that very thing which never has weight. Thinking is what we already know we have not yet begun; measured against the shape of writing, it is broached only in the epistēmē.
>
> Grammato*logy*, this thought, would still be walled-in within presence. (G 142/93)

The "index" of the future thus belongs to the thought of the closedness or the closure of the "age" of metaphysics. But that does not mean that there can be said to be a realizable possibility beyond that closure. Derrida is clear: notwithstanding metaphysics' closure, it may well never end. The necessity of the legibility of the erased writing conveys that same necessity of the "double bind": if the "old" writing (sign of a sign) is "generalized," then "the very idea of the sign falls into decay." But, equally, "it would be silly to conclude from its placement within an epoch that it is necessary to 'move on to something else,' to dispose of the sign, of the term and the notion" (G 26/14). Here the relation between the epochality of metaphysics and Derrida's indirectness becomes very clear: the critique of an epoch from which one cannot simply "move on" necessitates what he often calls the "strategic" use of these concepts. That is: to find a way to write in such a way that one can, in the same gesture, take into account both the necessity as well as the impossibility of the very terms one is using.[9]

Of the different titles that have frequently been given to these considerations of epoch, the future, the limit, and the beyond, perhaps the most prevalent is that of "overcoming metaphysics." It was Heidegger who initiated the use of these terms to explicitly characterize his central problem during a certain phase of his development (specifically in the 1930s). This was also the phase in which his primary sparring partner was Nietzsche. In that way, the title also came to characterize his famous interpretation of Nietzsche. This influential reading was one of the factors contributing to the general view that "overcoming metaphysics" signifies nothing less than the entire problematic horizon of what is called continental philosophy. It is also a welcome source of ridicule for that tradition, with Hegel, Nietzsche, Heidegger, and Derrida supposedly all claiming that they have finally succeeded in overcoming metaphysics, as opposed to their failing predecessors. But the title is also the source of the greatest misunderstandings surrounding the continental philosophical tradition. The misunderstanding lies in the idea that these thinkers took the overcoming of metaphysics to be a *task* at which they attempted to *succeed*. Instead, that title refers to a question and a problem. This becomes especially clear in the case of Derrida now that his terminology of epochality has been sharply distinguished from the idea that there is something "after" metaphysics. If the "movements of belonging or not belonging to the epoch are too subtle, the illusions in that regard are too easy, for us to make a definite judgment" (G 24/12), then indeed "overcoming metaphysics" ceases to designate a realizable task. It would not be something that one could carry out, would not constitute a "goal" for deconstruction, or even something that might become possible at some point in the future.

OVERCOMING PHILOSOPHY'S SELF-OVERCOMING

For Derrida, metaphysics itself is *already* the name for a self-investigative movement that is structured as overcoming. It has, according to Derrida, always been a relation-to-its-other; a self-interrogation in the attempt to recognize or understand the other in relation to itself. Deconstruction cannot be an attempt to overcome metaphysics because overcoming is itself one of the metaphysical motifs par excellence. This insight is not even a *result* of deconstruction. It is a central Derridean premise. This is clearly visible in the way certain of Derrida's texts from this period open, for example, in the opening of *Margins of Philosophy* (which I discuss in detail in chapter 4), where Derrida deals explicitly with the problem that questioning philosophy would require taking up a position "outside" philosophy, and in one of the most quoted instances at the start of "Structure, Sign and Play in the Discourse of the Human Sciences," where Derrida writes of Nietzsche, Freud, and Heidegger that:

> [. . .] all these destructive discourses and all their analogues are trapped in a kind of circle. This circle is unique. It describes the form of the relation between the history of metaphysics and the destruction of the history of metaphysics. There is no sense in doing without the concepts of metaphysics in order to shake metaphysics. We have no language—no syntax and no lexicon—which is foreign to this history; we can pronounce not a single destructive proposition which has not already had to slip into the form, the logic, and the implicit postulations of precisely what it seeks to contest. [. . .] But there are several ways of being caught in this circle. They are all more or less naïve, more or less empirical, more or less systematic, more or less close to the formulation—that is, to the formalization—of this circle. (*WD* 412/355)

There are "more or less naive" ways in which to be "caught up in the circle" of metaphysics. The discourses of Nietzsche, Freud, and Heidegger do not set out to "escape metaphysics" (which would be wholly naive), but they are already attempts to formulate and formalize the circle that makes such an escape impossible.

A similar point is found in the opening of Derrida's seminal 1964 essay *Violence and Metaphysics*. After positing a host of problems with respect to philosophy's "limits" (the "death" of philosophy, philosophy's opposition to "non-philosophy," the necessity for a philosophy *of* philosophy—a "community of the question about the possibility of the question"), he states that the *question* of philosophy can only be "indicated or recalled" because it *appears* (i.e., can be *presented*) "only through the hermetism of a proposition." That is: through the "hypocrisy of an answer [. . .] already initiated" (*WD* 118/98). In one sense, the question is a mere proposition that already anticipates its answer in a circular matter that leaves no room for alterity, rupture, or overflowing—the closure of metaphysics. But this "correspondence of the question with itself," in which it "comes to speculate, to reflect, and to question about itself within itself" (*WD* 119/99), makes enigmatic how philosophy then relates to itself, or whether philosophy can understand its own movement by its own means. So two figures of philosophy emerge here: on the one hand the philosophy "of the question" and on the other hand philosophy as "a determined—finite and mortal—moment or mode of the question itself." That is: "The difference between philosophy as a power and adventure *of* the question itself and philosophy as a determined event or turning point *within* this adventure." The point in all this is that according to Derrida it is "perhaps the most deeply inscribed characteristic of our age" that "this difference has come to light, has been conceptualized *as such*" (*WD* 119/99).

In other words: it is a premise for Derrida that several critical discourses (Nietzsche, Freud, Husserl, Heidegger, and I argue in Part II that one must include Hegel here) have already indicated the necessity of a certain overcoming of metaphysics *as well as* the impossibility of such overcoming. It also means that though these discourses, including Derrida's own, cannot be reduced to another moment in philosophy's perennial self-investigation, they cannot be detached from that interior dialogue either. But that would require a reinterpretation of what is meant there by "interior."

In *Violence and Metaphysics*, this means for Derrida that "the tradition's origin will have to be summoned forth and adhered to as rigorously as possible" (*WD* 120/99). He states that this places him in line with Husserl and Heidegger. But Derrida's goals are different here. What Derrida is after with respect to this "rigorous adherence" to metaphysics is its *strategic repetition*, as opposed to its "mere repetition." What is the difference?

As I indicated above, Derrida argues for a "faithful repetition" of metaphysics in order to "[make] it insecure in its most assured evidences." To oppose metaphysics or oppose something to it would mean to merely repeat it. It is this inability to oppose (oneself to) metaphysics that makes deconstruction "operate from the inside." And that is where repetition becomes strategy. One would appear to adhere to a certain position or philosopheme in positing it. But if one posits it again and again, inaugurating a certain track [*parcours*] or movement, one makes insecure *in* or *through* its repetition—a movement of showing in or through sentences and positions that are "mere" propositions only when left to themselves. Only on this level, when the explicit propositions and (op)positions in Derrida's texts are understood in the context of their broader movement of showing, can the status of Derrida's positions with regard to metaphysics become clear.

It is not that Derrida's irreducibility to the unequivocality of a "(theoretical) position" has received no attention. The early works of Simon Critchley and Rodolphe Gasché could be cited as two examples of good work in that direction.[10] Still, even in these works, *this very equivocality* is then shown to be *precisely what sets Derrida apart* from the philosophical tradition. In the case of Gasché, this is most clear: though knowledge of what he calls the "tradition of reflection" is necessary to understand the philosophical import of Derrida's work, that work itself is "irreducible to the philosophy of reflection" as it is written on the *tain* of that mirror. Put in extreme terms, this would amount to saying that the very impossibility of positioning himself outside metaphysics is what positions Derrida . . . outside metaphysics. Even if Gasché would not put it this way, and even if he does recognize Derrida's inextricability from metaphysics, this raises systematic and critical questions concerning Derrida's work that both Critchley and Gasché leave unanswered. They provide attempts to explain and to an extent defend Derrida's work. But Derrida himself consistently emphasized the aporetic complicity of his texts with what they put in question. Does that make Derrida "invulnerable to criticism" (which is in itself—we should not forget—a valid criticism)? And what does this mean for the critical force of these aporetic texts? These are the questions I respond to in the next chapter.

CONCLUSION

I have argued that for Derrida the question what exactly logocentric metaphysics is performatively complicates the possibility of answering that question. Instead of proceeding toward an answer, for Derrida the challenge consists in finding a mode of writing that could take this Heideggerian complication into account. In the absence of a definition, I proceeded to provisionally draw out some of the main characteristics of Derrida's use of the term metaphysics under the headings of demarcation, opposition, hierarchy, and presence. On the basis of this, I then argued that alterity (the question whether one can think or write "otherwise") is not reducible to externality.

My claim is that even though many often cite Derrida's famed phrase that one "cannot do without the concepts of metaphysics in order to shake metaphysics," still in the same gesture Derrida's work is too often presented as a move *away from* or *out of* logocentric metaphysics. In this view, the metaphysics that we are essentially "in" is the already familiar and thus more or less already known or determinable. Derrida's question of alterity (of how to think or write otherwise) would then be the question of how we can get out of it. I have shown the complications arising from this account by looking, first, at Derrida's conceptions of epoch, history, and the future; and, second, at the idea of overcoming philosophy's self-overcoming—an aporia that, I have argued, is not a result of deconstruction, but a premise. The question of alterity arises in the attempt to determine or question the very order of determination or questioning as such. In this sense Derrida takes philosophical self-interrogation itself to be thoroughly aporetic. Even if Derrida states that his work cannot be reduced to a mere moment in philosophy's perpetual self-questioning, the "(non-)place" from which he states deconstruction works expresses the complication that arises in the attempt to question philosophy. It is an explication of the implicit self-complication of the very Western rationality from which one cannot extricate oneself, and which is already in play the moment one asks, "what is . . . ?"

Only later (in chapter 9) am I able to show fully how this reflexive or performative problem of inextricability has ethical consequences in the form of an "irreducible complicity."

This changes the way in which the relation between undecidability and the unconditional necessity for action is conceived. Derrida's consistent attempt to take this performative complexity into account can then be understood as the attempt to affirmatively assume an intellectual or philosophical responsibility.

This performative complexity has important methodological consequences. For now, it is a matter of thinking through the consequences for the possibility of justifying and criticizing what Derrida is doing. One of these is that it no longer makes sense to interpret either the objections of performative contradiction or of the idea that a discourse is "still (too) metaphysical" as straightforward criticisms, whether of Derrida's own discourse or as critiques that Derrida would level at the philosophical tradition. We then arrive at the question of in what sense a critique of Derrida is possible, as well as in what sense Derrida's own discourse can be understood as criticism. I address these questions of the legitimacy and justification of Derrida's own non-positional discourse in the next chapter by asking to what extent Derrida is able to provide himself with any sure footing.

CHAPTER 3

THE QUESTION OF JUSTIFICATION AND THE LAW OF RESEMBLANCE

Empiricism—Skepticism—Critique

> That pathway must leave a track in the text. Without that track, abandoned to the simple content of its conclusions, the ultra-transcendental text will so closely resemble the precritical text as to be indistinguishable from it. We must now form and meditate upon the law of this resemblance.
>
> —Derrida (*Of Grammatology*)

Derrida's relation to metaphysics cannot be reduced to the very oppositionality that is constitutive of that metaphysics. If Derrida at times opposes metaphysics, this is never unequivocal and always part of a broader movement or strategy. This has consequences for what many of Derrida's defenders have thought they could successfully distinguish his writings from. In this chapter, I distinguish three of the most important of these figures: empiricism, skepticism, and critique. My aim is to show how the sword cuts both ways: deconstruction is not identical to either of these, but can neither entirely purify itself from, raise itself above, or claim to work at a deeper level than, each of these figures. We find a very interesting dynamic in each case: on the one hand, Derrida feels the need consistently to explicitly distance himself from each of these figures. He always does so in the form of the most direct, unequivocal proposition—propositions that Derrida's followers have often been eager to approvingly cite: deconstruction simply "is not" empiricism, skepticism, or (a) critique. Yet Derrida acknowledges a structural relation between deconstruction and each of these figures. What must be acknowledged is that it belongs to the vulnerability of deconstruction that it will never be able to definitively safeguard itself against these criticisms (a point on which, in stark contrast to both Hegel and Heidegger, Derrida tirelessly insisted). The aim in this chapter, then, is to qualify that structural relation in order to show how Derrida's explicit opposition to these figures is integrated in the broader movement of Derrida's writings. The aim of this with respect to my main question is to show that this results in problems for the extent to which these writings can be justified or provided with some theoretical or critical legitimation. Though many of Derrida's defenders *have* attempted to provide such a justification, I argue that such attempts may in fact risk obscuring the actual value of Derrida's work.

EMPIRICISM: DECONSTRUCTION AND METHOD

The concept of empiricism plays a fascinating role in Derrida's early works and in *Of Grammatology* specifically, as it plays a crucial role in its "Question of Method." In the French philosophical context, empiricism does not signify the view that knowledge is based on ἐμπειρία, or experience.[1] Instead, the term rather expresses an unfounded or arbitrary way of proceeding. In other words: empiricism concerns method. It signifies a lack of justification of one's method. One sees this at work in Derrida's texts when he equates empiricism simply with "non-philosophy," but also in the way in which Derrida groups the term together (in a telling, characteristic, and oft-repeated gesture) with relativism, skepticism, or nihilism.[2]

So to the extent that we are dealing with the non-philosophical as such, Derrida has an easy job of dispensing with empiricism and of distancing himself from it in an explicit way: deconstruction, quite simply, "is not" empiricism (or relativism, or nihilism, or skepticism . . .). This is the first part of Derrida's relation to empiricism: he explicitly distances himself from it, unequivocally positing the non-identity of deconstruction and empiricism.

Because empiricism denotes proceeding without justification, it is no surprise that the concept plays a vital role in *Of Grammatology*'s "Question of Method." What stands in need of justification in that section?

First of all, there is the choice of Rousseau's text as the "exemplary" (a notion that, you will recall, was said to be "strictly speaking, unacceptable") text with which to undertake the deconstruction of metaphysics. At the start of part two, Derrida states that Rousseau occupies a "singular" position within the "historical totality" that is metaphysics. That is: Rousseau made "a theme or a system of the reduction of writing profoundly implied by the entire age." Derrida adds to this, though, that "this abstraction [the focus on Rousseau and the abstraction from everything else that is implicated under the titles of 'greatest totality,' 'logocentrism,' 'history of metaphysics,' 'the West,' etc., JdJ] is partial and it remains, in my view, provisional." It remains provisional for a reason we are now familiar with: because "*all concepts hitherto proposed in order to think the articulation of a discourse and of an historical totality are caught within the metaphysical closure that I question here*" (G 146/99). Will Derrida's choices remain provisional and partial when he approaches the problem of justification directly in the "Question of Method"?

The "Question of Method" is titled "exorbitant," not only in reference to the exorbitant demands of a grammatology with respect to scientific, grammato-logical knowledge, but also because Derrida attempts to "broach" the "orb" of metaphysics. The question is whether the ex-orbitant (to occupy a place outside the orb, i.e. the circular trajectory of metaphysics) is possible, but the concept of the exorbitant also points to what for Derrida is *in fact* the status of his decisions: concerning the "formidable problems" of "justification" and of "method," he states, there is "no satisfying response" (G 231/161).

First of all, the "justification" of Derrida's reading (that strange reading that, we recall, was to "produce the problems of critical reading") will be "entirely negative, outlining by exclusion a space of reading that I shall not fill here: a task of reading" (G 227/158). Second, there is no "satisfying response" not only with respect to the choice of the example, but also when it comes to the ability to defend the claims that a grammatology would establish (e.g., "that there is no simple origin," that colloquial writing is founded upon a "general writing," etc.). I have argued that Derrida is not out to establish anything assuredly, and Derrida emphasizes that these claims signify "no knowledge at all": "only now," at this point in the essay, do "we know," and know it "a priori," that the text is a "system of a writing and of a reading" that is "ordered around its own blind spot," and this holds no less for the discourse that is *Of Grammatology* itself. But that knowledge, Derrida crucially indicates, is "not a knowledge at all" (G 234/164).

It is in these respects, in the use of "unacceptable" distinctions and examples, producing knowledge that is "no knowledge at all," and proceeding by way of what cannot be called a "method" (if that means a plan one would have beforehand, or an applicable program), that Derrida compares what he does to empiricism. At the end of *Violence and Metaphysics*, Derrida states that it is philosophy itself that has determined empiricism as nonphilosophy: empiricism is the "philosophical pretension to nonphilosophy, the inability to justify oneself." However:

> [. . .] this incapacitation, when resolutely assumed, contests the resolution and coherence of the logos (philosophy) at its root, instead of letting itself be questioned by the logos. Therefore, nothing can so profoundly *solicit* the Greek logos—philosophy—than this irruption of the totally-other [. . .]. (*WD* 226/190)

So now a second moment of Derrida's relation to empiricism emerges. At this point, empiricism becomes a *resource*. Empiricism is the "true name" of "this inclination to the Other, of this resigned acceptance of incoherent incoherence inspired by a truth more profound than the 'logic' of philosophical discourse, the true name of this renunciation of the concept" (*WD* 224/189).

Now it seems that there are two empiricisms, or two senses of empiricism. To the bad and naive empiricism we now add a good and profound one: "[. . .] the profundity of the empiricist intention must be recognized beneath the naïveté of certain of its historical expressions."

What distinguishes the dispensable from the resourceful empiricism, the profound intention from the naive expression?

Derrida clarifies in the same text: empiricism "has ever committed but one fault: the fault of presenting itself as philosophy" (*WD* 224/189). So the naive expression of empiricism is the one that still remains philosophical (whether by being determined as such by philosophy or by presenting itself as philosophy). But what does it mean for empiricism to remain philosophical? Derrida answers: "[. . .] it is the *dream* of a purely *heterological* thought at its source. A *pure* thought of *pure* difference" (*WD* 224/189).

Empiricism remains philosophical if it opposes itself to (or is opposed to) philosophy in such a way that the distinction between them is *itself* still rigorous, determinable, philosophical. Here is the paradox of the limit and of the outside of philosophy: the more strictly one wishes to *separate* alterity from philosophy ("a *pure* thought of *pure* difference"), the more one affirms the philosophical gesture of absolute and rigorous distinction (the "desire for purity," according to Derrida; desire for the integrity of distinction, delimitation, determination).

This means that the attempt to *increase the distance* between philosophy and whatever one would want to oppose to or distinguish from it in fact *inversely reduces* the latter's alterity with respect to philosophy—it in fact decreases that distance. Alterity, as I have argued, is not externality. *The more external, the less other.* Derrida stresses the point already in "Structure, Sign and Play in the Discourse of the Human Sciences," and he does so with reference to empiricism:

> [. . .] we condemn ourselves to transforming the alleged transgression of philosophy into an unnoticed fault within the philosophical realm. Empiricism would be the genus of which these faults would always be the species. Transphilosophical concepts would be transformed into philosophical naïvetés. Many examples could be given to demonstrate this risk: the concepts of sign, history, truth, and so forth. What I want to emphasize is simply that the passage beyond philosophy does not consist in turning the page of philosophy (which usually amounts to philosophizing badly), but in continuing to read philosophers *in a certain way*. (*WD* 421/364)

So now the situation is as follows: empiricism seemed to be the nonphilosophical, but it reveals itself *as merely philosophical* precisely to the extent that it is determined . . . as *non*philosophical! Derrida confirms: "[. . .] if we wanted to pose the problem of empiricism [. . .] in depth, we would probably end up very quickly with a number of absolutely contradictory propositions [. . .]" (*WD* 422/364).

In the midst of this apparent self-contradiction (which is the characteristic figure of *skepticism* that I discuss in the next paragraph), where do we find empiricism's *resource* for the "solicitation of the Greek logos"?

We can return to *Of Grammatology* to answer this question. In the "Question of Method," Derrida states that "within the closure," the "style of deconstruction can only be judged with recourse to "accepted oppositions" [*oppositions reçues*]. That style could then be said to be empiricist, "and in a certain way that would be correct." Derrida specifies that "the *departure* is radically empiricist":

> It proceeds like a wandering thought on the possibility of itinerary and of method. It is affected by nonknowledge as by its future and it *ventures out* deliberately. I have myself defined the form and the vulnerability of this empiricism. But here the very concept of empiricism destroys itself. To *exceed* the metaphysical orb is an attempt to get out of the orbit (*orbita*), to think the entirety of the classical conceptual oppositions, particularly the one within which the value of empiricism is held: the opposition of philosophy and nonphilosophy, another name for empiricism, for this incapability to sustain on one's own and to the limit the coherence of one's own discourse, for being produced as truth at the moment when the value of truth is shattered, for escaping the internal contradictions of skepticism, etc. *The thought of this historical opposition between philosophy and empiricism is not simply empirical and it cannot be thus qualified without abuse and misunderstanding.* (G 232/162)

It is to words like these that those who wish to defend Derrida often take recourse. Here is how one could reconstruct this thought: deconstruction is not a simple empiricism because the latter is defined in its *opposition* to philosophy, but it is the very opposition between philosophy and its other that Derrida is out to deconstruct. Ergo: deconstruction is not simply empiricism. In the following two paragraphs, I show that the same applies to deconstruction's distinction from skepticism and from critique.

Now on the one hand this insight is entirely correct: Derrida's works are not reducible to an empiricist position outside or against philosophy (I think here of the objections of the "anything goes" variety). Yet what these readings crucially miss is that this must also mean that Derrida cannot and does not fashion for himself an irreducibly singular place outside that very distinction, as if Derrida's operation of writing were somehow elevated above or below, superior to or deeper than, the discourse that would be either simply philosophical or nonphilosophical. A zeal to defend Derrida can lead to crediting him with a singular position with respect to the tradition that he deconstructs. But this goes against what I argue is the most valuable aspect of Derrida's work, which consists in its tireless insistence on its own irreducible complicity, on its irreducible "contamination," and on the naivetés of the supposed escape.

So although Derrida's work is not reducible to one side of the distinction between philosophy and empiricism, it cannot be placed simply

The Question of Justification and the Law of Resemblance 57

outside that opposition either. There is no unequivocal position opposed to that oppositionality. It is in that light that Derrida's insistence on the "(non-)place" with respect to philosophy must be understood. That indirect terminology does not signify the *possibility* of an irreducibly singular or absolutely incomparable place, but precisely the (im)possibility of a place that is at the same time *not* a place; a (non-)place that cannot itself be purified from the oppositionality it "deconstructs." This leads to essential problems of justification.

Where commentary has at times been overzealous is in the assumption that one can only argue for the worth or value of Derrida's texts if we provide him with some kind of (theoretical) legitimization or justification. That is: by attempting to grant deconstruction a superiority over the tradition that is, after all, being deconstructed. Derrida would then at least in some way work on a deeper level than that tradition. Even the image of the tain of the mirror, from which no doubt one of the best books on Derrida gets its title, still risks such a suggestion: that there is a whole metaphysical tradition of reflection, on the one hand, and that then there is Derrida, working on the *tain* of that mirror. Let me be clear: certainly in a period during which deconstruction was continuously faced with accusations of irresponsibility (mere empiricism, mere skepticism, mere nihilism, etc.), such defenses are absolutely necessary. But that does not diminish the risk to which I am pointing here.

Now we see, looking at the quote above, that Derrida is not out to argue that his own texts would *not* suffer from the "incapability to sustain on one's own and to the limit the coherence of one's own discourse" or from "being produced as truth at the moment when the value of truth is shattered." Deconstruction cannot simply be the attempt to *escape* "the internal contradictions of skepticism" (to which I return in the next paragraph).

So now the situation is this: on the one hand, Derrida does not wholly identify with either philosophy or empiricism in the sense in which the two are opposed (the possibility and impossibility of justification). On the other hand, Derrida equally cannot straightforwardly oppose that oppositionality or rigorously distinguish himself from it. It is with this total situation in mind that we must ask: how are we to understand Derrida's "position"?

And it is here, at this point of inability to rigorously distance himself from empiricism, that we see empiricism reemerge as a structural element of deconstruction: according to Derrida, deconstruction in a certain sense entails an "avowal of empiricism." It "necessarily" has this form of empiricism or even of "errancy" (*errance*: failure, wandering). The errancy is already evident in the, to an extent at least, unjustifiable choice for the example of Rousseau. The example is not unjustifiable because it would be inappropriate, contingent, or totally random, but because *any* choice of an *example* "supposes that we have *already* prepared the exit, determined the repression of writing as the fundamental operation of the epoch" (G 232/162). This determination would presuppose the very *determinability* of the epoch (as a *field* that one could "master") that it attempts precisely to deny.

So the errancy of *Of Grammatology* consists, first, in the theoretical impurity (or the violation of the "scientific exigency") of such a precomprehension or predetermination as a point of departure. Derrida does not attempt to wriggle out of that complication but, on the contrary, to bring it into focus and to expose its temporal, anticipatory character.

Second, as I have been arguing throughout, *Of Grammatology*'s errancy consists in the self-confessed impossibility of determining metaphysics as repression of writing (that this is no longer a "determination" at all, that this is a knowledge that is "not a knowledge at all," etc.). We can call this the inherent provisionality of the investigation.

In one of the most famous passages of the "Question of Method," Derrida does not deny, but *confirms* the structurally anticipatory and provisional character, this crisis of the scientific "rigor" of his own "method":

> No other trace is available, and as these errant questions are not absolute beginnings in every way, they allow themselves to be effectively reached, on one entire surface, by this description which is also a criticism. We must begin *wherever we are* and the thought of the trace, which cannot not take the scent into account, has already taught us that it was impossible to justify a point of departure absolutely. *Wherever we are*: in a text where we already believe ourselves to be. (G 233/162)

This irreducibility of deconstruction's being-in the very object of its deconstruction, its *own* complicity or contamination, is confirmed in all the places where Derrida describes deconstruction as a mode of "inhabiting" ("inhabiting [. . .] in a certain way, *because one always inhabits, and all the more when one does not suspect it*" [my emphasis, JdJ]; as "borrowing" from the structures of metaphysics, and in the explicit admission that "the enterprise of deconstruction always in a certain way falls prey to its own work" (G 39/24).

Deconstruction falls prey to itself. But: it falls prey to itself *in a certain way*. What is left to do now is to qualify this "in a certain way" [*d'une certaine manière*]. "In a certain way" functions like something of a central category throughout *Of Grammatology*, and it is this that is to mark the nonidentity of deconstruction and simple empiricism (e.g.: "It may be said that this style is empiricist and *in a certain way* that would be correct," G 232/162, my italics, JdJ).

Deconstruction inhabits "in a certain way" and falls prey to its own work "in a certain way." With that phrase, Derrida indicates his non-identity with both metaphysics and empiricism without being able to oppose either of them. Compare:

> [. . .] one must accentuate the "naiveté" of a breakthrough which cannot attempt a step outside of metaphysics, which cannot criticize metaphysics radically without still utilizing *in a certain way, in a certain type or a certain style of text*, propostions that, read within the philosophic corpus [. . .] have always been and will always be "naivetés," incoherent signs of an absolute appurtenance. (G 32/19, my italics, JdJ)

It is not by counter-positioning metaphysics, by opposing it, or by proposing *other* propositions (propositions that would, *per impossibile*, be "non-metaphysical") that it can be criticized. Rather, it is a matter of utilizing the (irreducibly metaphysical) propositions *in a different way*. Here we touch on the essence of Derrida's text as a movement of showing. It is *in the course of* (though the movement of, on the way of, along the path of) utilizing the oppositions of metaphysics *in a certain way* that one criticizes metaphysical oppositionality.

It also means that "when abandoned to the simple content of its conclusions," the "ultra-transcendental text will so closely resemble the precritical text as to be indistinguishable from it." That is: when focusing on the content of Derrida's isolated conclusions alone, deconstruction will be indistinguishable from empiricism, and from metaphysics for that matter. He even states in this regard that a *law* guides this resemblance, the very law he is out to formulate or articulate. Now one sees how it is possible that, in the commentary that sets out to defend Derrida, his *distinction* from empiricism has perhaps been overemphasized with respect to the *law of resemblance* between deconstruction and empiricism. Because the question becomes: how can a "radically empiricist departure," a "wandering" that professes to be "blind tactics" and to be affected by "nonknowledge," still take accurate aim, still be *rigorous,* still have an effect or be valuable for science, for philosophy, for thought? In response to that question, *it is not enough* to distinguish deconstruction from a simple empiricism. One must account for the law of their structural resemblance.

This entails making at least one concession that some of Derrida's staunch defenders may not like: that there is no way to *safeguard* the "ultra-transcendental" from the "precritical" text, or deconstruction from empiricism, if that means securing for Derrida a position outside it, or rigorously purifying his work from it. Nor, or so I argue, does Derrida's work need such purification to show its value. Derrida himself always stressed this impossibility to safeguard his texts:

> [. . .] what I say is *always* going to run the risk of being taken in an unfavorable light, it cannot fail to lead to misunderstandings, according to the very same law of contamination. There is no way out. As to the criticisms of deconstruction brought up earlier, one has indeed to assume the risk of being misunderstood, continuing to think in modest terms what is after all exceedingly ambitious, in order to prepare for these responsibilities—if they exist. (*N* 237)

That there is no safeguard from empiricism (no assured position beyond the oppositionality of philosophy and empiricism) was already evident in the necessity to "retain the old name," as discussed above. What could possibly guarantee that the "old name" (difference, writing, supplement, text) now have a new sense? No (pro-)position could guarantee it. There is no way to secure the ultra-transcendental meaning of the seemingly empiricist or precritical text.

Nevertheless, there is a way in which Derrida, if you will, testifies to or takes into account his non-identity with both philosophy and empiricism without opposing them, and this is that he does so *textually*. If there is a difference between deconstruction and empiricism, it is a difference not of position but a difference in the way in which the ("old") metaphysical op(positions) are utilized. It is a difference that lies in the movement of showing that his texts inaugurate. That difference is

The Question of Justification and the Law of Resemblance 61

therefore not posited; it is in a certain sense ("in a certain way") "nothing." It is "unheard of" (G 38/23). It is "the blank part of the text," the "necessarily indeterminate index of a future epoch of difference." "In a certain sense," it "means nothing" and "has no weight" (G 142/93). As such and for all these reasons, it is not presented or posited, but it is *marked*, *textually*. On that level, deconstruction ceases to be merely negative or destructive where it becomes affirmative without being simply positive (the ethical implication to which I return in chapters 8 and 9), where Derrida achieved the kind of "liberation" of which he was beginning to see signs "all over the world" (G 14/4).

I quote in full and at length the main passage in which Derrida makes this explicit. Important parts of it have already been discussed above:

> I believe that there is a short-of and a beyond of transcendental criticism. To see to it that the beyond does not return to the within is to recognize in the contortion the necessity of a pathway [*parcours*]. That pathway must leave a track in the text. Without that track, abandoned to the simple content of its conclusions, the ultra-transcendental text will so closely resemble the precritical text as to be indistinguishable from it. We must now form and meditate upon the law of this resemblance. What I call the erasure of concepts ought to mark the places of that future meditation. For example, the value of the transcendental arche [*archie*] must make its necessity felt before letting itself be erased. The concept of arche-trace must comply with both that necessity and that erasure. It is in fact contradictory and not acceptable within the logic of identity. The trace is not only the disappearance of origin—within the discourse that we sustain and according to the path that we follow it means that the origin did not even disappear, that it was never constituted except reciprocally by a nonorigin, the trace, which thus becomes the origin of the origin. From then on, to wrench the concept of the trace from the classical scheme, which would derive it from a presence or from an originary nontrace and which would make of it an empirical mark, one must indeed speak of an originary trace or arche-trace. Yet we know that that concept destroys its name and that, if all begins with the trace, there is above all no originary trace. (G 90/61)

Derrida indicates here that deconstruction's empiricism cannot entail a regression to a precritical state, short of the transcendental criticism of empiricism. It also cannot, however, simply identify with the latter. The only way to "exceed" transcendental criticism without reverting back to precritical empiricism is through a "track" [*parcours*; path, way, movement] that must be *marked* in the text. Without the mark of this movement, the text would be abandoned to the simple content of its conclusions. What exceeds the content of conclusions is neither an other conclusion nor the dream of a totally new and different writing (the "dream of a *pure* difference"), but the movement of a certain utilization of the "old" conclusions. That certain utilization is marked, for instance, by the erasure. The necessity of metaphysics, of "transcendental criticism," and of the "old name" in general is signified by the legibility of what is erased. The "originary trace," just like all the central Derridean concepts, as well as the production of necessarily contradictory propositions, performatively or demonstratively *marks* this movement.

I have argued that deconstruction should be neither delivered over nor opposed to empiricism—a predicament that is marked in Derrida's texts by the utilization of the "old names" *in a certain way;* strategically or following a certain path, way, or track through positions that shift from explicit opposition to empiricism to the law of resemblance that binds deconstruction to it. That does not, however, provide a defense or justification of deconstruction, nor does it rigorously distinguish it from either philosophy or empiricism. This becomes clearer in the context of the accusation of skepticism.

SKEPTICISM: DECONSTRUCTION AND SELF-CONTRADICTION

Skepticism has always been a key notion in criticisms of Derrida's work. From the moment Derrida's writings gained recognition, he has had to fend off accusations of "postmodern skepticism." Though some of these accusations may have arisen from misunderstandings of Derrida's works, the relation of deconstruction to skepticism is in fact highly complex and structurally similar to its relation to empiricism. At the center of these concerns are still questions of method and justification. But now they are focused specifically on the status of self-contradiction in Derrida's texts and the occurrence of negative or destructive theses in them. To understand the occurrence of such claims in Derrida's texts, it will again be a matter of qualifying their place within a broader movement or strategy.

First of all, it is noteworthy that in Derrida's massive oeuvre one does not find a sustained, systematic engagement with skepticism. This fact is as surprising as it is telling. Surprising, because skepticism has played such an important part (and often still does) in the reception of Derrida's work.[3] Telling, because in that reception (especially in the 1970s and 1980s), the term skepticism did not exceed the status of a pejorative label. This brought on an all-too-familiar polemic between critics and defenders of Derrida, centering around the occurrence of destructive theses in his work (about the indeterminacy or impossibility of interpretation, language, or meaning, for instance). Even those who defended Derrida's work against its reduction to a simple skepticism still often had trouble explaining those theses within that work.[4] They are right to emphasize both the irreducibility of Derrida's texts to a simple skepticism as well as the occurrence of skeptical elements within them.

That very fact should already be enough to realize that the purport of Derrida's writings cannot be exhaustively understood with reference to *claims* that would *posit*, say, the indeterminacy of language, even though some of the most sympathetic early readings of Derrida still leave room for such interpretations.[5] In such cases, the critic's work is all but done: Derrida is refutable as simply the next in a long line of relativists who end up "refuting themselves," if not through flagrant, explicit self-contradiction, then through a "performative" self-contradiction (Jürgen Habermas is probably the best-known proponent of the latter view).[6] All of this would also seem to be in line with the pejorative sense that Derrida lends to the term skepticism in his texts. As I indicated in the previous paragraph, he often simply groups the term together with empiricism, relativism, historicism, and nihilism, and unequivocally distances himself from it. In this way, both Derrida (or those writing in his wake) and his critics never really needed to engage: Derrida simply denies that he is a skeptic while his opponents think that, as a skeptic, Derrida refutes himself.

The binary, oppositional form of that polemic—which is essentially a polemic about the relation between the impossibility of knowledge (or of thought, certainty, or determination) and the impossibility of determining, knowing, or claiming that very impossibility—has structured discussions surrounding skepticism since its inception and will no doubt continue ad infinitum. For some, that very infinity is reason enough to leave the discussion to itself altogether: there will never be an answer anyway, and no new positions are possible. But in taking up such a negative meta-position with respect to the debate, one actually finds oneself recaptured in it. For what is the status of the insight into the infinity of the debate? Is it an endorsement of indeterminacy (because "we will *never know*") or an endorsement of determinacy (because "we *will never* know")? Is it that the difference between determination and indeterminacy is undeterminable, or that that difference can be *determined as* being indeterminable? Thus, in the attempt to exceed the debate in this way, one finds oneself recaptured in it.

Concerning Derrida's relation to skepticism, it is indeed a matter of exceeding the binary nature of the debate surrounding skepticism, but that excess cannot (just like with the relation to empiricism) have the form of a position *outside* that oppositionality. So, analogous to the discussion of empiricism, it is possible to identify several structurally necessary moments of Derrida's relation to skepticism.

The first moment is explicit denial. Deconstruction is not skepticism. Derrida posits that claim explicitly and unequivocally on several occasions. This will not come as a surprise, although the way in which he formulates it in the afterword to *Limited Inc* is surprising. There, he distances himself from

> a relativism, with everything that is sometimes associated with it (skepticism, empiricism, even nihilism). First of all because, as Husserl has shown better than anyone else, relativism, like all its derivatives, remains a philosophical position in contradiction with itself. (*LI* 137)

This is strange: how can Derrida distance himself from a form of thinking on the basis of a "contradiction with itself" when that figure is so clearly an essential part of his own writings? In his eagerness to distance himself from simple forms of relativism, Derrida neglects here the essential and internal relation, the "law of resemblance" between deconstruction and skepticism. That resemblance comes out better at other points in his texts.

First of all, and as we have seen in the discussion of empiricism, it is equally impossible to fashion for oneself a position simply outside the "internal contradictions of skepticism." This aspect is underrepresented in the commentary that is sympathetic to Derrida. To illustrate this, one could take the words of W. Fuchs, who states that Derrida cannot be a skeptic because skepticism is "totally ensnared in the metaphysics of presence."[7]

The thought, there, is that the oppositionality of skepticism (*can we* or can we *not* know?) belongs to the metaphysical tradition that Derrida *questions*. Now on the one hand that is exactly right. But I have already indicated in several ways that the supposition underlying that diagnosis—that Derrida cannot himself be ensnared in that tradition because he is the one who is questioning it, that he occupies some kind of meta-position with respect to it—is not simply possible and neglects the inescapable structures of "complicity" that Derrida attempted time and again to bring out. If there is no way *not* to be in some way ensnared in that tradition, then what does that mean for Derrida's skepticism? In an influential article by A. J. Cascardi ("Skepticism and Deconstruction"), he takes a similar approach: skepticism, according to Cascardi, moves in a circle (of self-refutation), whereas Derrida "is seeking to free himself from the skeptical circle in order to question the axis on which it turns." In this way, according to Cascardi:

> [. . .] the deconstructionist is [able] to fashion for himself what amounts to a utopian (non)place for his inspection and questioning of every determinate position in any "topographical" (i.e., propositional) logic—which is to say, any position pro or contra skepticism.[8]

Even though the irony is palpable in sentences such as these, they still allow for an interpretation in which skepticism is relegated back to a mere accusation, a pejorative label. This view obscures the structural analogy between skepticism's "self-refutation" and the movement by which Derrida's texts are not exempt from the instability and "incompetence of science" that they seek to expose.

This is where, out of the impossibility to simply oppose skepticism, the *second moment* of Derrida's relation to skepticism arises. Now it becomes a *resource*. At this point of structural resemblance to skepticism, not only do the critics have a point when they quote the "destructive theses" that appear in Derrida's texts, but Derrida gives the same arguments for the value of skepticism that he does for the value of empiricism:

> [. . .] within philosophy, empirical or skeptical discourses are incoherent and dissolve themselves, following a well-known schema. Nonetheless, the moments of empiricism and skepticism have always been moments of attention to difference. [. . .] One can see the empirical or skeptical moments of philosophy as

moments when thought meets the philosophical limit and still presents itself as philosophy. That, perhaps is the only weakness of skeptical or empiricist philosophy.[9]

The point is not whether there are skeptical theses to be found in Derrida's writings, because there evidently are. The point is that none of these, by itself, is unequivocally endorsed. In this light, it is strange that the accusation of performative self-contradiction was leveled at Derrida as a criticism at all. What does it mean to critique a discourse that so ostensibly contradicts itself in the name of performative self-contradiction? It is this question that makes the relation between deconstruction and skepticism so interesting, because from its earliest incarnations, the skeptical tradition has had to deal with the charges of self-contradiction and self-refutation.

When searching for forms of skepticism in the history of philosophy that might provide insight into Derrida's skepticism, the first step would be to discard those forms of modern skepticism that revolve around the possibility of knowledge about the existence of the "(outside) world."[10] Instead, one would have to look for a form of skepticism (a) that complicates itself in its very articulation; and (b) for which the very binary form of any distinction or determination is itself problematic, and which thus focuses on their "undecidability," or on the possibility of a "third way" with respect to such oppositions.

The *locus classicus* of such a third way is Sextus Empiricus's *Outlines of Pyrrhonism*. Of all the numerous modifications of philosophical skepticism, what distinguishes pyrrhonism is that it takes extremely seriously the reflexive implications of what it says for the very articulation with which it is said. The pyrrhonian skeptic articulates the third way in the attempt to avoid the respective weaknesses of two equally unattractive alternatives: dogmatism and relativism. Both are, in the eyes of Sextus, determined by a commitment: the former are committed to the truth that they "believe to have found," the latter to the claim that the truth cannot be found. The skeptic, according to Sextus, is "still searching."[11]

Sextus knows like no other that the impossibility of arriving at determinations with certainty does not let itself be (dogmatically) posited. His text everywhere exudes this tension inherent in the paradoxical enterprise of describing the "outlines" [ὑποτυπώσεις] of a "doctrine" of being "still-searching." It is a doctrine that is "not a doctrine";[12] one that has a goal, but a goal that is only reached "by accident";[13] and one for which it holds that everything that it states is "not claimed" or posited [αφασια].[14]

A very large part of Book I of the *Outlines* is devoted in such a way to explaining how its own claims should be interpreted nondogmatically.

Now, I am not out to posit an identity here between Derrida and the ancient pyrrhonian skeptics. It is *only* in the way in which Sextus attempts to consistently take into account the implications of the indeterminacy that he exposes for the articulations with which he exposes it that a reflexive complication presents itself that is similar to the one that forms the main philosophical challenge for Derrida. The comparison between skepticism and Derrida is fruitful in examining (1) how to respond to that challenge, how to explicitly account for—how to say—the interrelation between what is said and the act of saying it; (2) how to interpret the texts that attempt to take up this challenge, how their content in a certain way exceeds their content, that is: how they bring a movement into play that cannot be contained within the "content of its conclusions"; and (3) what the accusation of performative contradiction is worth and how to respond to it, especially when the criticized discourse not only affirms, but even flaunts its self-contradiction.

This is where the comparison between deconstruction and pyrrhonian skepticism ends. Derrida is not a pyrrhonian skeptic. The differences are so numerous and vast that one hardly needs to summarize them.[15] I briefly mention only the following here: first, Sextus's "third way" aims at a *practical way of living*; it involves a change in one's attitude toward knowledge that amounts to nothing less than *moral reform*, whereas Derrida has no such "way of life" in mind. Second, what is perhaps the most glaring difference between them: the "principle" [ἀρχη] of that way of life is the hope for the attainment of "tranquility" [ἀταραξια], which runs counter to the disturbance [*sollicitation, ébranlement*] that Derrida is after. Third, one may hope for tranquility by suspending [ἐποχη] judgement concerning only the things that are "not evident" [ἀδηλος]. Such guiding principles and distinctions would be unacceptable for Derrida, especially the distinction between what is "evident" [προδηλος, ἐναργης] and "not-evident" [ἀδηλος] and its correlates, such as the distinction of being from appearances—that basic Greek distinction that controls everything that Sextus writes (e.g., that the skeptic only states how the matter "appears" to him and not "what it is"). Derrida's "hesitation," moreover, is not the ἐποχη as it results from the availability of an "equal counter-argument," but from the "differential contamination" of opposites. In this way, these distinctions and principles are indispensable for the skeptical way of life, whereas for Derrida they are all deeply problematic.

Not only is Derrida not a pyrrhonian skeptic, but the very search for such identifications (is he a skeptic *or not?*) is itself delivered over to an oppositional thinking that deconstruction *and* skepticism *both* attempt to put in question. Such identifications thus reduce both of them to mere labels. At issue is understanding *both* the role of Derrida's explicit disavowal of skepticism *as well as* his own skepticism in the context of the broader movement of his writing. To better understand this, it is helpful to look at the role skepticism plays for Emmanuel Levinas.[16]

In his *Otherwise than Being or Beyond Essence,* Levinas uses the "model" of skepticism's return *in spite of* its refutation. That return is not the stubborn insistence of what should already have disappeared. Skepticism persists precisely in and through its consistent refutation. It is nothing other than the to-be-refuted of philosophy. For that reason, Levinas calls it the "refutable par excellence."[17] In the words of Levinas, this indicates skepticism's sensitivity to the "diachrony" (the incommensurable temporality or nonsimultaneity) between what is said [*le dit*] and its saying [*le dire*].[18] This means that skepticism brings to light the limits of what can be explicitly posited, stated, or claimed (the said) precisely *by* implicitly, performatively contradicting the said *in* the act of saying (e.g., in the performative self-contradiction of the adage that "nothing is certain"). Skepticism thus introduces this implicit dimension of the saying that cannot be reduced to "content of conclusions." Skepticism's "refusal" to "synchronize" saying and said precisely *demonstrates* their difference, a difference that cannot itself be *posited.* It therefore demonstrates the limits of what can be said or posited without opposing something to it. In this way, skepticism is exemplary for Levinas's own project, which revolves around the question of how to thematize the "unthematizable" (ethics) in the language of being and essence (ontology).[19]

In this way, for Levinas, skepticism exceeds the status of a mere accusation. A "truth" of skepticism is revealed, but one that cannot simply be of the order of the truth that the skeptic puts in question.[20]

That places Levinas in a certain tradition for which the truth *of* skepticism is not the truth that is suspended *by* skepticism. In contemporary philosophy, this position is most famously taken up by Stanley Cavell. Though skepticism's concern may be what he calls epistemological (can we know? can we be certain?), its very return *in spite of* its refutation already shows that the status and the value of skepticism cannot be reduced to epistemological concerns. There is no "answer" to skepticism, only what he calls a certain "range of response."[21] Skepticism's value does not lie in a denial of knowledge (because that would make it partake in the same "flight from the ordinary" in which the traditional response to skepticism consists, a flight that for Cavell forms the true "scandal of philosophy"[22]), but in displacing the role and value of knowledge in our relation to the world. Therefore, for Cavell, the "truth of skepticism" is that "the human creature's basis in the world as a whole, its relation to the world as such, is not that of knowing, anyway not what we think of as knowing."[23]

So how is skepticism understood in this reading? First of all, its "traditional" concerns are identified as being "epistemological." Then a dimension is contrasted to these (merely) epistemological concerns (in the case of Cavell: the *ordinary* and "ordinary language"). There have been several attempts at connecting the insights of this surpassing of epistemological skepticism to the work of Derrida. I mention only two of the more successful ones. A famous example is found in Simon Critchley's *The Ethics of Deconstruction*. There (with explicit reference to Levinas's project of saying the ethical in the language of ontology), the dimension that is contrasted to the epistemological is the *ethical*. But the most sustained discussion of the relation between deconstruction and skepticism is found in Ewa Ziarek's *The Rhetoric of Failure: Deconstruction of Skepticism, Reinvention of Modernism*. Ziarek combines the insights of Cavell and Critchley to understand Derrida neither as a skeptic nor as an anti-skeptic but as engaged in a "deconstruction *of* skepticism." For her, too, an epistemological skepticism is simply logocentric, and cannot progress beyond a "subject-object" scheme. But the true sense of skepticism for Ziarek does not lie in such concerns, but in questioning "the primacy of truth as a philosophical concern." This means that in the discussion of skepticism, one must make "a shift from the negative epistemological consequences of linguistic instabilities to the emphatic affirmation of the other of reason and the other of the subject"; a shift from the epistemological "logic of contradiction," or the "rhetoric of failure," to the affirmative "rhetoric of temporality," which consists in a "performative address to the other."[24]

In this way, in almost all of these examples, an "epistemological" skepticism is identified (which is tied to theoretical knowledge and the form of the constative) and then distinguished from a dimension that is irreducible to it: the saying, the ordinary, the ethical, the temporal. The problem in relating such a distinction to the work of Derrida is that this very distinction (ontology versus ethics, atemporal versus temporal, theoretical versus practical, constative versus performative, said versus saying) always risks, at least, being a modification of what Derrida insists is a "traditional" (and "logocentric") distinction between theory and practice that is suspect. I am not saying that these authors all in fact contrast a dimension of practice to that of epistemology. But I am saying that even if they are attempting to work toward truly broaching such a distinction, the schema within which they work essentially risks such a relapse. On the one hand, a true discussion of skepticism only starts to be valuable when one takes seriously the skeptical attempt to show or demonstrate the limits of epistemology. After all, the skeptic denies the terms of the epistemological debate as such. Skepticism cannot be reduced to a mere doubt that resides simply *within* epistemology; its purport is only understood when the concerns of epistemology as such are being put in question (such as Sextus's attempt to describe a different ethos, a different life in which one can attain tranquility in the face of contradictions). I wholly agree with this first step, which consists of the necessity to expose the limits of theoretical knowledge, and I believe that all of the authors mentioned above, as well as Derrida himself, are in agreement on this necessity. However, the risk (with which, I want to argue, one would end up running counter to Derrida's texts) is that one thinks one can expose these limits by *opposing* to the epistemological or the theoretical a dimension wholly foreign, *outside* of or *beyond* it. It is this that would be problematic from the point of view of deconstruction.

In conclusion, at issue in Derrida's relation to skepticism is the accusation of "self-contradiction," performative or otherwise. Derrida explicitly distances himself from a simple skepticism, yet he cannot simply position himself outside it either; deconstruction is no pure non-skepticism. Derrida's texts are *also* (among other things) skeptical, first and foremost, when they are "abandoned to the simple contents of their conclusions." This is why it makes no sense to defend Derrida against the self-contradiction that he so emphatically performs, but also why, left to itself, that accusation carries no weight against a discourse that readily admits to performing it. It is only in this far-reaching awareness of the interrelation between what is said and how it is said, in this performative awareness that his own discourse produces knowledge that is "no knowledge at all" and suffers from the "incompetence of science" that it exposes, that a comparison with ancient pyrrhonian skepticism suggests itself, even though I have indicated that Derrida is not a pyrrhonian skeptic and that in all other respects the differences are numerous and too vast.

That deconstruction is, however, not reducible to skepticism (pyrrhonian or otherwise) can only be shown, not by opposing him to skepticism, but with reference to the broader movement of showing of his texts, and by the marks of the textual interventions that set him apart from all traditional skepticism. I show what is meant by such textual interventions in detail in chapter 5. What the examples of empiricism and skepticism show is that if a critique of Derrida takes his indirectness seriously, then this requires rethinking the very model of critique as such. Because engaging with Derrida's texts fruitfully cannot mean criticizing a "position" that one extracts from them, we now have to take a closer look at the relation between deconstruction and critique.

CRITIQUE: DECONSTRUCTION AND VULNERABILITY

Critique is, in one sense of the term, like empiricism and skepticism, another name for something with which Derrida is, if you will, oppositionally entangled. On the one hand, Derrida dismisses critique propositionally, unequivocally: "deconstruction is not critique." Yet deconstruction still maintains an inherent, structural relation to it. In another sense, however, the figure of critique is not merely one figure among others. For one thing, "critique" has rarely served as an accusation. For many, if deconstruction is anything, it is a critique of philosophy or of metaphysics. The remarks gathered here concerning critique therefore go to the heart of what deconstruction is or does. If deconstruction is essentially or primarily a way of reading texts, of "inhabiting" them "in a certain way," then what I address here under the heading of "critique" overflows the boundaries of this chapter alone, and also prepares the discussion of Derrida's readings of Hegel and Heidegger in the chapters still to come. We are transitioning from the question of how to criticize Derrida to the question how we must understand the "critical" force of deconstruction itself. Moreover, in this section I directly address one of the main questions that drove the entire investigation: what does an adequate critique look like of a discourse of movement, which refuses to identify with the claims found within it? It is also in this section that, through the notion of the vulnerability of deconstruction, I address my main dissatisfactions with the available defenses of deconstruction.

I do not so much intend to provide an overview of Derrida's relation to all the possible forms and meanings of critique (transcendental, genealogical, immanent, etc.).[25] Rather, I want to investigate how Derrida uses the term and, above all, to wrest our understanding of Derrida's critical relation to the philosophical tradition from a scheme that is determined by the very oppositionality that Derrida (but also, in their own way, the skeptics: Hegel, Nietzsche, and Heidegger) attempted to put in question. I start, as I did in the previous sections, with Derrida's most explicit and unequivocal assurances on the matter.

As Rodolphe Gasché already indicates in his 1991 "Critique, Hypercriticism, Deconstruction": "[. . .] that deconstruction is not a critique is stated in a rather unambiguous and decidedly propositional manner throughout Derrida's writings."[26] He mentions two quotes. The first is from "Ja, Or the Faux-Bond":

> [. . .] deconstruction is not a critical operation; it takes critique as its object; deconstruction, at one moment or another, always aims at the trust confided in the critical, critico-theoretical agency, the deciding agency, the ultimate possibility of the decidable; deconstruction is a deconstruction of critical dogmatics.[27]

The second is a famous quote from the "Letter to a Japanese Friend":

> Deconstruction is neither an *analysis* nor a *critique* [. . .] in a general, or a Kantian sense. The authority of the *krinein* or of *krisis* (decision, choice, judgement, distinction) is itself, in the same way as the whole apparatus of transcendental criticism, one of the essential "themes" or "objects" of deconstruction.[28]

According to Gasché, because deconstruction sets out to complicate the very "criteriology" that is essential to critique, the idea of deconstruction as a "critique of philosophy" is a "misjudgment" that "could have easily been avoided by a more careful scrutiny of Derrida's texts."[29]

But things are not quite so simple, and the most careful scrutiny cannot safeguard Derrida from critique entirely. In reading Derrida, a certain necessity to oppose critique must be combined with a certain impossibility to unequivocally do so. This impossibility also complicates the possibility of dismissing Derrida's misreadings (that Derrida is a critic of philosophy) through a simple reference to a more careful scrutiny of his texts. There is a more internal and ambiguous relation between deconstruction and critique that needs to be qualified.

Gasché of course knows this, and with his opening comment he somewhat shortchanges the more nuanced work he does in what follows. Because things quickly get complicated: Derrida explicitly distances himself from critique, but Gasché soon indicates that deconstruction is not "anticriticism" either; it is rather an operation "upon" critique, but then he hastens to add that this does not mean that deconstruction is a "critique of critique."[30] Let's take a step back.

The structure of the way in which Derrida denies engaging in critique is by now familiar: deconstruction *is not* critique, because critique is itself one of its main "objects" or "themes." But the very fact that "theme" and "object" stand in need of quotation marks already signals that these claims cannot unequivocally sustain themselves. As a tracing of the limits of what can be explicitly thematized or made into a describable object at all, it is just as essential to deconstruction that it *cannot* rigorously separate itself from critique. The very distinguishability of deconstruction from critique is itself subject to the problems of the "critico-theoretical, deciding agency," the "ultimate possibility of the decidable," and the "authority of the *krinein* or of *krisis* (decision, choice, judgement, distinction)."

But we must take another step back. First let us ask: what exactly does critique mean here?

By referring the meaning of critique back to *krinein,* Derrida engages in a Heideggerian gesture that immediately places the concept of critique at a remove from the commonsense meaning of the term, as well as from its more conventional philosophical forms. Critique here stands for the very possibility of rigorous demarcation or of distinction that, for Derrida, always implies binarity: the distinction of this from that, or of pro from contra. To this, Derrida relates the very possibility of decision or of judgement. Gasché is right to point to Heidegger's *What is a Thing?* [*Die Frage nach dem Ding*], where the latter distinguishes *krinein* from a negative operation. In fact, *krinein* is presented there as the "most positive of the positive" [*das Positivste des Positiven*]. For Heidegger, it signifies to "sort" or sunder [*sondern*]: to separate, isolate, dissociate, seclude; to "sort out" [*absondern*] and to so "lift out" what is "of its own sort" or what in other words is special [*das besondere herausheben*], by contrasting it to what is of a different sort [*Abhebung gegen anderes*]. Such sundering (negation, distinction, differentiation) is only apparently negative according to Heidegger. It is in fact *positive* [*positiv*] precisely because it forms the very structure of *positing* [*Setzung*] or of what is determining or decisive in every positing or positioning [*die Setzung desjenigen, was bei aller Setzung als das Bestimmende und Entscheidende im voraus angesetzt werden muß*].³¹ This form of the positive, of what must be posited beforehand in order for anything to be posited, will form the basis of the "affirmative" nature of deconstruction as it "precedes" critique, insofar as it is implicit in every critical determination and decision. I return to this in detail in chapter 9.

In Heidegger's words we can recognize the very demarcation (position, opposition, determination, decision) that was the hallmark of what Derrida called metaphysics (see chapter 2 above). If deconstruction is the attempt to put this in question, then neither can there be an unequivocal, binary demarcation of deconstruction from critique. Gasché indeed stresses that deconstruction is neither a "critique of critique" nor an "anticriticism," but he does so to emphasize that deconstruction does not attempt to find "better" criteria but to question the very criteriology of decision, as well as to stress that deconstruction "does not destroy" critique but "leaves it intact."³² Both of these are very valid points, yet they also carry a certain risk. In contrasting deconstruction's "hypercriticism" to critique, Gasché's account still runs the risk of fashioning for Derrida a strictly singular position with respect to critique (incommensurable with the "anti-" *and* with "critique" *and* with "destroying" *and* with "leaving it intact," and so on). My point is that the impossibility of distinguishing deconstruction rigorously from critique does not signify its singular incommensurability *to*, but rather its oppositional contamination *with* it. There is no way to safeguard deconstruction from falling back into critique. It is to this unavoidable falling-back-into, the irreducible complicity with or the reaffirmation of what one "criticizes," that Derrida points with his insistence on "contamination."

To see this a bit more clearly, let me add to Gasché's two examples a third quote in which Derrida distances himself from critique. It is from Derrida's 1999 *The University Without Condition*. In employing the description "more than critical" for deconstruction, Derrida seems to affirm Gasché's notion of "hypercriticism":

> This university without conditions does not, *in fact*, exist, as we know only too well. Nevertheless, in principle and in conformity with its declared vocation, its professed essence, it should remain an ultimate place of critical resistance—and more than critical—to all the powers of dogmatic and unjust appropriation.

> When I say "more than critical," I have in mind "deconstructive." (Why not just say it directly and without wasting time?) I am referring to the right to deconstruction as an unconditional right to ask critical questions not only about the history of the concept of man, but about the history even of the notion of critique, about the form and the authority of the question, about the interrogative form of thought. For this implies the right to do it *affirmatively* and *performatively*, that is, by producing events (for example, by writing) and by giving rise to singular oeuvres [. . .]. ("Uni" 14–15/204)

Derrida goes on to state that the university should thus be a place in which "nothing is beyond question, [. . .] not even the traditional idea of critique, meaning theoretical critique, and not even the authority of the "question" form, of thinking as "questioning."" Derrida in this way tries to conceive of a "force of resistance" that passes as much "by way of critique, questioning, and, *beyond critical philosophy and questioning*, by way of deconstruction" ("Uni" 21/207, my italics, JdJ).

So, on the one hand, deconstruction is thus again clearly positioned "beyond" critical philosophy and questioning, and described as "more than critical" in a way that is similar to the other examples: his point here is that critical questioning cannot *itself* be exempt from critical questioning. Although there is a slight nuance here: it is the "traditional idea" of critique, which he calls "theoretical critique," that cannot itself be exempt from questioning. The only way in which this critique can itself be criticized is "affirmatively" and "performatively."

I come back at length to the meaning of "affirmatively," as it is related to the (im)possibility of questioning the very form of the question, in the final chapter of this book. At this point I point out only that Derrida explicitly stipulates that "the 'yes' of the affirmation is not reducible to the positivity of a position" ("Uni" 15n1/301n3).

But "performatively" here cannot simply mean that what is impossible "constatively" (a "theoretical" critique) would *become possible* "performatively" (critique of critique; fashioning a meta-level above what was already a meta-level; a point of arbitration or decision for the point of arbitration or decision). Instead of a "possibility" outside of critique, Derrida rather acknowledges how critique does (and to a certain extent must) implicitly, performatively undercut itself: there is no positivity, no position that deconstruction could afford itself that would not itself have to be complicated. This also means that "more than" or "hypercritical" cannot mean a position of incommensurable singularity with respect to critique (neither anti, nor critique of, nor operation upon, nor . . . , etc.) but rather the inextricability from critique, as well as the necessity of critique to fall prey to itself. In the first case, one attempts to make Derrida's operation absolutely and singularly incommensurable with critique; the singularity of deconstruction would elevate it above all these strictures. But no such point of complete incommensurability or noncomplicity with respect to critique is possible.

I have called this complicity of Derrida's texts their *vulnerability*. I did this because it is the point at which Derrida cannot be completely safeguarded against the accusations from which his works must nevertheless be tirelessly distinguished.[33] It is the aspect that, even in the best commentaries, still threatens to go underrepresented in the attempt to defend the singularity and the worth of Derrida's textual operation, and to defend it against charges of relativism, skepticism, and so on.

To illustrate this point, compare how Derrida describes the university without condition, which we now understand would be a "more than critical," deconstructive university: a place so "unconditionally" critical that the very critical operation is not exempt from critique, where the very authority of the question is not exempt from being put in question. I quote at length:

> One must insist on this again: if this unconditionality, in principle and *de jure*, constitutes the invincible force of the university, it has never been in effect. By reason of this abstract and hyperbolic invincibility, by reason of its very impossibility, this unconditionality exposes as well the weakness or the *vulnerability* of the university [my italics, JdJ]. It exhibits its impotence, the fragility of its defenses against all the powers that command it, besiege it, and attempt to appropriate it. Because it is a stranger to power, because it is heterogeneous to the principle of power, the university is also without any power of its own.
>
> That is why we are speaking here of the university without condition.
>
> I say "the university" because I am distinguishing here, stricto sensu, the university from all research institutions that are in the service of economic goals and interests of all sorts, without being granted in principle the independence of the

university; I also say "without condition" to let one hear the connotation of "without power" and "without defense." Because it is absolutely independent, the university is also an exposed, tendered citadel, to be taken, often destined to capitulate without condition, to surrender unconditionally.

Yes, it gives itself up, it sometimes puts itself up for sale, it risks being simply something to occupy, take over, buy; it risks becoming a branch office of conglomerates and corporations. This is today, in the United States and throughout the world, a major political stake: to what extent does the organization of research and teaching have to be supported, that is, directly or indirectly controlled, let us euphemistically say "sponsored," by commercial and industrial interests? ("Uni" 18–19/206)

It is impossible not to see in the risk of the university without condition that Derrida describes here—the risk he is consistently out to expose as a *structural* risk; as no mere "accident" but as *inscribed in the very structure of* . . . (here: the university)[34]—it is impossible not to see in this vulnerability of the university without condition the very vulnerability of deconstruction itself. Compare Derrida's remark elsewhere that "Deconstruction is not a project, it is not a desire, but something like a movement; the movement of deconstruction is unconditional, that is what it shares with justice" ("OR" 26).

On the one hand, the very irreducibility of deconstruction to the positivity of a position permits deconstruction to come back ceaselessly to "haunt" any and all positions. This is what makes up its "invincible force." Simon Critchley makes the point well when he compares this aspect of deconstruction to skepticism: their very ability to *return in spite of their "refutation"* is what marks their "invincibility."[35]

Yet there is a flip side to that coin that is emphasized much less in Critchley's book and in other commentary, and that is that this very "abstract and hyperbolic invincibility" at the same time constitutes precisely deconstruction's *vulnerability*, its "impotence, the fragility of its defenses against all the powers that command it, besiege it, and attempt to appropriate it." However much one wants to maintain that "deconstruction is not a method"—under such powers we cannot merely understand those who, as if from the outside, want to abusively turn deconstruction into a method, appropriating and "applying" for their own goals an operation that would "in itself" somehow be purified from such "application" given its essential ties to a certain empirical, nonteleological wandering. Such a model *cannot* hold, precisely because the very essence of what Derrida tries to show is that the "risk" of such appropriation is *structural*. Even if Derrida continually stresses that "deconstruction is not a method," it can also not be rigorously distinguished from, or opposed to, method. If in commentary deconstruction's non-identity with method is emphasized (or with critique, empiricism, skepticism, . . .), however necessary this may be, such an account will remain one-sided so long as the very attempt to so demarcate deconstruction is not itself shown to be compromised. Deconstruction's supposed "misreadings," its "assimilations" cannot be simply reduced to the risk of an extrinsic happening that may or may not befall Derrida's texts and from which they would need safeguarding or protection in commentary. And it is certainly not enough to counter simply with the claim that the accusers should simply read Derrida's texts. This can even function as a dangerous kind of reassurance mechanism: never mind the critics; they clearly haven't read the texts. Instead, what Derrida tirelessly attempts to put in question is the very impulse to safeguard in such a way. The risk of assimilation and supposed misreading is not an extrinsic one, but intrinsic to the operation of deconstruction. Derrida himself always most explicitly recognized this risk as an *inherent* one; let me repeat the quote I elaborated above in the section on empiricism: "[. . .] what I say is *always* going to run the risk of being taken in an unfavorable light, it cannot fail to lead to misunderstandings, according to the very same law of contamination."

I give a final example, in which Derrida makes this point even more emphatically. I quote at length from his *Passions: An Oblique Offering* (and it is no coincidence that this text takes aim at the figure of the "oblique," that is, the "indirect" character of deconstruction):

> Some souls believe themselves to have found in Deconstruction ["*la*" *Déconstruction*]—as if there were one, and only one—a modern form of immorality, of amorality, or of irresponsibility (etc.: a discourse too well known; I do not need to continue), while others, more serious, in less of a hurry, better disposed toward so-called Deconstruction, today claim the opposite; they discern encouraging signs and in increasing numbers (at times. I must admit, in some of my texts) which would testify to a permanent, extreme, direct, or oblique, in any event, increasingly intense attention, to those things which one could identify under

the fine names of "ethics," "morality," "responsibility," "subject," etc. Before reverting to not-responding, it would be necessary to declare in the most direct way that if one had the *sense* of duty and of responsibility, it would compel breaking with both these moralisms, with these two restorations of morality, including, therefore, the remoralization of deconstruction, which naturally seems more attractive than that to which it is rightly opposed, but which at each moment risks reassuring itself in order to reassure the other and to promote the consensus of a new dogmatic slumber. And it is so that one not be in too much of a hurry to say that it is in the name of a *higher* responsibility and a more intractable [*intraitable*] moral exigency that one declares one's distaste, uneven as it may be, for both moralisms. [. . .]

[. . .] one gives ammunition to the officials of anti-deconstruction, but all in all isn't that preferable to the constitution of a consensual euphoria or, worse, a community of complacent deconstructionists, reassured and reconciled with the world in ethical certainty, good conscience, satisfaction of service rendered, and the consciousness of duty accomplished (or, more heroically still, yet to be accomplished)? ("P" 14–15)

Derrida here clearly designates both the defense of deconstruction as well as its attack (the accusation of irresponsibility that is in the vein of those of skepticism, empiricism, nihilism, unjustifiability, lacking academic rigor, etc.), as moralisms that must be distrusted. Deconstruction cannot position itself "beyond" these oppositions ("in the name of a *higher* responsibility"). A vulnerability necessarily accompanies deconstruction that is as much its strength as its weakness. One cannot simply discard accusations of such a lack of justification as a misreading. What is poignant here is that the question of critique is placed in the context of the question of responsibility. Derrida's indirectness must not only be referred to the strictures or the entanglements of performativity, but it must ultimately be understood in the context of what Derrida understands as the motivation that drives deconstruction. If one were less skeptical of the term philosophy than Derrida, or at least understand it less as a rigorously "metaphysical" term, then this is ultimately a question about what one is doing when one is doing philosophy. In the last instance, this is a question of what the proper philosophical response is, or of what it means to assume the highest form of intellectual or philosophical responsibility. If I stress the lack of legitimacy of deconstruction, I do so not to refute it, but to distinguish its legitimacy from what Derrida calls its "justice," a distinction that takes us from deconstruction's theoretical to its ethical justification, and that I return to at length in chapter 9. But even if deconstruction is responsible or just, this still cannot be a legitimation through the back door. Its value, justice, and responsibility will never be separable from its vulnerability.

CONCLUSION

I have argued that in the zeal to defend Derrida and distinguish deconstruction from empiricism, skepticism, and critique, deconstruction's structural vulnerability has gone underemphasized (even though such defenses are necessary and justified to the extent that there is no simple identity between Derrida's works and these figures). Though Derrida is in an important sense vulnerable to such accusations, this does not mean that they are not reductive. Deconstruction is no simple unmethodical, unjustified empiricism, nor simply a self-refuting skepticism. Yet there is a "law" binding deconstruction to them: on the level of theoretical legitimation and positions, "abandoned to the content of its conclusions," deconstruction will never be able to rid itself of the appearance of empiricism and skepticism. That Derrida is not wholly delivered over to it either, is not because he opposes empiricism or skepticism but because his empiricist and skeptical theses are used "in a certain way," that is: through strategy or the following of a certain path, way, or track; a movement of showing of which the erasure (but also more generally the frequent implicit or explicit self-contradictions of the Derridean text) are the mark. This "unheard-of" difference between deconstruction and empiricism or skepticism (the difference that, in a certain way, "is nothing") can, for Derrida, only be *written*. That does not, however, provide either a defense, justification, or explanation of deconstruction, nor does it rigorously distinguish it from skepticism or empiricism. The very wish to do so is itself part and parcel of the metaphysical oppositionality that is being deconstructed. Therefore, the accusations cannot simply be countered by claiming that Derrida has been misread, because there is a more internal relation between deconstruction, empiricism, skepticism, and critique. To put it boldly: if criticizing Derrida means to point out that he does not take up a justifiable position, then this critique is, in an important sense, correct. In the wish to defend

Derrida, one risks losing what is most important about Derrida's writings: their very resistance to such safeguarding. Deconstruction's irreducibility to a position deprives it of the means to establish for itself a theoretical legality. This vulnerability is as much its strength as its weakness. If deconstruction is to be justified, it must be responsible or just in a way that incorporates this irreducible illegitimacy. That takes us into the direction of the distinction Derrida makes between legality and justice, where the question of justification moves from a theoretical to an ethical concern. This is the subject of chapter 9.

For Derrida, critique, in whatever sense of the term, is inherently metaphysical because it implies the possibility of binary distinction or decision. But if alterity is not just externality, if there is no way to successfully extricate oneself from critique or metaphysics, then the very relation of deconstruction to the tradition it "deconstructs" becomes essentially ambiguous. What I work toward in this book is showing how this thought of an "irreducible complicity" forms the basis for a Derridean ethics. For now, it is important that it complicates the relation of deconstruction to the tradition it deconstructs. Too often, deconstruction is construed as a critique of metaphysics in the sense of a distancing from metaphysics or as the diagnosis of a failure to be corrected. The primal form of such a critique is that the deconstructed discourse is "still (too) metaphysical," but, as I have shown in chapter 2, Derrida's work is misunderstood as an attempt to get out of metaphysics. The "metaphysical" discourses do not fail at something that deconstruction would supposedly get right. Instead, Derrida's texts are the attempts to account for the complexities one necessarily deals with when engaging in a non-naive attempt to explicate the limits of metaphysics. That this involves an "irreducible complicity" already shows that "still too metaphysical" could never signify a simple critique. In this sense, there is no articulation that is not still (too) metaphysical, including Derrida's texts.

That means we can start to think differently about Derrida in relation to the metaphysical tradition. We can then start to gauge the structural analogies between Derrida and those other "less naïve inhabitants" of the "metaphysical circle." That is what I do in Parts II through IV, focusing on those other great thinkers of the "movement" of philosophical positions: Hegel and Heidegger. The consequences of these insights are that (1) Hegel and Heidegger cease to be representatives of a tradition to which Derrida would no longer belong. And (2) if this is so, then a certain leveling of the playing field occurs: Hegel and Heidegger cease to be mere points of contrast to illuminate the question about Derrida that gave this investigation its initial impetus and that until now has determined its perimeter. Hegel and Heidegger can now become two philosophers of whom we can equally ask the question of the necessity for indirectness. If I am right, then whatever the result, it will in any case not be a matter of making a simple choice between these thinkers. This does not mean that there are no differences: in each case, the necessity for indirectness takes on a very different shape. But here the polemical scheme of critique and (op)position must make way for one of showing and movement.

PART II

MOVEMENT AND OPPOSITION

From Hegel to Derrida

CHAPTER 4

HEGEL'S MOVEMENT OF THE CONCEPT AND THE LIMITS OF THE UNDERSTANDING

> To this oppositionality . . . I oppose nothing . . .
>
> —Derrida (*Limited Inc*)

> . . . not . . . as if it would position itself *against* opposition . . .
>
> —Hegel (*Difference* essay)

For Derrida, the central challenge posed by the mutual complication or entanglement of philosophical exposition with its object (the metaphysical nature of the escape from metaphysics; the putting-in-question of the question, the (im)possibility of opposing opposition, etc.) was to find a way to "write otherwise" that could take these complications into account. No doubt the form of this problem—that the character of philosophical investigation is bound up with its object—cannot be attributed to any single philosopher or source. Any philosophy worth its salt must find a way to meaningfully account for and question its own procedures, rules, and criteria. This problem is as old as philosophy itself, and it is found dispersed throughout its history in myriad configurations. But if one were to write a history of that problem, then Hegel would certainly take up a decisive place in it.

First of all, Hegel is the first philosopher to explicitly locate the aforementioned entanglement right at the heart of the philosophical enterprise. In fact, it is this very entanglement that sets philosophy apart from all other scientific endeavors. This problem defines philosophy.

Unlike all the other sciences, philosophy for Hegel does not have the luxury of being able to define beforehand its method or field of inquiry. This means that from the outset, one of philosophy's main problems is the very possibility of its own exposition [*Darstellung*]. The awareness of this problem determines the reflexivity (or what some today might call the kind of "performativity") that characterizes all Hegelian philosophy: that it is the content of the philosophical investigation itself that must determine its path or method.

That the true object of philosophy thus can only be approached through its progression, development, or movement means that the philosophical investigation cannot be reduced to any one of the specific determinations through which that movement progresses. In that sense, Hegel is especially the philosopher of the *limits* of what can be unequivocally expressed in a specific determination or proposition. Here already we see that Hegel's relation to Derrida is more complicated than is sometimes imagined: it is especially Hegel—the philosopher whose "absolute" idealism is so often interpreted to mean that he *knew no limits,* or at least no "other," let alone a "wholly" other or "alterity"—who is much more of an ally to Derrida's negotiation of the limits of philosophy than is sometimes assumed. They share a skepticism of the possibility of a simple externality. This is especially evident when comparing the ambiguity of Derrida's (early) critique of logocentric metaphysics to that of Hegel's (early) critique of (the philosophies of) reflection. This may come as a surprise to those who approach Derrida from a French philosophical tradition in which the "other" plays such an important part. But if we see that alterity cannot be reduced to externality, this enables a reading of Hegel that is much closer to Derrida's main concerns than is often thought. The shared concern is the irreducibility of the proper object of philosophy (the movement of the concept) to the unequivocality of a specific proposition, opposition, or determination. This is what I focus on in my interpretation of Hegel in this chapter.

I start by showing the origins of Hegel's idea of conceptual movement by looking at some early texts from around 1800. To better understand what it means, and also to understand Hegel's concept of philosophical critique, I then reconstruct the role movement plays in Hegel's response to Kant. I show that the question of how an exposition of conceptual movement is possible determines the young Hegel's ideas about the task of philosophy. Such an exposition demands a certain kind of immanence that I later show is not so far removed from Derrida's concerns as is often thought. I then compare Hegel's early ideas on movement and exposition to his first mature and systematic formulation of them in the *Phenomenology of Spirit*. I show how the entanglement of method and object affirms the limitations of reflection in many ways: through the necessity of contradiction; the problematic ideas about philosophy's beginning and end; philosophy's non-identity with its results; and a certain preservation of skepticism. I end by studying Hegel's ideas about the type of exposition that would be required to perform the movement of the concept, namely his conception of a "speculative proposition."

What I show in this chapter should place Hegel at a remove from a certain prevalent image, namely that of "Hegelianism" or of "speculative dialectics" to which Derrida so often explicitly opposes his own writing operation. Such a Hegelianism consists, for Derrida, in the thoroughgoing reappropriation of the other, the reduction of alterity, and the reversion of negativity back to positivity. But here—as with empiricism, skepticism, critique, and the relation to logocentric metaphysics—the broader movement of Derrida's writing cannot be reduced to the oppositions that one finds in it. So not only do I in this chapter show that Hegel is not reducible to this Derridean image of Hegelianism, but in the next I show how Derrida's interpretation of Hegel is itself not reducible to his explicit opposition of Hegelianism. Positioning himself against Hegel would only serve to reaffirm the very oppositionality Derrida is out to deconstruct. Such explicit opposition is implicitly complicated by other gestures within the broader movement of showing that Derrida undertakes in his writing, and this is what I set out to show in chapter 5.

THE ORIGINS OF HEGELIAN "MOVEMENT" AND THE CRITIQUE OF THE UNDERSTANDING

For Hegel, the nature of philosophical exposition or method is inextricably bound up with its content. Because of the reciprocal determination of content and method, the true object of philosophy and the character of its exposition are fundamentally (in) movement. This movement raises the true content of philosophy decisively above what is determinable in the content of a proposition. The first question that I therefore ask is: whence the necessity, for Hegel, of philosophical "movement"?

Where do we start if we want to answer that question? First of all, the concept of movement [*Bewegung*], especially as pertaining to "the concept" [*Bewegung des Begriffs*], is one of the key concepts of Hegelian philosophy. In that sense, it is ubiquitous and is everywhere at work in Hegel's texts. It seems to be on a par with phrases like *an sich* or *für sich*—the kinds of determinations of which Hegel writes that they are so "basic," so "simple" [*einfach*] that one could call them "souls" if their concept did not denote something higher still. But even those souls are so called precisely because they are "pure self-movements" (*PH* 55/35). Second, because movement denotes the very movement *of the concept*, as such this concept of movement is surely no mere concept among others. It is at least a post-Kantian concept in the sense of a *category* to the extent that it belongs to a transcendental logic. This means that it is not merely an object *for* knowledge but plays a constitutive role *within* all knowledge. For Kant, a category is a concept that expresses relations under which concepts have "objective validity." This means that a category does not just "apply" to a supposedly pregiven reality, but that it structures any reality to which one could relate at all. Because Kant's transcendental logic aims at unfolding the concepts that are *constitutive* for reality—for Kant: the constitutive concepts for experience or for experiential knowledge—this means that the determinations of thought are no longer conceived *in opposition to* reality. Rather, reality is itself understood *in terms of* those categories (and this includes the very category of reality itself). Because these categories are constitutive of what it means to relate to an object at all—because they thus express the necessary "form of the object" as such—the problem of the objectivity of the categories is the problem of how "reason gives itself objective reality."[1] Arguably, Kant is never closer to Hegel than in formulations such as those, taken in this case from the preface to the *Critique of Practical Reason*. But even if we state that movement is no mere logical or empirical concept but at least operates on a transcendental level, then where does that leave us? First of all, what is it, what does it mean, for a concept (let alone "the" concept), to *move*?

Rather than looking at Kant, a second option would be to consult the *Science of Logic*. Is not movement the very name for the dialectic as such, and the *Logic* its presentation? And because it is the *Logic*'s operative concept, the *very operation of the concept*, we could look at the preface to the *Logic*, where we read that it is the "nature of the content" that is "responsible for movement in science," and that it is "the content's own reflection that first posits and *generates* what that content is" (*SL* 15/9–10).[2] Perhaps even better than the preface would be the very opening of the *Logic* itself, where the (onto)logical source of "movement" is found: it is the engendering or becoming [*werden*] of/as being and nothing's "passing over" and "vanishing" into each other (*SL* 82/59–60). And if we still would not be satisfied, because what is operative at the beginning of the *Logic* is only fully comprehended at the end of the *Logic*, one could look there.

But here the notions of generation, of engendering and movement, are to such a large extent *already* at work and in play that it still begs the question of their introduction, their origin, and their necessity within Hegelian philosophy. For a concept that is so ubiquitous *within* the Hegelian system, it is surprisingly seldom an explicit object for it; a specific subject of definition or elaboration. Put in the most basic terms: Hegel did not produce a treatise on what conceptual movement is. The (onto)logical source of movement, or being-as-movement that constitutes the content and the exposition of the *Science of Logic*, does not give us the answer to the question: when did it become necessary at all to think "the concept" as being "in movement"?

When did it become necessary? From what complication did it arise? What motivates its introduction? If we ask in this way, we should focus our attention on the early Hegel.

The introduction of the concept of movement roughly corresponds, I think, to Hegel's transition from Frankfurt to Jena around 1800. We are looking, then, at the phase of the development of what is called the Jena-system. The question or problem that dominates Hegel's Frankfurt and early Jena-period is that of the "unity of oppositions" and the task of philosophy. In the words of the 1802 *Difference* essay: that "the absolute must be construed for consciousness" [*Das Absolute soll fürs Bewußtsein konstruiert werden*] ("Diff" 24/94, translation amended, JdJ). Why is that question the title of a problem, and how is movement its answer?

To clarify this, I read some passages from Hegel's 1800 "Fragment of a System" [*Systemfragment von 1800*]. There, the subject is "life" and how it should be philosophically conceived. The subject of life is one of the key subjects from that early period (along with those of love and religion) with which Hegel addresses the problem of the "unity of oppositions."[3]

At the stage of the fragment where I want to pick it up, Hegel has tried to show that what is in opposition—here thought under the notion of the "manifold"—cannot be posited absolutely. That is, a manifold must simultaneously be thought in its *relation*. It is that relation that makes it possible to think a manifold as *vital* [*belebt*] and its elements as "organs"; Hegel speaks of "living spirit" [*in Beziehung auf den lebendigen Geist*]. But, so says Hegel, to think life in this way would engender a new opposition, because with the introduction of the concept of life, its opposition to "death" is now implied. Therefore, this determination would remain "incomplete" [*so würde damit eben noch etwas ausgeschlossen und bliebe demnach eine Unvollständigkeit und eine Entgegensetzung, nämlich das Tote*] ("Sys" 421/312).

Therefore, Hegel asks what it would mean to think life completely—a question that may be interpreted as a version of the problem of "construing the absolute."

Hegel maintains here that to be "complete," life would have to simultaneously [*zugleich*] be thought *both* as organ (that is: in relation) *and* as opposition [*das Leben kann eben nicht als Vereinigung, Beziehung allein, sondern muß zugleich als Entgegensetzung betrachtet (werden)*]. To think life completely, then, would be to think simultaneously synthesis or relation and opposition. But here this task becomes a problem, because with whichever concept one thinks the two simultaneously, this concept would in turn engender a new opposition and therefore a new, seemingly unavoidable incompleteness:

> If I say that life is the union of opposition and relation, this union may be isolated again, and it may be argued that union is opposed to nonunion. Consequently, I would have to say: life is the union of union and nonunion. In other words, every expression whatsoever is a product of reflection, and therefore it is possible to demonstrate in the case of every expression that with its positing, something else is not posited, or excluded. ("Sys" 421/312, translation amended, JdJ)

Here we encounter some key concepts. First of all, we recognize the famous expression, employed here to describe the structure of life, that guides Hegel's early system-conceptions and will later come to describe the very structure of reason, subjectivity, and being: a synthesis of synthesis and non-synthesis (later: an identity of identity and non-identity). Hegel here employs the phrase tentatively, searchingly: he writes, *ich müßte mich ausdrücken*; "I would have to" or "I would be forced to employ an expression such as . . ." One can see here that Hegel is aware that such a formula, which is so vital to him, is primarily the title of a problem, not of a solution. How does he elaborate it? He clarifies by saying that, "in other words," every expression is a "product of reflection," which means that it can be shown of everything, insofar as it is posited, that with its positing, something else is always not posited, or excluded. Thus, the question of the possibility of construing the absolute is the question of recognizing the limits of reflection: how can one get to the whole without engendering a new opposition? Before looking at Hegel's response to that question, it is necessary to pause at this concept of reflection itself.

Reflection is a notoriously difficult concept in Hegel's philosophy. It is used by him in a variety of ways throughout his works, and this problem is quite well documented.[4] This is because reflection is inherently bound up with limitation and negativity or finitude. Insofar as a "philosophy of reflection" is philosophy from a limited standpoint, Hegel uses "reflection" in a pejorative sense. This is most prevalent in the early works where Hegel accuses Kant and others of propagating a "mere philosophy of reflection." But the term subsists throughout the later works, for example, when he indicates that contemporary philosophy is in the grip of a "culture of reflection."

Reflection is not always to be denounced, however. This is insofar as these limits of reflection precisely constitute an essential or structural "moment" of truth or of reason. Or, as it is put later in the *Science of Logic*, a structural moment of the concept "in its self-realization."[5] This is how, for instance, the forms of reflection in the *Logic of Essence* must be understood. But already as early as the *Difference* essay, as Walter Jaeschke has convincingly shown, both pejorative and more positive uses of the concept of reflection can be found. In other words, in this second sense, reflection is a "moment" of philosophy that at a certain point or at a certain stage becomes an *object for* philosophy.

Finally, there is the "immanent" reflection of the Hegelian "method" itself. This is neither the pejorative reflection of the past "philosophies of reflection," nor reflection as it becomes a specific theme for or a specific moment of speculative philosophy. Rather, this is the form of reflection that constitutes the very movement of speculative philosophy itself. It is the "reflection-in-itself" [*Reflexion-in-sich*] that describes the structure of dialectical thought as such, from the earlier works through to the mature dialectic.[6]

With so many conceptions of reflection, how to understand the concept here, and how to proceed? The very multiplicity of the senses of reflection in Hegel already shows what I want to focus on: the extent to which the form of the philosophical investigation is itself a theme for it, which is in my view also the question that ties Hegel's work most closely to Derrida's. What Hegel took to be one of the main philosophical challenges (and this is what I would like to bring out most of all with my short reading of the *Fragment*) is the question: what must the character of philosophical exposition be, if it is to take into account this entanglement of method and object, of *thematized* ("external") reflection—or reflection as a *moment* of philosophy—and the ("immanent") reflection *that thematizes* it.

For that reason, it is as yet unclear whether reflection is used in a pejorative sense or not at the point in the *Systemfragment* where I left it. What is precisely at issue is that although on the one hand reflection is what is to be "overcome," this very reflection is itself structured by "overcoming." It is precisely because reflection cannot be overcome in any simple sense that it must turn into a "moment."

What is clear about reflection at this point? Reflection is limited. Or better: it is the name for the movement of limitation (of negativity, distinction, opposition) that is inherent to thought. Another name for thought-as-limiting is the understanding [*Verstand*]. The pejorative sense of reflection arises wherever the view is explicitly or implicitly endorsed that these limits of reflection are unassailable, or that philosophy should be restricted to reflection or to the rules of the understanding. That is the purport of Hegel's critique of Kant.

In what does this limitation consist? Hegel states that every expression is a product of reflection to the extent that when anything is posited, something else will always not be posited. This means that reflection or the understanding is the movement of determinations and, with that, of distinctions. To put it in more explicitly Hegelian terms, the understanding is the movement of *negation* to the extent that to determine is to negate: with something's being-posited, something else is always not posited. The movement of the understanding is thus the movement of determination through negation; that is, of limitation. Its object is therefore always determinate, which is to say finite. With this, we can return to our initial problem.

WHAT EXCEEDS REFLECTION IS ITS OWN MOVEMENT

Under whichever concept the unity of relation and opposition is thought, it seems that it would always be inadequate to the extent that every expression is a product of reflection, which means that it will always engender a new opposition (between what is posited and what is, with or in that positing, not posited). Hegel responds:

> This being driven forth without a point of rest [*Fortgetriebenwerden ohne Ruhepunkt*] must however above all be guided [*gesteuert*] by not forgetting that what, for example, has been called a union of synthesis and antithesis is not something posited, something of the understanding or something reflected, but that its only character for reflection is that it is a being outside of reflection. ("Sys" 421/312, translation mine, JdJ)

The question was: how can reflection construe the absolute if it deals only in determinate oppositions? What Hegel suggests here is that it seems that one must go beyond the understanding or reflection, that reflection must be overcome, because one must not forget that what is called the "unity of synthesis and antithesis" can only have a character such that it is "outside" of reflection [*ein Sein außer der Reflexion*]. But that is where that question becomes a problem.

Because the beyond or the outside [*außer*] *is itself a reflexive determination*. To think the limits of reflection as the line dividing reflection's inside and outside, to think of something "beyond" reflection, would mean to not take a single step outside reflection. It would mean doing precisely what it is that reflection or the understanding does: to step outside, or to engender an opposition.

This has led Walter Jaeschke to write: "[. . .] here Hegel comes closer to his later basic thoughts than anywhere else in his early writings, without however achieving them."[7] Jaeschke adds that last clause because of Hegel's phrase "being outside of reflection" [*Sein außer die Reflexion*]: one cannot think what lies beyond the limits of reflection *as a beyond* without repeating the constitutive gesture of reflection (opposition).

This would not only be the point at which Hegel is closest to his own mature philosophy, but also the point at which the true dialogue between Derrida and Hegel can start. This is because this insight is the discovery of the performative complication inherent in the attempt to articulate the limits, not only, for example, of thought or of discourse, but also recognizing thought and/or discourse as the very system or movement of limitation—the limits of which cannot be straightforwardly articulated. A consideration of these limits leads to the simultaneous insight that

(1) there is a necessity to overcome the movement of limitation, that it is not absolute, and that philosophy must recognize this. Philosophy must concern itself with what cannot be reduced to an opposition, must think together what for the understanding will always merely remain opposed. And (2) that any attempt to articulate these limits seems to serve to reaffirm or confirm them; that a performative complication arises out of the attempt to articulate these limits; that one cannot simply oppose opposition. A certain kind of self-contradiction or self-complication presents itself here as necessary.

For now, and for these very reasons, I would like to indicate that I think Hegel is, at this early point, aware of this performative complication. Another way of reading the above quote, such that Hegel perhaps falls less short of his mature philosophy than Jaeschke seems to suggest, is that indeed *for reflection* such a synthesis will always merely be an "outside." How else could reflection think it? But what is the function of this synthesis? It *guides* [*gesteuert*] the *progression*, the production of oppositions through the determinations of the understanding, the drive forward through determinations without a point of rest [*Fortgetriebenwerden ohne Ruhepunkt*] ("Sys" 421/312).

Here, then, we find a very early version of Hegelian movement. If we ask how movement is an answer to the problem of reflection, we should say: it names what exceeds the limits of reflection without opposing something to reflection. What exceeds the limits of reflection is not *something beyond* reflection, but it is reflection's *own movement*.

Looking ahead to my discussion of Derrida's "Tympan" that I undertake in the next chapter, it would already be helpful to keep in mind one of its epigraphs, taken from Hegel's *Science of Logic*. It shows very well how these early insights are carried over into the later *Logic*, and it prepares the discussion of the limit in relation to Derrida. The quote reads:

> The thesis and antithesis and their proofs exhibit nothing more, therefore, than the opposed claims that a limit is, and that the limit is just as much only a sublated one; that the limit has a beyond with which it is however connected, and towards which it is to be exceeded [*wohin über sie hinauszugehen ist*], but in which there arises, however, another such limit, which is no limit.

> The solution of these antinomies, as of those previously mentioned, is transcendental [. . .]. (SL 274/201)

One can see here again that any positing (thesis and/or antithesis) means that there is a limit, and insofar as this limit is constitutive for what is on either side of it, it is simultaneously sublated and cannot be conceived as unsurpassable or absolute. Because this limit, then, is in such a way just as much *surpassed* and transgressed (and is thus just as much *not a limit*—it is sublated [*aufgehoben*]), this would present a new limit that is equally in fact not a limit. The point here is that from the perspective of reflection, this is an antinomy that cannot be resolved. The "solution" resides in taking up another perspective (a perspective that is speculative and that Hegel here calls "transcendental"). What is important to point out here, however, is that this solution does not mean that the movement is arrested or that the performative contradiction *disappears*. It means precisely that the perspective of reflection alone is insufficient, that it cannot sustain itself or be absolute. It means that there must be a different point of view on the matter, one that exceeds the bounds of reflection (called transcendental here, speculative elsewhere, or the perspective of "reason" [*Vernunft*] in the *Systemfragment*). The expressions and propositions produced from this transcendental standpoint of reason remain problematic when approached from the perspective of the understanding alone.

So movement is the answer to the problem that the beyond of reflection—its limits; what makes every determination, in Hegel's words, "incomplete" or "one-sided"—cannot (or not merely) be thought as something opposed to reflection, as its outside, because reflection is itself the very system or movement of opposition and of the outside.

That insight, to put it in the words of a famous article by Fulda on the subject, forms the proper "origin of the Hegelian dialectic."[8] Indeed, this is what Jaeschke was missing in the *Sein außer die Reflexion*-quote. He approvingly cites Dieter Henrich, who observes that here we have Hegel's prototypical thought [*eigentümlicher Gedanke*]:

> [. . .] that though the relata in the opposition must be understood out of a whole, that this whole however *does not precede them* [*ihnen aber nicht vorausgeht*] as being or as intellectual intuition,—but that it is merely the developed concept of the relation itself [*nur der entwickelte Begriff der Relation selber*].[9]

In the *Difference* essay, Hegel sums up what this insight means for his relation to the philosophy of reflection, as well as to reflection more generally, in a passage that Derrida also cites in *Glas*:

> The sole interest of reason is to suspend such rigid antitheses [*Solche festgewordene Gegensätze aufzuheben*]. But this does not mean that reason is altogether opposed to opposition and limitation as such [*Dies ihr Interesse hat nicht den Sinn, als ob sie sich gegen die Entgegensetzung und Beschränkung überhaupt setze*]. For the necessary bifurcation [*Entzweiung*] is a factor of life, which develops by eternally opposing [*das ewig entgegensetzend sich bildet*], and the totality is only possible in the highest vitality [*in der höchsten Lebendigkeit*] through re-establishment out of the highest separation [*durch Wiederherstellung aus der höchsten Trennung*]. What reason opposes, rather, is the absolute fixation of bifurcation by the understanding, all the more when the absolute opposites themselves originated in reason. ("Diff" 20–21/90–91, translation amended, JdJ)

The interest of reason, according to Hegel, is to sublate [*aufzuheben*], that is, to think together or think the unity of oppositions everywhere where oppositions have become fixated, or posited as absolute or unassailable. Yet this sublation of, or resistance to, opposition cannot itself be an opposition. It would make no sense for reason to oppose opposition. Instead, opposition is here described as a "factor" of life, a life that realizes itself precisely *in and through* the eternal *movement* of opposition [*ewig entgegensetzend sich bildet*], through diremption or bifurcation [*Entzweiung*]. Reason does not oppose opposition; it opposes the *absolute fixation* of oppositions (i.e.: abstracting from their movement) by the understanding.

To fully understand how Hegel's movement of reason relates to the oppositionality of the understanding, it is helpful to consider his critique of Kant, because that critique was precisely a resistance to the mere reflection that reduced philosophy to the rules of the understanding. So in considering the critique of Kant, the question needs to be: how is the oppositionality of the understanding to be resisted if it is not simply opposed? This means asking: what is the precise relation between the understanding and reason? What role does movement play in this resistance? Asking in this direction should expose a Hegelian sensitivity to limits and finitude that is often underrepresented in views of Hegel as a thinker of "totality." And this is important for an adequate understanding of Derrida's reading of Hegel.

THE AFFIRMATION OF LIMITS IN HEGEL'S RESPONSE TO KANT

It is a well-known fact that Hegel's response to Kant is ambiguous: throughout his works, Hegel alternates between praise for the potential of the principle of Kantian thought (its "spirit" of "authentic" or "true idealism") and criticism of the way it is carried out (the "letter"). Kant's meritorious principle is the *self-justification of reason*. Hegel recognized this in, at least: (1) the question that guides the *Critique of Pure Reason* ("how are synthetic judgments a priori possible?"); (2) in the idea that neither concepts nor intuitions by themselves yield knowledge; and (3) in what Hegel called "one of the profoundest and truest insights to be found in the Critique of Reason," namely: that "the *unity* which constitutes the *essence of the concept* is recognized as the *original synthetic* unity of *apperception* [. . .], the unity of the '*I think*,' or of self-consciousness" (*SL* 254/515).[10]

What do these three things—synthetic a priori; interdependence of concept and intuition; original synthetic unity—all signify? They are all expressions of the task of self-justification as Hegel sees it: consciousness must recognize itself as the implicit unity of all its explicit oppositions. That self-consciousness is recognized by Kant as the "highest-point" of the justification of knowledge—this Hegel takes to be the greatest merit of Kantian philosophy and the fullest expression of its "spirit" of "authentic idealism" ("Diff" 8/79).

Yet we know that, according to Hegel, Kant achieved this true idealism only from a "limited standpoint" ("Skept" 250/340). At the heart of the various ways in which Hegel criticized Kant, we always find the objection that the "subjectivism" of Kant's exposition lies in his affirmation, in various ways and places, of the opposition of thought to being.

What I want to stress is that Hegel does not *oppose* this opposition between thought and being. Before explaining this, I note that this theme of opposition has consequences on different levels: on one level, it is a theme within Hegel's discussion with Kant, but on another it concerns the form of the relation between Hegel and Kant. The first is the problem of Hegel's relation to the limits of reflection: that Hegel cannot be seen to *add* a "third term," an "outside" or an "underlying" unity to the oppositionality of reflection. In other words: oppositionality cannot be *opposed*, nor can its limits be conceived by opposing something (a "third term") to it. This is important because so many interpretations of dialectics—especially those contrasting dialectics to deconstruction—use this terminology of sublation into a "third term" (and we will see that Derrida is no exception). On the other hand, there is the question of to what extent Hegel "opposes" Kant's philosophy of reflection.

But could those two levels be rigorously separated? Is not the entire question of Hegel's relation to Kant decided precisely by the question of how to understand his opposition to the reduction of philosophy to mere reflection? This means that, as I have tried to show in the case of Derrida in the previous chapter, the problem of the overcoming of reflection is intimately linked to the question of critique. I show that this holds as much for Hegel's relation to Kant as for Derrida's relation to the metaphysical tradition generally. What is at stake in that question, therefore, is that these relations are ill-conceived as oppositions of philosophical positions.[11]

This could be shown of all the major aspects of Kant's philosophy that Hegel famously contests. Hegel does not simply position himself against the unknowability of the thing in itself or against the antinomies, nor does he simply oppose Kant's critique of the validity of the ontological proof of the existence of God. In all these cases, Hegel rather affirms that these matters exceed the possibilities of the understanding. For Hegel, the opposition between thought and being is not false or wrong. On the contrary: its explication is one of Kant's finest achievements. Hegel even states that it is the merit of Kantian philosophy to have articulated this difference "in its highest abstraction and in its truest form." Thought and being is the "highest" opposition, the opposition of all oppositions. That their unity cannot be known *as per the rules of the understanding*, Hegel states explicitly, is one of Kant's "excellent discoveries" ("Skept" 251/340).

It is, then, a matter of affirming in a certain way—not of opposing—the limits of the understanding or of reflection. These are limits that imply a beyond (reason, speculation, dialectic) that cannot be an outside, but must rather be thought as the movement of the determinations of the understanding itself. Several important consequences follow from this.

First, the "sublation" [*Aufhebung*] of the oppositions of the understanding does not "resolve" them in such a way that the contradictions *disappear*. Hegel calls the identity of subject and object the "principle of speculation." Speculation means having to think together what for the understanding *remains* opposed. For Kant, "speculation" meant the transcendental use of the categories, resulting, among other things, in the antinomies. As early as the Frankfurt-fragment *Glauben und Sein* (1797), we see Hegel formulating the main problem of the antinomies in terms of neither opposing nor simply resolving but of *having to think together* the poles of the antinomies, something that the understanding or reflection itself can never do, and that will remain a problem for it. To trace the being-together of the poles of the antinomies means to trace the movement of thought itself *as* a continual bifurcation [*Entzweiung*]. Perhaps the most illustrative instance of this is Hegel's reformulation of the main problem of Kant's theoretical philosophy:

> How are synthetic judgements a priori possible? This problem expresses nothing but the idea that in the synthetic judgement subject and predicate (the former the particular, the latter the universal; the former in the form of being, the latter in the form of thinking), that these different kinds [*dieses Ungleichartige*] are simultaneously a priori, i.e. absolutely identical. The possibility of such positing lies in reason alone, which is nothing other than this identity of such different kinds.[12]

Hegel's reformulation of the Kantian guiding question thus entails having to think what is disparate and contrary *as* absolutely identical.

Second, this means that sublation cannot be a dissolution of the oppositions of the understanding into a third term, because such a term implies that one can oppose a third dimension to the oppositions of the understanding. If such oppositions are taken up in a third term, then neither does that term constitute the resolution of the antinomy in the sense of the disappearance of the contradiction (their *solution*), nor is any such term itself extricable from the oppositionality to which it is supposedly opposed. Again: a "whole" neither precedes nor exceeds the relata of the relation, but it is constituted by their development or movement.

Finally, not only can the "object" of speculation not be a third term beyond the oppositions of the understanding, but (even though Hegel contrasts reason or speculation to the understanding) the very distinction between reason and the understanding cannot itself be a mere opposition; cannot itself simply be a distinction *of* the understanding. The understanding's very movement, the "standpoint of reason" or of speculation, cannot itself be simply opposed to that of the understanding as the supposedly "neutral standpoint" from which the movement of the understanding could then be traced. There is no neutral standpoint from which to "understand" the movement of the understanding. Rather, a justification of reason entails a *self*-justification, a tracing of how the understanding itself moves, that is: how its determinations engender other determinations through immanent implication; how the determinations of the understanding "disappear into" their opposites (that is to say: are, when posited, "simultaneously" or at the same time also [*zugleich*] "sublated" [*aufgehoben*]).

The idea that the "opposition" between understanding and reason must itself be justified *by* reason marks the main transition from the early works to their first full systematic exposition, as it is found first of all in the *Phenomenology of Spirit*. This changes the task of philosophy, which now becomes tracing the understanding's own movement, not from the outside but "from within." Here movement becomes *self*-movement, and the understanding itself becomes a "moment" of speculation. The impossibility of opposing opposition in this way leads to the necessity of tracing a wholly "immanent" development, which corresponds to the transition from "reflection" to "reflection-in-itself" [*Reflexion in sich selbst*].[13] Though the transition is fully realized first in the *Phenomenology of Spirit* as the first systematic exposition of speculative philosophy as immanent self-development, one can already see it at work in the earlier formulations of the *Difference* essay, especially where Hegel speaks of tracing the absolute that becomes itself or as it becomes itself [*das sich selbst werdenden Absoluten*]. I now turn to that essay to consider Hegel's account there of the task of philosophy.

THE *DIFFERENCE* ESSAY AND THE NEED FOR/OF PHILOSOPHY

In the *Difference* essay, Hegel articulates the relation between understanding, reason, and reflection as follows: "[. . .] reflection, risen to the height of reason in sublating the finite, now lowers itself again to the level of the understanding when it fixates the activity of reason into opposition" ("Diff" 20/90, translation amended, JdJ). Reflection functions at the level of reason when what is finite is sublated. But when this activity [*das Tun*, i.e.: the movement of reason] is fixated in opposition, reflection is pulled back down to the mere level of the understanding.

Hegel speaks in these passages with an acid tongue of all the various ways in the history of philosophy in which fixed oppositions have been misrepresented as "products of reason" (he mentions spirit and matter, soul and body, faith and understanding, freedom and necessity). He describes how these oppositions have ultimately all transitioned into the general opposition between absolute subjectivity and absolute objectivity, just before distinguishing the sublation of oppositions from an opposition to opposition, and where he stresses that his objection is against the reduction of philosophy to the structure of opposition (speculation *against* reflection) and not to opposition as such, because these oppositions are precisely to be interpreted as "resulting" from reason [*aus der Vernunft entsprungen sind*].

It is where oppositions become independent—where they come to be taken as absolutes or where they lose their vital relationality, the relationality that gives them "life"—that the need for/of philosophy [*das Bedürfnis der Philosophie*] arises: against the reduction of "the intellectual and real world" to the opposition of fixed subjectivity and objectivity, philosophy must sublate that opposition in order to show the movement of/in such oppositions:

> When the might of union vanishes from the life of men and the antitheses lose their vital connection and reciprocity [*die Gegensätze ihre lebendige Beziehung und Wechselwirkung verloren haben*] and gain independence, the need of/for philosophy arises. From this point of view the need is contingent. But with respect to the given bifurcation the need is the necessary attempt to suspend the rigidified opposition between subjectivity and objectivity; to comprehend the *having*-become [*das Gewordensein*] of the intellectual and real world *as* a becoming [*als ein Werden*], and its being as products of a producing. In the infinite activity of becoming and producing [*der unendlichen Tätigkeit des Werdens und Produzierens*], reason has united what was sundered [*getrennt*] and it has reduced the absolute bifurcation to a relative one, one that is conditioned by the original identity. ("Diff" 21/91, translation amended, JdJ)

Here Hegel speaks of a "battle" [*Kampf*] between *Verstand* and *Vernunft*, but we now understand that reason does not go against the understanding, but against the *reduction* of the "intellectual and real world" to the perspective of the understanding.

For Hegel, the question of the need *for* philosophy is also the question of the need *of* philosophy, and the necessity of immanence has consequences for that very point here. The need of philosophy introduces the problematic of the "beginning" of philosophy, what philosophy needs in order to be possible, what must be presupposed or what conditions philosophy. These considerations have a methodological significance that continues through the preface of the *Phenomenology of Spirit* to Hegel's definitive treatment of the issue in the opening section of the *Science of Logic* titled: "With what must the beginning of science be made?" With an eye to the Derridean reading, I note here that this concern for philosophy's "beginning" is prominent in Derrida's questioning of the function of the preface with regard to the requirement of the immanence of Hegelian philosophy in his "Hors livre, préfaces"[14] ("outside" or "beyond the book") from *Dissemination*. It is helpful to note preliminarily that Derrida there questions the very possibility of any "rightful beginning" (perhaps a beginning is impossible, perhaps we have "always already begun"). Though Hegel never asks that question in such an aporetic fashion, there are remarkable similarities in the kinds of insight that cause the respective necessities of these two approaches.

Hegel treats the matter in the *Difference* essay in terms of how one makes the "entrance into" philosophy, and what (which presuppositions or principles) this would require. Talk of such presuppositions, writes Hegel, suffers from being talk of mere generalities and only serves to obscure the true entry into philosophy.[15] Instead he turns the matter around: *the need for* philosophy *is its only "presupposition"*—philosophy "begins with itself." (It is not insignificant that these are the remarks that form the third epigraph to Derrida's "Tympan") *In a certain way*, philosophy is presuppositionless, but as soon as the very need for/of philosophy itself (philosophy itself as its only presupposition) is expressed [*ausgesprochen*], it is "posited for reflection" [*für die Reflexion gesetzt*], which means that it succumbs to the necessary bifurcation [*Entzweiung*] and therewith this results in two presuppositions. I have already shown that the need arises out of the inability of the fixation of oppositions to sustain itself (the negation of the movement or life of the understanding), out of the reduction of reason to the understanding. Therefore, if one does attempt to *posit* (i.e., with the means of reflection) a kind of presupposition to philosophy—"a kind of vestibule" or forecourt [*eine Art von Vorhof*]—then this would have to consist in the absolute, on the one hand, and on the other hand in bifurcation or opposition [*das Herausgetretensein des Bewußtseins aus der Totalität sein, die Entzweiung in Sein und Nichtsein, in Begriff und Sein, in Endlichkeit und Unendlichkeit*] ("Diff" 23/93, translation amended, JdJ). Hegel confirms here that rather than opposing or dissolving finitude, it is a matter of recognizing the absolute *in* it:

> From the standpoint of bifurcation, the absolute synthesis is a beyond—the indeterminate and shapeless as it is opposed to bifurcation's determinacies. The Absolute is the night, and the light is younger than it; and the distinction between them, like the emergence of the light out of the night, is an absolute difference—the nothing is the first out of which all being, all the manifoldness of the finite has emerged. But the task of philosophy consists in uniting these presuppositions: to posit being in non-being, as becoming; to posit bifurcation in the Absolute, as its appearance; to posit the finite in the infinite, as life. ("Diff" 23–24/93, translation amended, JdJ)

For the standpoint of oppositionality, of reflection or of the understanding, the "absolute synthesis" can only be an outside [*ein Jenseits*]. It would be that which is simply opposed to its determinations: the shapeless and undetermined. But we know that reason is not simply the other of the understanding:

> Every being is, because it is posited, an opposite, conditioned and conditioning. The understanding completes its limitations by positing the opposite limitations as conditions. These need to be completed in the same way, so the understanding's task expands *ad infinitum*. In all this, reflection appears to be merely understanding, but *this guidance toward* the totality [*diese Leitung zur Totalität*] of necessity is the contribution and secret efficacy of reason. ("Diff" 25/95, translation amended and my emphasis, JdJ)

Hegel reiterates here that reason is *in* the understanding. With every position, something is not posited, which is then posited as the condition for the first, which in turn brings its negation with it, and so on ad infinitum. Hegel explicitly states here that reflection only seems to be reduced to the understanding, but that this movement of the understanding is precisely reasonable as movement or in its progression: this directedness, this-being-guided-toward totality is what is the reasonable.

In this way, philosophy begins at the limits of reflection and is necessitated by them. It begins at the need that arises out of those limits, and it is needed to the extent that these limits must be articulated and comprehended. Thus, the need for/of philosophy can only consist in reaching the "principle of the annihilation [*Vernichtung*] of all fixed opposition and relating what is limited to the absolute" ("Diff" 45/112, translation mine, JdJ). I emphasize that it is not opposition as such that is to be "destroyed," but it is "fixed" opposition that Hegel opposes. This is a point at which Gasché's influential commentary on Derrida and the philosophy of reflection runs a risk, because he describes Hegel as showing the "self-destruction" of reflection.[16] That "rhetoric of failure"[17] risks no longer being able to account for reflection's positive role as a *moment* (in the terminology of the later *Phenomenology*, *Encyclopedia*, and *Logic*), or as the "appearance" *of* the "self-production of reason" [*dieser Selbstproduktion der Vernunft, eine Entwicklung der Vernunft selbst*]. The absolute must be recognized *in* its appearance [*Das Absolute muß sich also in der Erscheinung selbst setzen*]. That means that for Hegel this appearance must "not be destroyed," but to the extent that it appears as opposition, the identity of these opposites must be construed [*diese nicht vernichten, sondern zur Identität konstruieren*] ("Diff" 46–47/115). It is only in the *fixation* of opposites that the understanding "destroys itself."

The terminology of reason as the "life" of oppositions continues throughout Hegel's works, right into the *Science of Logic*, where the "self-movement" [*Selbstbewegung*] of the "immanent development of the concept" [*die immanente Entwicklung des Begriffes*] is called its "spiritual life" [*ihr geistiges Leben*]. It is that spiritual life that "constitutes science" and of which science is the "exposition" [*Darstellung*] (*SL* 16/10).

So now the dilemma becomes: if the task of construing the absolute for consciousness means showing the very *life* of oppositions, their *movement*, but if every expression is "posited for reflection," then what must the character of philosophical exposition be? Hegel states: "The form that the need of philosophy would assume, if it were to be expressed as a presupposition, allows for a transition from the need of philosophy to the *instrument of philosophizing*, to reflection *as* reason" ("Diff" 25/94, my emphasis, JdJ).

HEGEL'S EARLY PROBLEM OF PHILOSOPHICAL EXPOSITION: SKEPTICISM AND THE NECESSITY OF SELF-CONTRADICTION

When Hegel distinguishes the immanent development of science from a philosophy that would either expose or would itself lay down "*foundations*" [*Ergründen* or *Begründen*], it is because there is no neutral place from which such foundations could be exposed. That reason must show itself to be "its own foundation" is because reflection is both the "instrument" and the object of philosophy.

Because the transition from the Jena-works to the more mature exposition of the *Phenomenology* marks the move toward the interpretation of the understanding *as* reason, we can now see why its preface can be read as a systematic meditation on the problem of philosophical exposition.

The purport of that problem for the present investigation is to show how it is *in* the propositions of Hegel's speculative exposition, in its movement, that something of the limits of the propositional form is expressed and affirmed. Here a certain necessary indirectness, a resistance to the presentation of an unequivocal standpoint or a theory, results from the mutual complication of object and method or instrument. Now the question of exposition is no longer a merely formal one because reasons ("content") demand a specific "form." Because speculation aims at tracing or showing the implicit unity of what is explicitly opposed, the speculative truths *must necessarily have the form of a contradiction* from the perspective of reflection or of the understanding. At issue, then, is the *necessity of contradiction in philosophical exposition*. How does Hegel explain this necessity?

Though the *Phenomenology*'s preface contains the well-known passages about the "speculative proposition," one can find indications of the necessary self-contradiction of philosophical exposition well before the already very specific and systematic project of the *Phenomenology*. One of Hegel's most brilliant essays from his Jena-period is his review of Gottlob Ernst Schulze's 1801 *Critique of Theoretical Philosophy* titled "On the Relationship of Skepticism to Philosophy, Exposition of its Different Modifications and Comparison of the Latest Form with the Ancient One" [*Verhältnis des Skeptizismus zur Philosophie. Darstellung seiner verschiedenen Modifikationen und Vergleichung des neuesten mit dem alten*]. What starts as a review ends up being a wholesale survey of the different species of skepticism and the relation of skepticism to philosophy as such. His terminology there very closely resembles that of the *Difference* essay.

In that review, Hegel states that there is no more complete document of true skepticism than Plato's *Parmenides*. This is so not only because Plato voices doubts about what Hegel calls the "truths of the understanding," but also because one finds there a "complete negation of all knowledge of the understanding." Such a skepticism, according to Hegel, does not stand in opposition to philosophical knowledge. On the contrary: it is one "side" of knowledge of the absolute. Hegel calls it the "negative" or "free" side of philosophical knowledge. In such a scheme, the positive side would be reason:

> This skepticism that comes on the scene in its pure *explicit* shape in the *Parmenides*, can, however, be found *implicit* in every genuine philosophical system; for it is the free side of every philosophy [. . .]. ("Skept" 229/324)

Hegel then continues:

> If in any sentence that expresses a cognition of reason, what is reflected in it—the concepts contained within it—is isolated, and the way in which they are related is considered, then it must become apparent that these concepts are simultaneously sublated or are *related contradictorily*, otherwise it would not be a sentence of reason but of the understanding. ("Skept" 229/324, translation mine and emphasis added, JdJ)

All knowledge of reason must necessarily have a form that for the understanding can only be a contradiction. If it is not a contradiction, it is a proposition of the understanding. What belongs to reflection are the concepts contained in the proposition only insofar as they are isolated. Hegel shows here that the understanding performs a kind of abstraction: it must isolate the concepts from their relation, and it will fixate on their contradiction. For reason, however, it is imperative not that the contradiction disappears, but that these concepts *relate contradictorily* [*auf eine solche Art vereinigt sind, daß sie sich widersprechen*]. The sublation in question does not cause the contradiction to disappear, but where the understanding sees exclusion, the perspective of reason shows contradiction to be a relation. The concepts are both, simultaneously, explicitly posited as well as implicitly sublated.

Hegel proceeds to give examples of what he means. One is from Spinoza's *Ethics*. Its opening definition reads: "By that which is self-caused, I mean that of which the essence involves existence, or that of which the nature is only conceivable as existent." Hegel proceeds to show that the concept of "essence" can only be posited by *abstracting from* existence—the one is only "definable as long as there is an opposition to the other": "[. . .] let both be posited bound together as one, and their bonding contains a contradiction, so that both are simultaneously negated." Hegel proceeds to argue similarly for Spinoza's claims concerning God or nature as "immanent cause" of the world and the one and the many concerning the identity of substance and its attributes ("Skept" 229/324).

According to Hegel, this is where what he calls the "principle of skepticism" shows itself "in full force": "παντι λογῳ λογος ἀντικειται" ("against every argument there is an equal one on the other side"), which means that the principle of non-contradiction contains "not even so much as formal truth" for reason. For Hegel, this means that self-contradiction is necessarily a defining characteristic of all true, that is, reasonable, knowledge:

> The so-called "principle of contradiction" is thus so far from possessing so much as formal truth for reason, that on the contrary every proposition of reason must in respect of concepts contain a violation of it. To say that a proposition is merely formal, means for reason, that it is posited alone and on its own account, without the equal affirmation of the contradictory that is opposed to it; and just for that reason it is false. To recognize the principle of contradiction as a formality, thus means to cognize its falsity at the same time.—Since every genuine philosophy has this negative side, or always sublates the principle of contradiction, anyone who has the urge can set this negative side in relief and set forth for himself a skepticism out of each of them. ("Skept" 230/325, translation amended, JdJ)

Hegel thus maintains that if a proposition does *not* contradict itself in such a way—that its concepts are posited as well as simultaneously negated—then it *cannot* be a proposition of reason. From the standpoint of reason, a proposition is "formal" if it is posited for itself, *without* its contrary being equally posited. From the standpoint of reason, it would therefore be false.

In this way, Hegel maintains that the exposition of the self-unfolding of reason necessarily contradicts itself from the perspective of the understanding. He also devotes considerable attention to the same issue in the *Difference* essay, where he claims that "the form of reflection appears as contradictory propositions" [*diese Form der Reflexion erscheint als widersprechende Sätze*] ("Diff" 24/94, translation amended, JdJ).[18]

These early considerations on the necessary contradiction of the speculative exposition are slightly amended and expanded upon in the famous preface to the *Phenomenology of Spirit*. That preface can be seen as a thoroughgoing reflection on the nature of philosophical exposition [*Darstellung*].

THE PROBLEM OF SPECULATIVE EXPOSITION IN THE *PHENOMENOLOGY OF SPIRIT*

The *Phenomenology of Spirit* opens with a complication that also guides the openings of Hegel's other major works. It concerns the inability to posit or to unequivocally present philosophical truth or the absolute. The entire preface is dedicated to this question: what is the character that a scientific exposition of the absolute must have?

Hegel's problem begins with a question of "presuppositions." The performative complication is that anything that would be written in a prefatory way would merely harbor or express unproven presuppositions that the investigation itself will first need to prove. Hegel says this would mean making use of a type of exposition of which the philosophical investigation itself sets out to show the inadequacy. The *Phenomenology* sets out to show the essential inadequacy of a certain type of exposition. How does Hegel conceive the (in)adequacy of philosophical exposition in the preface?

First of all, he starts with a meditation on what it means to take up a philosophical position and how that relates to philosophical truth. Because any given position is at odds with the absolute in virtue of its very determinacy, it will remain (in terminology that Hegel already used in the early Jena-works) "one-sided." The problem of philosophical exposition is the problem of how not to be one-sided, how not to represent a side in a debate. The reason for this is that such a debate between positions would always require an arbiter or some external criterion. The only way not to be one-sided is to supply one's own criterion. One must be, in Plato's words, "both jury and advocates at once."[19]

According to Hegel, this means to recognize "mutually necessary moments" in what only appears to be conflict and opposition.[20]

In terms of philosophical positions, this means for Hegel that one has to resist the "concern with aim or results" of having to "either endorse or contradict" given philosophical systems. Indeed, Hegel even claims that the very distinction between true and false must not be conceived as a "rigid opposition." Rather, it would be a matter of recognizing *in* the different philosophical systems the progressive "unfolding" of truth. Hegel makes the same point, perhaps more clearly, in the introduction to the *Phenomenology*, where he states that everything that presents itself as science must necessarily be appearance and not yet the movement of science in its actual exposition, because it finds itself in the midst of several conceptions or appearances of what it is to be science. Because all the arguments with which to prove itself as the true science are equally applicable by all the other appearances of science, the only possibility is to "turn against appearance as such" (by which he means "mere" appearance). This can only be done by showing in what way all the forms are appearances *of* science, that is: through an exposition of science in its appearance(s) [*Aus diesem Grunde soll hier die Darstellung des erscheinenden Wissens vorgenommen werden*]. This not so that one can discover the supposedly true science *behind* its mere appearances, but in order to show how true or actual science is found *in* its multiple appearances.[21]

Thus the absolute is found in the propositions of the philosophical exposition but cannot be reduced to the contents of its conclusions or to a single standpoint or position. As "the real issue is not exhausted by stating it as an aim, but by *carrying it out*," so the real result is not only the conclusion but it "together with its becoming" [*es zusammen mit seinem Werden*] (PH 12/2).

As the philosophical exposition cannot be reduced to any one position, it must attempt to free itself from one-sidedness, and this means that the very carrying through of the exposition is inseparable from the results that it produces. So what does the philosophical exposition look like?

In the preface, the "activity of distinction or separation" [*die Tätigkeit des Scheidens*] is still what signifies "the work or the power of the understanding." He also calls such separating activity "the negative as such" [*das negative überhaupt*]. Another name for this negativity is subjectivity: "subject" is the name for "pure simple negativity" [*die reine einfache Negativität*], that is, the "bifurcation of the simple" [*die Entzweiung des Einfachen*] or the "doubling that sets up opposition" [*die entgegensetzende Verdopplung*]. The fully developed basis for philosophical exposition (which can only be fully justified *through* that very exposition) is now famously formulated as follows: "In my view, which can only be justified by the exposition of the system itself, everything comes down to grasping and expressing the true not only as *substance*, but equally as *subject*" (PH 23/10, translation amended, JdJ). In another formulation, Hegel stresses that "living" substance is the "being that is in truth subject," where substance is now also called the "in-itself" and subject the "for-itself." Hegel makes the necessity of self-development explicit when he states what it means for substance to be shown to be in truth subject. Living substance is "the movement of one's self-positing or the mediation of one's becoming-other with oneself" [*die Bewegung des Sichselbstsetzens oder die Vermittlung des Sichanderswerdens mit sich selbst*] or the "reflection in otherness *within itself*" [*die Reflexion im Anderssein in sich selbst*] (PH 23/10, translation mine, JdJ). Here the operative concepts are always "*sich*" (oneself) and "in." The "other" of the understanding must be recognized as being "within" the understanding; the understanding must come to recognize itself *as* the movement of becoming-other, and "returns to itself" only in that very recognition.

Hegelian identity can therefore never be a simple self-presence, because thought finds itself only *in* its other. Insofar as any positivity or posited identity implies its negativity or difference, the standpoint of reason means: to recognize oneself in one's other or in the movement of one's becoming-other. The positivity of any given determination or opposition is always partial, and the understanding is in that sense always also beyond itself or negative. To *not* be one-sided, to bring the "whole" before consciousness (the construal of the absolute as the task of philosophy) thus means for reason to recognize itself in this self-movement of becoming-other.

Now we can understand that famous proposition from the preface that states that "the true is the whole" [*Das Wahre ist das Ganze*]. Whole, not because it is "everything," but because no outside could be *opposed to* it without creating an opposition that would revert the absolute back to one-sidedness. Hegel immediately specifies: "whole" is no "totality" in the sense of the greatest aggregate (which would be a "rigid" absolute, a totality in the merely reflective sense), but rather the whole is "the essence consummating itself through its development" [*das durch seine Entwicklung sich vollendende Wesen*]. This means that the absolute is no mere end result but that it is to be recognized *in* (the movement of) the specific, finite determinations of reflection. Hegel is explicit on the point: each "moment" is itself a "whole," and the absolute is to be recognized *in* the determinateness of the moment and cannot be simply *contrasted to* that determinateness:

> On the one hand, the *length* of this path has to be endured, because each moment is necessary; on the other hand, each moment has to be *lingered* over [*andernteils ist bei jedem sich zu verweilen*], because each is itself a complete individual shape [*individuelle ganze Gestalt*], and is only viewed in absolute perspective when its determinateness is regarded as a whole or as something concrete, or when the whole is regarded in

what is proper to that determination [*oder das Ganze in der Eigentümlichkeit dieser Bestimmung betrachtet wird*]. (PH 23/17, translation amended, JdJ)

If movement becomes self-movement, then this complicates some essential ideas generally belonging to the idea of philosophical development. First of all, because it is no movement *away from* or *toward* something else, this complicates the notions of beginning and end or goal. Indeed, a goal is generally conceived as being at rest, but as subject it is self-moving, which collapses (or rather: treats as movement instead of as rigid opposition) the distinction between beginning and end: truth is "the becoming of itself" [*das Werden seiner selbst*], which as such "presupposes its end as its goal" [*der sein Ende als seinen Zweck voraussetzt*] and as such "has it at the beginning" and is "only actual in its carrying out and its end" [*nur durch die Ausführung und sein Ende wirklich ist*]. This is why Hegel describes the movement of science as "circular," a determination that will remain throughout Hegel's later works. This movement or relativizing of beginning and end, which is also a relating/relativizing movement of concept and actuality and of self and other [*sichanderswerden*], is indeed circular, because it is a self-movement:

> The result is the same as the beginning, only because the beginning is the goal; in other words, the actual [*das Wirkliche*] is the same as its concept [*sein Begriff*] only because the immediate has the self or pure actuality in itself as goal. The goal that is carried out [*Der ausgeführte Zweck*] or the existing actuality [*oder das daseiende Wirkliche*] is movement and unfolded becoming; but this very unrest is the self [*eben diese Unruhe aber ist das Selbst*]; and the self is like that immediacy and simplicity of the beginning because it is the result, that which has returned into itself, the latter being similarly just the self. And the self is the sameness and simplicity that relates itself to itself [*die sich auf sich beziehende Gleichheit und Einfachheit*]. (PH 26/12, translation amended, JdJ)

This means that although the absolute may consist in an identity or a unity [*Gleichheit* or *Einfachheit*], it is neither a unity in the form of a conclusion (a "dead result"), nor an immediate or "original unity." Rather, it is unity as movement: as identity that relates itself to itself [*sich auf sich beziehende Gleichheit*]. This is Hegel's problem in the extended polemic against the "formalism" for which the absolute is either an immediate intuition or an original principle.

As immediate intuition, the exposition of the absolute is fundamentally opposed to the concept. This absolute-as-*jenseits,* as wholly other than or unrelated to the concept, is colloquially expressed in the kinds of terms of which Hegel had shown the conceptual movement in his early works: religion, life, love. As far as an original principle goes, Hegel mentions the "ich=ich" he so famously describes as the "night in which all cows are black." The fault with both lies in a "disdain" for determination or determinateness [*blickt verächtlich auf die Bestimmtheit*]; for "*den Horos*" (ὅρος, the limit or the marking of the limit). The disdain resides in considering reflection to reside in "mere finitud" and to consider the absolute as wholly unrelated to it. Instead, Hegel argues that to recognize the absolute means to recognize the infinity *of* or *in* reflection, that is, to recognize it as movement of reflection-in-itself. Hegel is explicit on the point: the understanding *as* becoming *is* the reasonable [*als dies Werden ist sie die Vernünftigkeit*].

What are the consequences of the insight that the absolute is in the understanding, for the question of the exposition of the absolute? Hegel picks up the topic of method about halfway through the preface. He will slowly work toward the inherent limits of philosophical presentation that culminate in the discussion of the speculative proposition. The problem that all the ideas of philosophical method and presentation that he denounces have (the "empty formalism," the application of preconceived "schemas," the distillation of philosophy into "tables," etc.) is the very idea that "method," "presentation," or exposition is in principle distinguishable from content at all:

> Science dare only organize itself by the life of the concept itself. In it, the determinateness (which is taken from the schema and externally attached to what exists) is the self-moving soul of the realized content [*des erfüllten Inhalts*]. (PH 50/31, translation amended, JdJ)

As always, the "death" that is here opposed to this "life" comes in one of the following two forms: it is either a reduction of philosophy to fixed or rigid opposition, or it is the introduction or application of a wholly external element:

> It is in this way that the content shows that its determinateness is not received from or attached to it by something else, but that it gives itself its own determinateness [*sondern er gibt sie sich selbst*] and ranges itself into a moment and into a position in the whole [*und rangiert sich aus sich zum Momente und zu einer Stelle des Ganzen*]. (PH 52/32, translation amended, JdJ)

Hegel's problem with method is therefore that it seems to imply the application of a preconceived, external scheme or presupposition; whereas self-movement demands "radical presuppositionlessness." I borrow the latter term from Stephen Houlgate, and I believe that the problem he rightly identifies as pertaining to the *Science of Logic* ("does Hegel have a method?") applies to Hegel's considerations in the *Phenomenology* as well.[22] The indistinguishability of method from content makes that the true exposition of it can only be found in the *carrying out* of the speculative philosophy:

> This nature of scientific method, which consists partly in not being separate from the content, and partly in spontaneously determining the rhythm of its movement, has, as already remarked, its proper exposition in speculative philosophy. Of course, what has been said here does express the concept, but cannot count for more than an anticipatory assurance. Its truth does not lie in this partly narrative exposition, and is therefore just as little refuted by asserting the contrary [. . .]. (PH 52/35, translation amended, JdJ)

it is possible that the understanding gains for itself "independence" and a "freedom" of its own. Such is, as he famously puts it, the "monstrous power [*ungeheure Macht*] of the negative." Philosophy is the resistance to this. This resistance must have the form of a "liquification" of the rigidity of the oppositions of thought. But, once again, this cannot be done "from the outside." How are fixed thoughts liquified?

> Thoughts become fluid when pure thinking, this inner *immediacy*, recognizes itself as a moment, or when the pure certainty of self abstracts from itself—not by leaving itself out, or setting itself aside, but by giving up the *fixity* of its self-positing [*sondern das Fixe ihres Sichselbstsetzens aufgibt*], not only the fixity of the pure concrete, which the "I" itself is

in contrast with its differentiated content, but also the fixity of the differentiated moments which, posited in the element of pure thinking, share the unconditioned nature of the "I." Through this movement the pure thoughts become concepts [*werden die reinen Gedanken Begriffe*], and are only now what they are in truth, self-movements [*Selbstbewegungen*], circles, spiritual essences [*geistige Wesenheiten*], which is what their substance is. (*PH* 37/20, translation amended, JdJ)

Thinking needs to recognize *itself* as moment. The "sublation" of the determinations and thoughts of the understanding is not a setting aside of the understanding. Hegel speaks of the necessity to "face" the negative and to "dwell" with it [*bei ihm verweilt*]. Instead of doing away with reflection, it is necessary to suspend the rigidity of its determinations. Then the concepts of the understanding can be conceived as the self-movements that they are: as "circles" or "spiritual" essences.

This means that the negative comes to essentially inhabit the philosophical exposition. It is not its defect, but its very *life*; its "soul" or what "moves" in it [*ist aber ihre Seele oder das Bewegende derselben*].

There is in this way, states Hegel, a certain necessity to engage with "the false." According to Hegel, it is ignorance regarding the relation of philosophical truth to negativity that presents the biggest obstacle for understanding speculative philosophy. First of all, the true and the false are among the concepts that we generally hold to be opposed and mutually exclusive (i.e.: rigid, without movement). But speculative thinking holds that substance is itself essentially negative, as "distinction and determination of content" and as "distinction simply, that is, as self or as knowing as such" [*als Selbst und Wissen überhaupt*]. So it is the negative within speculation (speculation's dwelling with it) that distinguishes that speculation from dogmatism. Dogmatism, according to Hegel, consists in the production of propositions that are fixed results. But the articulation of the speculative sense of concepts features a "moment of being completely other" [*Moment des vollkommenen Andersseins*]. According to Hegel, even propositions such as "unity of subject and object, of finitude and infinity or of being and thought" are problematic. For many, such phrases express the essence of the Hegelian dialectic, and it is true that to a certain extent Hegel is bound to them. But it is clear that for Hegel they are primarily titles of problems. Recall Hegel's reluctance to use formulations such as the "identity of identity and non-identity" in the *Systemfragment*. Here in the preface, Hegel indicates the risk in doing so: in the very expression of such utterances, the terms subject and object mean what they mean insofar as they are *not* united. What is meant with them in their unity is not what is actually said [*in der Einheit also nicht als das gemeint sind, was ihr Ausdruck sagt*]. The reason why they are not meant as they are said is that in the phrase "unity of subject and object," both subject and object are simultaneously canceled out, that is: sublated. In the same way, according to Hegel, the negative or the false is not a moment of truth "*as* false."

If there is an indirectness of the Hegelian discourse, it can be found here, where the absolute signifies the essentially implicit—where a certain kind of self-complication, a simultaneous positing and positing of the opposite is necessary. In the skepticism-article, Hegel described it as a necessary self-contradiction—if a proposition did not contradict itself, it could only be a truth of the understanding, never of reason. In the preface, Hegel is more nuanced about the form of the speculative exposition through his account of the speculative proposition.

THE SPECULATIVE PROPOSITION

Throughout the preface, Hegel generally distinguishes three forms of thinking: representational, formal, and speculative. To each belongs a certain mode of expression that is specific to the character of that kind of thinking. What characterizes both formal and representational thinking (and what distinguishes speculative thinking from them) is *fixation*.

Hegel only pays very little attention to representational thinking, though its temptations form a strong and highly common force that Hegel refers to as a "habit" (*PH* 55/35). Hegel calls it a thinking that is "entrenched in materiality" [*in den Stoff nur versenkt ist*] which is, therefore, "contingent" [*ein zufälliges Bewußtsein*]. It is merely contingent because it is unable to comprehend the subjectivity of its expressions: to represent is to reproduce a content that is wholly external, a content to which consciousness is delivered over and in which it fails to recognize itself. The externality and lack of self-consciousness of representational thinking is captured by A. V. Miller in his translation of it as "picture-thinking." What one acquires through picture-thinking is a "familiarity" [*Bekanntschaft*] with things. This familiarity, however, is not (proper) knowledge. In fact, Hegel states that knowledge *goes against* familiarity: "what is 'familiarly known' is not properly known, just for the reason that it is 'familiar'"—what is

Bekannt is not *erkannt*. Knowledge starts with analysis of what we believe ourselves to be already familiar with. This analysis has the character of breaking up the familiar or the represented "into its ultimate elements" and thus "returning upon its moments." This "action of separating the elements is the exercise of the force of understanding" (*PH* 33/18ff., translation amended, JdJ).

The thinking that is confined to this work of the understanding, Hegel calls *formal* thinking. He also speaks of *räsonnieren*, which has been translated as ratiocination or argumentation. Formal thinking thus reduces the activity of consciousness to proceeding from representation to thoughts by way of analysis. According to Hegel, such thinking is formal to the extent that it abstracts from the (material) content. It consists in "freedom from all content, and a sense of vanity towards it." This sense of vanity issues from its "negative attitude towards the content it apprehends: it knows how to refute it and destroy it." The decisive characteristic of formal thinking is to stop short at this merely "negative insight" and to "fail to see the positive within" it. It is naive with respect to itself because it fails to "get its very negativity as its content." The negative is always only a "dead end," and it will have to look beyond itself for "new content," which means that it never learns, but always starts over. Hegel's polemic here is with "mathematical" thought. It is to this formal thinking that Hegel contrasts *speculative* or "comprehending" [*begreifenden*] thinking. This is the thinking for which the negative is to be a "moment," for which the negative belongs to the content itself.

If we now look at the modes of expression or exposition proper to these forms of knowledge, then Hegel states that there is a fundamental difference between speculative thinking on the one hand and both representational and formal thinking on the other hand. According to Hegel, the latter two both stand in need of a "subject" as a solid, fixed, or "permanent ground." Their mode of expression is to append "accidents or predicates" to such a subject. However, as we have already indicated, the "object" of speculation is movement as such, and as such it cannot be adequately expressed through the connection of a predicate to a fixed subject. An example that Hegel gives of the desire to *represent* substance as subject is the proposition "God is love." According to Hegel, that proposition is not false, but it also does not express speculative truth. Here the truth is "merely posited" as subject. It is not, however, "presented as the movement of reflection in itself" [*nicht aber als die Bewegung des sich in sich selbst Reflektierens dargestellt*]. What is wrong with this exposition is that in this representation, the subject is presumed to be a "fixed point" to which predicates can be "appended," whereas the "actuality of the concept" consists in fact in its "self-movement" (*PH* 27/40).

Hegel's idea of a speculative proposition is thus meant to resist the idea of a proposition in which predicates would be appended to a fixed subject. This does not mean that such a proposition has a fundamentally different form. On the contrary, it still has the form of a propositional sentence. However, it is a sentence that is designed to inaugurate a movement in such a way that this very form is simultaneously "sublated." Sublated in such a way that with the speculative proposition, "representational thinking suffers a counter-thrust" [*Das vorstellende Denken [. . .] erleidet, [um] es so vorzustellen, einen Gegenstoß*]. This is a counter-thrust to the subject as the supposedly solid basis or ground [*feste Boden*] to which general predicates are appended:

> If the concept is the object's own self, which presents itself as a becoming, then it is not a passive subject inertly supporting its accidents [*nicht ein ruhendes Subjekt, das unbewegt die Akzidenzen trägt*]; it is, on the contrary, the self-moving concept which takes its determinations back into itself. [. . .] The solid ground which ratiocination has in the passive subject is therefore shaken, and only this movement itself becomes the object. (*PH* 57/37, translation amended, JdJ)

So the object of the speculative proposition is the movement of what for ratiocination (whether representational or formal thinking) is a fixed subject to which predicates are appended. How is the counter-thrust to the propositional form realized?

The speculative proposition stages a conflict between the content of its expression and its propositional form. According to Hegel, the propositional form presupposes the distinction of subject from predicate. The speculative proposition, however, expresses the "identity" of that distinction and thus runs counter to "the form of any proposition whatsoever" [*Form eines Satzes überhaupt*]. Speculative or "philosophical" proposition thus provides the counter-thrust to the very propositional form, a form that is "corrupted" [*zerstört*] by the philosophical concept. Usually *zerstört* is translated as "destroyed" (this is also what Miller does), and though that is an adequate translation in itself, it is potentially misleading: Hegel soon (and crucially) stresses that the distinction of subject and predicate that constitutes the propositional form is not "annihilated" [*vernichten*] (*PH* 59/38).

The example that Hegel gives of a philosophical proposition is "God is being" [*Gott ist das Sein*]. What is the difference between "God is love" and "God is being"? Why is only the latter a speculative proposition? Hegel states that "*das* Sein" indicates that being has a substantial meaning here: God is not this or that being, but being *as such*. With that, "is being" ceases to be a specifying predicate properly speaking. But if God is being as such, then "God" ceases in turn to signify a particular subject of which something general could be predicated. Now the predicate, instead of signifying the accident, signifies essence, whereas the subject is "lost": it "disappears into" the predicate [*vergeht [. . .] in seinem Prädikate*]. Ratiocination expands its knowledge and expresses it through addition of the accident or predicate to the solid basis of the subject. But in the philosophical proposition, the subject disappears into the predicate. According to Hegel, thought is now "thrown back" onto the subject because of its loss. It is discovered in the predicate, which expressed not accident but essence. In this way, what at first presented itself as a subject (here: God) that was *posited*, together with the added qualification of being "being," initiates a movement whereby the subject is not posited at all but rather lost, and through that loss is rediscovered in the predicate. Hegel adds the example of "the actual is the general" [*das Wirkliche ist das Allgemeine*], which also is not meant to convey that the actual is posited as "being general," but rather that the actual moves into the general, which expresses its essence (*PH* 60/39).

This loss of the subject, its disappearance or transition into its predicate, is what forms the counter-thrust to the ratiocinative conception of the proposition, and it is what according to Hegel obstructs or inhibits (*hemmen*: to hinder, obstruct, frustrate) all nonspeculative thinking. Truly speculative exposition expresses not just this hindrance or resistance (the purely negative result that would be the dead end for ratiocination) but above all the very movement by which the subject is rediscovered in the predicate [*diese entgegengesetzte Bewegung muß ausgesprochen werden*]. That is what Hegel calls the "dialectical movement of the proposition itself"; it is the "truly speculative," and its expression truly constitutes "speculative exposition":

> The sublation of the form of the proposition must not happen only in an *immediate* manner, through the mere content of the proposition. On the contrary, this opposite movement must find explicit expression [*muß ausgesprochen werden*]; it must not

just be the inward inhibition mentioned above. This return of the concept into itself must be set forth [*dies Zurückgehen des Begriffs in sich muß dargestellt sein*]. This movement which constitutes what formerly the proof was supposed to accomplish, is the dialectical movement of the proposition itself. This alone is what is actually speculative, and only the expression of this movement is a speculative exposition. (PH 61/39–40, translation amended, JdJ)

So what is the proper speculative exposition? It consists in the articulation of the movement that is brought about by the speculative proposition. What is that movement? The speculative proposition arrests ratiocination by depriving it of the solid base it finds in the subject (the becoming-subject of substance), but most especially it is the movement of rediscovery of that subject in the predicate, which now ceases to be a mere accidental addition to a solid subject, but rather proves, on the contrary, to unveil its essence (the becoming-substance of subject). The dialectical movement is the movement whereby what externally appears to be accidental predicate shows itself to be expression of essence. Philosophical exposition thus shows how the essence that was lost in the loss of the subject is rediscovered in the predicate.

Is this conception of the speculative proposition still the same as the one from Hegel's article on skepticism? There he primarily affirmed that all truths of reason necessarily violate the principle of non-contradiction. His conception in the preface to the *Phenomenology* seems to be more specific. The contradiction between God and being or between the actual and the universal is not of the same kind as the way in which the notion of *causa sui* contradicts itself. On the other hand, the philosophical proposition does have the form of a proposition while simultaneously providing a counter-thrust to that very form, thereby simultaneously "sublating" it. In that sense, Hegel's immanent method requires the use, in the words of Stephen Houlgate, of "negative or self-undermining expressions,"[23] and the philosophical exposition is necessarily self-contradictory.[24]

CONCLUSION

I have attempted to show how for Hegel a certain kind of self-complication is necessary in philosophical exposition. This self-complication is the mark of a philosophy that is speculative, which means that it is essentially involved in the explication of what is essentially *implicit* (the exposition of *movement*).

I have shown that for Hegel philosophy cannot be reduced to the level of mere understanding or of reflection. At the same time, however, the attempt to *exceed* reflection immediately falls back into it: the very values of excess, outside, beyond, and opposition are themselves "products of reflection." This does not mean that the understanding is absolute in the sense that it would have no limits; it means that its limits cannot be conceived as the line dividing its inside from its outside (itself a merely "reflexive" conception of limit). Instead, what "exceeds reflection"—the absolute with respect to which any given determination or proposition is necessarily "one-sided"—is reflection's *own movement*.

This means that there can be no fixed presentation of the absolute (so no ultimate expression, theory, proposition, no ultimate end point or goal), and the limits of reflection are not "sublated" or overcome in any naive sense. Hegel's explication and affirmation of the limits of reflection are therefore constrained between the two equally unattractive extremes, between which Derrida's deconstruction of logocentric metaphysics is also constrained: (1) an opposition to the oppositionality of the understanding or of reflection, and (2) delivering philosophy over to the rules of the understanding (as Kant's "philosophy of reflection" did, according to Hegel). The first constraint necessitates the radical *immanence* of Hegelian thought. The second constraint means that this immanence cannot be the internality of an aggregate that would "contain" everything; Hegel's *Ganze* (whole) cannot be an all-encompassing field or overarching unity.

But the two go hand in hand. That the immanence of Hegel's philosophical systematicity does not revert all negativity and finitude back to positivity and totality is already evident from the very performativity of its development *as a self*-development. Hegel *affirms* the limitations of reflection and exposition precisely by showing that the absolute does not exceed them but is what is essentially implicit in them: reflection's own movement.

Concerning the way in which this movement is expressed, one can see these limitations in the necessarily self-contradictory character of the philosophical exposition; in the irreducibility of philosophical truth to any one unequivocal position or to the content (or even the form) of propositions, or to any given method.

In this way, Hegel's "absolute" idealism must be interpreted as an affirmation of the limits of reflection. He stresses that the absolute cannot be understood (contrary to popular opinion) either as an end result or as an added third term. Instead, I have stressed in various ways that the absolute is to be understood as being *in* reflection.

In that sense, Hegel's philosophy is exemplary as a critique of simple externality, of the *jenseits* or the outside, as well as of the attempt to explicate the excess within; the movement of what appears to be a fixed position. True infinity is the infinity of the movement *of* and *in* reflection: it is a reflection "in itself." With this, I have proposed a reading of Hegel that features the elements that I identified in Derrida's early work: the performative complication of the resistance to simple exteriority and the corresponding complication of simple interiority or *movement* that forms the "excess within." But in doing so, I have mentioned at least two interrelated aspects of Hegelian thought that are typically thought to go squarely against everything that Derrida stands for.

The first is the radical immanence of Hegelian thought and the resistance to externality. Compare this to the following passage taken from *Dissemination*'s "Hors livre, préfaces," which is probably one of Derrida's most emphatic and explicit affirmations of externality:

> To allege that there is no absolute outside of the text is not to postulate some ideal immanence, the incessant reconstitution of writing's relationship to itself. [. . .] The text affirms the outside, marks the limits of this speculative operation, deconstructs and reduces to the status of "effects" all the predicates through which speculation appropriates the outside. If there is no-thing outside of the text, this implies, with the transformation of the concept of text in general, that the text is no longer the snug airtight inside of an interiority or an identity-to-itself [. . .], but rather different placements of the effects of opening and closing. (*D* 42/36)

This immediately announces the second aspect that I had in mind: that Derrida in his analyses of Hegel seems to consistently return to the phrase that dialectic or speculation stands for the "appropriation of the outside," that is, the *reduction* of the outside, or: "to revert all negativity back to positivity."

So how to reconcile my reading of Derrida as well as my reading of Hegel with these passages?

The key to answering this question lies in the need to recognize these seemingly unequivocal positions (deconstruction "affirms the outside," Hegel "appropriates the outside," dialectic "reverts all negativity back to positivity") are themselves no definitive Derridean "positions." They are relativized and comprehended as moments within a broader movement of showing that makes Derrida's relation to Hegel much less unequivocal than the positivity of these propositions suggests.

CHAPTER 5

DERRIDA'S "TEXTUAL MANEUVERS"

Exceeding the Opposition to Hegelianism

> Consequently, to luxate the philosophical ear, to set the loxōs in the logos to work, is to avoid frontal and symmetrical protest, opposition in all the forms of anti-, or in any case to inscribe antism and overturning, domestic denegation, in an entirely other form of ambush, of *lokhos*, of textual maneuvers.
>
> —Derrida ("Tympan")

In the previous chapter, I pointed out how for Hegel a certain self-complication of the philosophical exposition is necessary. Speculative philosophy traces the *movement* of or *in* determinations and apparently fixed oppositions. The form of philosophical exposition becomes necessarily (in the words of the skepticism-essay) self-contradictory or (in the words of the preface to the *Phenomenology*) necessarily forms a counter-thrust to the propositional form. In that way, Hegel is a thinker of the limits of reflection. But that is not the way Hegel has often been interpreted, especially in the context of the complex French Hegel-reception of the second half of the twentieth century.

Derrida's own relation to Hegel has also primarily been construed in terms of an opposition: attention has been paid, for instance, to their different views on the sign and the subject of language. One can identify two lines of thought here. On the one hand, there is quite a lot of recent work on Hegel's and Derrida's respective views on language as a subject.[1] This is understandable not only given Derrida's own focus, but also in light of Jean Hyppolite's view that Hegel's philosophy is essentially a philosophy of language. (Hyppolite was also instrumental in introducing an interpretation of Hegel that emphasized the limits of reflection, but he did so under the heading of "finitude."[2]) But how does Hyppolite conceive this language? He states that "human language, the Logos, is this reflection of being into itself [. . .] without ever positing or postulating a transcendence distinct from this internal reflection."[3] With that, Hyppolite identifies under the heading of language the very structure of "reflection in itself" that I identified at the heart of Hegel's thought. If we take seriously Derrida's announcement that the "problem of language" was never merely "one problem among others," then the subject of language is no longer an end in itself. Instead, it must be related to the reflexive entanglement of the content and the exposition of philosophy. For me, this is the way to go in studying the relation between Derrida and Hegel: the performative complication of Derrida's "problem of language" should be compared, not so much to Hegel's thoughts on the "subject" of language [*Sprache*], but above all to Hegel's (methodological) thoughts on philosophical *exposition* [*Darstellung*].

Most of the literature on Hegel and Derrida, however, follows the second line of thought, comparing Hegelian difference to Derridean différance. Many construe the distinction in the following fairly unequivocal terms: Hegelian difference would be mere "negativity," and as such would still be subordinated to the oppositionality that Derrida's différance is out to "deconstruct." Then the focal point of their relation becomes showing how différance not only differs from, but also goes a step further than, Hegel's *sichanderswerden*. The same holds for their respective counterparts: to contrast Hegelian immediacy to the Derridean impossibility of "presence,"[4] or to counter Hegel's ubiquitous notion of the "self" (self-consciousness, self-movement, return to self, self-reflection, etc.) with Derrida's notion of a thoroughly aporetic self; a self that is always already other than itself, as Derrida elaborates it in, especially, *Voice and Phenomenon*. No doubt there are important differences here, but if difference and différance name the movement that exceeds what is presented, then how to compare here? At certain strategic points in his work, Derrida has emphasized that différance was his way of formulating a "difference without negativity." But he also knows that one can neither oppose the oppositionality of such "merely negative" difference nor identify Hegel's own work simply with such oppositionality. This should complicate the possibility of a "comparison" from the outset.

The reason why Hegel is so important and interesting from a Derridean point of view is precisely that Derrida's relation to Hegel is *not* reducible to a simple oppositional scheme. Derrida's relation to Hegel is inherently ambiguous, and this is so for essential reasons. Not only is Hegelian "difference" not reducible to docile negativity, which Derrida knows very well, but even if it was it would make no sense to oppose it. So opposition must be a strategic device within the broader movement of Derrida's writings. And Hegel takes up a privileged position within that strategy.

SITUATING HEGEL IN DERRIDA'S DEVELOPMENT

That Hegel takes up a privileged position with respect to Derrida's problem of strategy is already clear from what may be the most telling sign of Derrida's relation to Hegel. It concerns a development that seems to have occurred, if you will, behind the reader's back. In Derrida's dissertation of 1953/1954 (not published until 1990), *The Problem of Genesis in Husserl's Philosophy*, a clear commitment to Hegel is evident on every page, only to evaporate almost completely in the space of about ten years. The terminology in question is that of an "(originary) dialectic" that is ubiquitous throughout *The Problem of Genesis* but that has virtually disappeared in Derrida's first major publication, *Edmund Husserl's Origin of Geometry: An Introduction* from 1962. So much has changed in that decade that it is difficult to indicate precisely how Derrida's attitude toward Hegel changed. As Marian Hobson notes in her preface to the English translation of *The Problem of Genesis*, it is "completely different from the way Derrida would write less than ten years later."[5] She notes a "turn in style, and possibly in what Derrida expected of philosophy."[6] When on the occasion of its publication in 1990 Derrida reflects on some aspects of his dissertation in a new preface, one of them is the ubiquity of the concept of "dialectic" throughout the dissertation—a "philosophical name," he writes there, "that I have had to give up." At that point, he reduces this change to circumstance. He calls it "a phrase that was famous at that time" and points to both the "disappearance" of the dialectic in his later *Introduction* and *Voice and Phenomenon*, as well as, much stronger still, to the fact that dialectic in those later works even came to designate "that *without which* or *separate from which* difference, originary supplement, and trace had to be thought." He states this even as those later works were still driven by the "law of originary contamination" that Derrida states "will not have stopped commanding everything I have tried to prove." When Derrida says that these twists in his use of the concept of dialectic are perhaps signs of "the philosophical and *political* map according to which a student of philosophy tried to find his bearings in 1950s France," he seems to reduce his use of the term entirely to circumstance, as well as its disappearance and Derrida's "separation" of "difference, originary supplement, and trace" from it.[7]

I argue that the twists and turns in Derrida's relation to Hegel cannot be so easily reduced to historical context and circumstance. Instead, I propose that we must try to understand what the character of Derrida's relation to Hegel is in and through its frequent explicit opposition to a certain "Hegelianism."

I have already mentioned some propositions that Derrida explicitly opposes: there is the *immanence* of Hegelian philosophy, whereas according to Derrida the "text *affirms* the outside," and I have held that Hegel does not "revert all negativity back to positivity," whereas Derrida suggests precisely that in numerous places where he speaks of "Hegelianism" or of "(speculative) dialectic." It is a matter, then, of providing a reading of Derrida's relation to Hegel that is not exhausted by these isolated propositions.

Where Derrida's relation to Hegel is initially implicit in his use (and decision to stop using) the concept of a dialectic, his explicit references increase after the *Introduction*, though they still amount to little more than isolated references.[8] Derrida's most explicit works on Hegel follow in the period surrounding that other breakthrough year of 1972, in which are published *Margins of Philosophy*, *Positions*, and *Dissemination*. In that period, work has also started on the Hegel column of *Glas*, which was to appear in 1974. Some of Derrida's best-known reflections on Hegel are to be found in these works (most notably in the interviews in *Positions* and in "Différance" from *Margins of Philosophy*).

To be able to trace the essential ambiguity of Derrida's remarks on Hegel, including the important but isolated comments such as the ones from *Of Grammatology*, I start with a reading of "Tympan," the opening essay of *Margins* that serves as an introduction of sorts to the ten essays that make up the collection. The themes that I have dealt with in reading Hegel come together there. I first address what seems to be the biggest question regarding the relation between Hegel and Derrida: the status of the outside and of limits. The Hegel that Derrida most emphatically opposes is the one who ultimately reduces alterity to identity, negativity to positivity—dialectics as a mere movement of reappropriation. By contrast, Derrida states that the "text affirms the outside." But we know that this cannot be a matter of opposing a beyond to it, as there is "no outside-text." Instead, for Derrida, thinking the other of philosophy would mean to "surprise" it, which is for him essentially a matter of "timbre" and of "style," of "textual maneuvers"—of "writing otherwise."

This means that the difference between Derrida and Hegel is highly nuanced. I therefore proceed to show that there are multiple Hegels in Derrida's texts that are not all reducible to the "appropriating dialectics" that Derrida will at times oppose. Derrida chooses his point of departure *in* Hegel for essential reasons, and he departs *from* Hegel in a manner that is more than just oppositional.

"TYMPAN": THE LIMITS OF PHILOSOPHY AND THE NEED TO WRITE OTHERWISE

"Tympan" is first and foremost a text on the limit: it introduces the ten texts that make up *Margins of Philosophy* as "[working] toward the concept of the limit and the limit of the concept" (*MP* i–xxv/xvii). I have stressed that the self-complication of philosophical discourse concerns the limit of what can be said or stated unequivocally, directly or propositionally. The investigations of Derrida and Hegel have introduced a *problem* of the limit: it seems to imply a beyond that cannot be thought as a beyond. Though in a sense this is a shared insight, it is also the point at which Derrida departs from Hegel. Derrida needs to strategically oppose Hegel in order to articulate his reformulation of the limit—now as an "undecidable," perhaps "impossible" limit: as *margin*.

To that end, Derrida opens the left column of his text with the comment that the words "being at the limit" [*l'être à la limite*] could "engender almost all the sentences in this book," "provided," however, and crucially, "that one plays upon it." The book, then, promises to be a play on being at the limit. What does this mean?

Before those opening lines, one finds three epigraphs, two of which have already made their way into my reading of Hegel: first, Hegel's remarks from the *Logic* about how a limit necessarily implies a beyond (the limit implies its transgression *ad infinitum;* a movement that implies "a limit which is no limit"). Second, the remark from the *Difference* essay in which Hegel states that philosophy is its own presupposition. Third, Hegel's opposition to the tendency to view philosophy as an activity of supplying or construing "foundations" or "principles." These epigraphs pose the question: if there can be no "foundation" for/of philosophy outside itself, and if it does not begin except with itself, then what does this mean for the "limits of philosophy" and for their "transgression"?

Derrida opens his essay with the thesis that I described at the end of chapter 2, that philosophy itself is structured by overcoming and that therefore there is an essential relation between philosophy and the limit. According to Derrida, philosophy has always "meant to say" the limit, and it "has always insisted upon assuring itself mastery over the limit (*peras, limes, Grenze*)." "Mastery" over the limit means that it does not "remain foreign," and that means that philosophy "has appropriated the concept [of limit] for itself." If the concept of the limit, and with that the concept of the "other," is appropriated or *internalized* by philosophy, then the other that it thinks is "its" other. The limit is thus as much "the" limit as it is "its own" limit; insofar as determination is a form of delimitation, philosophy's engagement with its other goes hand in hand with its engagement with itself: its other is "that which delimits it, and from which it derives its essence, its definition, its production" (*MP* i/x).

The question that Derrida now asks concerns this other as "its" other: can the other be thus "sublated" or internalized? In Derrida's words:

> To think its other: does this amount solely to *relever* (aufheben) that from which it derives [. . .]? Or indeed does the limit, obliquely, by surprise, always reserve one more blow for philosophical knowledge? (*MP* i/xi)

What is Derrida's point of departure? Already we see a double bind on which Derrida tirelessly insists. First, there is the awareness that one does not simply explicate the limits of philosophy *philosophically*. The question of what philosophy is entails a confrontation with what is not or is no longer completely philosophy, and this cannot itself be a matter that is wholly internal to philosophy. The concept of the limit (and that of the other that it implies) cannot be so sublated without losing something of itself, without ceasing to be itself. Second, however: the awareness on which Derrida insisted perhaps even more tirelessly is that any articulation, any thought of another of philosophy is immediately bound up with, caught up in philosophy; that is, that philosophy has always been "of the limit." There cannot be said to "be" some "thing" beyond philosophy, not even a "possibility" beyond philosophy without articulating this by the very means of the categories most central to philosophy (being, possibility, etc.). That is why and how the question of the limit is, first and foremost, deeply problematic.

Derrida's point is not to take sides in this matter. Instead of working through this problem, he steps back from it to tease out the aporetic implications of this double awareness. For him, these implications are that the *very possibility* of philosophical determination (determination of philosophy and determination by philosophy, its relation to its other, etc.) is now at stake, and that the question is now what kind of questioning would be able to take this awareness into account.

"Tympan" poses the question how a confrontation with philosophy's other would be possible that would be neither a simple reduction to philosophy nor the naiveté of a point of simple externality with respect to philosophy. And because the question of the limit is bound up with delimitation and definition, what is at stake is as much the possibility of alterity as the very definition of philosophy itself: a conception of philosophy that does not naively distinguish itself from what it takes to be outside it—a conception of philosophy that cannot be identical to what Derrida takes to be its *self*-understanding:

> If philosophy has always intended, from its point of view, to maintain its relation with the non-philosophical, that is the antiphilosophical, with the practices and knowledge, empirical or not, that constitute its other, if it has constituted itself according to this purposive *entente* with its outside, if it has always intended to hear itself speak, in the same language, of itself and of something else, can one, strictly speaking, determine a nonphilosophical place, a place of exteriority or alterity from which one might still treat *of philosophy*? (*MP* iii/xii)

A similar double-edged sword or twofold risk that exists for the conception of philosophy, exists for the conception of the "other" of philosophy. The first risk is that this other would *dissolve*, and that as such it would no longer be effective *as* a *disruption* of philosophy. Here Derrida cites Nietzsche and Zarathustra's question of whether it would have to be a matter of "the sound of cymbals or tympani, the instruments, always, of some Dionysianism." But does a penetration of philosophy still truly take place in confronting it with non-sense *tout court*—with madness or white noise? And even then, these are still *philosophical* names, and therein lies the second risk of such a "negative without effect." My claim is that for Derrida this was always the greater concern: that the conception of the other remain precisely a *conception*, that is: an other "of" philosophy. This is the risk of domestication: "[. . .] *its* outside is never its *outside*" (*MP* viii/xvi). The risk of philosophizing "with a hammer" is that one subjects oneself to the "law of the inner hammer":

> [. . .] in relaying the inner hammer, one risks permitting the noisiest discourse to participate in the most serene, least disturbed, best served economy of philosophical irony. Which is to say, and examples of this metaphysical drumming are not lacking today, that in taking this risk, one risks nothing. (*MP* v/xiii)

My claim would be that what sets Derrida apart from the so-called postmodernists or poststructuralists is that though he shares with them a certain sense of the necessity of discontinuity, rupture, alterity, externality, and so forth, the *greatest risk* resides in the domestication of that alterity, the reaffirmation of logocentrism in a naive attempt to overcome it. In short, the greatest risk is that of achieving mere reversals, and thereby achieving nothing:

> Consequently, to luxate the philosophical ear, to set the loxōs in the logos to work, is to avoid frontal and symmetrical protest, opposition in all the forms of anti-, or in any case to inscribe antism and overturning, domestic denegation, in an entirely other form of ambush, of *lokhos*, of textual maneuvers (*MP* vii–viii/xv).

It is at this point that Hegel and Derrida are in closest proximity, in the double insight of (1) the ubiquitous or constitutive nature of reversal and opposition for the very nature of conceptuality, and (2) the aporetic character of the question of the limits of such oppositionality. But from this point of proximity, Derrida departs very differently. For Derrida, this complication raises questions about the very idea of an outside of philosophy, of a philosophical determination of the other, of a rupture of philosophy:

Can one then pass this singular limit which is not a limit, which no more separates the inside from the outside than it assures their permeable and transparent continuity? What form could this play of limit/passage have, this logos which posits and negates itself in permitting its own voice to well up? Is this a well-put question? (*MP* viii–ix/xvi)

To these questions Derrida gives "no answer." For him, the limits of language present themselves in the form of questions that remain undecided. If these questions do not allow passage toward a solution but are rather to be understood as presenting an aporia, then what is "enabled" by these questions is not a move forward but a step back. It means that what is necessary "cannot be achieved by means of a simply discursive or theoretical gesture" (*MP* xvi–xvii/xxi).

Several themes from *Of Grammatology* resurface here. Derrida's question (what if the margin "is no longer a secondary virginity but an inexhaustible reserve?") echoes the question from *Of Grammatology* concerning the sign (what if "'signifier of the signifier' no longer defines accidental doubling and fallen secondarity?"). Just like that conception of the sign would destroy the very idea of the sign, so a margin that would not be secondary would destroy the very idea of the margin and of the body of the text in opposition to which it has received its meaning (prompting Derrida's plays on Hegel's phrase "to philosophize *à corps perdu*"). This does not lead to a solution, but to "overflows and cracks [. . .] A lock opened to a double understanding no longer forming a single system" (*MP* xx/xxiv). This also recalls *Of Grammatology*'s necessity for a certain kind of empirical wandering: "[. . .] what legal question is to be relied upon if the limit in general [. . .] is *structurally* oblique? If, therefore, there is no limit *in general,* that is, like a straight and regular form of the limit?" (*MP* x/xvii).[9]

It is at this point of undecidability that, after the epigraphs, the first explicit references to Hegel are found in "Tympan," even though the spirit of Hegel is present everywhere in that text. It is present everywhere where Derrida writes *relève,* which is his translation of the Hegelian *Aufhebung.* Though Derrida is very sensitive to the multiple senses of that term, in this text he clearly associates it most strongly with sublation in the sense of a solution that domesticates the limit, the margin, and the other:

Which does not amount to acknowledging that the margin maintains itself within and without. Philosophy says so too: *within*

> because philosophical discourse intends to know and to master its margin, to define the line, align the page, enveloping it in its volume. *Without* because the margin, *its* margin, *its* outside are empty, are outside: a negative about which there seems to be nothing to do, a negative without effect in the text *or* a negative working in the service of meaning, the margin *relevé* (*aufgehoben*) in the dialectics of the Book. Thus, one will have said nothing, or in any event done nothing, in declaring "against" philosophy that its margin is within or without, within and without, simultaneously the inequality of its internal spacings and the regularity of its borders. (*MP* xx/xxiv)

This double entendre of the margin that is not conceivable from a "single system" is also inconceivable by stating that it must be conceived as both "within" *and* "without." Such a compromise would still be nothing more than a domestication of alterity, a repetition of the philosophical gesture par excellence: to maintain within itself the opposition between within and without, and thereby to remain unperturbed by its outside, because it is, after all, merely outside. These two moments reinforce each other: either philosophy *relates* to its outside, in which case it is important to it but appropriated, or there is no such relation, in which case it is harmless, empty—"a negative without effect." Hegelian dialectics—identified now with the *Aufhebung*—is associated here with mere reappropriation and domestication of negativity. This is the Hegel in opposition to whom Derrida defined his own project: dialectics as mere movement "in the service of meaning."

The "limitrophic violence" of Derrida's own text would have to consist in "textual maneuvers." Instead of providing a resolution or an answer, confronting philosophy with its other would have to mean "*to write otherwise*." Such a writing is not simply "possible." The concepts Derrida uses for such a writing are "surprise" and "play." He writes of the necessity to "unhinge" by *marking* a limit. By writing otherwise, "overflows and cracks" would have to become visible within the body of the philosophical text, which would then have to overflow into the margin. It is through "structures of expropriation" such as "timbre, style and signature" that an "obliterating division of the proper" is to be realized (*MP* xiii/xix).

The Nietzschean notion of play signifies the relation between signifiers in contexts of meaning that would (in the words of *Margins'* closing essay "Signature Event Context") lack a "center of absolute anchoring" in a determinate signified (*MP* 381/320). How does it play its part here in raising the question of the limits of philosophy? The other would have to "surprise" philosophy.[10] How does "Tympan" surprise?

That finally brings me to the single most obvious characteristic of the text. Most striking about "Tympan" is, of course, that its text is made up of two columns, one to the left and a narrower one to the right. *I have been quoting exclusively from the left column.*

That is not a coincidence. It is an indication of the kind of gesture that the confrontation of the columns brings about: the movements of philosophy are movements of appropriation and therefore of reduction. In this case, I have (so far) actively reduced the text to its left column to make the text "understandable" (what it is about, which issues and questions it raises, what it "means to say"). A further reduction: I have until now completely ignored, for the sake of making the text understandable, its very title and the way it recurs in all its different modifications. It is in these different modifications of the "tympan" that we find the "play" of a signifier that Derrida refuses to anchor down in one determined signified.

I am not out to mimic Derrida's performative gesture, nor do I recount all of the modifications of "tympan" here. I do, again, reduce that play to the role it plays for my present question, which still is: in what way does the play that is performed in "Tympan" force the necessary dislocation that is implied by the question of the limits of philosophy? I therefore attempt to make understandable, or to clarify, that play.

Such clarification can only happen if I do in fact anchor down the meaning of "tympan(um)" in a determinate meaning and list its connotations. Such an attempt could look like this: the tympanic membrane is the eardrum, and it separates the inner from the outer ear. Derrida's text is a questioning of the integrity of the distinction between inner and outer. The ear hears *spoken* language. The metaphysical conception of speech or the voice consists in a reduction of the specific kind of difference that Derrida names in a way that can be written but not heard: différance. In that sense, there is a *complicity* between metaphysics, speech or phonocentric writing, and knowledge or science. Derrida plays on that here: the ear *hears* or *understands* [*entendre*]. "Tympan," as a text on philosophy's "other," thus deals with the limits of what can be understood or made understandable. The Hegelian gesture consists in the recognition that the understanding's limit cannot be simply *understood*. These limits must have the form of a surprise. So Derrida asks about the possibility of rupture or penetration of the tympanic membrane. Recall the passage on Nietzsche:

> To philosophize with a hammer. Zarathustra begins by asking himself if he will have to puncture them, batter their ears (Muss man ihnen erst die Ohren zerschlagen), with the sound of cymbals or tympani, the instruments, always, of some Dionysianism. In order to teach them "to hear with their eyes" too. (*MP* iii–iv/xiii)

Not only does the play extend to the tympani as drums, but Derrida also indicates that one finds in the inner ear "the handle of a 'hammer.'"

How long would a commentary like this one have to continue, and what purpose would it serve? Would it be possible to extract all the multiple layers of meaning that are implied in the use of these "tympani" by Derrida? To what end would one do so?

It should be clear that in trying to "make understandable" Derrida's play, I am performing a specific kind of reduction and am connecting signifiers (tympan) to determined signifieds (eardrum, drum, hammer, without even having spoken of printing press, waterwheel, architectural feature, etc.).

In my "making understandable" of Derrida, I am going against one of the most consistently performed movements or motifs of the text. The multiple senses of tympan and the layers of meaning that they introduce are a part of the strategy of surprise, because according to Derrida "about this multiplicity philosophy has never been able to reason." Again the quote from before:

> How to put one's hands on the tympanum and how the tympanum could escape from the hands of the philosopher in order to make of phallogocentrism an impression that he no longer recognizes, in which he no longer rediscovers himself, of which he could become conscious only afterward and without being able to say to himself, again turning on his own hinge: I will have anticipated it, with absolute knowledge.

Derrida's text is an attempt, in writing of philosophy's limits, to estrange philosophy from itself. To stage a confrontation of philosophy with that in which the philosopher would not recognize himself, not so foreign to philosophy as to leave it undisturbed, and not so close to philosophy as to do no more than repeat it. Derrida's writing of the limit of philosophy involves staging a misrecognition of philosophy. What is the effect of this confrontation? "Will the multiplicity of these tympanums permit themselves to be analyzed? Will we be led back, at the exit of the labyrinths, toward some *topos* or commonplace named *tympanum*?" (*MP* xxiii–xiv/xxvii). That would be the reduction that I started to perform above in "making understandable" Derrida's text.

What the effect of Derrida's text is, is that such a writing, writing otherwise, brings to the surface both an other of philosophy that is closer to what is in fact foreign to philosophy; as well as a philosophy that may not be what the philosopher recognizes himself in, but is closer to what is in fact the movement of philosophy. They do not have the form of a claim about the essence of philosophy, one that would give us a better, or more determinate conception both of philosophy and of the other. Instead, on the contrary, the text makes more enigmatic the supposed integrity of the border between philosophy and its other. As such, it is, in carrying it out, precisely a discourse on the very limits of what one can make determinate, understandable, what one can directly state or present.

It is for the articulation of those limits that a certain indirectness is necessary. "Tympan" is a labyrinthine writing. It functions "obliquely, by surprise." This obliqueness, surprise, play, necessary equivocality is part of the "strategy" that Derrida experimented with most in the period in the early 1970s when his dialogue with Hegel was most explicit. It is that strategy that is developed further in *Dissemination* and *Glas*, the two main other works from the period in which it is clear that it is Hegel who is, implicitly and explicitly, at work in Derrida's texts. These texts are marked by a textual extravagance—a style that is motivated by reasons of content and as such ceases to be "mere" style. The large-scale textual complexity of *Dissemination* or *Glas*, however, is already prefigured in the smaller-scale written interventions of the visible erasure (the trace) or of the "a" in différance. The double question of "Tympan" is not only how to find an alterity that is no mere externality, but also how the other of philosophy could still be made to resonate. Can it leave a trace? That question of the exposition of différance is dealt with explicitly in the first of the texts that "Tympan" introduces: the essay "Différance." I take a short look at this essay before looking at the multiple Hegels in Derrida's *Dissemination*.

In various ways, Derrida distinguishes the necessary textual operations, which are to surprise philosophy, from a presentation. I quote at length:

> What am I to do in order to speak of the a of différance? It goes without saying that it cannot be exposed. One can expose

> only that which at a certain moment can become present, manifest, that which can be shown, presented as something present, a being-present in its truth, in the truth of a present or the presence of the present. Now if différance ~~is~~ (and I also cross out the "~~is~~") what makes possible the presentation of the being-present, it is never presented as such. It is never offered to the present. Or to anyone. Reserving itself, not exposing itself, in regular fashion it exceeds the order of truth at a certain precise point, but without dissimulating itself as something, as a mysterious being, in the occult of a nonknowledge [. . .]. In every exposition it would be exposed to disappearing as disappearance. It would risk appearing: disappearing. (*MP* 6/6)

The impossibility of presenting différance includes the irreducibility of différance to words, concepts, to an essence or origin, to the "question of essence" ("what is?"), which would trace the movement of différance back to an actor or origin, a unity or foundation, a principle or beginning (*archè*). Therefore, Derrida states that his discourse will resemble that of negative theology "occasionally even to the point of being indistinguishable" from it (*MP* 6/6; another "law of resemblance").

Immediately after having formulated the excess of différance with respect to being, presence, and truth, Derrida stresses that this différance that is wholly irreducible to presentation, manifestation, and so forth is not nothing either, does not "dissolve" or is not "mysterious" or "occult," that is: simply beyond truth and presence. Such a reversal would only reaffirm and achieve nothing: it would risk disappearing "as" disappearance—the mere outside "of" philosophy.

Even though différance is announced as neither word nor concept, it is treated like one "for strategic reasons." The passages that follow (on différance's double meaning of deferral/difference) are well-known and conclude with the necessity "to put in question the secondary and provisional characteristics of the sign, to oppose to them an 'originary' différance." Yet, because that would "put into question the authority of presence," "the name 'origin' no longer suits it" (*MP* 12/11).

But even if it is not the "origin" of signification, the unpresentable différance would still have to make itself felt in the language of metaphysics. Derrida then introduces the terminology (equally insufficient, equally metaphysical) of différance "producing" signification, of differences as the "effects" of différance. Yet just as an "original" différance is not "somehow before" the differences that originate in it, "in a simple and unmodified—in-different—present," so too do the "effects" of différance "not find their cause in a subject or a substance, in a thing in general, a being that is somewhere present." At the heart of différance we therefore find a duplicity about which "we must not hasten to decide":

> Here we are touching upon the point of greatest obscurity, on the very enigma of différance, on precisely that which divides its very concept by means of a strange cleavage. We must not hasten to decide. How are we to think simultaneously, on the one hand, différance as the economic detour which, in the element of the same, always aims at coming back to the pleasure or the presence that have been deferred by (conscious or unconscious) calculation, and, on the other hand, différance as the relation to an impossible presence, as expenditure without reserve, as the irreparable loss of presence, the irreversible usage of energy, that is, as the death instinct, and as the entirely other relationship that apparently interrupts every economy? It is evident—and this is the evident itself—that the economical and the noneconomical, the same and the entirely other, etc., cannot be thought together. If différance is unthinkable in this way, perhaps evidentiality which would make short work of dissipating the mirage and illogicalness of difference and would do so with the infallibility of calculations that we are well acquainted with, having precisely recognized their place, necessity, and function in the structure of différance. (*MP* 20/19)

Though there are other places in the essay in which Hegel is referenced more explicitly (Derrida mentions Hegel's "*differente Beziehung*" and suggests that différance might be a good translation of the German *different*), it is in the above passage that a clear point of divergence between Derrida and Hegel emerges.[11]

This point is where Derrida explicitly states that the two moments that contradict each other (here: the detour that aims at coming back to presence and différance as the relation to an impossible presence, but the *content* of the distinction is less important here than its general form, as is indicated by the "etc." in "[. . .] the economical and the noneconomical, the same and the entirely other, etc.")—that these two moments "cannot be thought *together*." Différance could not be their "unity." Here we find a certain reversal of the Hegelian philosophical task, as the entire problem of the "limits" of the understanding would not even arise if we did not have to think together [*zugleich*] the general and the particular, the finite and the infinite, the relative and the absolute, and so forth. It is clear why Derrida wants to say this here; his words are not meant to function as unities, even if these unities do not resolve, but rather precisely affirm the contradiction that is left undecidable.

These are the points in which one can recognize a "critique." And immediately after the passage just cited, it is not Hegel, but nevertheless an interpretation of différance through the lens of a "Hegelianism" (Derrida himself puts it in quotation marks) *against* which Derrida operates. "Hegelianism" is now another name for "philosophy," for what is to be "displaced." Its central moment is the "*relève*." But Derrida's relation to Hegel, too, is structured by the "law of resemblance" of oppositional entanglement: the need to distance himself oneself from it while at the same time "maintaining relations of profound affinity with Hegelian discourse" and "unable to break with that discourse." With his textual maneuvers, of which the writing of the "a" of différance is one, Derrida hopes to "operate a kind of infinitesimal and radical displacement of [Hegelian discourse]" (*MP* 15/14):

> As rigorously as possible we must permit to appear/disappear the trace of what exceeds the truth of Being. The trace (of that) which can never be presented, the trace which itself can never be presented: that is, appear and manifest itself, as such, in its phenomenon. The trace beyond that which profoundly links fundamental ontology and phenomenology. Always differing and deferring, the trace is never as it is in the presentation of itself. It erases itself in presenting itself, muffles itself in resonating, like the a writing itself, inscribing its pyramid in différance. (*MP* 23–24/23)

What cannot be represented must nevertheless leave a trace within the language of metaphysics and the order of truth. This trace itself can no longer signify the absence of a presence, and so "erases itself" and "muffles itself in resonating." As such, the trace "must have maintained the mark of what it had lost." According to Derrida, this is the paradox that in metaphysical language results in contortions that mark that metaphysics is traversed rather than surrounded by its limit:

> The paradox of such a structure, in the language of metaphysics, is an inversion of metaphysical concepts, which produces the following effect: the present becomes the sign of the sign, the trace of the trace. It is no longer what every reference refers to in the last analysis. It becomes a function in a structure of generalized reference. It is a trace, and a trace of the erasure of the trace.
>
> Thereby the text of metaphysics is comprehended. Still legible; and to be read. It is not surrounded but rather traversed by its limit, marked in its interior by the multiple furrow of its margin. (*MP* 25/24)

As I indicated in chapter 3, the harder you push for the externality of alterity, the more internal it shows itself to be (or rather: internality and externality show themselves to be incomplete categories). This means that even though such alterity is unpresentable, it must still leave some trace, must be the trace of a trace. That is the function of the "old names" of "origin," "produce," "effect," "movement" in the "Différance" essay. They must be used in spite of their inadequacy in order to distinguish the radical alterity of différance from a mystical or ineffable externality that would be merely opposed to philosophy. In other words: metaphysics opens *itself* up to the other, which for Derrida means that there is no longer such a thing as a rigorously determinable metaphysics "itself." These are precisely the points that Derrida makes more expansively in *Dissemination*. There, in the text that I turn to next, he argues that the oppositions of metaphysics have "never constituted a *given* system." Also, and perhaps above all: "[. . .] the 'closure of metaphysics' can no longer take, can indeed never have taken, the form of a circular line enclosing a field, a finite culture of binary oppositions, but takes on the figure of a totally different partition" (*D* 31–32/25).

"HORS LIVRE" AND THE MULTITUDE OF DERRIDA'S HEGELS[12]

There are at least two Hegels at work in Derrida's texts. This was already announced clearly in *Of Grammatology* (where we found the "last philosopher of the book" and the "first thinker of writing" [*G* 41/26]), although that work lacks the analysis necessary to support the claim. Even though Derrida is quite explicit on that point, the general agreement in commentary is that, in the last analysis, Hegel is primarily the philosopher of the book.

This seems to be confirmed by the publications from 1972 onward, where Derrida so often used the name "Hegelianism" for the type of "reappropriating dialectics" against which he defined his work. But there is no such last analysis, and the ambiguity of Derrida's relation to Hegel should be taken seriously. Of the two texts that embody and express this ambiguity best, "Hors livre, préfaces" and *Glas*, I discuss the former in detail to demonstrate this.[13]

"Hors livre, préfaces" is a preface to *Dissemination* that thematizes prefaces. It asks whether prefaces "exist" in order to show that one would have to conclude simultaneously (1) that *all* writing has a "prefatory" structure, and (precisely because such an interminable preface would no longer be "pre-" and would thus destroy its very concept) that (2) the preface is "impossible," or, rather: that it effaces itself. The text specifically focuses on Hegel's prefaces because Hegel in his own way already quite explicitly identified the "self-effacing" nature of prefaces.

The very first sentence of "Hors livre, préfaces"—"This [(therefore) will not have been a book"—indicates that the very possibility of beginning of a justified point of departure will be complicated. The possibility of the beginning is (like that of the end) tied to the possibility of the "book." The book is the "model" of the totality or whole that would have determinable borders: it would "begin" and "end" at the limit that "surrounds" it (see chapter 1). The future perfect of "will have been" indicates the complex anticipatory structure of temporality that belongs to the nature of a preface, and corresponds to the way prefaces are traditionally conceived: often written after the main body of the text, it nevertheless anticipates, that is, explains what will be shown in advance, thus simultaneously functioning in advance but already presupposing the conclusion of the work and its "overview."

To the extent that a preface, conventionally, presents the main body of the text, and as such presupposes its manageability or the determinability of what is "contained" within the text, the very concept of the preface complies with the model of the book. Derrida writes therefore that "the question astir here, precisely, is that of *presentation*," and so *Dissemination* is a part of Derrida's general project of "dismantling" the form of the book. This is done by "writing processes" that "*practically* [question] that form." To distinguish his "resistance" to that form from a simple opposition, Derrida introduces the term *restance*.

Derrida confirms the necessity to "retain the old name"; the "double" character of the deconstruction of philosophy; the unavoidability of reversal as an "insufficient but indispensable phase" of the double operation of deconstruction ("to remain content with reversal is of course to operate within the immanence of the system to be destroyed"); and that these operations are called "work" or "practice" rather than (op)positions. If the "outside of the classical oppositions" is no longer a boundary surrounding, but rather a limit traversing, those oppositions, then this does not only tell us something about the outside and the limit, but it also complicates the very possibility of that system as it was conceived:

> [. . .] these oppositions have never constituted a *given* system, a sort of ahistorical, thoroughly homogeneous table, but rather a dissymmetric, hierarchically ordered space whose closure is constantly being traversed by the forces, and worked by the exteriority that it represses: that is, expels and, which amounts to the same, internalizes as one of *its* moments. (D 11/5)

What the impossibility of opposing opposition shows is that there was never a pure opposition to oppose: "[. . .] the "metaphysical" is a certain determination or direction taken by a sequence or "chain." It cannot as such be opposed by a concept but rather by a textual labor and a different sort of articulation" (D 12/6). This textual labor can be contrasted to Hegel's *Arbeit am Begriff*, yet it is a departure from Hegel at the point where Derrida and Hegel are closest.

The "method" of dialectics as well as that of deconstruction must consist in tracing the *movement* of the concept beyond its simple self-identity. For Hegel, the tracing of the movement of the concept means that the exposition must "justify itself" and that no preexisting program or justification is available. The refusal to uncritically adhere to such external or unjustified principles, axioms, or programs is the source of the necessity for immanence and self-movement. For Derrida, that lack of justification or program means that one must apply a "strange strategy without finality" and that one must to a certain extent and in a certain way *wander* (the law of resemblance that binds deconstruction to empiricism). Both originate in the impossibility of knowing beforehand where one is going and what one's "method" is. That is what complicates the possibility of the preface and of "already having anticipated everything that follows": "[. . .] the *pre* reduces the future to the form of manifest presence" (D

13/7). That is a critique of a very specific "Hegelianism" and of a very specific conception of what "absolute knowledge" means.

In his discussion of Hegel's prefaces to the *Phenomenology*, the *Science of Logic*, and the *Encyclopedia*, Derrida stresses that Hegel, in all of his prefaces, "with unflagging insistence," disqualifies the preface. In chapter 5, we have seen why: every distinction must be justified within the investigation itself. Everything stated preliminarily, anticipatorily, and so forth is mere supposition. This holds for everything that would be external to the actual carrying out of philosophy (in the main body of work), for example, principles, foundations, axioms, suppositions, premises, and so forth. This demand of immanent self-movement is what defines philosophy and what separates it from all the other sciences. Hegel expresses in his preface to the *Phenomenology* his irritation not only with formalism and empiricism, but also with the hasty preoccupation with "aims and results" that makes the actual carrying out into the "unessential" part of philosophy—a haste that is amplified by the prefatory character of the preface itself. Derrida finds a similar disqualification in the preface to the *Science of Logic*, where he ties it more explicitly to the problem of method:

> The form of this movement is dictated by the Hegelian concept of method. Just as the Introduction (which follows the Preface) to the *Phenomenology of Spirit* critiques that critique of knowledge which treats the latter as an instrument or a milieu, so also the Introduction to the *Science of Logic* rejects the classical concept of method: an initial set of definitions of rules external to the operations, hollow preliminaries, an itinerary assigned beforehand to the actual route taken by knowledge. [. . .] If the path of science is itself science, then this method is no longer a preliminary, external reflection; it is the production and the structure of the whole of science as the latter exposes itself in logic. (D 21/15)

Now Derrida stresses this duplicity inherent in the self-effacement of the Hegelian preface: Hegel continually stresses the superfluous nature of the preface *in a preface*. It can therefore be reduced completely neither to the content of the text nor to a mere externality (in which case it would wholly dissolve). And even if the preface *were* taken to so dissolve in the face of the content of philosophy, because it fulfilled a "didactic" function in dispelling the still (contingently) prevalent formalism and empiricism of the culture, then this very negation of empiricism and formalism itself was still a moment of truth. So the preface is as such either a mere part of the philosophical exposition, in which case it "has no specificity," or it "escapes this in some way, in which case it is nothing at all" (D 21/15).

At this point, Derrida contemplates the preface's irreducibility to the classical oppositions:

> If one sets out from the oppositions form/content, signifier/signified, sensible/intelligible, one cannot comprehend the writing of a preface. But in thus *remaining*, does a preface *exist*? Its spacing (the preface to a rereading) diverges in (the) place of the χώρα.
>
> We have come to a remarkable threshold [*limen*] of the text: what can be read of dissemination. Limes: mark, march, margin. Demarcation. Marching order: quotation: "Now—this question also announced itself, explicitly, as the question of the *liminal*." (D 22/16, final quotation in different typeface in the original, JdJ)

What happens here?

I can give no precise description of what these lines "contain," and to convey or to *enact* precisely this is perhaps their primary function. It is at this point that we see Derrida's "textual intervention" even more explicitly than at the previous points in the text where, already, a relation of a concept to another is suggested without being determinately bound to it (where a concept is made to *move* in a direction not completely known)—an explicit intervention and a writing otherwise. What can we unpack of the different layers of meaning implied in these lines? Let's start another provisional attempt to "make understandable" what is going on here.

To start with: the irreducibility of the preface to the "classical oppositions" is stated. This is not surprising, and we have seen that the self-effacement of the preface was already explicitly at work in Hegel. It is important to emphasize that at this point Derrida does not go against Hegel. The question of the "existence" of the preface is therefore meant to expose the "undecidability" of the self-effacement of the preface that is already present in Hegel's prefaces. This irreducibility to oppositions is the "remarkable threshold" that the preface introduces. "Dissemination" is the name Derrida employs for the irreducibility of meaning to something contained within determinable borders.

Because the limit of oppositions confronts us with a radical alterity that must however make itself felt, the question is indeed "what can be read of dissemination," of this limit that is not a surrounding border. This is what introduces the references to *limen, limes,* and liminal: the liminal is a *threshold,* which conventionally means a limit beyond which one can no longer feel or register (a limit without a beyond, if you will). What the quote refers to, however, is the "liminary" in the discussion of Mallarmé in "The Double Session" [*La double séance*], which concerns the "*pre*-liminary." Thus, at once, Derrida enacts (by quoting from what is to come) the preliminarity of the preface (also one of its conventional functions) while questioning its possibility in doing so: what could pre-liminary mean? The liminary is the threshold of demarcation, which introduces the elaborate play of de-marcation, margin, mark, march. I discussed the margin above, as well as its relation to the problem of demarcation. The function of the "mark" is also clear in its relation to writing: the limit is always *marked*, is both what is characteristic of the mark as such, as well as what must "leave a mark" (in the sense of a trace). And then: movement. "March." If the meaning of the mark (its "content") is not "contained" within an interiority with determinable borders, then it is always already ahead of itself; more, less, or other than itself; never what Derrida calls a "full self-presence." Only insofar as content is therewith determined as/by movement could this be one of those points, as Derrida famously stated, of "almost absolute proximity to Hegel" (*Pos* 60/44).

But this is also the point of departure *from* Hegel through the enactment of this act of writing. The impossibility of rigorous demarcation (which does not let itself be formulated in any rigorously demarcated sense) implies movement, "marching orders." The very passage itself (how it moves from the irreducibility to opposition, to limit, liminal, *limen*, preliminary, demarcation, mark, march; from content to quote, etc.) is the enactment of this very movement: to "reconstitute a chain in motion." "Act of writing," "textual intervention," and so forth: all these must therefore be taken not a literary sense, but rather in the technical sense of the "new" concept of writing that I discussed in chapter 1. It is the "enactment" of that notion of writing that theoretically destroys itself, the performance of that self-complication.

Returning to the text, Derrida states that "the liminal space is thus opened up by an inadequation between the form and the content of discourse or by an incommensurability between the signifier and the signified." A lot hinges on how we interpret the following proposition of

Derrida's about Hegel, namely that "[. . .] the inadequation between form and content should erase itself, however, in speculative logic, which, in contrast to mathematics, is at once the production and the presentation of its own content" (*D* 25/18).

In the pages that follow, Derrida performs a self-complication that is exemplary, both for his entire project and for its relation to Hegel. Its structure is roughly this: (1) he develops an interpretation of Hegel as someone out to reduce completely the difference between form and content. Then (2) he argues (this would be the colloquially "postmodern" moment) that this is incommensurable with a thought of the "*débord*," of what de-borders or exceeds borders. (3) Derrida then, however, turns the tables and argues that this "critique" cannot sustain itself and that, moreover, this Hegel-interpretation is one-sided. (4) He then proceeds to show the other side of Hegel, until eventually (5) he *departs* from Hegel with the second very explicit "textual intervention" of the essay.

Derrida first argues that for Hegel the "inadequation between form and content [. . .] should erase itself in speculative logic." His first step is to recognize in the introduction to the *Science of Logic* a different but still *analogous* problem to the problem of the preface. Different, because Derrida concedes that the relation of the introduction to the *Science of Logic* is "less historical, less circumstantial" than its relation to the preface. The introduction "deals with general and essential architectonic problems," whereas the preface operates from a "more empirical historicity; they obey an occasional necessity that Hegel defines, of course, *in a preface*" (*D* 24/17). Analogous, however, because the non-place of the preface, its self-effacement with respect to the philosophical content, holds equally for the introduction: "[. . .] the Introduction, too, should disappear, should (shall) have disappeared, along with the Prefaces, in Logic" (*D* 24/17). Hegel is clear enough on the point: the concept of logic "is generated in the course [*Verlauf*] of this elaboration and cannot therefore be given in advance [*vorausgeschickt*]" (*SL* 35/23). Consequently, according to Hegel:

> What is anticipated in this Introduction, therefore, is not intended to ground as it were the concept of logic, or to justify in advance its content and method scientifically, but rather to make more intuitable, by means of some explanations and reflections of an argumentative [*räsonnierendem*] and historical nature, the standpoint from which this science ought to be considered. (*SL* 35/23)

Derrida acknowledges that this "constraint" of the introduction is "accidental." It serves to dispel the "lemmatism, mathematism, formalism" of his time and of his culture. But Derrida's point here is that the very scientific negation of those forms is itself a part of the actual self-movement of science:

> But this error being a form of negativity that cannot be avoided or eliminated [. . .] we find it thought out, internalized, sublated by the movement of the concept, and in its turn negated and absorbed as an integral part of the logical text. The necessity of this movement sounds paradoxical or contradictory only if it is observed from the exteriority of a formalist instance. This contradiction is rather the very movement of speculative dialectics in its discursive progression. (D 26/20)

Now Derrida is approaching the Hegel of whom he stated in *Of Grammatology* that he is both the last philosopher of the book and the first thinker of writing: according to Derrida, Hegel is "at once as close and as foreign as possible to a 'modern' [here: Derridean, JdJ] conception of the text or of writing." Why?

> The signifying pre-cipitation, which pushes the preface to the front, makes it seem like an empty form still deprived of what it wants to say; but since it is ahead of itself, it finds itself predetermined, in its text, by a semantic after-effect. But such indeed is the essence of speculative production: the signifying precipitation and the semantic after-effect are here homogeneous and continuous. Absolute knowledge is present at the zero point of the philosophical exposition. Its teleology has determined the preface as a postface, the last chapter of the *Phenomenology of Spirit* as a foreword, the *Logic* as an Introduction to the *Phenomenology of Spirit*. This point of ontoteleological fusion reduces both precipitation and after-effect to mere appearances or to sublatable negativities. (D 26–27/20)

Hegel, first thinker of writing: in recognizing the self-effacement of the preface, in the necessity of immanence and therefore the necessity of self-*movement*, in his recognition of the entanglement of method and object, Hegel recognizes that "nothing precedes textual generality absolutely." There is no preface, no program, or at least: "[. . .] any *program* is already a *program*, a moment of the text, reclaimed from the text by its own exteriority."

Surely the comparison between Derrida's "text" and the self-movement of Hegel's logic cannot be this clean, but Derrida recognizes a point of convergence here between his textuality and Hegel's logic.

But is this not the same absolutist Hegel from whom Derrida had to distance himself, the Hegel who ultimately "erases" the "inadequation between form and content"? That would be the Hegel for whom "there would then be no more discrepancy between production and exposition, only a presentation of the concept by itself, in its own words, in its own voice, in its logos." This would constitute the "end of the preface," and indeed this is the Hegel "against" or "in opposition to" whom Derrida has had to define himself:

> But Hegel brings this generalization about by saturating the text with meaning, by teleologically equating it with its conceptual tenor, by reducing all absolute dehiscence between writing and wanting-to-say [*vouloir-dire*], by erasing a certain occurrence of the break between anticipation and recapitulation: a shake of the head.
>
> If the preface appears inadmissible today, it is on the contrary because no possible heading can any longer enable anticipation and recapitulation to meet and to merge with one another. To lose one's head, no longer to know where one's head is, such is perhaps the effect of dissemination. (D 27/20)

The inadmissibility of the preface "today" is the inadmissibility of (this) Hegel. Which Hegel? The one who ultimately "erases the break" "reduces the dehiscence." The last philosopher of the book. "Inadmissible today" means: this is behind us, this is what we can unequivocally oppose. A philosophy that is of no use to us anymore. "No possible heading can any longer. . . ." This is not a hesitant standpoint, a perspective of ambiguity or indirectness (let alone of *necessary* ambiguity or equivocality). Derrida emphasizes:

> If it would be ludicrous today to attempt a preface that really was a preface, it is because we know semantic saturation to be impossible; the signifying precipitation introduces an excess

facing [*un débord*] ("that part of the lining which extends beyond the cloth," according to Littré) that cannot be mastered. (*D* 27/20)

The part of the lining that extends beyond the cloth: "tain" of the mirror, margin, χώρα. What follows is a now familiar elaboration of the "impossibility" of mastering ("they will miss it in their very attempt to master it"). At this point, the opposition to Hegel is raised to its highest point. "Hegel" now means: reverting all difference back to positivity. "Derrida" here means: "dehiscence," "structurally irremediable," rupture, break, alterity, interruption, aftereffect. This would be an all-too-familiar (postmodern or otherwise) critique of Hegel, of which one would do well to ask whether it targets more than a ghost or a caricature. But Derrida knows this well.

For what comes after the highest point? Derrida shows that such a "critique" cannot sustain itself. Now we see the "insufficiency" of that (no less necessary) "phase of reversal": because such a standpoint, such a position that opposes Hegel, such an unhesitating, unequivocal, unambiguous stance, *must* be the self-sufficiency of a *knowledge*:

> But the question of meaning has barely been opened and we have not yet finished with Hegel. We *know*, said we, a minute ago. But we know something here which is no longer anything, with a knowledge whose form can no longer be recognized under this old name. The treatment of paleonymy here is no longer a raising or a regaining of consciousness.
>
> No doubt Hegel, too, allows for the insistence of a certain gap between the form and content. (*D* 27–28/21)

Hegel, philosopher of movement, indirectness, writing. And Derrida, without simply being a relativist, must admit to a certain empiricism or wandering: "to lose one's head."

Amplifying the impossibility of unambiguous resistance to Hegel, Derrida proceeds by arguing for the Hegel who does *not* reduce the gap between form and content. He mentions, among other things, the *Phenomenology of Spirit* as "precisely the history of such discrepancies." More importantly, Derrida points to Hegel's problems with mathematical method and "presentiment." They satisfy "curiosity" rather than "knowledge" (recall that what is *bekannt* is not *erkannt*) because they depart from something *externally* and uncritically *given* (for Hegel, it makes no difference whether this assumes the form of given axioms, foundations, or principles; or of "inspiration" or "prophecy").

This means, according to Derrida, that speculative dialectics "must overcome the opposition between form and content, just as it must overcome all dualism or duplicity, without ceasing to be scientific. It must *scientifically* think out the opposition between science and its other" (*D* 28–29/22). The decisive question is whether one must interpret such formulas as Hegel's ultimately reverting science back to one of the two poles of its opposition, the sublation in the sense of solution of science's other by itself. The question, therefore, is of the status of this "third term." Derrida points to an important clue that such a view of sublation goes squarely against Hegel's intentions and his entire project in his discussion of formalism. Formalism "corrupts" the dialectic: when "fixed" in a "schema or a table of terms," it tears up the "life" of the concept. It is the life of the concept that is the unopposed other of opposition, its movement. No duality is self-sufficient, yet their movement is no third thing.

And indeed as Hegel's irritation with the preoccupation with "aims and results" already showed, it is also such "static classification of dual terms" that is precisely a "thinking of the preface." Because this is what prefaces generally do: they supply a formal schema of the true science that resides only in the actual carrying out in the body of the work. Derrida knows this: "[. . .] in contrast to this triplicity of death, the speculative dialectic favors the living triplicity of the concept, which remains beyond the grasp of any arithmetic or of any numerology." He quotes Hegel on the point: "In general, the numerical form of expression is too thin and inadequate to present true concrete unity. The Spirit is certainly a trinity, but it cannot be added up or counted. Counting is a bad procedure" (*D* 31/24).

It is at this point that the final moment in the movement I described commences. To this second Hegel, the Hegel that is attuned to difference, or rather to these two Hegels, Derrida opposes nothing, but *departs* by means of a textual gesture. Hegel here still forms the point of departure: dissemination is introduced as another way of working with numbers. Partly true to the workings of the conventional preface by anticipating his discussion of Sollers's *Nombres* in *Dissemination* (but untrue to it to the extent that it does so only *obliquely*, in line with a "modern" idea of the preface), Derrida launches into the problematic of resisting both "the two of binary oppositions" and the "three of speculative dialectics." With respect to such schemes and numbers, he shows of his "categories" (difference, *gramme*, trace, etc.) how "the movement of these marks" makes that "they can never be enclosed within any finite taxonomy." "They 'add' a fourth term the more or the less"; "the opening of the square, the supplementary four [. . .] the more or less which disjoins dissemination from polysemy," and thus:

> Two/four, and the "closure of metaphysics" can no longer take, can indeed never have taken, the form of a circular line enclosing a field, a finite culture of binary oppositions, but takes on the figure of a totally different partition. (*D* 31–32/25)

CONCLUSION

On the one hand, in numerous places Derrida has done his best to present "speculative dialectics" as the sublation of the negative into the "third term": the reduction of difference. On the other hand, Derrida has shown that arguing against this dialectic only reaffirms it, and that reversal betrays itself. Not only does he not simply oppose a dialectics of the "third term," but at other times he emphasizes that Hegel *himself* resisted it.

This is how Hegel, in his resistance to opposition that is not itself an opposition, forms a *point of departure* for Derrida. It is from out of this "crisis of versus" (playing on Mallarmé's *Crise de vers*) that Derrida departs, by "destroying" the "trinitarian horizon" "*textually*," that is, through the marks of dissemination. He chooses *in* Hegel his point of departure but also does something other than Hegel, so that neither simple identity nor simple juxtaposition seems appropriate. Derrida presents this necessary duplicity with respect to Hegel—in which he is both the first thinker of writing as well as of the "irreducible difference" that exceeds "speculative dialectics"—as an "uneven chiasmus":

> We are in an uneven chiasmus. In Hegel's reason for disqualifying the preface [. . .], how can we avoid recognizing the very question of writing, in the sense that is being analyzed here? The preface then becomes necessary and structurally interminable, it can no longer be described in terms of a speculative dialectic: it is no longer merely an empty form, a vacant significance, the pure empiricity of the non-concept, but a completely other structure, a more powerful one, capable

of accounting for effects of meaning, experience, concept, and reality, reinscribing them without this operation's being the inclusion of any ideal "begreifen." (D 41/35)

The preface is necessary in spite of (or in light of) its self-effacement. And though Hegel recognized it, it cannot be described by a speculative dialectic. The relation to Hegel is irreducibly ambiguous.

In this way, Derrida needs Hegel's "speculative dialectics" as a point of contrast, but he is aware that Hegel cannot be reduced to those terms. In the end, "speculative dialectics" is at once a "model" to oppose, but also itself an "effect" of a "new" textual economy or movement of difference. But this "new" text does not let itself be presented or stated unequivocally, without also "erasing itself in its own production." The more radical Derrida presents himself as moving beyond Hegel, the more emphatically his allegiance to Hegel is reaffirmed.

Derrida is at his best when he testifies to this very fact, when his writing is guided by the awareness of this predicament, this inescapability, when he performs the textual operations with which he inaugurates a movement of showing irreducible to any unequivocal position. He is at his worst (and this, too, is found not unfrequently in his writings) when he attempts to forge a breakthrough that is too radical, too clean, too naive, and therefore too much of a reversal. Indirectness is essential to the *crisis of versus* at which Hegel and Derrida both operate.

PART III

HEIDEGGER

The Preservation of Concealment

CHAPTER 6

THE TRANSITION TO TRANSITIONAL THINKING

From *Being and Time* to the *Contributions*

> The being that we, ourselves, in each case are, is ontologically the furthest.
>
> —Heidegger (*Being and Time*)

Whereas the relation between Derrida and Heidegger is usually considered in terms of to what extent deconstruction surpasses hermeneutics or phenomenology, I consider it from the perspective of indirectness. With respect to Hegel's *Darstellung* and Derrida's textuality, Heidegger's development can be seen as a progressive intensification of the complication of the consequences of what he is saying for how he is saying it. For him, this is not primarily a problem of method or system, but he explicitly treats this as the complication of philosophical *language*.

The question of the very possibility of philosophical articulation is already an explicit theme in *Being and Time*. The neologisms that abound in that work signal the necessity of a new language for the articulation of its radical critique of representation and Western objectivity. But the Heidegger from the *Contributions to Philosophy (Of the Event)* deems the language of *Being and Time* still insufficient, and he states this objection in a form with which we are by now familiar—the language of *Being and Time* is said to be "still too metaphysical," "still too representational." But if, as I have shown, this cannot simply be a critique, then what does it mean for a language to "fail"? And is such a failure accidental or essential to Heidegger's question of being? Is there a "right" language here?

My thesis is that Heidegger's attempt is not so much to overcome the failure to say being (a view of Heidegger as, in Derrida's words, being on the quest for "the right word"), but to find a language that would take into account, recognize, and preserve a certain necessary failure-to-say with respect to (the question of) being.

Therefore, to defend my claim I need an account of the transition from *Being and Time* to the *Contributions*. More precisely: my claim is that the way Heidegger himself relates to his own works is essentially related to what in the later works (and in the *Contributions* in particular) becomes an explicit theme: the insufficiency of language. Understanding the transition from *Being and Time* to the *Contributions* therefore becomes essential for understanding the *Contributions*' "transitional thinking." One cannot simply separate Heidegger's so-called *Kehre* after *Being and Time* from the "*Kehre im Ereignis*" that is the pivotal structural figure of the *Contributions*.

Though Heidegger's *Contributions* is a "middle period" work, it can read like the end of a certain development. It anticipates so many of the central themes of the middle and later works: everything that falls under the privileged heading of *Ereignis* and the "turning" therein or thereafter—language, poetry, history, technology, and so on. But even more than in terms of its content, it is the *Contributions*' explicitly self-aware style, the radicality of which arguably places it at the end of a gradual intensification of the awareness of the inseparability of "style and content." The *Contributions* pushes to the limit, in the most explicit fashion, the question of how to speak in the face of the "destruction of the genuine relation to words" (*CP* 3/5). That depletion is a consequence of what Heidegger in the *Contributions* calls "machination" [*Machenschaft*], the all-pervasive rationality of calculation and "explainability" that characterizes Western thought. The question of language is therefore embedded in a problem of "being-in" that is first systematically developed in *Being and Time*: if machination is what we are essentially and irreducibly "in," if it is the pre-structure of all our relations to reality, then how to *question* it? These are the *Contributions*' questions.

That means that it is still a matter of an irreducible inextricability. But in Heidegger's post-phenomenological hands, that inextricability takes on a form that differs decisively from Hegel's approach. The key to any phenomenology lies in the locution "always already in." Such a "being-in" is no longer Hegelian immanence. Hegel's "essentially implicit" now takes on the form of what one is "always already in" in such a way that it cannot be put "before" oneself as a "describable object" [*Gegen-stand*]. The essentially implicit then becomes a "hiddenness." What guides Heidegger's indirectness is not an implicit movement, but an irreducible *concealment*. The form of the question is now: if in our time, in our life, in our world, the truth of beyng essentially "withdraws" or passes us by in silence, does it nonetheless still "resonate" in our history? Can we conceive of the limits of the history of being ("our" history), and can we conceive (of) an "*other* beginning," other than the (our) "first beginning"?

For that reason, my goal in this part is to understand the relation between *Being and Time*'s "being-in" and the emphasis on language in the *Contributions*. It is a matter of showing how the *concealment* of *Being and Time*'s "being-in" is essentially related to the refusal, reticence, withholding, or "self-withdrawal of beyng" of the *Contributions*. It is in the articulation of what withdraws that language needs to preserve instead of overcome a certain failure-to-say, which Heidegger calls "bearing silence" [*Erschweigung*]. It is therefore a matter of understanding Heidegger's thesis that "above all, the concealment of the inceptual must be preserved" (*CP* 188/148).

This not only complicates the relation between Heidegger's early and later works—insofar as that is taken to be a story of a development from a "still too representational" language toward a saying of "being itself"—but it also complicates Derrida's relation to Heidegger. If Heidegger is out to expose an irreducible failure-to-say with respect to beyng, then the difference between Heidegger and Derrida can no longer simply or only be—as Derrida *at times* claims it is—an opposition between Heidegger's "onto-hermeneutical" project of *meaning* and Derrida's Nietzsche-inspired "plurality of styles." Derrida knows this. That is why, in the final part of this book, I investigate how Derrida's indirectness plays out in his relation to Heidegger, and I show how Derrida conceives the inability to oppose or go beyond Heidegger as an expression of an affirmative responsibility.

But first, this chapter is devoted to *Being and Time* and the transition to the *Contributions*. I show the implicit self-complication of *Being and Time* in relation to its guiding motif of "(always already) being in." That complication gives rise to a (phenomenological-hermeneutical) method of self-explication ("showing of itself by itself") that maintains an irreducible relation to concealment. I show in various ways how *Being and Time* turns the question of the possibility of its own exposition into an explicit problem. This allows me to provide an introduction to Heidegger's "transitional thinking" in the *Contributions*. I embed that thinking in the thematics of the present investigation by showing how the "transition" is neither a reversal nor a transcendence, but is to be conceived in terms of the performative complexity of a "transcendence of transcendence." This raises questions about the relation between *Being and Time* and the *Contributions*, especially whether the new language of the *Contributions* is an attempt to rectify a failure of the ("still too representational") language of *Being and Time*. I end this chapter by formulating the precise questions about the relation between Heidegger's early and later work, with which I engage the *Contributions* in chapter 7.

I argue against a certain standard account of the relation between *Being and Time* and the later work, which is that Heidegger moves from an investigation of "a" being (*Dasein*) to being "itself." This reading appears to be confirmed by Heidegger's own later dissatisfaction with his earlier work. Instead, I argue that this dissatisfaction must be interpreted differently and that there is a clear continuity of concern throughout the early and the later works, which lies in the performative awareness that both exceeds and can only be approached through beings—an awareness that takes on different modes.[1] After *Being and Time*, Heidegger increasingly comes to identify that complication under the heading of "language." But the idea that the turn to language marks an essential turning in Heidegger's way of thinking belongs to another prejudice: that *Being and Time* would have deployed a relatively conservative style that would be "still too metaphysical." The performative complication later identified under the heading of language is however already a main concern of *Being and Time*, but one must know where to look. This should not be surprising if we consider what a radical attempt *Being and Time* was to overcome certain metaphysical tendencies. The transition to the later works is better understood as the increasing thematization, under the heading of "language," of the performative complexity of the unavoidable yet insufficient metaphor of "overcoming."

THE MOVEMENT OF SHOWING OF ITSELF BY ITSELF: THE CIRCULARITY OF *BEING AND TIME*

From the beginning, the basic problem of *Being and Time* is tied to a performative complication. On the untitled opening page, before the actual investigation starts, Heidegger indicates that we have no answer to the question of what the word being means, but we are also in no way "perplexed at our inability to understand the expression 'being'" (*BT* 1/1). With that, Heidegger immediately points out the implicit character of being: no one is unable to grasp the sense of this most mundane of concepts, no one has problems using it, but nobody is able to give a definition of it either, or make its sense unequivocally explicit. What this means is that *Being and Time* will not investigate "being" directly. It is not a work of ontology in a conventional sense: "being" is not its "object of investigation." Instead, first the sense that such a question ("what is the sense of being?") could possibly have must be investigated. So before telling us anything "about" being (and the entire project of *Being and Time* aims at showing that being is not "something" that one can talk "about"), this rather tells us something about the being that asks such a question: the being that "we" are or the particular being "for whom its being is its issue" [*das Seiende, dem es um seinem Sein geht*]. This is not to say that *Being and Time* would *not* be about being, but only that the question of the sense of being will not straightforwardly be answered. Rather, Heidegger attempts to show in *Being and Time* how the very positing of the question of being (1) involves a confrontation with the *limits* of what can be talked "about" (thematized, represented, objectified—approached "directly"); and (2) how the positing of that question enables a new ("fundamental-ontological") way of thinking or understanding ourselves and our relation to reality—a way of thinking for which objective knowledge is only a derivative mode.

This is confirmed by Heidegger's immediate insistence that being cannot be defined. The unproblematic use of (the concept of, the word) being and the loss of the sense of the *question* of being (the "forgetfulness" of being [*Seinsvergessenheit*]) are, according to Heidegger in the introduction, sanctioned by three prejudices that have arisen out of the history of metaphysics: being's generality, its indefinability, and its self-evidence. According to Heidegger, it is the very generality of the concept of being that makes its meaning "obscure." That generality has always been peculiar: "The 'generality' of Being '*surpasses*' any generality of genus" (*BT* 3/2, translation amended, JdJ). Heidegger mentions how Hegel's conception of being is still consistent on this point with Aristotle's insight that the generality of being is not of the order of the genus (a conception that itself works through in Aquinas's conception of being as "transcendens"). Being's indefinability has, according to Heidegger, traditionally been deduced from its peculiar generality: because the generality of being is not that of the genus, this means that being cannot be defined qua *definitio fit per genus proximum et differentiam specificam* (subsumption under a genus and specification through differentiation of its species). From this Heidegger concludes that the method that is used to define beings is not fit to define being: being is not something like "a being" ["*Sein*" *ist nicht so etwas wie Seiendes*] (*BT* 4/3).

If *Being and Time* is an investigation into limits, then the limits in question are those of the way of thinking or understanding that can only treat everything as a being or in terms of beings; or of the "ontological difference" between being and beings. It is beings that can be talked "about," (re)presented, objectified. If being cannot be reduced to beings, it is equally the case that it cannot be some thing that simply transcends beings, or that would be external to, say, the "realm" of beings. Thing, transcendence, externality, realm—all of these belong to the conceptuality that is appropriate for beings. Here the complication in positing the question of being already becomes visible: in Heidegger's marginal notes from his own copy of *Being and Time,* at the sentence "'being' is not something like a being" ["*Sein*" *ist nicht so etwas wie Seiendes*], we read: "No! Rather: decisions cannot be made about beyng [*Seyn*] with the help of such conceptuality" [*nein! Sondern: über Seyn kann nicht mit Hilfe solcher Begrifflichkeit entschieden werden*] (*BT* 4n/3n, translation amended, JdJ). To say that being "is" not a being already shows the performative complication involved: the positing of the question of being already relies on the very conceptuality (appropriate for beings) that it precisely attempts to put in question.

The final prejudice was also already announced before the investigation started: being's self-evidence ("everybody understands 'The sky *is* blue,' 'I *am* merry,' and the like," *BT* 4/3). For Heidegger, the very self-evidence of the concept of being proves the necessity to posit the question: "The fact that we always already [*je schon*] live in an understanding of being and that the meaning of being is at the same time shrouded in darkness proves the fundamental necessity of retrieving the question of the meaning of 'being'" (*BT* 4/3, translation amended, JdJ). Positing the question of being means therefore to interpret this very situation: that the sense of the concept of being is shrouded in darkness and that yet, at the same time, "we always already live in an understanding of being." When looking at the specific form of the problem as Heidegger takes it up, especially in contrast to Hegel and in relation to Derrida, it is the terms "always already in" [*je schon in*] that are decisive. They characterize the entire setup of the investigation of *Being and Time*, in its point of departure as well as what is analyzed at every level. *Being and Time* can be seen as an analysis of the various ways in which Dasein is "essentially always already in . . ." (called *Existenzialien*).

This is the self-complicating form of the question for Heidegger: how does one thematize (objectify or place before oneself, according to Heidegger's conception of objectivity) what one is always already in?

The meaning of being cannot have the form of a determination of being, in the sense in which beings are determined: "being—not 'a being'" [*Sein—kein Seiendes*]. The elaboration of the meaning of being "demands a mode of exhibiting that is proper to it" [*fordert eine eigene Aufweisungsart*] and "requires a conceptuality of its own" [*verlangt eine eigene Begrifflichkeit*]. At the same time, this proper exposition is not *external to* beings, but: "'being' means the being *of* beings" [*Sein besagt Sein vom Seiendem*]. This means for Heidegger that what the question of being looks for (what is the sense of being?) is "what determines beings as beings" [*das, was Seiendes als Seiendes bestimmt*]. This means that being has an essentially implicit character, as "that in terms of which beings have *always already* been understood no matter how they are discussed" [*das, woraufhin Seiendes, mag es wie immer erörtert werden, je schon verstanden ist*] (*BT* 6/5, translation amended and emphasis added, JdJ). And that makes any direct approach to being impossible—the being *of* beings can only be interrogated *through* beings.

So for Heidegger, the specific way in which he conceives the implicit character of being shows itself in that double modality of always already living in an understanding of it [*Seinsverständnis*], yet not such that it is a knowledge, a conceptual knowing, or explicit comprehension: "What is sought in the question of being is not completely unfamiliar, although it is at first totally ungraspable" (*BT* 6/5). The questioning of being therefore proceeds indirectly as the questioning of the specific being that "we" are. As an investigation into the limits of our understanding of being in terms of beings, this involves clarifying and awakening the sense of the *question*:

> Thus to work out the question of being means to make a being—one who questions—transparent in its being. Asking this question, as a mode of *being* of a being, is itself essentially determined by what is asked about in it—being. This being, which we ourselves in each case are and which includes inquiry among the possibilities of its being, we formulate terminologically as *Dasein*. The explicit and lucid formulation of the question of the meaning of being requires a prior suitable explication of a being (Dasein) with regard to its being. (*BT* 7/7)

It is in these formulations that Heidegger starts to unpack the reflexive or performative complications that positing the question of being opens up. It is crucial for an understanding of *Being and Time* that Heidegger is not out to transform the implicit or vague understanding of being into an explicit theoretical conception (in short: to answer the question of the sense of being). Rather, he is out to interpret as itself essential this specific form of always-already-being-in: "this indefiniteness of the understanding of being that is always already available is itself a positive phenomenon which needs elucidation" [*diese Unbestimmtheit des je schon verfügbaren Seinsverständnisses ist selbst ein positives Phänomen, das der Aufklärung bedarf*] (*BT* 5/4). It is for this reason that the investigation focuses on that being for which questioning is itself a way of being [*Seinsmodus*]. In this way, the question of being becomes the "making transparent" of the specific being that is Dasein. And with that idea—that clarification of the question first requires clarification of Dasein itself—the self-complication of *Being and Time* emerges as the problem of its *circularity*.

The first circle that Heidegger makes an explicit point of is methodological: a (specific) being [*Dasein*] is to be interrogated with respect to its being, so that on the basis of this the sense of the question of being can become clear, so that the question can then finally be posited. Heidegger explicitly recognizes the circle, but distinguishes it from the "vicious" kind of circle that is detrimental to certain types of proof. Though it is true that the interpretation of the "average understanding of being" [*durchschnittlichen Seinsverständnis*] is only truly possible with an "explicit concept of being" [*ausgebildeten Begriff des Seins*], it is still possible to articulate it "provisionally" [*vorläufig*].[2]

Heidegger distinguishes his exposition from the kind of proof for which such circularity would be vicious:

> A "circle in reasoning" cannot possibly lie in the formulation of the question of the meaning of being, because in answering this question it is not a matter of grounding by deduction [*eine ableitende Begründung*], but rather of laying bare and exhibiting the ground [*eine aufweisende Grund-Freilegung*]. (*BT* 8/7)

This means that responding to the question of being can't have the form of deductively producing a conclusion that would follow from certain premises or presuppositions. Rather, Heidegger aims to show, "exhibit" [*aufweisen*], or lay bare [*Freilegung*] such presuppositionality (the "average understanding of being") as itself belonging to the "essential constitution" [*Wesensverfassung*] of Dasein.

At this point, Heidegger announces that the theme of the investigation is inherently complicated:

> "Circular reasoning" does not occur in the question of the meaning of being. Rather, there is a remarkable "relatedness backward or forward" of what is asked about (being) to asking as a mode of being of a being. The way what is questioned essentially engages our questioning belongs to the innermost meaning of the question of being. (*BT* 8/7, translation amended, JdJ)

This circularity or "remarkable 'relatedness backward or forward'" can be seen in the question's pre-involvement with what it asks after [*das Gefragte*; the sense of being] as well as in Dasein's ontic characteristic of *being ontological*, and it has important methodological consequences. Heidegger puts the problem succinctly: "Dasein is ontically not only what is near or even nearest—we ourselves *are* it, each of us [*wir* sind *es sogar je selbst*]" (*BT* 15/15). It is impossible to abstract from the theme in question in order to fashion a methodological point of neutrality from which to carry out the operation. As a self-explication of Dasein, especially one in which Dasein must explicitly recognize its implicit understanding of being as the explicit answer to the question of being, in order for it to be posited, it is clear that such an investigation faces "peculiar difficulties" [*eigentümlichen Schwierigkeiten*]. Wherein do these difficulties lie? "[. . .] in the mode of being of the thematic object and the way it is thematized [*In der Seinsart des thematischen Gegenstandes und des thematisierenden Verhaltens selbst*]" (*BT* 16/16).

This complication casts doubts on the procedure of the investigation as Heidegger sketches it out in the introduction. This is a temporally linear procedure: the analytic of Dasein is to "prepare the way" for the possibility of asking the question of the sense of being. This preparation is achieved by "clearing the horizon" [*Freilegung des Horizontes*] within which the "most original exposition of being" [*ursprünglichste Seinsauslegung*] could take place. Once that horizon has been cleared, it *then* would require a *repetition* of the analytic of Dasein on this new, "higher, genuinely ontological basis" [*auf der höheren und eigentlichen ontologischen Basis*] (*BT* 17/17).

In these paragraphs on method, Heidegger seems to combine two aspects that are in tension with one another, and this is the tension that arguably forms the arch of the entire work: Heidegger attempts to work out a linear plan of steps of sorts, a program for the elaboration of the question of being. Yet this question is inherently complicated, necessitating an indirect approach that is preliminary, incomplete, and that essentially undermines the very possibility of presentation or thematization. In fact, the book's central theme is that this very preliminarity, the pre-structure of "always already in," is itself the essential structure of Dasein. So how can that insight itself be thematized, presented? Can it itself be established securely or without preliminarity? And if so, would that constitute the success of the investigation—or rather its failure? Would it perform what it states it cannot do—thematize Dasein; determine Dasein's being without presupposing a conception of being; determine Dasein precisely as that being in whom or in which something is always still standing out [*daß im Dasein immer noch etwas aussteht*] (BT 236/227); determining it as such—*without* leaving anything standing out?

In *Being and Time*, the struggle with this complication is often very explicit and always in the background. It concerns the way in which the form or the way of the investigation suffers the consequences of what is thematized within it.

In Heidegger's work, everything about this complication can be traced back to the "always already being in"-character of Dasein: the question always already moves within an understanding of being, Dasein always already moves within that question and that understanding, and this is what initially presents Heidegger with the (albeit preliminary) "solution" to his methodological problems: if the "average understanding of being" of Dasein, in which Dasein always already finds him-/her-/itself, is itself an essential way of being of Dasein, then a fundamental ontology cannot start with the *explicit conceptions* Dasein has of him-/her-/itself (Heidegger mentions some: psychological, biological, anthropological, ethical, political, poetic, biographical, historical, etc.). Instead of such "dogmatically constructed" explicit self-knowledge, according to Heidegger, "[w]e must rather choose such a way of access and such a kind of interpretation that this entity can show itself in itself and out of itself [. . .]" [*das dieses Seiende sich an ihm selbst von ihm selbst her zeigen kann*]. Instead of its own explicit conceptions of itself, Dasein must therefore be shown "*initially and for the most part*—in its average *everydayness*" (BT 16/16). And Dasein must be thus shown, as it is in itself, *by* or out of itself. This is a methodological fusion of phenomenology and hermeneutics.

The phenomenological character of *Being and Time* resides in the call to have being "show itself as it is in itself."[3] It refers to Husserl's idea of phenomenology as the mere explication or description of the matter at hand [*die Sache*] as it gives itself, where "no conceivable theory can make us err."[4] Though worked out in a completely different way, this is one of the few points of convergence with Hegel's phenomenology: the demand that the philosopher purely be an onlooker [*reines zusehen*]. This phenomenological moment is fused with the hermeneutical requirement that it must show itself in itself *by* or from out of *itself* (BT 16/16).[5] Heidegger relates φαινόμενον to "what shows/manifests itself" [*das, was sich zeigt, das Sichzeigende, das Offenbare*] and λόγος to ἀποφαίνεσθαι, or to "reveal" (BT 28ff./26ff.). To the extent that this also means to "discover" (to take beings [. . .] out of their concealment; to let them be seen as something unconcealed; to *discover* them" [*aus seiner Verborgenheit herausnehmen und es als Unverbogenes (ἀλήθεια) sehen lassen; entdecken*]), λόγος is related to truth (BT 33/31).

By thus relating phenomenon, truth, and *logos* to revealing, disclosing, and unconcealment, we can already see the basis for what will become the central thrust of Heidegger's thinking after what is commonly called the *Kehre* (roughly from the question of the "nihilating nothing" [*nichtende Nichts*] in the 1929 inaugural lecture *What Is Metaphysics?* onward): that the phenomenon as unconcealment maintains an original relation to concealment, and so that the elaboration of these themes, at least partly (and to this Heidegger gives increasing importance) requires a thinking of what is essentially implicit or undisclosed. In Heidegger's terminology: of what is concealed or of what in the language of the later *Contributions* is called reticence or withdrawal. This can be seen in *Being and Time*'s seventh section on method. That section is set up so as to already indicate a more originary sense of phenomenon, *logos*, and hermeneutics. Its decisive characteristic is that it relates essentially to the concealed:

> What is it that phenomenology is to "let be seen"? What is it that is to be called "phenomenon" in a distinctive sense? What is it that by its very essence becomes the *necessary* theme when we indicate something *explicitly*? Manifestly it is something that does *not* show itself initially and for the most part, something that is *concealed* [*verborgen*] in contrast to what initially and for the most part does show itself. But, at the same time, it is something that essentially belongs to what initially and for the most part shows itself, indeed in such a way that it constitutes its meaning and ground.

> But what remains *concealed* in an exceptional sense, or what falls back and is *covered up* [*Verdeckung*] again, or shows itself only in a *"disguised"* ["*verstellt*"] way, is not this or that being but rather, as we have shown in our foregoing observations, the *being* of beings. (*BT* 35/33)

Here Heidegger distinguishes the more originary sense of *logos* as "showing" [*sehenlassen*, letting-be-seen] or disclosing/uncovering [*entdecken*] from its metaphysical derivatives, including the sense of truth as correspondence. The same holds for the phenomenon, as he indicates in the above quote. The interest there is to distinguish it from appearance [*Erscheinung*]. The peculiar character of the phenomenon as the object of the phenomenology of everydayness [*Alltäglichkeit*] in which the existential analytic finds its point of departure is that primarily it is not adequately understood as what "appears," because appearance invariably has the sense of "mere appearance" or of illusion [*Schein*]. Rather, what the existential analytic is out to uncover, discover, or disclose (the being *of* beings) is precisely what at first does *not* show itself, but what nonetheless essentially belongs to what *does* show itself, as its sense and its ground. He is clear: it is what "*remains* concealed in an exceptional sense" [*Was aber in einem ausnehmenden Sinne verborgen bleibt*] (*BT* 35/33, my italics, JdJ). So the object of the phenomenology of being aims at showing what remains hidden "in an exceptional sense."

How does one show what *remains* hidden? Does it remain hidden after showing it? One thing is certain: the explication that is *Being and Time* cannot transform the implicit *into* the explicit. Its explication must have a different relation to the implicit—to keep hidden its object, or to explicate it *as hidden*.[6]

In *Being and Time*, that hiddenness results from Dasein's "hermeneutical situation," in virtue of which it is inextricably bound up with (or "in") what it investigates. A short overview of the first steps of the investigation will show how being-in "orients" its progression.

THE COMPLICATION OF "BEING-IN" AND THE OPENING OF *BEING AND TIME*

Heidegger conceives Dasein's "average everydayness" terminologically as "being-in-the-world" [*in-der-Welt-sein*]. Though he states that this is composed of three elements—the "world," the specific "being" that is in that world (the "who?"), and "being-in" as such—it is clear from the introduction of the phenomenon of being-in-the-world in §12–13 that being-in as such "orients" the further discussion. Heidegger starts with his analysis of the "world" as what Dasein is always already in, showing how traditional metaphysical explicit knowledge (and the epistemological problems of knowledge of the world in terms of a gap that needs bridging) rest upon a phenomenally prior mode of being-in. This includes the critique of traditional representational objectivity (the "present-at-hand" [*Vorhandenheit*]) as a derivative mode of the phenomenally more original "ready-to-hand" [*Zuhandenheit*]. The analysis of the "world" starts with an analysis of what it means to be "in" it.

Heidegger famously argues that one is not "in" the world "as the water is 'in' the glass, or the garment is 'in' the cupboard." Being-in is not "to be in." What is the difference? "These beings whose being 'in' one another can be determined in this way all have the same kind of being—that of being present [*Vorhandensein*] as things occurring 'within' the world." (*BT* 54/54), which is the term Heidegger uses for what he calls the traditional notion of *existential*: to exist "simply." To existential in this traditional sense Heidegger opposes *Existenz*, as the way of being of Dasein. The difference between the being of Dasein and the being-present-at-hand of "things" in the world is precisely Dasein's existence, which is the peculiar way of "being-in" the world of a being that is *da*. That "[t]he essence of Dasein lies in its existence" means that the hallmarks of Dasein that are to be produced by the existential analytic are not properties of a being that would be present-at-hand, but rather "always possible ways of being" [*je ihm mögliche Weisen zu sein*]. This is also why Dasein cannot be grasped ontologically as "a case and instance of a genus of beings objectively present." (*BT* 42/42).

What does all this signify? That the object of *Being and Time*—the being of beings, as well as the object of the existential analytic: the being of the being that is Dasein—is for Heidegger essentially not objectifiable according to the narrow sense he gives to that term. This is what determines the specific shape of the relation between *Being and Time*'s content and the gesture of its exposition. It results in a performative tension that essentially complicates the investigation's own objectivity.

First of all, in terms of "content": the results or conclusions of the existential analytic are inherently ambiguous, because *Being and Time* is "completed" only to the extent that the self-explication of Dasein reveals its irreducible incompleteness. Let me show this by providing a short consideration of the course of the investigation. The formal result of existential analytic that starts with the "average everydayness" of Dasein's being-in-the-world is the determination of Dasein as care [*Sorge*]. The technical formulation is that Dasein is essentially "being-ahead-of-itself-in-already-being-in-a-world" [*Sich-vorweg-im-schon-sein-in-einer-Welt*] (*BT* 192/185). So what care designates is the various (essentially: three) ways in which Dasein is irreducibly involved, embedded, or situated: Dasein is always already "*ahead of* itself," "already *in* (a world)," and "already *with*." What binds these three equiprimordial moments of the ways in which Dasein essentially is "care" insofar as that means an involvement in something, that is, *ahead of* itself, *out of* itself, or *with* (others). In slightly different terminology, it means that Dasein is irreducibly always already *possibility* [*Seinkönnen*]. This means that Dasein is not essentially a determinable finished article or totality, but rather that in Dasein, "something is always still standing out" [*immer noch etwas aussteht*]. That is nothing less than a reformulation of the fact that Dasein exists. Precisely *that* is Dasein's characteristic: that it is always already outside itself, ahead of itself, or essentially "involved in. . . ." Now the question becomes whether a self-explication of such a being could be complete. And if not, what consequences does this have for the possibility of answering the question of being?

The question is a recurring theme in the remainder of *Being and Time* in the form of the seemingly somewhat formal considerations of "architectonic" and of the possibility of "completing" the investigation. Only if we recall the setup of *Being and Time* (that a determination of Dasein was required both in response to the question of being as well as in order to be able to posit it in the first place) does the question of Dasein's possible completeness cease to be a merely formal concern.[7] For this reason, Heidegger remains ambiguous when in §45 he asks whether with the determination of Dasein as care, Dasein has been comprehended completely.[8] He states that it is "questionable" whether a being whose essence is existence (who exists essentially in the "between" between birth and death) can be comprehended "as a whole." Heidegger proceeds to state that the interpretation of Dasein was not yet "original," because it was analyzed only from the point of view of its everydayness. The original interpretation, which is meant to show the "horizon" within which the everyday or inauthentic Dasein is, reveals Dasein's temporality and is the central focus of *Being and Time*'s second part.

Time, however, does not "solve" the problem of completeness. Its explication is merely the original interpretation of the "horizon" within which Dasein can be "ahead-of-itself as already in a world as being with." In all these structural elements of Dasein as care, an element of "transcendence" was implied, or an essential prepositionality: Dasein is *in* a world, *with* others, and *ahead* of itself. Time now stands for this prepositionality or "transcendence" that Dasein essentially *is,* and the second part of *Being and Time* aims at showing the "temporal sense" of these three "ecstasies" as relations to past, present, and future. In this way, Heidegger can in §65 posit temporality as the "ontological sense" of care, and claim that temporality means "the primordial, 'outside of itself' in and for itself" [*das ursprüngliche "außer-sich" an und für sich selbst*] (BT 329/314). Dasein's self-explication is complete only in its recognition of its irreducible incompleteness.

Second of all, in terms of *Being and Time*'s own language: Heidegger seems to manage to avoid discussing the question of *Being and Time*'s *own* language in his reflection on the subject of language, that is: his discussion of *Sprache*, which is phenomenally grounded in *Rede*. But even if they are not found under the explicit heading of language as a subject (as he will increasingly do in the later works), questions of performativity still guide the methodological reflections on circularity, completeness, preliminarity, and being-in (the "hermeneutic situation" of the question of being). Already early on in *Being and Time*, Heidegger defends his frequent use of "negative expressions"; this negativity is said to be "appropriate" [*angemessen*]. In fact, this negativity is even called "positive" (!) because it announces what is proper to the phenomenon (BT 58/58). And aside from this, there is the constant reminder, on every page, that Heidegger's attempt to regain the originary horizon of Western metaphysics is couched in a plethora of neologisms.

But even more than in all these matters, the question of performativity is implicit in Heidegger's analysis of objectivity. The derivative status of what is objectively present-at-hand [*Vorhanden*] with respect to the more original ready-to-handness [*Zuhandenheit*] is reflected in the treatment of the *assertion*. The explicit proposition or judgment is a "derivative mode of interpretation" [*abkünftiger Modus der Auslegung*]. This means, with an eye to the philosophical tradition, that the judgment cannot be seen as a basic form of thought or as the "most basic phenomenon of expression" [*das einfachste Aussagephänomen*] (BT 157/152, translation amended, JdJ). For Heidegger, all explicit conceptions or expressions are phenomenally grounded in the *implicit* understanding [*Verstehen*], which is always already "before" or "pre-"; everything explicitly conceived must be *already implicitly disclosed*. This affirms the explicative character of the investigation as an explication of what we are always already in. This is in line with the essentially explicative character of the investigation (the phenomenological-hermeneutical "showing of itself by itself") that Heidegger distinguishes from mere representation or objective description when he points to the original senses of phenomenon, *logos*, and *hermeneia*.

The distinction of the method of *Being and Time* from a representation itself resonates in the analysis of truth. There he argues that truth is not primarily a relation of correspondence, but a matter of the *Sache* (the matter at issue) as *Sichselbstzeigendes* (what shows itself). Heidegger aims at revealing the "traditional" conception of truth—*adequatio intellectus et rei*; correspondence or representation of thought with things[9]—to be a derivative[10] mode of the original sense of truth as unconcealment (Heidegger's conception of the original sense of the Greek ἀλήθεια):

> To say that a statement *is true* means that it discovers the being in itself. It asserts, it shows, it lets beings "be seen" (ἀπόφανσις) in their discoveredness. The *being-true (truth)* of the statement must be understood as *discovering [entdeckend-sein]*. Thus, truth by no means has the structure of an agreement between knowing and the object in the sense of a correspondence of one being (subject) to another (object). (*BT* 218/210)

What the methodological analyses and those of objectivity show is that the results or conclusions of the existential analytic essentially complicate the very language that articulates them. That is what I want to focus on in thinking about Heidegger's development. From *Being and Time* onward, these central performative complexities are gradually gathered under the heading of "language."

From this complication, Heidegger more and more radically draws the conclusion that the question of being necessitates a special kind of enactment of language. What I have emphasized is that in *Being and Time*, this problem is not primarily discussed under the heading of language, but in terms of method: the circularity of the investigation, the possibility of its completeness, its preliminary status, and the main hermeneutical complication of how to thematize or gain access to what one oneself irreducibly *is*, or what one is inextricably "in." It is in that light that I read Heidegger's *Contributions to Philosophy (Of the Event)*.

But isn't this emphasis on the complication of Heidegger's own language exactly what is often regarded as the main characteristic of the works after the "still too representational" *Being and Time*? That is why, at the end of my introduction to the *Contributions* in the next paragraph, I formulate the questions concerning Heidegger's *Kehre* that guide my interpretation of the *Contributions* in chapter 7.

INTRODUCTION TO THE "TRANSITIONAL THINKING" OF THE *CONTRIBUTIONS TO PHILOSOPHY (OF THE EVENT)*

In the opening of the *Contributions*, Heidegger announces that the text will not speak "about" anything: "The issue is [. . .] neither to describe nor to explain, neither to promulgate nor to teach" [*hier wird nicht beschrieben und nicht erklärt, nicht verkündet und nicht gelehrt*]. Rather, the *Contributions* are to enact a movement of saying: "Here the speaking is not something over and against what is to be said but is this latter itself as the essential occurrence of beyng" [*hier ist das Sagen nicht im Gegenüber zu dem Sagenden, sondern ist dieses selbst als die Wesung des Seyns*] (CP 4/6).

The entirety of the *Contributions* can be seen as an attempt to respond to the question of how to conceive the limits of what one is so essentially involved in, that it already permeates the very attempt to articulate those limits. In that way, the structure of "being-in" that controls *Being and Time* and the "remarkable 'relatedness backward or forward'" of the question of being, still guides the path of the *Contributions*. By way of an introduction, I preliminarily indicate how this thematic of "being-in" relates to the concealment that was so important in the discussion of *Being and Time*. Shortly thereafter, I situate my discussion of the *Contributions* within the broader framework of the present investigation, by showing Heidegger's critical relation to metaphysics to be irreducible to both a "reversal" and to "transcendence." I do this to clarify the "cessation of overcoming" that marks the *Contributions*' "transitional thinking."

In the *Contributions*, Heidegger frames the question of the limits of what one is inextricably in as the question of the possibility of an "other beginning." This would be a beginning other than the "first beginning" of Western history or of metaphysics. In the *Contributions*, Heidegger calls the situation of Western metaphysical mankind "machination" [*Machenschaft*]. Machination stands for the ubiquitous and pervasive power of a technological understanding of being that prestructures "our" world; a "thorough and calculable explainability" [*dürchgängigen berechenbaren Erklärbarkeit*] (*CP* 132/104) that Heidegger will later call *Technik*. According to Heidegger, machination is the ground and the original essential determination of what Nietzsche understood under the concept of "nihilism" (*CP* 119/95). Like Derrida's logocentrism, machination must be understood to denote both a historical circumstance as well as a structural figure.

This means that the question of an other beginning is a question born out of a *distress* [*Not*] or a *plight*, and that plight necessarily has a peculiar structure. Heidegger speaks of "the concealed plight of *a lack of a sense of plight*" [*der verborgenen Not der* Notlosigkeit] (*CP* 11/11). Machination is so pervasive that the inability to conceive its limits is not even experienced *as* a plight, and *this* itself is the distress out of which Heidegger's questions are born.

One can think here of similar motifs in Kierkegaard's work, such as the "universality" of the "sickness unto death" and its dialectical character (that the "most cherished and desirable place to live" of despair is precisely *concealed* in the "heart of happiness").[11] Similarly, Heidegger states that the abandonment by being is strongest, precisely there where it is most decisively hidden (*CP* 110/87).[12] Aside from Kierkegaard, the influence here is, as in so many other places in the *Contributions*, Nietzschean. The most distressing characteristic of modern European man is not that God is dead, but man's lack of distress in the face of this fact. This is the distinguishing feature of the modern form of nihilism, the "European disease," that we live among the remnants of a religion we no longer believe in (liberal democracy being the most important of those ruins), but that we are no longer able to conceive of ourselves as the creators of our values. Because we are not even able to experience God's death *as distressing*, it is necessary for Nietzsche to philosophize "with a hammer." Kierkegaard, Nietzsche, and Hölderlin are the *Contributions*' three guiding inspirational figures (*CP* 204/160) because of this kind of plight that is structured by a prevailing lack of plight. All three in their own way realized that announcing such a plight would require a fundamentally different kind of saying.

Given the pervasive nature of machination, raising the question of its limits also raises the question of the limits of what or who we are. For Heidegger, this means that the very ability to truly ask this question would have to transform the questioner. Just like questioning the limits of metaphysics for Derrida always means no longer wholly participating in it, so raising the question of machination requires a transformation of the one who asks the question. In the *Contributions*, that transformation is conceived as the transformation of "man"—that is, the "humankind" of Western metaphysics, the *determination* of man—into "*Da-sein*," that is, into a being for whom its relation to beyng is no longer obscured or already distorted by machination.

The thinking of the *Contributions*, in that way, is a "*transitional* thinking" [*das übergängliche Denken*]. It is the transition from the first to the other beginning, and from man as "a" (determinate) being to Da-sein.

In several ways, Heidegger sharply distinguishes this transition from a movement *counter* or *opposed* to metaphysics:

> For transitional thinking, however, what matters is not an "opposition" to "metaphysics," since that would simply bring metaphysics back into play; rather, the task is an overcoming of metaphysics out of its ground. (CP 172–73/136)

Now, metaphysics can obviously mean a great many things, and what Heidegger has named with that title has differed throughout his works. Quite soon after *Was ist Metaphysik?* the concept of metaphysics no longer designates an original kind of questioning. The word metaphysics, in other words, became "too metaphysical."

In the case of the *Contributions*, Heidegger quite consistently understands under the heading of metaphysics the questioning that proceeds by way of the "guiding question" [*Leitfrage*]. The guiding question is the question of the being of beings, the question that drives and defines metaphysics. From this, Heidegger distinguishes what he calls the "basic" or "grounding question" [*Grundfrage*]; the one that "inceptual" thinking attempts to ask: the question of the truth of beyng, or, more precisely: the question of "how beyng essentially occurs" [*wie Seyn west*]. Now what would it then mean to overcome metaphysics "out of its ground"? And how is it different from going counter to it? Throughout the *Contributions*, two main reasons can be discerned for why overcoming metaphysics cannot mean opposing metaphysics. They can be identified under the headings of (a) *reversal* and (b) *transcendence*.

a) *Reversal*. The first problem with going against metaphysics is that this would constitute a "mere reversal" [*Umkehrung*] that would only reaffirm metaphysics: all attempts, according to Heidegger, to go against metaphysics are reactions that therefore remain fundamentally dependent on what they react to:

> Not a *counter-movement;* for all counter-movements and counter-forces are essentially codetermined by that which they are counter *to,* although in the form of an inversion. Therefore a *counter-*movement never suffices for an *essential* transformation of history. [. . .] Beyond counter-forces, counter-drives, and counter-arrangements, something utterly different must commence. (*CP* 186/146)

The thinking of the other beginning must be utterly different from a counter-force. Instead of going "counter to," Heidegger is targeting a transformation. Heidegger elaborates (in a language that anticipates Derrida's use of the figure of the future as "monstrosity") by stating that "future decisions will not be made in previous domains" to the extent that the latter are "still upheld by counter-movements." Instead, the "uniqueness of beyng [. . .] lies anterior to all the oppositions in the previous 'metaphysics.'" As such, the other beginning stands *outside opposition*:

> The other beginning is not a counter-trend to the first; rather, as something *utterly different,* it stands outside of the "counter-" and outside of all immediate comparison.
>
> Therefore this confrontation is also not an opposition, neither in the sense of crude rejection nor by way of a sublation of the first in the other. The other beginning, on the basis of a genuine originality, procures for the first beginning both the truth of its history and thereby its inalienable, most proper otherness, which becomes fruitful only in the historical dialogue of thinkers. (*CP* 187/147)

The talk of "outside opposition" [*außerhalb des Gegen*] of course conveys the performative complication that is at stake: the attempt to distance oneself from opposition requires the oppositional articulation of the *außerhalb*. Perhaps just as telling is that in the *Contributions,* it is of all people Nietzsche who is cited time and again as falling back into metaphysics (albeit "through the back door" [*CP* 218/171]), because Nietzsche allegedly understood his own thinking in terms of an "inversion" [*Umkehrung*] of Platonism. (This is a hardly credible diagnosis of Nietzsche, and here we must, just like in the writings of Derrida, emphasize that there is also consistently a second Nietzsche present in the *Contributions.* This ambiguity with regard to Nietzsche is neither a coincidence nor an incoherence.)

So if inversion and reversal are gestures of reaffirmation, and if Heidegger targets a transformation into what is utterly different, then it would seem that Heidegger sets out to *overcome* or *transcend* metaphysics.

b) Transcendence. But for Heidegger, as for Derrida after him, transcendence *characterizes* metaphysics. For Derrida, transcendence stands for the figure of reappropriation; the internalization of the exterior as it culminates in the dialectic of Hegelianism; philosophy as always being philosophy "of *its* other." Heidegger traces transcendence back to a "mode of representation" [*Vorstellungsweise*] arising out of Plato:

> Arising out of the Platonic interpretation of beings is a mode of representation which in various forms radically rules over the subsequent history of the guiding question and thereby also over Western philosophy as a whole. The determination of the ἰδέα as the κοινόν turns the χωρισμός into a sort of being, and that is the origin of "transcendence" in its various forms, especially if even the ἐπέκεινα is grasped as οὐσία on account of this determination of the ἰδέα. (*CP* 216/169)

Transcendence arises there where the Platonic idea, as what is "common" to the beings partaking in it, is posited as *separate* from beings. This is especially so if through an act of reification (which Heidegger takes to be characteristic of Christianity and ontotheology more broadly speaking) the ἐπέκεινα, the "beyond," is itself interpreted as being. According to Heidegger, what this leads to is that one remains stuck within metaphysics or within the mere questioning of the guiding question concerning the being of beings [*ein Steckenbleiben in der Frageweise der Leitfrage, d. h. in der Metaphysik*] instead of being able to ask the grounding question (of the truth of beyng) (*CP* 218/170). So the problem with transcendence is not so much Derrida's problem of drawing the limit, of de-termining and thereby employing the constitutive structure of metaphysics, but rather the problem of a specific interpretation of being; of remaining within the forgetfulness of being.

For Heidegger, the problem with such transcendence lies not so much in the conception of a beyond, but rather with the conception of *diesseits*—of what lies on *this* side of the limit—that it implies. Transcendence implies that the indeterminable only begins beyond the borders of what is itself essentially unproblematic or determinable; the "already known": "[. . .] the human being can be taken as what one is already essentially familiar with [*was man in seinem Wesen schon kennt*], as the being in relation to which and on the basis of which all 'transcendence' is determined" (*CP* 25/22). In other words: transcendence according to Heidegger implies "departing from known and familiar 'beings' and going out in some way beyond them" (*CP* 218/170). Heidegger's problem with transcendence is not so much the creation of a mystery, but that this mystery is located outside of the confines of what is supposedly unmysterious or already familiar. His problem is with the false sense of familiarity the figure of transcendence bestows on what lies on *this* side of the limit. The risk of the figure of transcendence is that it locates the mystery in a beyond, whereas it should serve to first make enigmatic what "we" are.[13]

So now it seems that the very idea of transcendence must disappear. That seems to leave us with the necessity of somehow transcending transcendence, or overcoming overcoming?

THE "CESSATION OF ALL OVERCOMING"

In the *Contributions*, the idea of an overcoming of overcoming is conceived as a "leap over transcendence": "the task is not to surpass beings (transcendence) but, instead, to leap over this distinction and consequently over *transcendence* and to question inceptually out of beyng and truth" (*CP* 250–51/197). Its more famous articulation, however, can be found at the end of Heidegger's lecture "Time and Being." In that lecture, Heidegger announces that he will speak of the attempt "to think being without regard to its being grounded in terms of beings." At the start, Heidegger gives a "little hint" to his audience: "The point is not to listen to a series of propositions, but rather to follow the movement of showing" [*Es gilt, nicht eine Reihe von Aussagesätzen anzuhören, sondern dem Gang des Zeigens zu folgen*] ("TB" 2/2). The lecture ends by pointing out that it will have produced merely propositions, and that as such the very form of the lecture and the form of the proposition is an "obstacle" [*Hindernis*] in the saying that it has attempted. There Heidegger formulates the need to overcome overcoming:

> The task of our thinking has been to trace being to its own from appropriation [*Ereignis*]—by way of looking through authentic time without regard to the relation of being to beings.

> To think being without beings means: to think being without regard to metaphysics. Yet a regard for metaphysics still prevails even in the intention to overcome metaphysics. Therefore, our task is to cease all overcoming, and leave metaphysics to itself.
>
> If overcoming remains necessary, it concerns that thinking that explicitly enters appropriation [*Ereignis*] in order to say it in terms of it about it [*um Es aus ihm her auf Es zu—zu sagen*].
>
> Our task is unceasingly to overcome the obstacles that tend to render such saying inadequate.
>
> The saying of appropriation [*Ereignis*] in the form of a lecture remains itself an obstacle of this kind. The lecture has spoken merely in propositional statements [*Aussagesätzen*]. ("TB" 25/24, translation amended, JdJ)

Heidegger starts by confirming that the attempt to overcome metaphysics is itself metaphysical. Here we recognize what we could call Derrida's starting point: how to think both philosophy and its other if philosophy was always already philosophy of the other; of *its* other? Heidegger then concludes that if the attempt to overcome metaphysics is itself metaphysical, then the task would be to cease all overcoming and leave metaphysics to itself.

This would be in line with a certain prevalent interpretation of Heidegger's *Kehre*: whereas in *Being and Time*, being is thought with regard to a specific being (Dasein), being must now be thought *without* regard to beings, which, so he states here, means thinking being without regard to metaphysics. So it may seem that the saying that attempts to say *Ereignis* is so radically heterogeneous to metaphysics that it "leaves it to itself" in the sense of leaving it behind. But that interpretation cannot hold. It is already incommensurable with the lines that follow, because Heidegger, right after having left metaphysics "to itself," *reintroduces* the hypothesis of the necessity of its overcoming [*Wenn eine Überwindung nötig bleibt* . . .]. If such an overcoming consists in the attempt to prepare the thinking of *Ereignis*, to clear the way for the possibility of its saying, to "overcome the obstacles" that stand in its way, then this task holds "unceasingly" [*unablässig*].

So now the question becomes how to understand the transition of the "transitional thinking" of the *Contributions*. It is transitional in several ways. As a transition from the "first" to the "other beginning," this transition cannot consist in leaving metaphysics behind or in its reversal or its transcendence. Heidegger is most clear on the point in §85 of the *Contributions*. There he opens with the thesis that to gain a foothold in the *other* beginning means *to originarily appropriate* [*Zueignung*] *the first beginning and its history*. It is therefore through an originary appropriation *of* metaphysics that one gains a foothold in the other beginning: "Only now can 'metaphysics' be known in its essence" (*CP* 171/135). So metaphysics is "overcome" *only* when it becomes possible to inquire into its essence inceptually. This is also the juncture at which the second Nietzsche (aside from the one who "merely reverses" Platonism) enters the scene in the *Contributions*. Because the other side of Nietzsche's gesture was that he explicitly and unrelentingly identified Platonism as the inceptual heart of metaphysics.[14]

But matters are still inherently complicated. This inquiry into metaphysics' essence does not finally yield "knowledge" about that essence, or a more precise determination of it. Instead, "in transitional thinking all talk of 'metaphysics' becomes equivocal" [*kommt alle Rede von »Metaphysik« in die Zweideutigkeit*]:

> *The question*, what is metaphysics?, situated in the domain of the transition to the other beginning (c.f. the lecture connected to Being and Time and to "On the Essence of Ground"), inquires into the essence of "metaphysics" already in the direction of a first acquisition of a vanguard position toward the transition into the other beginning. In other words, it already inquires out of the other beginning. What it makes visible in its determination of "metaphysics" is already no longer metaphysics but, rather, is the overcoming of metaphysics. The aim of this question is not the clarification—which means the perpetuation—of the previous and, moreover, necessarily confused representation of "metaphysics" but is instead the impetus into the *transition* and thereby into the knowledge that *every sort* of metaphysics is at an end and must be so if philosophy is to attain its other beginning. (*CP* 171–72/135)

The reflection on metaphysics itself is not simply a matter of "determining" metaphysics. As a reflection on determination as such, the question does not aim at providing a new, better, or other "representation" or "clarification" of metaphysics, as that would itself be metaphysical. That would mean to hold on to the previous or "old" modes of representation. Instead, that *every* form of metaphysics must come to an end means that the positing of the question of metaphysics *already* inaugurates a thinking that is irreducible to representation because it questions representation as such. As such, it is "already no longer metaphysics but, rather, the overcoming of metaphysics." The "other" thinking, out of the other beginning, is nothing other than the ability to finally be able to ask the question of who or what we are, which is to say what are our limits, which is—if the limits are to truly be limits instead of mere reversals or beyonds—to (already) broach these limits in a certain way.

This brings me back to my starting point in this paragraph: "this presentation does not describe or explain." Instead, Heidegger attempts to *enact* a transformation through the "transitional" thinking-saying language [*denkerisches Sagen*] of the *Contributions*.

Here, still, the risk of reversals looms. The very idea that such a transformation could be *effectuated* (as something one could "do") itself belongs to machination. An entire tradition of the "critique of subjectivity" lurks in the background of that thought, and indeed in the *Contributions* Heidegger speaks of Da-sein as an "overcoming of all subjectivity" [*Überwindung aller Subjektivität*] (*CP* 259/204; 303/240). Of that entire tradition, it is once again Kierkegaard and Nietzsche of whom one cannot fail to think here. It is one thing to conceive of a "critique of the subject," but quite another to recognize that such a critique necessarily complicates itself in its very articulation. What Kierkegaard and Nietzsche bring to this problematic is the awareness that such a critique would require, at some decisive moment, a suspension of "self-mastery" that essentially complicates the very idea of resistance to subjectivity itself (hence the extended and explicit self-interrogations of their *own* position as author, thinker, and questioner throughout their respective oeuvres, most clearly in Nietzsche's *Ecce Homo* and in Kierkegaard's texts on his "point of view"). In staying with the *Sickness unto Death*, the analogue of this self-complicating gesture would consist in the fact that the most intensified form of despair ("in despair to will to be oneself: defiance") consists in the recognition of despair in the very attempt to rid oneself of it; the wish to be someone else or to actively change oneself. Kierkegaard recognizes that despair is most intense in this attempt to effectuate by oneself one's release from despair: the attempt to bring about one's own salvation.[15]

Because the transformation of man into Da-sein cannot be *effectuated by man*—on his own terms, as it were—Heidegger conceives this transformation as the "occurrence" of a *turning* [*Kehre*], more specifically a *Kehre "im Ereignis"* (in the event, event of appropriation, eventuation, enowning). The unfolding of the full sense of the concept of *Ereignis* is something I can only gradually work toward here. For now, I focus on the transformation as a "turning."

With the introduction of the concept of the *Kehre*, we can start to appreciate just on how many different levels Heidegger's thinking is "transitional."

WHAT TURNS? FROM *BEING AND TIME* TO THE *CONTRIBUTIONS*

Aside from the structural figure of the *Kehre im Ereignis* that plays such a pivotal role in the *Contributions*, Heidegger has described his own development after *Being and Time* in relation to a *Kehre* or a turning. That is the *Kehre* that most people know about. The two cannot be separated. How one understands the "transitional" character of the *Contributions* depends intimately on how one understands the transition from *Being and Time* to the *Contributions*.

The *Contributions* are, among other things, also the site of an explicit critique of *Being and Time*. That critique consistently takes on a form that is by now very familiar to us. Heidegger consistently characterizes his own earlier writings as "still too representational," "still too metaphysical." But because I've already shown how that in itself cannot constitute a critique, what does that mean for the relation between *Being and Time* and the *Contributions*?

My goal is to show that a certain account of Heidegger's development is insufficient. That account consists of the following interrelated thoughts about the transition from *Being and Time* to the *Contributions*. In this way of thinking, Heidegger's *Kehre* would amount to:

1. A move *away* from the attempt to posit the question of being by way of the existential analytic of Dasein *towards* a saying of being "itself" (in the sense that the transformation would be a change of object: from "a being"—Dasein—to "being itself");

2. A transition from the representational, metaphysical language of *Being and Time* to the "poietic" language of the *Contributions*;

3. This makes the *Contributions* into the "direct" attempt to say being "itself," for which the "still too representational" language of *Being and Time* is, then, insufficient. Heidegger's development, therefore, is one in which he attempts *to find the right language,* the *right word,* or to *overcome the failure to say* "being itself."

There is a textual basis for all these thoughts. Heidegger does indeed speak of a shift towards a saying of "beyng itself," the inadequacies of the still too metaphysical language of *Being and Time,* and the task of finding a language with which to speak from out of the truth of beyng itself. But the question is how to interpret these claims. I suggest the following alternatives:

1. The transition from beings to beyng is not a change in "object"—if the ontological difference taught us anything, it is the absolute dissymmetry between beings and being which means precisely that being was always the being *of* beings. There cannot be said to "be" such a thing as "being itself." If there is a turn towards "being itself," this can neither mean a difference in "object," nor a shift away from beings.

2. The problem with the distinction between representational and poietic language is that it risks sounding like these are two different languages. One can no more "leave behind" representational language than one can regard speaking poietically as a "possibility" (something one can *do*) with which one can then "get it right." Moreover, *Being and Time* was already a radical critique of representation and an attempt at a "new language." *There is no more pure representation than there is a pure poietics*. Instead, if there are limits to representation, they must show themselves through a poietic movement of showing *in* the "metaphysical" propositions (the "pathway" *in* or *through* seemingly objective propositions).

3. Consequently, Heidegger's development cannot be understood as a quest to find the "right language" or to *overcome* his earlier failure to say being in *Being and Time*. The "turning" from *Being and Time* to the *Contributions* is not simply

a possibility, nor a transcendence, nor a reversal. Instead of overcoming, the transformation aims at *recognizing and preserving* a certain failure-to-say being.

To show this, it is vital to understand what Heidegger means when he states that (1) the "saying" that he is after is in fact a "saying that accomplishes the utmost reticence" or a "bearing silence" [*Erschweigung*], and that (2) nothing essential can come to pass if the "basic disposition" [*Grundstimmung*] of unassertiveness, restraint or "reticence" [*Verhaltenheit*] is lacking.

Only if reticence is recognized at the heart of the Heideggerian exposition can the relation between representational language and poietic language truly come to the fore. When the poietic is recognized as the movement or the pathway "in" the representational, then one can understand Heidegger's *Kehre* from *Being and Time* to the *Contributions*, as well as the *Kehre im Ereignis*. That *Kehre* consists in the "recuperation" of beings "out of the truth of beyng," beyng's concealment or sheltering precisely *in* beings [*Bergung, verbergen, entbergen*], or *Ereignis* as the *self-withdrawal* of beyng in or through which beings "come into their own."

If the only "intimation" we have of beyng is precisely an intimation of beyng's *refusal*, if in a world that is abandoned by beyng, if it "resonates" precisely *as withdrawal*, then "this already indicates that the task here is not the description, explanation, or ordering of something objectively present." Instead, writes Heidegger, thinking faces a different burden (*CP* 108/86). Already early in the *Contributions*, Heidegger links the required "transformation into Da-sein" to the problem of language and what must exceed the "proposition":

> In philosophy, propositions are never subject to proof. This is so not only because there are no highest propositions, from which others could be derived, but because here "propositions" are not at all what is true, nor are propositions simply that about which they speak. All "proving" presupposes that those who understand, as they come to stand before the represented content of the proposition, remain the same, unaltered in following the representational nexus that bears the proof. And only the "result" of the course of the proof can require a changed mode of representation or, rather, require the representing of something previously unheeded.

> In philosophical knowledge, on the contrary, the very first step sets in motion a transformation of the one who understands, and this not in the moral-"existentiell" sense, but rather with respect to Da-sein. (*CP* 13/13)

What is to be said in philosophy is not reducible to representation because it is not on the basis of what Heidegger writes, but *through*, *in*, or *with* this saying that a transformation is to occur. This is a saying that would have to "accomplish the utmost reticence." It is this that I try to understand in the next chapter.

CONCLUSION

In this chapter, I have shown in what way *Being and Time* anticipates the reticence and hesitation of the *Contributions*, even if their style and systematicity are so different. *Being and Time* points from the start to an implicit self-complication in the question of being that creates essential difficulties for the exposition of a fundamental ontology. I have shown how the irreducibility of "being-in" leads to a phenomenological-hermeneutical kind of self-explication of Dasein (the "showing of itself by itself") that (1) complicates the possibility of "completing" the investigation, (2) is essentially "circular" and therefore irreducible to a sequence of "steps," (3) complicates the investigation's own "objectivity" because it shows the objective knowledge of the proposition to be a "derivative mode" of a more originary being-in, and *moreover* (4) maintains an irreducible relation to concealedness. The objectivity of the exposition in *Being and Time* is not the correctness of a representation because Dasein's self-explication is completed in the very recognition of its irreducible incompleteness. This means that this explication must to an extent recognize and preserve a certain incompleteness and concealedness as belonging essentially to what Dasein is (an incompleteness and concealedness that is identified at so many different levels of the investigation—from "being-in" to "standing out," from "care" to "temporality"—but that has its source in Dasein's existence in the technical sense that Heidegger gives to that term).

If *Being and Time* is already an explication of an irreducible concealedness and therefore a complication of the possibility of philosophical exposition, then how to qualify Heidegger's later remarks that *Being and Time* was "still too representational"?

I have argued that this question of Heidegger's transition after *Being and Time* (the famous *Kehre*) cannot be separated from what becomes more and more of an explicit theme for the later "transitional thinking" (the less famous *Kehre im Ereignis*). The *Contributions*' transitional thinking is neither reversal nor overcoming, but it targets a kind of "overcoming of overcoming" in order to arrive at an inceptual inquiry into the essence of metaphysics. This paradoxical overcoming can neither be a better representation, nor be a matter of choice or a possibility. Instead, it is an event that consists in a transformation that Heidegger will ultimately call the *Kehre im Ereignis*. Heidegger increasingly thinks this as an event of language or the enactment of a kind of saying. The transition from the inquiry of a specific being—Dasein—in the existential analytic to the attempt to speak out of the "truth of beyng itself" can neither be interpreted as a change from one object to another, nor in a turning away from beings. The same holds for the "still too representational" language of *Being and Time:* the move toward the explicit performativity of the *Contributions*' "poietic" language cannot be understood as the move *away from* representational language. Whereas the idea of a new language would only reaffirm metaphysics, the transformation consists in a transformation of the relation to the "old" language; of being *attuned* to it differently. That is what I try to understand in my interpretation of the *Contributions to Philosophy (Of the Event)* in the next chapter.

CHAPTER 7

RETICENCE AND EXPOSITION

Heidegger's *Contributions to Philosophy (Of the Event)*

> The concealment of the inceptual must be safeguarded above all. Every distortion of it through attempts at explanation must be avoided [. . .].
>
> —Heidegger, *Contributions to Philosophy (Of the Event)*

STYLE AND SYSTEMATICITY: THE CONJUNCTURE OF THE *CONTRIBUTIONS*

The *Contributions* clearly differs from *Being and Time* in its systematicity. There are several ways in which Heidegger announces that the *Contributions* will not be "a 'work' in the previous style." The "previous style" would be a representation: it would speak "about" a subject and "present something objective" [*ein Gegenständliches darzustellen*] (CP 20/18). By contrast, Heidegger presents his indirectness in terms of a (path)way. The systematicity of the *Contributions* is called a "a *course* of thought" [*Gedanken-gang*]. Heidegger is accustomed to describing his style of thinking—in contrast to a "work"—as a path, track, or way (one need only compare some titles: *Holzwege, Wegmarken, Unterwegs zur/der Weg zu Sprache, der Feldweg, Mein Weg in die Phänomenologie*, etc.). And, of course, the motto Heidegger appended to his collected works is "ways—not works" [*Wege—nicht Werke*].

The "way" is not only temporal (one must *traverse* a way, one cannot get it "in one go"), but it can also "come to an abrupt stop where the wood is untrodden" (this is the primary sense of *Holzwege*). That has the double signification of, negatively, the possibility of dead ends (and byways, wandering, errancy), as well as that of, positively, arriving at previously unexplored territory. As Heidegger indicates later in the *Contributions*: "In inceptual thought, domains of the truth of beyng must be *traversed* in order for them then to step back again into concealment precisely when beings flare up. This taking of byways belongs essentially to the indirectness of the 'efficacy' of all philosophy" (*CP* 17/16, translation amended and emphasis mine, JdJ).

There is an internal connection between the saying that accomplishes reticence and the path or way: "the more necessary the thoughtful speaking about beyng, the more unavoidable reticence becomes regarding the truth of beyng in the *course* of questioning" (*CP* 19/17). It is apparently through traversing a *course of questioning* that the reticence in which one ceases to speak "about" being is to be accomplished. This is the subject of the *Contributions*' first proper section: the *Contributions* question "along a way that is paved only now." More precisely: a way that is paved *in* the questioning [*Die "Beiträge" fragen in einer Bahn die* [. . .] *erst jetzt gebahnt wird*] (*CP* 5/6).[1]

Given the entanglement of the saying and what is to be said in the *Contributions*, the text is not linearly structured. Instead, the *Contributions* has the form of what Heidegger calls *eine Fuge*—a (con)juncture or fugue of/for what he calls "inceptual thinking." Playing on the meanings of *Gefüge*, *Verfügung*, and *Fügung*, Heidegger states that this conjuncture has a threefold sense: (1) in its architectonic or in its construction [*im Aufbau*], it must possess a philosophical rigor ("to apprehend the truth of beyng in the completely developed fullness of its grounded essence") even if what corresponds to such a rigor turns out to be the impossible; (2) that, as a "way," it is "only one way and the way of only one," and so in traversing it one necessarily abstains from the possibility of overseeing other ways; and (3) that it is clear from the outset that the attempt at inceptual thinking remain a "dispensation" or "providence" [*Fügung*] *of* beyng (*CP* 81/64ff.). In this way, Heidegger emphasizes that both the rigor and the trajectory of the *Contributions* do not conform to theory, assertion, or representation to a project that would oversee its object or field. Instead, that "object" (the truth of beyng) is itself what is to be *enacted*. In this way, it is a performative radicalization of Heidegger's conception of phenomenology as a "showing of itself by itself."

It is clear from this perspective that Heidegger distinguishes the *Contributions* from a "system." A system, according to Heidegger, is the necessary form of philosophy insofar as it is led by the "guiding question" [*Leitfrage*] of the being of beings, rather than the grounding question [*Grundfrage*] of inceptual thinking: the question "how beyng essentially occurs" [*wie Seyn west*]. Here it may seem as if these questions have a different "object": from beings to beyng. Instead, the difference must be more subtle, because their difference is precisely that the first has an object at all (beings) and is guided by it (with Kant, it turns into the question of the objectivity of the object), whereas the grounding question asks out of the awareness that it lacks an object properly speaking—it aims at an articulation of what essentially conceals or withdraws. If such articulation cannot be systematic or linear, then what is its structure?

The "conjuncture" [*Fuge*] of the *Contributions* consists of six "junctures," fugues, joinings, or joints [*Fügungen*] that have the following headings: "The Resonating" [*Der Anklang*]; "The Interplay" [*Das Zuspiel*]; "The Leap" [*Der Sprung*]; "The Grounding" [*Die Gründung*]; "The Future Ones" [*Die Zu-künftigen*]; and "The Last God" [*Der letzte Gott*]. These six junctures are preceded by a "Prospect" or preview [*Vorblick*], from which I have primarily been quoting so far. Heidegger says of the six junctures that though every one "stands in itself," this is only "so as to make the essential unity more impressive." This confirms Heidegger's awareness of the entanglement or inextricability of the saying and what is to be said: "[. . .] in each of the six junctures, a saying of the same about the same is attempted, but in each case out of a different essential domain of that which is called the event" (*CP* 81–82/65).

Now, just because the *Contributions* are no system, that does not mean that there is no systematicity to them. Heidegger says that there is "a hidden interweaving among them." With what has been said so far, it is already possible to introduce these headings and their interweaving, so as to get a preliminary grasp on what is at stake in each of them.

We return to the thought of entanglement, the inextricability of "being-in." The question of an other beginning was the question of the possibility of relating to beyng in a world that is dominated by machination or by questionlessness. What was called "forgetfulness of being" in *Being and Time* is now conceived as the "abandonment by being."[2] In this light, if the project is to get started at all, there must be an "inkling" or *intimation* [*Ahndung, Wink*] of beyng in a world that is abandoned by it. Beyng, in other words, does not "appear," but must nevertheless somehow "resonate" in a world of machination. This is the first question: in a world of machination, or in an age of metaphysics, how does beyng nevertheless resonate? Therefore, the sections we find in this juncture concern the specific form that machination takes in our world. This juncture also contains what one could call Heidegger's philosophy of culture. It deals with the abandonment by being, the prevailing (lack of) plight and thoroughgoing questionlessness, and the ways in which machination reigns in experience, (public) discourse, and the sciences.

Heidegger's answer to the question of how beyng can resonate at all in a world of machination is that beyng resonates precisely *as* that which is concealed: as self-refusing. The lack of beyng is a distress that is structured as "the plight of the lack of plight." An intimation of an *other* beginning therefore initially arises only in the identification of machination itself. The plight arises only when machination is recognized as such; it is the distress that accompanies the recognition of the lack of distress in the face of the abandonment by being. This means that beyng "resonates" or finds resonance in a world of machination when an interrogation of (the limits of) what one is "in" takes place. Such an interrogation means interrogating the "first beginning," and that is what Heidegger means by the second juncture: *interplay* [*Zuspiel*]. This is how Heidegger says it: "The interplay first takes its necessity out of the resonating of the plight of the abandonment by being" (*CP* 16/17), and: beyng resonates precisely "*in its refusal*" (*CP* 10/10).

Interplay signifies the interrogation of the first beginning, through which the very thought of an "other" beginning is to arise (it is also the thought of the possibility of a "transition" to another beginning, though it will be shown that strictly speaking no "transition" between the two is possible, as is evidenced in the necessity of the "leap"). Therefore, this juncture contains Heidegger's history of Western philosophy, a version of the task that in *Being and Time* was envisioned as the "destruction" of the history of ontology. What the interplay reveals as the *first* beginning is the nature of *truth*. The history of the West, of metaphysics, is the history of truth. Probably the clearest line of continuation between *Being and Time* and the works that come after it is the continual rethinking of truth in terms of (un)concealment. At this point, one can clearly see the continuation between the *Contributions* and Heidegger's famous contemporaneous essay on the origin of the work of art. In that essay, truth is understood as clearing-concealing [*lichtende Verbergung*], as what hides itself precisely *in* the "play" of beings, the play wherein or whereby it is decided what "is" or what counts as being (the present/presenting [*das Anwesende*]). This means that in the interrogation of the first beginning, one recognizes how beings "shelter" truth. *Sheltering* [*Bergung*] is the "preservation" [*Verwahrung*, literally the "be-truth-ing"] of the "cleared-concealed," such that:

> It is exactly this preservation [*Verwahrung*] which first allows beings *to be* and indeed *as* the beings they are and can be in the truth of the not yet thematized being [*Sein*] and in the way this truth is unfolded. (*CP* 71/57)

This means that the interrogation of the first beginning in the interplay leads to the recognition of the movement by which what counts as being [*was als seiend gilt*] is decided. To recognize that in Western history that which counts as a being is conceived in a limited way is precisely to recognize the very movement (the *event*) in which or by which beings "come into their own." That is a preliminary indication of the sense of *Ereignis*.

In this way, resonance and interplay form the first two moments of inceptual thinking, and Heidegger states that they "prepare" the "leap" ("Resonating and interplay are soil and field for the first run-up of inceptual thinking to the leap into the essential occurrence of beyng" [*CP* 82/65]).[3] The conclusion that these two introductory moments lead to, however, is that there is no fixed path or introduction for what is to be thought. The interplay shows that what is essential is what is irreducibly concealed. All exposition will have already been caught up in the unconcealment that is only its "consequence." It is here that a "leap" is required: the transition from an assertive discourse into the "thinking-saying" [*denkerische Sagen*] of the *Contributions* ("To thinking there remains only the simplest saying [. . .] in purest reticence," *CP* 72/58). This is also the reason why the "way" of the *Contributions* is consistently described as only *anticipation* and *attempt*. There is something essentially resisting "fulfillment," "realization," or even "possibility" of what is to be "thought-said." It is in this context that the "future ones," as well as the "few and the rare" that the *Contributions* frequently references, must be understood. What is to be said not only resonates for the few and the rare in a world of machination. It is *essentially* unheard-of, and its articulation is not simply "realizable." Rather, it is a matter of awakening a sense of precisely one's limits, and with that a sense of plight, through a path of questioning. To speak "from" *Ereignis* is therefore not to attain or assert a position or to actualize a possibility.

Recognizing the limits of truth and the way in which it conceals thus requires a leap out of the realm of truth and metaphysics that controls all articulation. What the interplay gives is not a "new" or more original ground of truth, but the ungrounded character of truth. The leap is therefore a leap into the "abyss" [*Abgrund*]. This juncture therefore focuses on beyng in relation to the abyss or *Zerklüftung*, and especially on nothing, non-being, being-toward-death, and beyng's "essential occurrence" [*Wesung*].

Only out of the recognition of the abyss does the necessity for "grounding" arise (juncture 4). This is the thematization of the "recuperation" of the relation of beings to beyng. This juncture could therefore be called the juncture of the, if you will, *reconception* of beings out of the truth of beyng. The "grounder" of the "truth of beyng" is Da-sein, and because that cannot be a voluntaristic type of act by an entity called "man," this is also the section on the reconception of "man" as "Da-sein" and on turning and transformation. Its two largest parts are dedicated to Da-sein and truth. Here it is helpful to point to what Heidegger writes in §193 of the *Contributions*: that Da-sein "does not lead out of beings" (*CP* 314/249; cf. 424/336). This in light of what has been a guiding thread throughout this book, namely: that Heidegger works toward a conception of "our limits" (specifically: the limits of machination as the loss of the relation to beyng) in full awareness that such limits cannot be conceived as opposing beyng to machination or to beings as what would be outside or beyond it. It is a matter not of the possibility of an "other world" but of recognizing one's limits so as to be able to relate differently to one's own. To this end, it will be necessary to understand what it means that beings "shelter" (thus conceal *and* preserve; *Bergung, bergen, verbergen*) the truth of beyng, which is what the juncture of grounding ends with.

Concerning the final two junctures (the future ones and the last God), the first refers to an irreducible "unrealizability" of what is to be articulated. We must take as seriously as possible the claim that the *Contributions* are fundamentally an "attempt"—that is: an "anticipation" does not anticipate a simply realizable future or a task that one could voluntaristically carry out. The problem with the idea of such a realizable future is that it puts the focus on some other world or possibility, rather than on relating differently to oneself and one's own world, and successful resolution, solution, and accomplishment are perhaps the most prototypically machinational notions. As Heidegger states with regard to machination, what is absent in this "age of complete questionlessness" is not a sense of new possibilities, but the exact opposite: machination is a world in which everything has become *merely possible*. What is necessary, and what has disappeared from it completely, is any sense of the *impossible* (or of the *mystery* [*Geheimnis*], to which I return below).[4]

I therefore leave the preliminary introduction of the last two junctures in order to proceed with the examination of the main problem of the *Contributions*' explicit relation to the limitations of its own articulation. As Heidegger states in §95 of the *Contributions*: "The concealment of the inceptual must be safeguarded above all. Every distortion of it through attempts at explanation must be avoided" [*Vor allem muß die Verborgenheit des Anfänglichen gewahrt warden. Zu vermeiden ist jede Veranstaltung durch Erklärungsversuche*] (*CP* 188/148). Instead of taking something out of its concealment, the concealment of the inceptual must be "preserved." And this is why "attempts at explanation" will "distort" what is to be said. So what strange kind of philosophical exposition is Heidegger targeting here? If it does not unconceal, then is such a movement still a "showing"?

THE *CONTRIBUTIONS*' "REFLECTION" ON ITS OWN LANGUAGE: *DENKERISCHES SAGEN* AND THE LIMITS OF REPRESENTATION

Heidegger articulates the problem of the *Contributions*' own articulation in numerous places, for instance at the opening of §40:

> The work of thought in the age of transition [. . .] can only be, and must be, a *course* of thought, taking this word "course" in its two senses at once: a proceeding and the path on which the proceeding takes place, thus a path that itself proceeds [*ein Gehen und ein Weg zumal, somit ein Weg, der selbst geht*].
>
> Can such a thing be given form in saying, so that the simplicity of this task comes to light? And to such a thing does there correspond the conjunction *Of the Event*? (*CP* 83/66)

The "simplicity" of the task does not mean that the task is easy. The task is "simple" or "basic" [*einfach*] to the extent that creating the pathway and following it cannot be distinguished, and must somehow be accomplished in one and the same gesture. That complicates the possibility of philosophical presentation as representation:

> Because, in philosophical knowledge, in each case everything is transformed at once—the being of humans into its standing in the truth, the truth itself, and thereby the relation to beyng—and because, accordingly, an immediate representation of something objectively present is never possible, philosophical thinking will always seem strange. (CP 14/13)

This performative problem of the inextricability of creating and following the path raises the question of its relation to philosophical reflection. Because "I" myself am entangled with what is to be my "object," saying and what is to be said are indistinguishable. Heidegger confirms this structure as guiding inceptual thinking, though he stresses that both "reflection" and "self" (with its connotations of "subjectivity") are to be avoided. If this project were conceived as man's reflection on "himself," then this would neglect that both the determination of "man" and the determination of "self" are part of what is in question: "The meditation of inceptual thinking is, rather, so original that it first asks how the *self* is to be grounded, in whose domain 'we,' you and I, in each case come to our *selves*" (CP 67/54). At issue for a thinking of *Ereignis* is to show originally how beings "come into their own" [*ereignen*]. Though "we" are at stake, this showing cannot proceed on the basis of some pre-given "self," but rather should show precisely how a being comes to have an "itself" or comes into itself: "The selfhood of the human being [. . .] is a realm of occurrences [*ein Geschehnisbereich*], a realm in which human beings are appropriated to themselves [. . .] wherein an appropriation can occur" (CP 51/42). In this way, Heidegger can state that "The meditation of inceptual thinking concerns us (ourselves) and yet does not" (CP 68/55).

In my view, Heidegger here expresses an insufficiency of traditional accounts of subjectivity and self-consciousness while at the same time acknowledging that he is operating at the heart of the concerns of such accounts. Heidegger adds that this *ambiguity* with respect to the self (inceptual thinking is a self-reflection and it is *not* a self-reflection) is "unavoidable" and corresponds to the risk of seeing in it an "anthropological existential meditation in the usual sense." This is further qualified in §19, where Heidegger asks (in a manner that anticipates the type of questioning that Derrida later picks up on) to what extent it is clear who "we" are, or even to what extent that question is intelligible at all. How are "we" *already* thought when positing the question of who we are? Heidegger stresses *both* (1) that meditation or reflection [*Besinnung*] is necessarily self-reflection (meditation *on oneself*) and (2) that the question of "who we are" cannot already depart from a preconception of a "we" as objectively present in whatever capacity (*vorhanden*; whether as "myself," "man," a "people," a "human being," etc.). In other words, it cannot be a "consideration turned back upon ourselves as 'given' beings." On the contrary: it is a meditation that forces one to grapple with what cannot be "given" or presented in precisely such a way.

It follows from this entanglement or inextricability of saying and what is to be said that the "truth of beyng" does not let itself be said "in ordinary language, which is ever more comprehensively used up today and degraded through idle chatter." Thus Heidegger asks whether the truth of beyng can be said at all, or whether perhaps a "new language" could be found to say beyng.

His answer is resolute: "No," it cannot be a matter of a "new language." Inasmuch as there can be no position outside metaphysics for Derrida, and inasmuch as for Hegel there can be no reason outside or opposed to the understanding, so for Heidegger there can be no "new" language that would be "suitable" to say beyng. Heidegger goes even further: even if *per impossibile* one would devise such a language, it would still "not be one that speaks" [*selbst wenn dies gelänge [. . .] wäre diese Sprache keine sagende*] (CP 78/62). Analogous to the thought of the "*recuperation of beings*" [*Wiederbringung des Seienden*] (CP 411/326, my translation, JdJ) is the thought of a "transformation of language" [*Verwandlung der Sprache*] that cannot be a transformation *into* something other or new. Instead, this is the task: "Thus all that matters is this one thing: to say the most nobly emerged language in its simplicity and essential force, to say the language of beings as the language of beyng" [*die Sprache des Seienden als Sprache des Seyns sagen*] (CP 78/62).

So it is not a matter of an other language, but rather of saying the (same) language of beings *as* language of beyng—to *recuperate*, in other words, the language of beings and restore its relation to beyng. This involves at least a different attitude with respect to words. Heidegger states, concerning his own terminology:

> Therefore something is said of the "renunciation of pursuance," of the "clearing of concealment," of the "appropriating event,"

of "Da-sein"; and this is not a mere plucking of truths out of words but is the opening of the truth of beyng *in* this sort of transformed saying [. . .]. (*CP* 78/62, my italics, JdJ)

In other words: one is not expected to "find" in the new words a previously hidden truth so as to be able to pluck or "claw it out of them" [*Herausklauben*]. Instead, the very use of these words serves as the attempt to open the truth of beyng *through* a transformed saying.

This means that to the extent that language "fails" to say beyng, this failure must be qualified in a very nuanced way. This question, what it means for language to fail and whether that failure can be remedied, moreover raises all the stakes implied in the discussion of Heidegger's own development: if Heidegger states that his language in *Being and Time* was "still too metaphysical," then what does this signify? Is the *Contributions* an attempt to write something that would be no longer metaphysical? Is there a (new, other) post-metaphysical language? I have suggested that there is not, and this means that Heidegger's development must be understood differently. It also means that Derrida's relation to Heidegger must be reinterpreted if Derrida sees in Heidegger the onto-hermeneutical project of *meaning*, as the nostalgic search for "the right word." This reconsideration I undertake in Part IV.

What does Heidegger say about the failure of language in the *Contributions*? First of all, one could say that the exhaustion of language forms the very point of departure of the *Contributions*. Looking at the first page, we see Heidegger distinguishing the "public title" (*Beiträge zur Philosophie*) from the "essential heading" (*Vom Ereignis*). Philosophy, according to Heidegger, cannot be announced any other way, since all essential titles have become impossible because all the "basic words" have been exhausted or "used up" [*Vernutzung*], and the real or "authentic relation to the word" [*des echten Bezugs zum Wort*] has been "destroyed" [*Zerstörung*]. Further down, Heidegger is more specific about the failure of language:

> Words fail us [*Es verschlägt einem das Wort*]; they do so originally and not merely occasionally, whereby some discourse or assertion could indeed be carried out but is left unuttered, i.e., where the saying of something sayable or the re-saying of something already said is simply not carried through. Words do not yet come to speech at all [*Das Wort kommt noch gar nicht zum Wort*], but it is precisely in failing us that they arrive at the first leap.

> This failing is the event as intimation and incursion of beyng [*Das Verschlagende ist das Ereignis als Wink und Anfall des Seyns*].
>
> This failing us is the inceptual condition for the self-unfolding possibility of an original (poetic) naming of beyng. [*Die Verschlagung ist die anfängliche Bedingung für die sich entfaltende Möglichkeit einer ursprünglichen—dichtenden—Nennung des Seyns*]
>
> Language and the great stillness, the simple nearness of the essence, and the bright remoteness of beings, when words once again are effective. When will such a time come?
>
> Restraint: creative withstanding in the abyss [*Die Verhaltenheit: das schaffende Aushalten im Ab-grund*]. (CP 36/30)

Words fail "originally." It is *in* the failure of words that an intimation of beyng is found. If there is to be a "naming of beyng," then the failure of the word is an "inceptual condition."

What kind of naming can have as its condition a *failure of the word*? That question can only be answered with reference to two central concepts within Heidegger's reflection on the language of the *Contributions*: silence as it plays a part in the locutions *Schweigen, Erschweigung, Verschweigung,* and the concept of *Stimmung* (mood, attunement, or disposition), specifically the "basic" or "grounding" disposition [*Grundstimmung*] of *restraint* [*Verhaltenheit*]. First, however, it is important to have more clarity about how exactly representation and proposition relate to the "failure" to say the truth of beyng. Or, perhaps better: how does beyng relate to the failure-to-say? The central question is: is Heidegger's goal to find a language that could (finally, successfully) say beyng? Or is he on the way to expose rather than amend a failure-to-say as belonging essentially to beyng?

DO THE *CONTRIBUTIONS* PRESERVE OR OVERCOME THE FAILURE TO SAY BEYNG?

Heidegger opens §276 of the *Contributions*, titled "Beyng and language" [*Das Seyn und die Sprache*], with a numbered series of headings, presumably those under which the problems surrounding the relation between beyng and language could or should be elaborated. The first two of these read: "1. Language as assertion and saying [*Die Sprache als Aussage und Sage*]. 2. The saying of being [*Das Sagen des Seyns*]." He proceeds to, first and foremost, make clear that for an "inceptual" determination of language [*anfängliche Bestimmung der Sprache*], it could never be what it has traditionally been for philosophy of language or linguistics: "a present-at-hand object" [*ein vorhandener Gegenstand*], one "alongside other objects" [*neben anderen Gegenstanden*]. Because language cannot be treated as a being, Heidegger states that the "first question" would have to be "the question of the relation of language to beyng." And even the question of a "relation" between language and beyng would still suffer from the risk of treating language and beyng as two beings that one could subsequently relate. For that reason, Heidegger asks instead: "How does language essentially occur in the essential occurrence of beyng?" [*wie west in der Wesung des Seyns die Sprache?*].

So Heidegger also wants to expose the limits of the propositional form, assertion, and representation without opposing an other or new language to it. The risk inherent in distinguishing representation (and its privileged form of the *Aussage*) from (thinking-)saying or from a "poietic"[5] language is that this very distinction risks falling prey to itself, as if asserting and thinking-saying are two languages that there are or that one has, two "beings" or else two "possibilities." Rather, assertion and saying are, so to speak, the linguistic analogues of the ontological difference: it is a matter of showing the saying *of* representation, or to recuperate language and to restore its relation to being. In fact, Heidegger criticizes the very notion of the ontological difference for this very reason in the *Contributions*. Though even in *Being and Time* being was always the being *of* beings, the very articulation of that difference risks going counter to what it wants to express: it may enlarge rather than reduce the risk of conceiving being as a being, because one finds it *next to* or *distinguished from* beings. For that reason, Heidegger states in the *Contributions* that it is no longer a matter of the ontological difference, but rather of showing the "simultaneity" [*Gleichzeitigkeit*] of beyng and beings.

In one sense, everything that Heidegger does has the form of a critique of representation and assertion. On the other hand, he stresses that there is no new or other language outside representation. Even the poets are delivered over, if not to representation as such (though often enough this too), then at least to the "old words." They do not speak an *other* language, but they reawaken a relation to beyng *in* (the "old") language. What I have called Heidegger's *recuperation* of language sets out to restore the relation of the proposition to beyng. In *Being and Time*, he did this by showing how the assertion is rooted (albeit as a "derivative" mode) in

Auslegung, *Rede*, and ultimately in *Sorge*, which is itself ultimately rooted in temporality. How does he do this in the *Contributions*?

In §41, Heidegger states that "every saying of beyng takes place in words and namings":

> Every saying of beyng is couched in words and namings which, as expressions of beyng, are liable to be misunderstood when taken in the sense of the everyday view of beings and thought exclusively in that sense. What this requires is not at all primarily a failure of the question (within the realm of the thoughtful interpretation of beyng); rather, the word itself already reveals something (something familiar) and thereby conceals that which is supposed to be brought into the open in thoughtful saying.
>
> Nothing can remove this difficulty. Indeed, the attempt to remove it already signifies misunderstanding of all saying of beyng. The difficulty must be accepted and must be grasped in its essential belonging (to the thinking of beyng). (*CP* 83/66)

The word, in its colloquial or ordinary sense and usage, is already a revealing word, and as such, in that very revealing, it is also concealing what would have to be brought to light in thinking-saying. To want to *erase* this "difficulty" would already be to negate what it would mean to say beyng. Rather, says Heidegger, this difficulty must be "taken up" and shown to belong essentially to the thinking of beyng.

The thinking of beyng thus does not set out to erase or amend the inability to say beyng. Rather, it sets out to bring that inability to light as an inability that does not "happen occasionally," but that is *original*.

The only way in which to bring to light this original inability is by being *unassertive*. That does not mean that one cannot utter assertions, nor is it merely negative. Its twofold "positive" sense is an essential part of the *Contributions*. The first is that for this reason the philosophical explication in the *Contributions* must be involved in a "logic of *silence*" [a *Sigetik*], by which Heidegger does not mean a lack of utterance or muteness. This "bearing silence" is the subject of the next two sections, where I look at Heidegger's Parmenides-lectures and his essay on the essential occurrence of truth [*Vom Wesen der Wahrheit*]. The second is that if a saying is to be distinguished from representation, but not by way of a new language, then it must be a matter of being differently *disposed* or *attuned* to the old one. Inceptual thinking, therefore, requires a *basic disposition* [*Grundstimmung*] without which nothing essential can come to pass ("If the basic disposition is lacking, then everything is a forced clatter of concepts and of the mere shells of words" [*ein erzwungenes Geklapper von Begriffen und Worthülsen*], CP 21/19). The basic disposition lies precisely in being unassertive; it is the dis-position of the exercise of restraint [*Verhaltenheit*]. Only in the disposition of restraint can "the highest thoughtful reticence" be accomplished, which is the subject of the final sections of this chapter.

BEARING SILENCE, WITHDRAWAL, AND ΛΗΘΗ IN THE *PARMENIDES*-LECTURES

It is now possible to see why Heidegger would ask: "Which saying effects the highest thoughtful reticence [*Erschweigung*]?" In §37, titled "Beyng and its bearing silence (Sigetics)" [*Das Seyn und seine Erschweigung (die Sigetik)*], Heidegger calls bearing silence the "logic" of philosophy, insofar as it asks the grounding question out of the other beginning. This means to inquire into the truth of the essential occurring [*Wesung*] of beyng. And that truth is "the intimating-resonating concealment (the mystery) of the event (the hesitant withholding)" [*die winkend-anklingende Verborgenheit (das Geheimnis) des Ereignisses (die zögernde Versagung)*] (CP 78/63). What does *Erschweigung* signify?

I have been stressing that the problem of the *Contributions* is a radicalization of *Being and Time*'s problem of being-in: of articulating and recognizing the limits of what one is essentially "in" and therefore cannot oversee or objectify. It is the problem of how to question the dominant or pervasive understanding of being, especially if that understanding always already controls the very means with which to question it. This is already evident from the reconceptualization of some central terms, notably the transformation of *Being and Time*'s existence or "standing-out" into the *Contributions*' *Inständigkeit* or "standing *in*." But nowhere is the problem of being-in more prominent than in the necessity to bear silence. Here it is clear how Heidegger is still a phenomenologist: a world of machination is characterized by the abandonment of being, yet that does not mean that beyng's essential occurrence takes place outside who or what "we" are, but that it takes place within machination precisely *as concealment*. This is what the opening question of *Being and Time* focused on: the unrepresentable because essentially implicit character of (our understanding of) being. Now that issue is radicalized by focusing on what self-withdraws as such: in a world of machination, one can only hope for an "intimation" of beyng, which is not some voice from an *other* world, but precisely what in this world resonates precisely *in, through, or as* hesitant withholding or concealment. The necessity to bear silence directly relates to the withdrawal of the truth of beyng, or beyng's essential occurrence [*Wesung*] *as* withdrawal. Here the "entanglement" of method and object is in full force: the *Contributions* do not attempt to perform an *Erschweigung* because it would "correspond" to the truth of beyng. Rather, it is only *in* reticence and in hesitant withholding (in *un*assertion) that the truth of beyng can resonate *as* what withholds itself in a world of machination.

This at least partly gives to philosophical explication a task of preserving concealment, a motif that can be traced throughout Heidegger's development and into the later works in which the theme of language becomes so prominent. In this context, it is helpful to look at Heidegger's 1942/43 lectures on Parmenides. There Heidegger confirms where the necessity to bear silence arises: "The proper relation to the rare is not to chase after it but to leave it at rest by acknowledging the concealment" [*Der gemäße Bezug zum Seltenen ist nicht die Jagd darnach, sondern das Ruhenlassen als das Anerkennen der Verbergung*] (*Par* 92/62). In that sentence, I would like to highlight the importance of "letting" [*Ruhenlassen*] and "acknowledging" [*Anerkennen*]. What is at issue here is how philosophical exposition, explication, disclosure, or showing relates to concealedness. Heidegger maintains here that exposition and explication do not simply *un*-conceal, are not opposed to concealment. In the same lecture, Heidegger stresses that this cannot be the case by describing the relation of forgetting to concealment. (This means that here we learn about how to read the "forgetfulness of being" with which *Being and Time* opens. Is that book the attempt to remedy that forgetfulness and replace it with a remembrance, or rather to first recognize and preserve that forgetting?)

Heidegger states in the Parmenides-lecture that with the transition of truth as unconcealment [ἀ-λήθεια] to correctness [ὁμοίωσις, likeness, being of the same kind, *adequatio*] a transformation coincides, beginning with Plato, of λήθη (concealedness) and the remembrance (ἀνάμνησις) that is its opposite. According to Heidegger, the event of withdrawing concealment of ἀλήθεια changes into the distinctly "human comportment of forgetting" (*Par* 124/185). In this way, what is *opposed* to λήθη [*was gegen die λήθη steht*] is now thought in terms of a "fetching back again" [*Wiederzurück-holen*] by man. However, Heidegger states that so long as the Platonic ἀνάμνησις is conceived in the (modern, subjective) sense of remembering and forgetting, it is not possible to appreciate the ground of its essential occurrence [*Wesensgrund*] (*Par* 185/125). Heidegger identifies this essential ground in the myth of λήθη at the end of Plato's *Republic* as the "hidden counter-essence to ἀλήθεια": "This withdrawing counter-essence to disclosedness 'withholds' unconcealedness but at the same time also holds in itself the essence of unconcealedness" [*Dieses entziehende und die Unverborgenheit »vor-enthaltende« Gegenwesen zur Entbergung enthält im voraus ihr Wesen*] (*Par* 127/189). As such, this counter-essence is "neither simply the opposite, nor the bare lack, nor the rejection of it as mere denial." Concealedness does not relate to unconcealedness as either opposite, rejection, lack, or denial. Instead:

> Λήθη, the oblivion of withdrawing concealment, is that withdrawal by means of which alone the essence of ἀλήθεια can be preserved and thus be and remain unforgotten. Thoughtless opinion maintains that something is preserved the soonest and is preservable the easiest when it is constantly at hand and graspable. But in truth, and that now means for us truth in the sense of the essence of unconcealedness, it is self-withdrawing concealment that in the highest way disposes human beings to preserving and to faithfulness. For the Greeks, the withdrawing and self-withdrawing concealment is the simplest of the simple, preserved for them in their experience of the unconcealed and therein allowed to come into presence. (*Par* 189/127)

Forgetfulness, now, if conceived in its original relation to concealment, is precisely that through which the essence of truth can be *preserved* and thus *remain unforgotten*. Heidegger distinguishes "preservation" here from keeping present at hand. He does this to indicate that forgetfulness *itself* can be a symptom or a telling phenomenon in which the truth (unconcealment) is preserved.

Two important consequences follow. First of all, the purport (already of *Being and Time*) is misunderstood as an attempt to deny or counter the forgetfulness of being.[6] Rather, it aims to recognize and preserve that forgetfulness as such, or interpret it originally. Heidegger's reconceptualization of the forgetfulness of being as the abandonment by being in the *Contributions* therefore serves to counter the possible association of forgetfulness with something that could be simply remedied or undone. This reinforces the sense that being's concealment not only resides in "our" forgetting, as something that "we" would somehow "do," but that this concealment must itself be conceived as an essential occurrence of beyng. Secondly, this means that philosophical explication is not *opposed* to the preservation of what is concealed. Such a preservation must be active in philosophical "showing." This is why Heidegger states, also in the Parmenides-lecture, that:

> The "open mystery" [*Das »offene Geheimnis«*] in the genuine and strict sense, on the contrary, occurs where the concealing of the mysterious is simply experienced as concealedness and is lodged in a historically arisen reticence. The openness of the open mystery does not consist in solving the mystery, thus destroying it, but consists in not touching the concealedness of the simple and essential and letting this concealedness alone in its appearance. (*Par* 93/63)

Rather than an active "construction" of sentences, words, or theses aiming at a kind of showing that would take its object out of concealment, philosophical showing, or explication now assumes the more passive form of not touching or a *letting*: "letting alone in its appearance." One *lets* or preserves (in the sense mentioned above) concealment precisely by *sheltering it in reticence*. It is in this "letting alone in its appearance" that we see the relation to the properly phenomenological motif of *Being and Time*, the method of which was guided by the attempt to let what shows itself be seen as it shows itself (explication as *sichzeigenlassen*).

In the *Contributions*, this terminology is still present, especially there where the role of *attunement* is discussed. Such a *letting* is by definition, if not unassertive, then at least a certain disposition or attunement of or to the assertion and assertiveness. Such unassertiveness is diffidence or *Scheu*, and it is when Heidegger discusses the role of diffidence for the saying of the *Contributions* that he states that "[f]rom diffidence in particular arises the necessity of reticence; the latter is what allows an essential occurrence of beyng as event and thoroughly disposes every comportment in the midst of beings and toward beings" (*CP* 15/15). The full extent of the role of *lassen* in philosophical explication does not come into comprehensive focus until the texts published under the heading of *Gelassenheit*, but the attunement of the *Contributions* prepares the way for those texts.[7]

The "mystery" [*Geheimnis*] in the quotation above refers to a term that is introduced in "On the Essence of Truth." Famously, Heidegger indicates in his "Letter on 'Humanism'" that it is with that text that something of the turning or *Kehre* from *Being and Time* to its projected third part, "Time and Being," becomes visible. What does this pivotal text between *Being and Time* and the *Contributions* then teach us about Heidegger's development concerning the language that would have to preserve concealment?

RETICENCE AND SHELTERING IN "ON THE ESSENCE OF TRUTH"

In the "Letter on 'Humanism,'" Heidegger states:

> The adequate carrying out and completion of this other thinking that abandons subjectivity is surely made more difficult by the fact that in the publication of *Being and Time* the first division of the first part, "Time and Being," was held back. Here everything is reversed [*Hier kehrt sich das Ganze um*]. The division in question was held back because thinking failed in the adequate saying of this turning [*im zureichenden Sagen dieser Kehre versagte*] and did not succeed with the help of the language of metaphysics. The lecture "On the Essence of Truth," thought out and delivered in 1930 but not printed until 1943, provides a certain insight into the thinking of the turning from "Being and Time" to "Time and Being." This turning is not a change of standpoint from *Being and Time*, but in it the thinking that was sought first arrives at the locality of that dimension out of which *Being and Time* is experienced, that is to say, experienced in the fundamental experience of the oblivion of being. ("LH" 327–28/249–50, translation amended, JdJ)

Heidegger's own additions to the text are as revealing as these words themselves. First of all, Heidegger states here that a thinking beyond subjectivity, as he attempts not merely to *describe* it but to *carry it out* [*Nach- und Mit-vollzug*] in *Being and Time*, was complicated because its third part was held back. In that third part (the title of which reverses the main order of the concepts of the first title—"Time and Being"), according to Heidegger, "the whole thing turns around" [*Hier kehrt sich das*

Ganze um]. In his notations, he further qualifies this "whole" as a turning in the "what and how of what is thoughtworthy and of thinking" [*im Was und Wie des Denkwürdigen und des Denkens*]. According to Heidegger, the third part was held back because thinking failed in saying this turning sufficiently and could not do so with the help of "the language of metaphysics." He specifies the sufficient saying [*zureichenden Sagen*] in his notations as *Sichzeigenlassen* (letting-itself-be-seen or "letting itself show" ["LH" 328n/250n]). The saying in question would then have to be a letting itself be seen of the turning from *Being and Time* to "Time and Being." What is it that thinking would have to let be seen?

Heidegger adds that it is the lecture "On the Essence of Truth" that gives a certain insight into the thinking that thinks the turning from "being and time" to "time and being." He then emphasizes that this is not a turning away from *Being and Time*. Rather, it is the transformation that is implied in and required by the very project (of surpassing subjectivity or metaphysics) that *Being and Time* inaugurated. When Heidegger states that the "standpoint" of *Being and Time* remains unchanged, he specifies in his notes that the standpoint of *Being and Time* is the "question of being." This question obviously remains *the* question for Heidegger. Instead, in that turning the thinking that was attempted arrives in a certain place [*Ortschaft*] of the dimension out of which *Being and Time* was experienced, and this experience is further qualified as the basic experience [*Grunderfahrung*] of the forgottenness of being [*Seinsvergessenheit*].

Everything comes together as he adds this remarkable string of words in his notations: "Forgottenness—Λήθη—concealing—withdrawal—expropriation: event of appropriation [*Vergessenheit—Λήθη—Verbergung—Entzug—Enteignis: Ereignis*]" ("LH" 328n/250n). This movement, path, or course exemplarily embodies the trajectory from *Being and Time* to the *Contributions* by way of the different modifications of concealment. What a sufficient saying would have to let be seen is concealment as such. It is in that sense that transformations of both the thoughtworthy and the thinking itself are demanded by *Being and Time*'s premise (the premise of the forgottenness of being). It is indeed the lecture on how truth occurs essentially ("On the Essence of Truth" [*Vom Wesen der Wahrheit*]) that directs the explicit attention to concealment, Λήθη or untruth.[8] I therefore now turn to that lecture.

"On the Essence of Truth" opens with a discussion of truth as it is "vulgarly" thought and intends to explicate what is implicit in that conception. Heidegger seems to start at a familiar point, with truth as correspondence [*Übereinstimmung*]. Where some would perhaps expect a more straightforward critique of this notion, Heidegger is more sensitive here to the sense of *Stimmen* implied in it (to which I return below—it has the sense of correctness as well as of tuning; *Stimmung* also translates as "attunement" or "mood," which is essential for the *Contributions*). Heidegger reconstructs in a now familiar way how truth as correspondence [*Übereinstimmung*] or correctness [*Richtigkeit*] is possible. Heidegger states that for a true proposition to be such that it says things as they in fact are ["in such a way as": *so-wie*], the "thing" must already be conceived as an object to which a sentence could *correspond*. In this way, Heidegger states that what makes it possible for a proposition to be true in a colloquial sense is if the essence of that proposition already consists in a "letting stand over against" or "letting stand in opposition" of the thing as object [*Entgegenstehenlassen des Dinges als Gegenstand*]. Only in such letting stand in opposition can there be a "correspondence," which is now conceived as "re-presentational approximation" [*vor-stellende Angleichung*]. But in recognizing this, the proposition is already no longer the locus of truth. Truth does not essentially occur in the proposition, but in the "standing open" of the relation [*offenständigkeit des Verhaltens*]. The "thing" must precisely be pre-given [*Vorgeben*] *as* object; it must already be *disclosed* as such or revealed. What follows in the text is a meditation on the essential nature and possibility of such revealing.

Heidegger now states that if the proposition is not the locus of truth, *Entgegenstehenlassen* must rather be understood to be *Seinlassen des Seienden* (this is also the transition from a *representational* language to an *explicative* language, from letting-stand-over-against to letting-be-seen). The openness of the open [*das "Da" ist, was es ist*] consists in the *revealing* of beings as such [*die Entbergung des Seienden als eines solchen*]. The dynamic of *Entbergen* (revealing) and *verbergen* (concealing) is in the *Contributions* picked up under the general heading of *Bergung*, which can be translated very well as "sheltering." Sheltering conveys exactly what is at stake: what is sheltered is both preserved and concealed.

Here is the point that Heidegger is after: there can be no *Entbergen*, no revealing, without something being concealed [*verbergen*]. There is an original, not a merely contingent or posterior, relation between truth (unconcealment) and concealment: "The letting-be is in itself simultaneously a concealing" [*Das Seinlassen ist in sich zugleich ein verbergen*]. Indeed, what Heidegger is after in his text is to conceive concealment as basic or grounding occurrence [*Verbergung als Grundgeschehnis*]. Or: truth's ownmost untruth, the untruth that essentially occurs in truth [*die dem Wahrheitswesen eigenste und eigentliche Unwahrheit*]. Indeed, to the extent that the being-revealed of beings depends on the concealment of being as such, Heidegger calls untruth "older" than openness (I note in parentheses that this is exactly the terminology that Derrida will use when he states that "in a certain and very strange way," différance "is 'older' than the ontological difference or than the truth of Being." I return to this notion at length in chapter 9.) Another way of putting it would be to say that the movement by which beings come to stand in the open as beings (or, to use the terminology of "The Origin of the Work of Art," that also finds its way into the *Contributions*: the movement of the *Lichtung* of beings) is reconceived as the movement of the concealment of the concealed [*die Verbergung des Verborgenen*]. The concealment of the concealed is what Heidegger calls *das Geheimnis* (the secret, often translated as the "mystery," that we already encountered in the quote from the Parmenides-lecture). If the concealment of the concealed is not a posterior but an original occurrence, then (and this is what Heidegger does in the *Contributions*) the secret from "On the Essence of Truth" must be reconceptualized as the *self-concealment* of being.

There is hardly a better description of what Heidegger conveys under the heading of *Ereignis* than that one. *Ereignis* is the movement by which being withdraws itself, such that beings "come into their own" or become what they are (precisely: beings), or: the appropriation of beings in the self-withdrawal [*Entzug*] of being.

In the "Letter on 'Humanism,'" Heidegger called the forgetfulness of being the basic or grounding experience [*Grunderfahrung*] of *Being and Time*. I would say that this forgetfulness, reconceived as abandonment by being in machination, also forms the distress or plight [*Not*] out of which the *Contributions* were born. My claim has been that it was not Heidegger's contention that we should get "out of" machination. "On the Essence of Truth" confirms this: the "untruth" and forgetfulness that essentially accompany Dasein's fallenness in *Being and Time*, as it results essentially from the history of the West or of metaphysics, is in "On the Essence of Truth" reconceptualized as "errancy" [*Irre*]. Because untruth has now so explicitly been recognized as originary, Heidegger emphasizes that man cannot simply *not* err: "Humans err. Human beings do not merely stray into errancy. They are always astray in errancy" [*Der Mensch irrt. Der Mensch geht nicht erst in die Irre. Er geht nur immer in der Irre*] ("ET" 196/150). This means that *not* erring is not a possibility. It is not possible to break through the forgetfulness of being by asking the question of being. For man to be man, being must withdraw. Must man then forever remain wholly blind to being and its *Ereignis*? No, what is at stake is not to conceive the breakthrough as a movement away (away from oneself, from "man," from metaphysics, from what one is and what one is "in") and toward an outside or an other (an other position, place, language, world, etc.). Instead, Heidegger states that the only possibility of not erring is *to experience errancy as such*: "by experiencing errancy itself and by not mistaking the mystery of Da-sein" [*indem man die Irre selbst erfährt und sich nicht versieht am Geheimnis des Da-seins*]. To experience errancy is not to remove it, but rather to show and preserve, to *shelter* it.

This is directly related to the question of a "sufficient saying" and the need to bear silence. The only way the text itself could participate in the essential occurrence of truth is if in some way or to some extent it would also conceal, or "name by unsaying." This is confirmed in the Remark [*Anmerkung*] that Heidegger appended to the text in 1949. There he reflects on the language of the text itself, its mode of presentation, and the kind of saying that would have to be able to articulate the necessary turning. That turning is now—instead of as the movement from *Being and Time* to "Time and Being"—articulated in the form of a sentence that would constitute the "answer" to the question wherein the essential occurrence or the essence of truth lies. It reads: "*the essence of truth is the truth of essence*" [*das Wesen der Wahrheit ist die Wahrheit des Wesens*] ("ET" 198/153). In the Remark, Heidegger calls truth "sheltering that clears as the fundamental trait of Being" [*lichtendes Bergen als Grundzug des Seyns*]. He therefore reformulates the sentence as: "Sheltering that clears is—i.e., lets essentially unfold—accordance between knowledge and beings" [*Das lichtende Bergen ist, d.h. läßt Wesen, die Übereinstimmung zwischen Erkenntnis und Seiendem*]. He states that the sentence is "not dialectical" or in fact a proposition. Rather, the "answer to the question of truth" requires:

> the saying of a turning [*die Sage einer Kehre*] within the history of Beyng. Because sheltering that clears belongs to it [*Weil zu ihm lichtendes Bergen gehört*], Beyng appears originarily in the light of concealing withdrawal [*im Licht des verbergenden Entzugs*]. The name of this clearing [*Lichtung*] is ἀλήθεια. ("ET" 201/154)

Answering the question of truth would require saying a turning to which belongs the concealing-withdrawal of beyng. Heidegger adds that (just like with *Being and Time*) a second section in which things would be turned around [*Von der Wahrheit des Wesens*] was projected but held back for reasons indicated in the "Letter on 'Humanism.'"

What is Heidegger doing here? One could view this holding-back as resulting from a failure of the "too metaphysical" language of the text. But now we come to an absurd point: wasn't "On the Essence of Truth" the text Heidegger himself indicated—*in* the "Letter on 'Humanism,'" no less!—to be the text that shows something of how the thinking of the turning would have to be carried out?

One can only make sense of these remarks if one reevaluates the meaning of failure and the status of the remark that a text is "still too metaphysical." Heidegger himself gives some hints in the very same Remark.

Insofar as the third part is held back, insofar as it "leaves open the decisive question," the lecture has the appearance of remaining within the orbit of metaphysics [*in der Bahn der Metaphysik*]. And yet, according to Heidegger, "in its decisive steps" it belongs also to the overcoming of metaphysics. The decisive steps are the transformation of the question of truth from a question of correspondence into, ultimately, a question of concealment and errancy. In other words: the overcoming of metaphysics is not assertive or direct. Heidegger states that not only have, as in *Being and Time*, all anthropology and subjectivity been left behind, but the *very way, path, or proceeding*; the *movement* of the lecture [*der Gang des Vortrags*], in the very *sequence of its steps* [*die Schrittfolge*], appropriates itself to think from "this other ground" (from "Da-sein" rather than the "man" of subjectivity, anthropology, or metaphysics):

> The *course* [*Schrittfolge*] of the questioning is intrinsically the *path* of a thinking that, instead of furnishing representations and concepts, experiences and tests itself as a transformation of its relatedness to Being [*sich als Wandlung des Bezugs zum Sein erfährt und erprobt*]. ("ET" 202/154, my italics, JdJ)

What the text does, instead of providing concepts and representations, is attempt to *carry out, enact,* or *effectuate* a transformed relation to being. One finds this same thought in the *Contributions*, when Heidegger stresses that the more necessary "the thoughtful speaking about beyng" [das denkerische Sagen vom Seyn] becomes, the more unavoidable it becomes to bear silence with regard to the truth of beyng *through the course* of questioning [*umso unumgänglicher wird das Erschweigen der Wahrheit des Seyns durch den Gang des Fragens*].

THE PHILOSOPHICAL NECESSITY TO BE UNASSERTIVE: *STIMMUNG* AND ITS DISTINCTION FROM *ERLEBNIS*

Returning now to §37 of the *Contributions*, I left it by concluding that the saying (the letting-be-shown, the language) of the *Contributions* must bear silence; what is to be shown is what withdraws as such. Heidegger cross-references that section of the *Contributions* with a pivotal point in the lecture course on Nietzsche that is called "Nietzsche's Fundamental Metaphysical Position" [*Nietzsches metaphysische Grundstellung im abendländischen Denken. Die ewige Wiederkehr des Gleichen*]. There Heidegger articulates how, with Nietzsche, the metaphysics of the guiding question comes to an end. This does not mean that nothing after Nietzsche can come to pass, because it is in the occurrence of this bringing-to-an-end that the question of an *other* beginning is made possible. Such questioning Heidegger there calls a thinking of "the world as such." He explains that truly thinking the (this, our) world implies thinking its limits and thus a thinking "out beyond the world, and so at the same time back to it" (*NI* 415/207). This characteristic of the relation to a world that is no mere object *for* thought but that one is essentially "in" recalls the ec-static character of Dasein from *Being and Time* and what is called *Inständigkeit* in the *Contributions*. It is a thinking "in the direction of that sphere within which a world becomes world." Of the articulation of the thinking of that sphere, Heidegger now states:

> Wherever that sphere is not incessantly called by name, called aloud, wherever it is held silently in the most interior questioning, it is thought most purely and profoundly. For what is held in silence is genuinely preserved; as preserved it is most intimate and actual. [. . .]
>
> Supremely thoughtful utterance does not consist simply in growing taciturn when it is a matter of saying what is properly to be said; it consists in saying the matter in such a way that it is named in nonsaying. The utterance of thinking is a telling silence [*das Sagen des Denkens ist ein Erschweigen*]. Such utterance corresponds to the most profound essence of language, which has its origin in silence. As one in touch with telling silence, the thinker, in a way peculiar to him, rises to

the rank of a poet; yet he remains eternally distinct from the
poet, just as the poet in turn remains eternally distinct from
the thinker. (*NI* 423/207–8)

So Heidegger distinguishes bearing silence [*Erschweigen*] from a simple
muteness or lack of utterance [*verschweigen*]. Instead, "the saying of thinking is a bearing silence" [*das Sagen des Denkens ist ein Erschweigen*] means
that at stake is "to say it in such a way that it is named in not-saying"
[*es so zu sagen, das es im Nichtsagen genannt ist*]. Here the thinker rises to
the rank of the poet, though he remains eternally distinct from him.[9]
So to bear silence is not to be silent. In that sense, David Farrell Krell's
translation of *Erschweigung* as "telling silence" is potentially misleading.
By a "telling silence" we usually mean a somehow significant muteness.
Instead, *Erschweigung* is a saying, but a saying that names by not-saying; so
one that speaks differently or otherwise, but speaks nonetheless.

It is a saying, thus, that relates in a different way to its "object."
That is why Vallega-Neu coined the apt phrase *poietic* saying: the saying
stands in a productive rather than a representative relation to "what" it
says. How does this work? This is where the concept of *Stimmung* is vital.

If it is not through a new, other, or different language; or through
muteness or a lack of language, but through a recuperation of the "old"
language, that the possibility of an other beginning comes into view, then
this is possible only if one has a different attitude toward ("one's own,"
the "old") language. This attitude is called *Stimmung*; attunement, mood, or
disposition. *Stimmung* is what makes the difference between representational
and poietic or enacting language. I have already indicated that Heidegger
states that without what he calls the *basic disposition* [*Grundstimmung*] of
restraint or reticence [*Verhaltenheit*, nothing essential can come to pass.

With the concept of *Stimmung*, Heidegger introduces a dimension
that is irreducible to the content of propositions. Rather than finding new
words, it is a matter of being *attuned* differently to what will otherwise
always only be "mere propositions." *Stimmung* is alternately translated as
mood, attunement, and disposition. It might seem, then, that the mood
introduces a dimension that exceeds the propositional; mood is beyond
the limits of what can be propositionally represented. To some extent,
one cannot avoid speaking of limit and excess in such a way. But the
function of the basic disposition is such that only *in* or *through* it, the
language of beings can be said *as* the language of beyng.[10] This means

that rather than denote a realm outside the propositional, the attunement is an attunement *of* or *to* the propositional, such that its relation to being can be restored. For this reason it is helpful, before studying the basic disposition in more detail, to see how Heidegger distinguishes it from what is vulgarly conceived as a non-propositional "realm" outside of or opposed to language: that of *experience*.

The Excess Beyond the Propositional: Erlebnis

It is the very metaphysical nature of language that makes it so that the limit to thought, language, or understanding is usually conceived in terms of an outside or a beyond. There are many colloquial names for those things that, as we say, defy comprehension, description, or representation: one can think of a singular experience that does not let itself be represented; a "feeling" or an "emotion" (such as mourning or ecstasy, when we say—and I insist that we *say* it—that "there are no words"). Alternatively, one can think of the "body" and the physical; the "aesthetic" or the sublime. What the vulgar conceptions of these phenomena have in common is that they are formulated as the beyond or outside of comprehension (the body *and not* the mind; feelings *and not* understanding; emotional *and not* rational; the experience *and not* the mere representation). However, in that very *opposition* to comprehension or description, these conceptions betray something of the structure of the secret or mystery that belongs to them. Heidegger gathers this general structure under the heading of *Erlebnis* ("lived experience").

With *Erlebnis*, Heidegger targets the way in which the "mysterious," while apparently opposing the calculative rationality of machination, nevertheless belongs to machination in virtue of being precisely its "mere opposite." *Erlebnis* thus signifies *the domestication of the mysterious within machination*.

The primary characteristic of machination is questionlessness: nothing is essentially question-worthy because everything can be "done" as long as one "wills" it. But that very will has determined beforehand, according to Heidegger, what counts as possibilities for action (what can be projected or planned). That is to say: what can be represented as a possibility—machination signifies the "interpretation of beings as representable and represented": "beings as such are the represented, and only the represented is a being" [*Auslegung des Seienden als des Vor-stellbaren und Vor-gestellten; das*

Seiende als solches ist das Vor-gestellte, und nur das Vorgestellte ist seiend] (*CP* 108–9/86). "Representable" means, according to Heidegger, "accessible in opinion and calculation" and "providable in production and implementation" (*CP* 109/86). So machination signifies the will that wills a certain choice from among the "options" that are (already) present-at-hand, that have been limited beforehand as options by their representability to that will. It is for that reason that Heidegger stressed that for machination, nothing is essentially "impossible." Machination may know "problems" and "difficulties," but only as "an impetus to progress" [*Anstoß in den Fortschritt*] (*CP* 109/86). If it knows of a *limit,* it knows it only as a motivation to go "further" and "make progress."

Now, according to Heidegger, *Erlebnis* is the domesticated guise of the question-worthy within the questionlessness of machination. According to Heidegger, *Erlebnis* stands for the domesticated mystery: the "exciting," the "provocative," and the "stunning," as they are "necessitated" by machination:

> [. . .] an ever greater, ever more unprecedented, and ever more loudly proclaimed "lived experience" [*Erlebnis*]. "Lived experience," understood here as the basic form of representation belonging to the machinational and the basic from of abiding therein, is the publicness (accessibility to everyone) of the mysterious, i.e., the exciting, provocative, stunning, and enchanting—all of which are made necessary by what is machinational. (*CP* 109/87)

Thus, *Erlebnis* stands for the "enchantment that is carried out precisely by the disenchantment itself." It is *as* machination's opposite that *Erlebnis* belongs to it. And to the extent that *Erlebnis* monopolizes the space "outside" of machination, it makes impossible the recognition of machination itself. In that sense, machination is "concealed" by *Erlebnis*. Such is the pervasive nature of machination, that it withdraws behind the *Erlebnis,* which "seems to be its extreme opposite and yet which completely and utterly remains under its domination." The more decisive machination hides itself in that way, "all the more does it press toward the predominance of that which seems completely opposed to its essence and yet is of its essence, i.e., toward *lived experience* [*Erlebnis*]" (*CP* 127/100).

At one particular point in the text, it may seem possible to see in *Erlebnis* a tiny gesture of hope in the world of machination. The passage concerns the origin of *Erlebnis*, in §51. Heidegger there suggests that the need for such a domesticized question-worthiness stems from the fact that "this destruction of question-worthiness, even in the age of the complete absence of questioning, is perhaps at bottom not fully possible" (*CP* 109/87). But what reveals itself here is the opposite, the most deeply cynical part of the pervasive rationality of machination—the "law" that it is only affirmed by the gesture that seems to go against it: "the more lived experience is unconditionally prescriptive for correctness and truth [. . .], all the more hopeless does it become that from here a knowledge of machination as such could be acquired." Vallega-Neu states the predicament well:

> What is most frightening in this occurrence is that the abandonment of being is masked by an occurrence which appears to be most alive. For Heidegger, this "life" engendered in lived experience suffocates any need to question be-ing. Beings are not only calculable and producible—thus satisfying our need for security—but are also pleasurable and exciting—thus satisfying our need for discovery and novelty. What else should one look for?[11]

The Excess Within the Propositional: Stimmung

I started the discussion of "experience" to clarify something about the way *Stimmung* (disposition or attunement) functions for Heidegger as a crucial element that exceeds representationality, propositionality, and determination. Its very articulation thus presents a fundamental problem: "[. . .] the clarification of a disposition is never a guarantee that it is actually *disposing* instead of merely being represented" (*CP* 15/14). To understand what role *Stimmung* plays, it is essential to realize that with attunement Heidegger is precisely not after what is outside, beyond, or in opposition to the proposition, as that would revert right back to that very propositionality. Instead, attunement is essentially attunement *to* the proposition. It names a change in attitude toward the propositional. The considerations about *Erlebnis* should therefore have made two things clear: (1) that attunement does not simply exceed the proposition as its beyond or outside, and (2) that Heidegger's references to disposition and attunement cannot be interpreted in the conventional sense of moods, feelings, or experiences, insofar as the vulgar understanding of them contrasts or opposes them to what is sayable, thinkable, understandable, or conceptual.

So if not as the outside of propositionality, then how does *Stimmung* name a limit of representation?

In the longish fifth section of the book (titled "For the few—For the rare" [*Für die Wenigen—Für die Seltenen*]), Heidegger introduces the concept of a basic or grounding disposition, attunement, or mood [*Grundstimmung*]. He distinguishes several modes of attunement, and this gives his initial discussion the air of hierarchy and systematicity, but that specific hierarchy never returns in the remainder of the *Contributions*. He states that the basic disposition that is to guide the thinking of an other beginning "oscillates" or sways [*schwingt*] in or between the following moods: "shock" [*das Erschrecken*], "restraint" [*die Verhaltenheit*] and "diffidence" [*die Scheu*]. Though in this apparently hierarchical initial analysis he calls *die Scheu* (diffidence) the basic disposition, elsewhere it is *die Verhaltenheit* (restraint) that he clearly marks as the basic disposition. I shortly consider how Heidegger conceives these moods.

According to Heidegger, shock and restraint both name modes of attunement that belong to intimation [*die Ahndung*]. I have already discussed the importance of intimation: relating to beyng is not a simple or realizable possibility, as reality, possibility, goal, will, and all other concepts implied in such a "possibility" belong to metaphysics. If beyng is to nevertheless "resonate" in a world of machination, if one is to have an intimation of beyng, then it does so only in the recognition of the very limits of machination—of what one is or is essentially in. The modality in which this occurs, the mood that embodies the recognition of these limits, is shock and restraint.

Shock, as the intimation of an other beginning, is what Heidegger contrasts to the basic disposition of the first beginning, namely "wonder" (θαυμάζειν; the mood in which, according to both Plato and Aristotle, philosophy begins).[12] Instead, the intimation of beyng in the recognition of one's limits is first and foremost, according to Heidegger, the shock of being "taken aback [. . .] from the familiarity of customary behavior." This is a mood of shock because "what was hitherto familiar shows itself as what alienates and also fetters." Heidegger specifies the kind of shock he has in mind: "Shock lets us be taken aback by the very fact [. . .] that beings are and that being has abandoned and withdrawn itself from all 'beings' and from whatever appeared as a being" (*CP* 15/14). Again we see the same dynamic: shock is not the experience of, for example, the contingency or relativity of the world or the possibility of a *different* world. Rather, it is a recognition of what one's world is (the very fact *that* beings *are*) and what is withheld in it (that being has abandoned and withdrawn itself from all beings). It is to recognize the withdrawal of beyng *in* the being of beings.

This is why Heidegger stresses that shock is not a merely negative mood, a "mere shrinking back" or "bewildered surrender." This is so because shock *reveals* the withdrawal of beyng:

> [. . .] because in this shock it is precisely the self-concealing of beyng that opens up, and because beings themselves as well as the relation to them want to be preserved, this shock is joined from within by its own most proper "will," and that is what is here called restraint. (*CP* 15/14)

What I would like to call attention to here is Heidegger's emphasis that beings as well as the relation to them "want to be preserved" [*bewahrt sein will*]. Heidegger frequently plays on the relation between *Wahrheit* (truth) and *bewahren* (preservation) to show that it is a matter of restoring the relation of beings to beyng and of recognizing beyng's withdrawal *in* the being of beings or the fact that beings are. The "willingness" to recognize the withdrawal of beyng in the being of beings, Heidegger now calls *Verhaltenheit* (restraint). This is why he calls restraint "the pre-disposition of readiness for the refusal as gift" [*die Vor-stimmung der Bereitschaft für die Verweigerung als Schenkung*] (*CP* 15/14). That is: it is the readiness or willingness to *recognize* what withholds or withdraws itself; to interpret what refuses itself *as* a gift.

Gift here is *Schenkung* (the occurrence of giving or "bestowal"), which, occasionally as *Verschenkung*, never occurs in the *Contributions* without conjunction with terms such as *Verweigerung* (refusal), *das Sichentziehende* (the self-withholding), *Versagung* (both self-refusal and, literally, refusal-to-say), *Zögerung* (hesitation), or *sich-verbergen* (self-concealing).[13] In "Time and Being," it is through the *Es gibt* that Heidegger questions being and time. After all, one says: *Es gibt Zeit* and *Es gibt Sein* ("TB" 4/5). These are not just propositions: "we must also consider the possibility that, contrary to all appearances, in saying 'there is (it gives) being,' 'there is (it gives) time,' we are not dealing with statements that are always fixed in the sentence structure of the subject-predicate relation." In attempting to identify originally what is expressed in these sentences, the identification of the "Es" seems to resist the possibility of identifying, as one does normally in and through propositions, the "subject" to which one could append a predicate. Heidegger concludes that the *Es gibt* must be understood "in the light of the kind of giving that belongs to it: giving as destiny" [*aus der Art des Gebens her, das zu ihm gehört: das Geben als Geschick*] ("TB" 19/19). What Heidegger calls *Geschick* is "[a] giving which gives only its gift, but in the giving holds itself back and withdraws" ("TB" 8/8). Instead of *identifying* (clarifying, determining, bringing to light) the *Es*, it rather would be a matter of recognizing it *as* what withdraws *in* a giving. If one were to push the question of the *Es*, of *what it is* that gives in the giving, then there can only be an answer that is necessarily unsatisfying from a standpoint of logic. The answer is *Ereignis*. It is unsatisfying to the extent that, if we were to ask further *what Ereignis is*, a certain turning takes place. Because *Ereignis* was the name for the dynamic that was to account for the "is" of the *Es gibt,* the question of what *Ereignis* itself "is" would introduce a circle.

To this circle corresponds the point at which, in the words of the "Letter on 'Humanism,'" "the whole thing is turned around [*Hier kehrt sieh das Ganze um*]" ("LH" 328/250, translation amended, JdJ). The answer to the question can only have a form that exceeds the way in which propositions have sense. The turning around is not only already evident in the turning from *Being and Time* to "Time and Being," or in the turning that produces the (non-)proposition that "The essence of truth is the truth of essence" ("ET" 198/153). Heidegger states it like this:

> What remains to be said? Only this: Appropriation appropriates [*Das Ereignis ereignet*]. Saying this, we say the Same in terms of the Same about the Same [*Damit sagen wir vom Selben her auf das Selbe zu das Selbe*]. To all appearances, all this says nothing. It does indeed say nothing so long as we hear a mere sentence in what was said, and expose that sentence to the cross-examination of logic. ("TB" 24–25/24)

From the perspective of logic, nothing has been said. It is only *in the course of questioning*, in its *movement*, that something will have been shown. This requires no longer hearing mere propositions in what is said, that is, a different *attunement* to what is said.

Returning to the *Contributions*, restraint thus names the willingness to recognize, or the openness to, what gives itself *as* or *in* its refusal, withholding, concealment, or withdrawal.[14] In that way, the "being taken aback" of restraint is at the same time a turning *toward* [*Zukehr zu*] the "hesitant self-withholding" [*zögernden Sichversagen*] *as* the essential occurrence of beyng [*der Wesung des Seyns*]. Heidegger goes on to say that in this way restraint determines or attunes [*bestimmt*] the "style" of inceptual thinking. Later, Heidegger calls the "style" of *Verhaltenheit* the "law" of the carrying out of truth [*vollzugsgesetz der Wahrheit*] insofar as truth has the sense of "sheltering in beings" [*im Sinne der Bergung in das Seiende*]. Indeed the "recuperation" of beings or of their relation to the truth of beyng is such that the task consists in showing how the truth of beyng is sheltered *in* beings.

CONCLUSION

I have waited until my conclusions to present the elliptical epigraph with which the *Contributions* opens. I give the German original:

> Hier wird das in langer Zögerung
> Verhaltene andeutend festgehalten
> Als Richtscheit einer Ausgestaltung

What was held back [*Verhaltene*—we recognize the basic disposition] in long hesitation is held fast here indicatively [*andeutend*] as the straightedge of a configuration. *Ausgestaltung* is a configuration or a certain arrangement, a shape of exposition. So what will function as determining the *Contributions*' setup, determining the shape of the exposition of what is to be said, is the reticent [*das Verhaltene*]; that which was held back. What was held back in long hesitation is here held fast, but only indicatively. So what hesitatingly does not give itself is both what is "indicated" here (the "subject" or "object" of the investigation; that toward which it is directed), but also what indicates or points the way, what will form the guiding criterion for the shape of the exposition (the principle of its "method"). The hesitant or reticent is therefore both the "object" of the investigation and what guides its "method" or the shape of its exposition.

In the previous chapter, I showed how *Being and Time*—even if the style and systematicity of that work are so different from that of the *Contributions*—anticipates this reticence and this hesitation. We must take Heidegger very seriously when he stresses that the saying of *Ereignis* is always only preliminary and anticipatory [*vor-läufig, vor-sichtig*] and that inceptual thinking is an "attempt" and that it is inherently "futural" [*kün-*

ftig, Zu-künftig]. Heidegger's thinking is not transitional because it at some point *arrives* at a realizable future; it is *inherently* preliminary, anticipatory, transitional, and an "attempt" because it *structurally* relates to our limits or to what is irreducible to prevailing norms.[15]

Whoever has spent serious time thinking through all that Heidegger attempts in the elliptical *Contributions* will have trouble suppressing an incredulous smile in reading Heidegger's remark at the start of the next big beyng-historical work (the 1941/42 *Das Ereignis*) that the presentation of the *Contributions* itself is "in places too didactical."[16] Heidegger's development did not consist in finding a language that would finally succeed in speaking out of the truth of beyng, but rather in recognizing and preserving an inherent failure-to-say with respect to beyng. Such a failure-to-say is anticipated in *Being and Time*, and the performative complexity of such a showing can be recognized in progressive levels of complexity throughout Heidegger's development. That Heidegger recognized and preserved a certain failure-to-say as the very to-be-said can be seen in the progressive importance of withdrawal or concealment. This starts with *Being and Time*'s (un)concealment, moving through the *nichtende Nichts* of the early 1930s to the *Erschweigung* and *Verhaltenheit* of the *Contributions* and into the *Entzug* and ultimately *Enteignis* of the works after the *Contributions*.

That does not mean that everything is already there in *Being and Time*, but the thought of "being-in" does anticipate the later thought of *Ereignis*. Consider how Heidegger says it in "Time and Being":

> Thus appropriated, man belongs to appropriation. [*So geeignet gehört der Mensch in das Ereignis*] This belonging lies in the assimilation that distinguishes appropriation. [*Dieses Gehören beruht in der das Ereignis auszeichnenden Vereignung*] By virtue of this assimilation, man is admitted to the appropriation. *This is why we can never place appropriation in front of us*, neither *as something opposite* us nor as something all-encompassing. This is why thinking which *represents* and *gives account* [*das vorstellend-begründende Denken*] corresponds to appropriation as little as does the saying that merely states [*das nur aussagende Sagen*]. ("TB" 24/23, my emphasis, JdJ)

It is in virtue of man's "being-in," his inextricability from the "object of investigation," that no counter-positioning, reversal, representation, or proposition can be adequate to what is to be said. Heidegger states there that the "basic experience" [*Grunderfahrung*] of the *Contributions* is "not the expression, the proposition, or consequently the principle" [*nicht die Aussage, der Satz, und demzufolge der Grundsatz*], but rather "the holding itself back of restraint." But that restraint must nevertheless be brought "to word." When reticence is brought to word, according to Heidegger, what is said is always *Ereignis* [*ist das Gesagte immer das Ereignis*].

> [To] understand this saying means to carry out the projection and leap of knowledge into the event. The saying that bears silence is what grounds [*Das Sagen als Erschweigen gründet*]. Its word is not by any means merely a sign for something quite other. What it names is what is meant, but the "meaning" assigns only as Da-sein, i.e., in thinking and questioning. [*Was es nennt, ist gemeint. Aber das »Meinen« eignet nur zu als Da-sein und d. h. denkerisch im Fragen*]. (CP 80/64)

"What is said is what is meant." Here Heidegger identifies a norm of exactness in the saying of *Ereignis* that is different from the calculative exactness of science, technology, or machination. This saying of what is meant does not consist in the articulation of a correct representation.

In the *Contributions*, this becomes explicit when Heidegger identifies the "failure of the word" as an "inceptual condition," which necessitates a *Sigetik* or a "logic of silence" as the proper form of philosophical exposition. Such "bearing silence" [*Erschweigung*] does not consist in a new language, a move away from the old one, or even in muteness. Nor does it consist in a silent and mysterious "experience" that would be *opposed* to what can be expressed theoretically (the "mysterious" *Erlebnis* that, because it is opposed to calculative rationality, is in fact the complicit counterpart of machination). It rather consists in a transformation of one's relation *to* (one's own, the "old") language, in a different *attunement* to it. That attunement is reticence or restraint, the unassertiveness that is able to recognize the movement of showing *in* or *through* the "old" assertions.

What I have been arguing is that such a different attunement does not lead to "new insights" or "possibilities," but precisely to impossibility or to an experience of limits. Heidegger is very explicit on that point: it is not that in machination nothing essential is *possible* anymore, but that for machination nothing essential is still *impossible* (CP 108/86). In the age of complete questionlessness, it is "above all" the "concealment of the inceptual" that must be "preserved" [*Vor allem muß die Verborgenheit des Anfänglichen gewahrt werden*] (CP 188/148).

PART IV

OF DERRIDA'S HEIDEGGERS

Style, Affirmation, Responsibility

CHAPTER 8

THE QUESTION OF STYLE

Heidegger, Nietzsche, and the
Heterogeneity of the Text

> Is this unavoidable? Can one escape this program? No sign would suggest it, at least neither in "Heideggerian" discourses nor in "anti-Heideggerian" discourses. Can one transform this program? I do not know. In any case, it will not be avoided all at once and without reconnoitering it right down to its most tortuous ruses and most subtle resources.
>
> —Derrida (*Of Spirit*)

On the one hand, the ambiguity of Derrida's relation to Heidegger structurally resembles his relation to Hegel. This is the subject of the present chapter. There are several different Heideggers at work in Derrida's text. Even though Derrida shows some of them to be subtler than others, it is essential for Derrida's modus operandi that he shows how these different tracks imply each other, meaning that it can not be a matter of a simple choice between these different Heideggers.

I show this through a reading of Derrida's 1978 *Spurs: Nietzsche's Styles* [*Éperons: Les styles de Nietzsche*]. That text is a movement through a multitude of positions pro- and contra-Heidegger, and it is also a text *on* the limits of oppositions and reversals, especially on the place of Nietzsche's often venomous and bombastic positions within the broader movement of his writing. The question is whether Heidegger's interpretation of Nietzsche, as it is so often accused of doing, reduces the "plurality of styles" that Derrida shows to be essential to Nietzsche's writings. *Spurs* deals with the problem of reversal, opposition, and style through a discussion of Nietzsche's writings on "woman." I show why Derrida argues that Nietzsche's numerous instances of vehement antifeminism are "congruent" with the plurality of styles that Derrida calls a "feminine" operation. Though it is this very feminine operation that Heidegger has failed to acknowledge in Nietzsche, that is not the only Heidegger at play in Derrida's text. I show how Derrida shows the mutual co-implication of both these Heideggers through a performative, stylized practice [*pratique stylée*] around the notions of spurs, style, and Nietzsche's fragment "I have forgotten my umbrella." That passage has rightly become a classic of deconstructive reading, but not always for the right reasons.

On the other hand, the question of sexual difference introduces a different kind of critical relation of Derrida to Heidegger, which he does not have to Hegel: a critique that centers around ethical questions of responsibility. In a cluster of texts in the 1980s, Derrida interrogates Heidegger with an eye to what one could call certain underrepresented themes, which are conspicuously absent from Heidegger's work. The most important of these are *Geschlecht* in all its different senses (race, gender, heritage, family), animality, the body, and politics. These thoughts culminate in the publication of *Of Spirit: Heidegger and the Question*. This other type of critical relation to Heidegger, and the relation between indirectness and responsibility, is the subject of the next and final chapter.

NIETZSCHE'S "FEMININE 'OPERATION'"

A deliberate effect of Derrida's virtuoso essay *Spurs: Nietzsche's Styles* is that it is difficult to pinpoint exactly or exclusively what the text is about. Derrida purposefully maximizes the number of connotations and layers of meaning that are at play in the text's subjects (woman, style, Nietzsche, feminism, truth). Derrida's central concern throughout the text is a disruption of what he calls the "mode of *pro et contra*." This applies not only to the opposition between man and woman. The text is also an attempt to show how Nietzsche's explicit and blatant oppositionality (to almost all the subjects he touches on, but specifically here to women) and his reversals must be understood as part of (as "congruent with") a "plurality of styles" or a broader movement of writing that cannot itself be reduced to the unequivocality of a position. According to Derrida, that excess makes Nietzsche's writing into a "feminine 'operation,'" and this prompts the essay's central question: how to account for Nietzsche's vehement antifeminism within this feminine operation? (*Sp* 57)

Derrida carries out his deconstruction of sexual difference through the undecidable notion of "style." The "question of style" was the subject of the colloquium at Cerisy-la-salle in 1972, where Derrida presented an early version of the paper. In a virtuoso display of writing, Derrida makes it impossible to unambiguously pin down the meaning of style; itself a performative enactment of the "feminine 'operation'" and the deconstruction of the opposition between man and woman, both of which are shown to be unstable notions.[1] The style is the *objet pointu*, the pen that writes and inscribes but also the weapon, the dagger or stiletto [*stylet*] that cuts [*coup*]; it is the phallus that penetrates and the understanding penetrating through the veil of mere appearance. In this sense, the style is man's style. This would make woman the reverse: the equivocal, the to-be-ruptured veil of mere appearance; the distant, to-be-unveiled [*dévoilement*] who is hidden behind veils or sails [*voiles*]. But what is essentially implicit cannot simply be unveiled or (re)presented. What is veiled or "withdrawn from the here and now" is what cannot be simplified so as to be done in one go ("in a single stroke/cut" [*d'un seul coup*]; *Sp* 39). In a manner reminiscent of Heidegger's remark that the proper relation to the concealed is not to "hunt after it" but rather to *let*, so Nietzsche writes that to woman's "efficacy in distance" [*Wirkung in die Ferne, eine* actio in distans] "belongs, first and foremost—distance!" [*dazu gehört aber, zuerst und vor allem—Distanz!*].[2]

Because the style that inscribes is also the style of writing. As mere externality, opposed and secondary to "content," it is what can hurt philosophy and what must be kept at a distance. But at the same time, it is that against which, precisely by keeping it at bay and maintaining its externality, philosophy identifies itself and maintains the integrity of its self-determination. In that way, the style, the dagger, is both attack and protection. And it is through his plurality of styles that Nietzsche's writing is termed "feminine." Because the veil [*voile*] can also attack; the surging forth of the sailing (*vaisseau voile*) that cleaves the "hostile surface" of the sea or that rocky point [*éperon*] on which the waves break so as to protect the harbor. The styles are also those of that other undecidable figure of attack and protection that gives the text its name: the spur [*éperon*, the German *Spur*: trace, wake, indication, mark]. And the question is: who is spurring on whom? Because in the famous opening of *Beyond Good and Evil*, if truth were a woman [*Vorausgesetzt, daß die Wahrheit ein Weib ist*], then the dogmatic philosopher's attempts to win her over (an "easy" woman, no less—*gerade ein Frauenzimmer*] have been thoroughly unsuccessful in their "terrible seriousness and clumsy importunity" [*der schauerliche Ernst, die linkische Zudringlichkeit*]. Now man is helpless and clumsy, his weapons impotent. The power relation reverses. Distance, Derrida writes, is the "element of woman's power"; she "seduces from a distance." And one must "keep one's distance from distance" (*Sp* 49). But if woman is "distance itself," one can no longer speak of an "itself" of distance. Distance is the very receding from presentation and the present. Woman therefore "names the non-truth of truth," and as such she "distorts the vestiges of essentiality." In a particularly suggestive and recurring phrase, Derrida writes of a (feminine) "spreading" or of a "divergence within truth" [*cet écart de la vérité*]: "There is no truth of woman but that is because this abyssal divergence of truth, this non-truth is the 'truth.' Woman is a name for this non-truth of truth" (*Sp* 51, translation amended, JdJ). It is not only man's style that ruptures. In fact, it is woman spurring on man: "In its maneuvers, distance strips the lady of her identity and unseats the philosopher-knight. That is, if he has not already been twice-spurred by the woman. The exchange of stylistic blows or the thrust of a dagger confuses sexual identity [. . .]" (*Sp* 53).

And so the equivocality of style enacts the complication of any determinate sense of man or woman. And that very operation, that "effect" or "efficacy" [*Wirkung*], is feminine. Whether that itself constitutes a new "unveiling" will, according to Derrida, forever remain an open question (*Sp* 107). One cannot simply oppose a certain indeterminacy of "woman" against the (op)positionality of the metaphysics (of presence, of truth, of man—what Derrida calls "phallogocentrism") without repeating its constitutive gesture. *Spurs* is an exemplary text on the strictures of complicity and the unavoidable risk of reaffirmation. The philosopher who believes (and it is the philosopher who "believes") in the non-truth of truth has "understood nothing" (*Sp* 53).

The necessity of indirection, here in the form of a multiplicity of styles, announces itself in this impossibility to state, posit, or (re-)present the non-truth of truth. According to Derrida, Nietzsche does not state or posit this non-truth, but he *inscribes* truth. The "divergence within truth" is "elevated" in style. Nietzsche *suspends* truth by putting it in quotation marks: "truth" puts us at a distance from truth without counter-positing truth. This suspension of truth through its inscription is "the feminine 'operation'" [*"l'operation" féminine*] (*Sp* 57).

This is why Derrida explicitly affirms the plurality of senses in his text (such as those of style, woman, and, famously and explicitly, the sense of "I have forgotten my umbrella," to which I return below). After all, the "*figure* of the woman" or of "feminin*ity*" would no longer be about "woman—a non-identity, a non-figure, a simulacrum." As such, the text is a performative enactment of the plurality it argues for. So any attempt to explicate this excess must take into account its consequences for style:

> Without discrete parody, without writing strategy, without difference or a spreading of pens/feathers [*sans différence ou écart de plumes*], without style, therefore, the grand one, the reversal would amount to the same [*revient au même*] in the noisy declaration of the antithesis.
>
> Hence the heterogeneity of the text. (*Sp* 94, translation amended, JdJ)

If not through a simple (op)position, then the excess, according to Derrida, can only be inscribed through an act of writing; a *coup*, a cutting, or an intervention in the form of a stylized practice [*pratique stylet, pratique stylée*], in a heterogeneous text or in a plurality of styles.

The question to what extent Derrida has, with this text, strengthened the cause of feminists was never easy to answer and is still very much alive.[3] On the one hand, the nuances of the risk of reaffirmation through reversals may seem to have little to offer to the nitty-gritty, real-world problems of feminism as an emancipatory social movement (the fight for recognition, for equal wages, etc.). The "risk of reaffirmation" may not get in the way of the immanent necessity to oppose the existing hierarchy. But this may misunderstand the purport of Derrida's work. It's not that one *shouldn't oppose*; it's that *opposition cannot be enough*. One must oppose, but if the goal is real change then opposition cannot be allowed to become an end in itself. This is where Derrida's concern becomes political: insofar as one can't simply oppose opposition, it can at best be one moment within a veritable transformation. What is at stake therefore is the self-understanding of any emancipatory discourse (or movement of protest or resistance) and the role of opposition within it (to which it cannot be reduced). This is how Derrida's persistent insistence on the "risk of reaffirmation" expresses an irreducible complicity in or with what one is resisting, emancipating from, or arguing against. And this changes both the self-understanding of the resisting movement as well as its understanding of what is to be resisted. At stake, therefore, are the consequences of the performative complexity of "opposing opposition" for emancipation, for the self-understanding of social transformations, and for the direction of political negotiation.

That is also the broader context in which Derrida's specific question in *Spurs* becomes interesting: how is it possible that the most radical critique of Western, male-dominated rationality contains, as a moment of its movement, the most explicit and vehement forms of misogyny and antifeminism?[4] If Nietzsche's writing, as a suspension of ("phallogocentric") truth through its inscription, is a "feminine 'operation,'" then how is this "appearance of feminism" to be reconciled with Nietzsche's "enormous corpus of voracious antifeminism"? Derrida can only state that the "congruence" of Nietzsche's feminism and antifeminism is "rigorously necessary" if the operation of Nietzsche's writing is not reducible to its reversals and (op)positions (*Sp* 57).

But the primary focus of this chapter was to establish Derrida's structural ambiguity with regard to Heidegger. Where does he come in?

DOES HEIDEGGER REDUCE THE PLURALITY OF NIETZSCHE'S STYLES?

At issue in the text is Heidegger's famous interpretation of Nietzsche. Derrida claims that the "thesis" of Heidegger's *grand livre* is "a lot less simple than is generally acknowledged" (*Sp* 73, translation amended, JdJ). What is that generally assumed thesis? That, as a mere inversion [*Umdrehung*] of "Platonism," Nietzsche would be "still metaphysical." In other words: that Heidegger himself reduces in the most metaphysical way the very "plurality of styles" that, for Derrida, forms the hallmark of Nietzsche's "feminine 'operation.'" A suppression, in short, of Nietzsche's *writing*.

Derrida mentions three of Heidegger's remarks on Nietzsche with which to frame the discussion: Heidegger warns (1) against reading in Nietzsche an "aesthetic confusionism"; (2) that Nietzsche's "grand style" is not to be confused with his "pseudo-transgressive exuberance"; and (3) that Nietzsche must be read in light of the confrontation with Western thought as such, that is: that the "accepted ideas" [*idées reçues*] are insufficient to judge the work (*Sp* 75). On the one hand, these theses show Heidegger as the prototypically male philosopher, attempting to penetrate through Nietzsche's styles to the essential content of his works. On the other hand, they show Heidegger's sensitivity to the fact that the movement of Nietzsche's writing is not reducible to a simple aestheticizing opposition to Western thought. In other words, the importance of style is not reducible to the loud oppositional surface or the rhetoric of Nietzsche's positions. Derrida then raises his own questions: should we or can we say that Nietzsche "contradicts himself" concerning woman (vehement critique of Western rationality yet vehement antifeminism), and what would it mean to say that Nietzsche is "still metaphysical" in his "inversion" of Platonism?

The point that Derrida quickly makes is that, contrary to popular opinion, Heidegger does not restrict himself to this scheme in which Nietzsche's writings ultimately only serve to reaffirm metaphysics. So what Derrida is after is to show that (1) Nietzsche's counter-movements, reversals, and oppositions are only part of a larger "grand style" and how (2) Heidegger himself is also not merely content to point to Nietzsche's self-contradictions but that these too belong to a greater movement in the interpretation of Nietzsche. It is clear from Derrida's text that this holds for Nietzsche and Heidegger alike:

> Heidegger, however, does not restrict himself (as it is often supposed) to this schema of an inversion. Not that he abandons it purely and simply. The work of reading and writing is no more homogeneous in his case than it is in Nietzsche's, and his seeming leaps from *pro* to *contra* are not without a certain strategy. Thus Heidegger remarks that, although Nietzsche might seem, or perhaps even ought, to employ the method of *Umdrehung*, it is nonetheless apparent that he "is seeking something else" (etwas anderes sucht). (*Sp* 79, translation amended, JdJ)

So it will be a matter of identifying, in Nietzsche and Heidegger both: what is this other thing, that is sought beyond reversal and reaffirmation [*cet autre qui ne fait plus couple dans une opposition de renversement*]? And what (no less "rigorously necessary," after all) place or function do reversals still have within it? Derrida approaches these questions initially with reference to the famous "History of an Error" [*Geschichte eines Irrtums*] from Nietzsche's 1888 *Twilight of the Idols* [*Götzen-dämmerung*]: "How the 'True World' Finally Became a Fable" [*Wie die "wahre Welt" endlich zur Fabel wurde*] (*Sp* 79).

First of all, Derrida points out how, in interpreting that passage, Heidegger has located the site where Nietzsche veritably exceeds metaphysics and Platonism: "In his consideration of the problematic of *Umdrehung* Heidegger emphasizes the very strongest of torsions, that in which the opposition which has been submitted to reversal is itself suppressed" (*Sp* 81). This shows itself most clearly in the passage's staggering ending: that in getting rid of the true world, we have also abolished the apparent one ("We have abolished the true world. Which one remained? The apparent one perhaps? . . . But no! Along with the true world we have also abolished the apparent one!"). This transformation is no inversion or reversal within an existing hierarchy. It is, according to Derrida, a "transformation of the very value of hierarchy." This is itself "not merely a suppression of all hierarchy," no mere "an-archy," but a "transformation of the hierarchical structure itself" (*Sp* 81).

At this point it would seem that Heidegger has located more in Nietzsche than a mere inversion of metaphysics. And it is at this point that Derrida asks the question of whether Heidegger's intention is itself here still "a form of question more proper to a hermeneutic, and consequently philosophical, order, the very order that Nietzsche's operation should have otherwise *put out of order*" [*déranger*] (*Sp* 83). And is it a coincidence that this Heidegger "analyzes all the elements" of Nietzsche's "History of an Error," but "with the sole exception of the idea's becoming-female [*sie wird Weib*]?" (*Sp* 85).

This is the moment of the more straightforward Derridean critique of Heidegger's Nietzsche-reading. The purport of the objection is this: Heidegger would be too male, too philosophical; this is for him still (merely) a "critical question"; he is too interested in reducing Nietzsche's writing-operation and his plurality of styles; rather like those clumsy dogmatic philosophers who have not learned the art of seduction or to keep one's distance from distance.

But how must we understand the kind of critique that criticizes Heidegger—as Derrida does here—for still engaging in "critical questioning"? And if "still too metaphysical" even means "too critical," then how should we qualify Derrida's own questioning? (In what sense) is this still a critique? Derrida, very explicitly, leaves the matter as an open question: "[. . .] all these weapons circulate from one hand to another, passing from one contrary to another, the question remaining as to just what I am doing here at this moment" (*Sp* 57).

If we try to take some stock, we end up with a still too metaphysical Nietzsche in the eyes of Heidegger, a still too metaphysical Heidegger in the eyes of Derrida, and even a still too metaphysical Derrida in the eyes of Derrida, who affirms the complication of his own mode of interrogation. But Nietzsche, Heidegger, and Derrida are aware of this, and attempt to write at these limits of oppositionality. For Derrida, style, strategy, and writing name the other side of that movement, a textual practice—"*pratique stylet, pratique stylée*" (*Sp* 83). In the subsection titled "positions," Derrida explains on what level Nietzsche operates. Not only was he under "no illusion" that he would "know" of truth or woman, but the level at which Nietzsche operates is that of the analysis of that very illusion, as he "took care to avoid" the negation of the system of negation and reversal; the simple erection of a system *against* [*élever un discours simple contre*] that system.

The remainder of the text demonstrates this in two ways. The first is by formulating a formalization of the principle that is at work in Nietzsche's heterogeneous propositions concerning woman. Derrida does this, however, only in order to subsequently show "the essential limit of such a codification and the problem of reading that it determines" (*Sp* 95, translation amended, JdJ). It is this essential limit that the enactment of Derrida's text is meant to show, the limit of what can be formalized and contained or "codified" in propositions. The "essential limit" lies in the very irreducibility of heterogeneity and style. The second way is an enactment of that "problem of reading" through a writing on or around the fragment "I have forgotten my umbrella."

Starting with the first: what, then, is the "principle" that is active throughout Nietzsche's heterogeneous propositions on woman? Derrida identifies three kinds of proposition on woman: (1) she is debased, censored, despised as figure of *falsehood*; (2) she is debased, censored, despised as figure of *truth*; (3) she is recognized and affirmed as an affirmative power. In the first two cases, Derrida recognizes a negation that is fundamentally "reactive" (i.e.: a reversal): in the face of falsehood, man reacts "in the name of the truth and metaphysics"; in the second case, woman is accused by a prosecutor who "does not escape the inversion of negation." In the third proposition, however, woman names that which transcends the entire "economy" of reversal, negation, and reaffirmation, "beyond that double negation." It is no longer man who affirms her, but she affirms herself.

"Antifeminism is in its turn reversed, he didn't condemn woman but to the extent that she was responding to the man of two reactive positions." The "anti-" of antifeminism, the economy of reversal and reaffirmation, is itself, "in turn" [*à son tour*], "overturned" [*renversé*]. The turnings of oppositionality are *overturned* (*Sp* 97, translation amended, JdJ). The movements are by now familiar. What is at stake here?

Derrida is often hailed as one of the great thinkers of the "disruption" of essentialism or of metaphysical oppositionality, but what is disrupted above all is the very attempt to formulate an alternative to it that would itself be unproblematic. More than a desire for disruption, it is an awareness of the risk of reaffirmation in doing so that drives Derrida's texts. In Nietzsche, this plays out in terms of an absolute appearance that deconstructs both the real and the apparent world, and of an irreducible superficiality that deconstructs the opposition between surface and depth.[5] Thus, a "codification" such as the one above is an attempt to make positive what does not let itself be posited as a position: "each value implied in the three schemes would have to be decidable into a couple of oppositions as if there were a contrary to each term"—the very decidability that the affirmation of the third proposition challenges. Here the "essential limit" that Derrida was out to show is the one posed to the "pertinence of these hermeneutic or systematic questions." That essential limit is the "margin" that is always there to limit the "control" over sense and code. This margin does not let itself be posited. In analyzing what to conclude from this, it is once again clear that Derrida is not aiming at creating possibilities, but rather that his concern is with recognizing (by showing or performing) a certain impossibility. *One cannot "side with" the heterogeneous or the parody*, which would precisely mean to reduce them once again [*ce serait encore les réduire*]; nor does it mean that the "master sense" is "unique" and "unfindable" and that as such it belongs to Nietzsche's "ungraspable power." One cannot "outmaneuver" the "hermeneutic mold" [*déjouer la prise herméneutique*], for that would mean falling back [*retomber*] even more surely into what one was trying to elude (*Sp* 99).

At this point, Derrida leaves the question irreducibly open. That the heterogeneity of Nietzsche's text is "unassimilable" means for Derrida that, to a certain irreducible extent, Nietzsche *himself* "did not see very clearly" [*n'y voyait pas très clair*]. Not, however, as a lamentable contingent blind-spot, but as a regular, rhythmic blindness [*aveuglement régulier, rythmé*] with which one is never finished [*avec lequel on n'en finira jamais*] (*Sp* 101). Recall the "errancy" of *Of Grammatology* discussed in chapter

3: the irreducible wandering that is inseparable from its method. Derrida recognizes it in the text of Nietzsche and as such finds an ally there (as he already did in *Of Grammatology*, in pointing out that Nietzsche had already "contributed a great deal to the liberation of the signifier" [G 31/19]). The question of style becomes the question of writing.

And so Derrida writes that there is no "truth of Nietzsche" or of his text in order to make the point that the question of the woman in it "suspends the decidable opposition of the true and non-true; founds the epochal regime of parentheses," a regime that according to Derrida disqualifies the "hermeneutic project," whereby "reading is freed from the horizon of the meaning or truth of being" (*Sp* 107). That brings us back to the question of the critique of Heidegger, and at this point Derrida clearly opposes Heidegger's ontological hermeneutics. We get a clue immediately after Derrida has used this most emphatically thetic, oppositional language. Because if "the [. . .] spurring operation [*opération-éperonnante*]" is understood as being "more powerful than all content, any thesis, all sense"; as the "styled spur traverses the veil," Derrida asks: does such a conception not still amount to an "unveiling"? "That question *as question* (between *logos* and *theoria*, saying and seeing) interminably remains" (*Sp* 109, translation amended, JdJ).

With that, the "problem of reading" disqualifies Heidegger's "hermeneutic project" but cannot just oppose it. Now two Heideggers emerge that make up the framework within which the necessary ambiguity of Derrida's relation to Heidegger takes place.

DERRIDA'S TWO HEIDEGGERS: *EREIGNIS* OUTSIDE THE HERMENEUTIC CIRCLE

On the one hand, Derrida construes a version of Heidegger against which he defines himself. The form of that Heidegger is not so different from the reappropriating dialectics of Hegelianism. Here, Heidegger is identified with "hermeneutics" and with the "hermeneutic circle." Derrida associates hermeneutics with a project that aims at *sense* or *meaning*. Throughout his work, the figure of the circle is always a pejorative for Derrida. It invariably stands for what merely keeps coming back to the same.

What Derrida will show is that in one sense this hermeneutical Heidegger reduced the plurality of Nietzsche's styles, writing and woman— Heidegger was "still metaphysical." Then Derrida proceeds to describe an "oblique movement," even a movement through which Heidegger's thinking would be "regularly disoriented," another discourse in Heidegger's work, that would be "outside of the hermeneutical circle." That discourse is marked by *Ereignis*.

First movement: Did Heidegger ask the question of sexual difference? Derrida states that it would appear not: the matter seems subordinated to the question of being, whereas Derrida has tried to show that the question of woman is not reducible to a demarcatable field. This is not because every question is inherently sexual, but because the question complicates the structure of determination in terms of demarcation. This is why matters are "not so simple" and why Derrida chose to interrogate the question of woman out of "a certain Heideggerian landscape" (*Sp* 73).

Toward the end of the text, Derrida states that the concepts involved in Nietzsche's analysis of sexual difference are based on what he terms a process of "*propriation* (appropriation, expropriation, *prise, prise de possession, don et échange, maîtrise,* servitude, etc)." Propriation is the "sexual operation." Derrida then embarks on a series of negative remarks concerning the modes of investigation and articulation that would be *incapable* of asking the question of propriation. To sum up: if propriation as the oppositioning of "give and take," of "possess and possessed," is ultimately "produced by the hymen's graphic," then it "escapes not only dialectics, but also any ontological decidability"; therefore the question of "what *is* the proper?" is "no longer possible"; propriation "organizes all ontological statements"; the proper cannot be "derived" from "an onto-phenomenological or semantico-hermeneutic interrogation." The question of the truth of being, according to Derrida, is *not capable* of the question of the proper. In short, that question reveals the "limit" of the "onto-hermeneutical horizon." The question of being "falls short" of it, as it is "already inscribed" in what is designated under the heading of "propriation" (*Sp* 109).

But then, Derrida recognizes that Heidegger cannot be seen to be simply deficient.

Second movement: Derrida calls the "limit" to the onto-hermeneutic interrogation a "singular" limit, as it concerns neither an "ontic nor an ontological region" but the "very limit of being itself" [*la limite de l'être même*]. The more one pushes, however, this excess of the question of being (of dialectics, of onto-hermeneutics, ontology, phenomenology, sense, etc.) toward an *outside* of these, the more one merely reaffirms and accomplishes nothing:

> Equally naïve though would be to conclude that, since the question of the proper is no longer a derivative of the question of being, it is thus available to direct examination, as if one *knew what it is*, the proper, propriation, exchange, giving, taking, debt, price, etc. Failing to elaborate on this problem, maintaining a discourse comfortably installed in this or that determined region [*champ*: field, domain, JdJ], one remains in the onto-hermeneutic presupposition, in the pre-critical relation to the signified, in the return to the presence of the spoken word [*la parole présente*], to natural language, to perception, visibility, in a word, to consciousness, and to its entire phenomenological system. (*Sp* 113, translation amended, JdJ)

To the extent that the question of the proper, and with that the question of sexual difference, exceeds the "onto-hermeneutic" horizon, this does not mean that Heidegger's *avoidance* of the question of woman and of sexual difference (as a simple deficiency on his part) can now be amended by approaching that question only directly. One must keep one's distance from distance—there is no way around this. Inasmuch as the question of sexual difference exceeds the question of being, the question of propriation does not open up some *other* domain in which one could "settle comfortably." Derrida states of what is "often taken to be" the central thesis of Heidegger's Nietzsche-reading—that Nietzsche, in *completing* metaphysics, still *belonged* to it—that it is indeed a matter of whether one is able to determine the unique sense of the value of "belonging" (i.e.: what "belongs" to "belonging"). Though in one direction of both Heidegger's and Derrida's readings one will always "still belong," in another direction Heidegger's Nietzsche (but also Heidegger's entire philosophical project) already works toward the very limit that Derrida tirelessly tries to explicate: what Derrida calls "the de-limitation of the ontological problematic." According to Derrida, Heidegger did indeed exceed "the hermeneutic space of the question of the truth (of being)." This happens "every time that Heidegger submits or opens up the question of being to the question of the proper, of propriating, or of propriation (*eigen, eignen, ereignen,* above all *Ereignis*)" (*Sp* 115–17, translation amended, JdJ).

So the Heidegger that Derrida distances himself from is the Heidegger who remains within the confines of sense and of truth, of the ontological hermeneutical investigation of the sense of the truth of being. But in the direction of *Ereignis*, this reading is "opened up" to "another reading" that "refuses to be contained there" (*Sp* 115).

Now it is true that for Derrida *Ereignis* is not simply opposed to the hermeneutical project. This reading "does not exact its toll of a critical or destructive effect," but it "reinscribes the hermeneutic gesture" (*Sp* 115). *Ereignis* is no simple critique of the hermeneutical project. And for that reason Derrida can point to some elements of *Being and Time* that anticipate *Ereignis*.[6]

But Derrida still thinks that *Ereignis* falls outside the problematic of the "hermeneutic circle." I think Derrida is right concerning the proximity of what he is trying to articulate—the *limit* to a certain hermeneutical horizon—to what Heidegger thinks under the title of *Ereignis*. That is: it is fundamentally a thinking of a certain essential limit, concealment, withdrawal, and the question of how to articulate it. And it is not surprising that Derrida is most content with *Ereignis* as it later develops into *Enteignis*, with how *Ereignis* intimately relates to "the abyssal structure of the proper" (*Sp* 117, translation amended, JdJ).

But Derrida can only do this by construing a false opposition between the thought of *Ereignis* and the hermeneutic circle. Even if Derrida admits it is no simple opposition, he fails to recognize the internal relation between the hermeneutic circle and the thinking of *Ereignis*, as I have outlined this development in chapters 6 and 7. Hermeneutics was never simply a project of *positive sense*, and the circle never just meant a return to the same. The "hermeneutic situation" of the question of being ("being-in") and its circularity tie that question irreducibly to concealment. This also means that the thought of *Ereignis* is by no means an "oblique movement," let alone a movement by which Heidegger's work would be "regularly disoriented" (*Sp* 117).

But that is how Derrida would have it, because it enables him to refer Heidegger back to Nietzsche's structural and irreducible *heterogeneity* and his own methodological *errance*. I believe that especially the *Contributions* and the subsequent "beyng-historical" works (which Derrida could not have read at the time of writing) show decisively that, for Heidegger, this is no disorientation.

But it is clear why Derrida would write these things. From the very start, the question of woman was the question of what withholds or conceals. At stake is to what extent a transformation of hierarchy (e.g., feminist emancipation) can be achieved by speaking up for what has been suppressed. Derrida's claim is that such transformative movements cannot be exhausted by opposition or by *making present* what was absent within the hierarchy. At stake in the question of woman is the "strategy" or "style" necessary for the "presentation" of what refuses itself or cannot be presented. Here both Heidegger and Derrida negotiate a point where "the opposition between metaphysics and non-metaphysics in turn encounters its limit, which is the limit itself *of* that opposition, of the form of opposition" (*Sp* 117, translation amended, JdJ). Because both attempt to negotiate that limit, Derrida is not out to oppose Heidegger (whether "critically" or "destructively").

But that there is no unambiguous critique does not mean that there are no differences. For Derrida, the "other discourse" outside of the hermeneutic circle must have the form of an *enactment* of the heterogeneity of the text. It is in this light that the famous final section of the text must be read. In that section, Derrida considers the fragment "I have forgotten my umbrella," as it was found, "isolated in quotation marks, among Nietzsche's unpublished manuscripts" (*Sp* 123).

PERHAPS: "I HAVE FORGOTTEN MY UMBRELLA"

The section on Nietzsche's fragment is arguably the most famous part of *Spurs*, and it stands in the literature as an exemplary instance of the Derridean or the deconstructive gesture. One could reconstruct a popular story about the significance of the passage roughly as follows: the story about the fragment commences after Derrida announced an "other" discourse about Nietzsche. "Other" means other than Heidegger, which means: other than metaphysics or outside the confines of the ontological-hermeneutical question of the truth of being. A non-metaphysical reading of Nietzsche that pays attention to the plurality of Nietzsche's styles. In such a reading, Derrida would defend the thesis that all text (including Nietzsche's) is constituted as "fragment"—it is impossible to determine its meaning exhaustively with reference to context, authorial intention, history, psychoanalysis, or whatever signified would have to arrest the play of signifiers that essentially constitutes the fragment. Thus, the passage is an exemplary instance of Derrida's position: the endless proliferation of meaning in the play of signifiers as it constitutes all textuality.

In chapter 3, I have already discussed at length the problem of such a relativist interpretation of Derrida. The point is that such an interpretation itself reduces what is most essential to Derrida's writing operation: the plurality of Derrida's own styles, the reflexivity of its deliberate self-complication. The point is that the "metaphysical" reading of Nietzsche does not let itself be opposed to, or substituted by, an "other" point of view—one cannot simply oppose an "endless play" to "full meaning." First of all, the standard account reads this passage as too much of an unequivocal critique of a too unequivocally metaphysical or hermeneutical Heidegger. Secondly, this other discourse cannot have the form of a position or thesis on the essential indeterminacy of language. What is sometimes baffling in Derrida's reception is that one can find (often in one and the same text) both the thesis that Derrida is "not a relativist" *and* the *assurance* of the indeterminacy of meaning; the "view" on language as "endless play." Such an account is unable to recognize the role that "relativism" (reversal, opposition, negation, self-violation) plays necessarily as a mere moment within a total movement that does not lead to reassurances, least of all concerning the nature of meaning or of language.

So it is a matter of reading this final passage of *Spurs* differently. To do this, I quote at length from *Beyond Good and Evil*. It is a passage that Derrida does not treat explicitly but that is found in the opening of the Nietzsche-book to which he devotes most of his attention:

> The grounding faith of metaphysicians is *the faith in the opposition of values.* Not even to the most cautious among them did it occur to doubt already here at the threshold, where it was after all most necessary; even when they vowed themselves to "*de omnibus dubitandum.*" For one may doubt first whether there are oppositions at all, and second whether those populist valuations and value oppositions upon which the metaphysicians have pressed their seal are not perhaps mere foreground valuations, mere provisional perspectives, even more, *perhaps* from an angle, *perhaps* from below, frog perspectives as it were, to borrow an expression familiar to painters? For all the value that may be attributed to the true, the truthful, the selfless, *it would be possible* that a higher and more fundamental value for all life would have to be ascribed to appearance, to the will to deceive, to self-interest and craving. *It might even be possible* that *what* constitutes the value of those good and honored things consists precisely in their being insidiously related, allied, linked, *perhaps* even essentially identical to those wicked, seemingly opposing things. *Perhaps!—But who has the will to be concerned with such a dangerous Perhaps!* For this, one really has to await the arrival of a new species of philosopher, those

who have some other kind of reverse taste and inclination from their predecessors—*philosophers of the dangerous Perhaps in every sense.*—And in all earnestness: I see such new philosophers emerging. [emphases added, JdJ]⁷

The belief in the *opposition* of values defines metaphysics. But here it is necessary to doubt at the threshold, as this belief may merely be "of the foreground," may be merely temporary, or, even more radically, mere "frog-perspectives" (in painting or photography, the frog-perspective makes the subject look bigger, more imposing than it is in reality). Not only *is it possible* that *perhaps* a higher value for life than truth, truthfulness, and selflessness is to be found in appearance, deception, or self-interest (their *opposites*, in short). But, more radically, *it is possible* that *perhaps* that which makes up the worth of those "good" things is in fact in some duplicitous manner entangled or intertwined with, *perhaps* in essence even the same as, these "bad" things that it is *supposedly opposed* to. *Perhaps!*

Nietzsche challenges metaphysics not by opposing it but by marking the belief in opposition itself as its very hallmark. What this leaves is the strategy of what is *also possible*. That signifies an *opening* of conceptuality, an open space or what Derrida would term an undecidability. Its central operative category is the "perhaps." The post-metaphysical or supra-metaphysical philosopher, the philosopher who would be capable finally of seeing metaphysics for what it is, is a philosopher who does not substitute the metaphysician's belief for a different one, but whose concern is the "dangerous perhaps."

Compare this to the opening of the passage on Nietzsche's umbrella in *Spurs*. I quote the French original:

"J'ai oublié mon parapluie."
Parmi les fragments inédits de Nietzsche, on a trouvé ces mots,
    tout seul, entre guillemets.
Peut-être une citation.
Peut-être a-t-elle été prélevée quelque part.
Peut-être a-t-elle été entendu ici ou là.
Peut-être était-ce le propos d'une phrase à écrire ici ou là.
Nous n'avons *aucun moyens infaillible de savoir* où le prélèvement
    a eu lieu, sur quoi la greffe peut prendre.
Nous ne serons *jamais assurés de savoir* ce que Nietzsche a voulu
    faire ou dire en notant ces mots. (*Sp* 122, all emphases
    mine, JdJ)

Perhaps the fragment was a citation, *perhaps* picked up somewhere, *perhaps* heard, *perhaps* a sentence to be written here or there.

Perhaps.

Barbara Harlow's English translation inexplicably misses the mark here. It is as if she felt that starting a sentence four times with the word "perhaps" was an affront to good *style*. She goes through all kinds of trouble to avoid the emphatic repetition of the "perhaps" in these sentences (the first is translated with "maybe," the second with "it might," the third is omitted by conjoining two sentences, and the fourth with "perhaps").[8]

"Perhaps" (*Vielleicht!*) is for Derrida the central Nietzschean category, and it provides the key to reading him.[9] What the perhaps does is "suspend" truth in the manner discussed above; it points to an inability to know for sure. Perhaps signifies: something else is also possible ["es wäre möglich," *peut-être*, "could be"].

That is also how Derrida structures his text around Nietzsche's fragment. It is possible that Nietzsche didn't even *mean* or *want* to say anything with it. It is possible that it isn't even Nietzsche's. And even if somehow, through some "act of diligence" and/or "good fortune," the "context" of the fragment (the circumstances of its inscription, its "place" in the corpus, etc.) were successfully reconstructed, then what Derrida calls "such a factual possibility" would still leave open a certain structural, always open possibility that is essentially related to the very structure of the fragment: that it would remain intact in its severance from any specific context.

What are we to conclude from this? The "we cannot know" is not brought forward as a thesis that would itself bring assurances. This would be nothing "dangerous," and it would not be very "perhaps" either. But what is often regarded as the *thesis* of the section on Nietzsche's umbrella is this: "However far one pushes conscientious interpretation, one can never suspend the hypothesis that the totality of Nietzsche's text might, perhaps, in its enormity be of the type 'I have forgotten my umbrella'" (*Sp* 133, translation amended, JdJ). But the text is not set up so as to *defend* this thesis. It rather points to the impossibility of *excluding* the *hypo*thesis that, *perhaps*, the entirety of Nietzsche's text would be of a fragmentary structure. Instead of a defended thesis, Derrida leaves us with an open question: what kind of a discourse, what kind of a writing, would be able to take into account such a structural perhaps? According to Derrida, "at least we will never *be able to* know it, and this inability must be taken into account" (*Sp* 127, translation amended, JdJ). How, through what kind of writing, could or should one "account for" this possibility of not being able to know?

First of all, Derrida states that at least the *opening* of the perhaps creates a remainder [*restance*], "like a trace," which is subtracted "from any assured horizon of a hermeneutic question." According to Derrida, as a movement of opening, reading consists in the "perforation" of such a horizon (rupture of/through the style, through the *pratique stylet*) (*Sp* 127). Derrida associates the "circular trajectory" of the "hermeneutical circle" with what can be contained within a "proper itinerary" from origin to end. Here Derrida's opposition to Heidegger or to "onto-hermeneutics" serves the same function as his resistance to dialectics: as a necessary phase of reversal, it reaffirms them in order to mark an "internal" opening in its very movement.

In the same way, Derrida reaffirms the necessity of the hermeneutic operation in *Spurs*:

> To account, in the most rigorous possible manner, for that structural limit, of writing as the marked remainder [*restance*] of the simulacrum, the deciphering must [. . .] be pushed to the furthest lengths possible. The limit does not circumscribe a knowledge and announce a beyond [*Telle limite ne vient pas border un savoir et annoncer un au-delà*], it traverses and divides a scientific work of which it is also the condition, and which it opens to itself. (*Sp* 133, translation mine, JdJ)

To account for the structural limit, the essential and irreducible possibility of something else, therefore of not-knowing, this structural lack of assurance, the process of "deciphering" must not be given up, but can only be pushed to its limit. To give it up here means to fashion for oneself an other position on language, interpretation, or meaning. But the "essential limit," according to Derrida, is not the outer border of knowledge (does not circumscribe knowledge; delimit, determine it), nor does it proclaim a beyond. Instead, it traverses and divides a "scientific" work; it is at work *in* the scientific work and can "open it up to itself."

The discourse that would want to account for this limit, that would want to be *unassertive* (perhaps veiled, withheld to some extent; indirect; going against itself, implicitly complicating itself, maintaining ambiguity, etc.)—such an exposition would require *other forms*: "If Nietzsche wanted to say something, is it not that very limit of the will to say [*de la volonté de dire*], as the effect of a necessarily differential will to power, always divided, folded, multiplied [*divisée, pliée, multipliée*]?" (*Sp* 133, translation amended, JdJ).

CONCLUSION

On the one hand, Derrida attempts in *Spurs* to mark off the movement of Nietzsche's positions, his plurality of styles, against the horizon of meaning of the hermeneutical circle. With that, Derrida recognizes Nietzsche as a thinker of movement. On the other hand, Derrida continually complicates that very gesture. He does so (1) on the level of its content by continually reemphasizing the risk that this very point will have been a new "unveiling," the risk that one ends up once again *opposing* the plurality of styles to the onto-hermeneutical horizon and thereby merely reversing the order, and for that reason (2) his reading is also an enactment of the plurality of styles, a departure from the Heideggerian approach to Nietzsche, especially in the opening of the text (following the movement of the multiplied of the senses of *éperon*, *style*, and *voile* that is reminiscent of "Tympan") and in his emphasis on the "dangerous perhaps" in his reflection on Nietzsche's umbrella-fragment.

At the same time, Derrida stresses that Heidegger too cannot be simply restricted to that hermeneutical horizon, and he points to the explosive potential of *Ereignis* with respect to the confines of the hermeneutical circle. It belongs to the "divided and multiplied" character of Derrida's discourse that he does not make a simple choice between these two Heideggers. The virtue of that undecidability lies in its potential to open the texts of these thinkers and resist reducing them to the content of an unequivocal thesis.

So far, Derrida's engagement with Heidegger is structurally similar to the structural ambiguity he maintains with respect to Hegel that I discussed in chapter 5. But the question of woman already indicated the political nature of the question of performativity. Derrida's discussion of Heidegger is indeed, much more so than his discussion of Hegel, a discussion with ethico-political stakes and consequences. This comes out best in Derrida's *Geschlecht*-series that culminates in *Of Spirit*, to which I now turn my attention.

CHAPTER 9

STRATEGY AND RESPONSIBILITY

Derrida, Heidegger, and the Ethics of Complicity

> Even if all forms of complicity are not equivalent, they are irreducible. The question of knowing which is the least grave of these forms of complicity is always there—its urgency and its seriousness could not be overstressed—but it will never dissolve the irreducibility of this fact. This "fact" [*fait*], of course, is not simply a fact. First, and at least, because it is not yet done [*fait*], not altogether [*pas tout a fait*]: it calls more than ever, as for what in it remains to come after the disasters that have happened, for absolutely unprecedented responsibilities of "thought" and "action."
>
> —Derrida (*Of Spirit*)

One of Derrida's most sustained engagements with Heidegger is found in his 1987 *Of Spirit: Heidegger and the Question*, based on a lecture given that year at a conference in Paris titled "Heidegger: Open Questions." That text is the result of a development of Derrida's thinking about Heidegger to which the *Geschlecht*-series also belongs. *Of Spirit* is not part of that series, but continues a path along the lines of "five foci of questioning" at the end of *Geschlecht II*.[1] In *Of Spirit*, Derrida ties these focal points to the concept of spirit [*Geist*] and its modifications (*geistig, geistlich*) as the "knot" that ties or weaves these threads together. He directly thematizes Heidegger's "avoidances" and articulates critical questions about some implicit gestures hidden in Heidegger's work (a hidden teleology;

a hidden privilege of the question that itself remains "unquestioned"; a hidden desire for non-contamination). The most famous of these avoidances was Heidegger's silence after World War II about his affiliation to the Nazi Party. Partly because of this, *Of Spirit* is often mistakenly thought to have been written in response to Victor Farias's *Heidegger and Nazism*, the work that sparked the so-called "Heidegger affair." This is in fact not the case, as the books appeared almost simultaneously.[2] But *Of Spirit* does address Heidegger's silence and avoidance, and at the center of it is the question of whether there is a responsibility to respond.

Derrida's critical questions center around absence, avoidance, and hiddenness. All of these questions (woman, style, animal, *Geschlecht*, *Geist*, question, etc.) in one way or another relate essentially to concealedness. What ties the problems of spirit and avoiding to my present concerns is that it relates the limits of thematization to responsibility. An important part of Derrida's conception of responsibility is that there is something like a necessary absence or avoidance. Derrida shows that there is a necessity to respond, but also that neither that which Heidegger avoided, nor that which is "suppressed" in Western metaphysics (whether that be woman, body, animal, race, etc.), can be rehabilitated by simply taking it out of its concealment or by (re-)presenting it. Derrida's central question is: *how to account* for such an irreducible concealment in a writing?

In terms of Derrida's critical relation to Heidegger, this means that Derrida cannot be understood to unproblematically oppose Heidegger's hidden teleology, desire for purity, and "unquestioned privilege of the question." Derrida shows that such opposition is impossible without reaffirming the opposed. This becomes especially clear in Derrida's idea of an affirmation that would "belong to the unquestionable itself in any question"; a performative notion of the (un)questionable that grounds an affirmative concept of responsibility.

Derrida develops his concept of responsibility more elaborately in later texts. In the debate about the "ethics of deconstruction," interpretations have tended to work within a Levinasian framework, which understands ethics primarily with reference to the "other." That is quite right, but there is a risk if the other is confused with the external. I show that *Of Spirit* provides the material for an interpretation that has its basis in deconstruction's indirectness in order to formulate an account of Derrida's ethics based on his thought of "irreducible complicity."

With the question of the responsibility of the indirect discourse, the question of the relation of (op)position to the movement of showing becomes a political question. Opposition is a necessary structural feature of social or political transformation (emancipation, protest, resistance, disobedience). But opposition simultaneously undermines their transformative potential. In that sense, the making-present (the re-presentation) of "repressed" or "avoided" groups or themes is a vital moment, but only one moment, within the total movement of emancipation. This is what Derrida expresses with the notion of irreducible complicity. If saying no is at best one moment within a broader movement, then this changes the structure of political deliberation or of what Derrida called "negotiation." It's not that one cannot or should not take up a position, it's that taking up a position is *not enough*: it does not or not yet take into account the irreducible complicity in the act of saying no (it is thus also a form of the very desire for purity that was being contested). Therefore, the possibility of transformation requires a broader strategy.

This book ends by pointing to where these political consequences would have to begin. Working them out in detail will have to be done elsewhere. What I am able to show is where Derrida's indirectness is at its most positive—what its most positive motivation is and what distinguishes indirectness (as the accusation often goes) from evasiveness, negativity, or a relativizing or destructive discourse. This means returning to the question of critique discussed in chapter 3, but now by approaching the question of justification as an ethical or normative question. We move from deconstruction's theoretical to its normative legitimacy (in the words of *Force of Law*: from *justesse* to *justice*). On the other hand, I show that the positivity of the "affirmation" is not the positivity of a position. There is an "ethical turn" in Derrida's development only on a superficial level, and it did not consist in the assumption of a particular ethical stance that would be at odds with his indirectness. To assume responsibility, for Derrida, is not primarily, exclusively, or ultimately to take up an unequivocal standpoint. Instead, the indirectness is itself the attempt to assume a meaningful intellectual or philosophical responsibility.

OF SPIRIT AND THE UNAVOIDABLE

Derrida concedes that the choice of spirit [*Geist*] as a central concern for a meditation on Heidegger may seem strange, because that concept does not seem to be one of Heidegger's "major themes and major terms" such as "being, *Dasein*, time, the world, history, ontological difference, *Ereignis*, etc." (*OS* 16/4). For Derrida, however, spirit does deserve such a place. In *Being and Time*, as well as much later in the text on Trakl, Heidegger explicitly warns that *Geist* is a term that should be avoided. Yet at certain other points (notably the rectorial address of 1933³), Heidegger explicitly made use of *Geist* and *geistig*. Therefore, Derrida asks: "Could it be that he failed to avoid what he knew he ought to avoid? What he in some sense had promised himself to avoid? Could it be that he forgot to avoid? Or else, as one might suspect, are things more tortuous and entangled than this?" (*OS* 12/2).

The entanglement in question here is the inherent relation of the question of being with a certain avoiding [*vermeiden, éviter*]. Here, referring to his own text "How to Avoid Speaking: Denials" [*Comment ne pas parler: Dénégations*], Derrida clarifies that avoiding does not necessarily mean avoidance [*l'évitement*] or denegation, because such a discourse "does not take into account the economy of *vermeiden* in those places where it exposes itself to the question of being" (*OS* 13/2). In other words: the avoidance of *Geist* in Heidegger's work is not a simple absence or a form of repression. Instead, there is an internal relation between the question of being and avoidance. To translate the question of *Of Spirit* into the terms of my present investigation: is there a necessary avoidance? What would it amount to? Would it not have to be said (i.e.: not avoided) if it were necessary?

Where does such a necessity show itself? Derrida writes:

> I'm thinking in particular of all those modalities of "avoiding" which come down to saying without saying, writing without writing, using words without using them: in quotation marks, for example, under a non-negative cross-shaped crossing out [*kreuzweise Durchstreichung*], or again in propositions of the type: "If I were yet to write a theology, as I am sometimes tempted to do, the word 'Being' ought not to appear in it," etc. (*OS* 13/2)

So Derrida will ask the question of a necessary avoidance by tracing the terms *Geist*, *geistig*, and *geistlich* in Heidegger's work.

When Derrida establishes that *Being and Time* is predicated upon the avoidance of certain terms (subjectivity, *Geist*, anthropology; in short: what "belongs to metaphysics"), this can mean several things. The problem is analogous to that of "overcoming": either this avoidance serves to make room for a wholly new, non-metaphysical questioning (beyond or outside what is avoided) that would *substitute* the old discourse; or it gives new meaning to the "old" metaphysical concepts and questions, giving rise to a different *attunement* to them. It is an important element of Heidegger's self-understanding that he develops a different discourse after *Being and Time*, but without simply opposing what he did there. In a televised interview with Richard Wisser from 1969, Heidegger states that the thinking he develops after *Being and Time* demands "a new care with respect to language [*eine neue Sorgfalt der Sprache*]." He clarifies: "not the invention of new terms, as I once thought [*keine Erfindung neuer Termini, wie ich einmal dachte*], but a return to the inceptual content of the language that is our own but that is understood in its continual decay."⁴ That Heidegger does not go against the old discourse is already clear in *Being and Time* itself, where he does not oppose the subject-object distinction but rather demands an original meditation on its sense. He says the same of *logos*—which he does not go against but of which he demands a "sufficient determination" [*zureichende Bestimmung*]⁵—and, famously, of technology ("I am not against technology" [*ich bin nicht gegen die Technik*]).⁶ Derrida is right to point out that the avoidance of a certain metaphysical vocabulary was an essential part of Heidegger's strategy to reach an originary or sufficient determination of the sense of what was thought under these "old names."

And so matters become "more tortuous and entangled." Derrida distinguishes: (1) Heidegger's explicit call to avoid *Geist*; (2) Heidegger's avoiding-but-no-longer-avoiding it by putting it in quotation marks; and (3) Heidegger's emphatic use (even "celebration" and "exaltation") of the concept of *Geist* in the rectorial address "The Self-Assertion of the German University" from 1933. What does that mean for Derrida's "critical" relation to Heidegger? Just as it is clear that Derrida has never approached Heidegger without reservations, so it is equally clear that those reservations could never lead simply to the identification of inconsistencies in Heidegger's texts. One great example of this can be found in Derrida's early 1964/65 seminar on *Heidegger: The Question of Being and History*.⁷ I regret there is no room here for an elaborate analysis of that text. Already there, Derrida shows that for both Hegel and Heidegger a relation to the philosophical tradition can never be a "refutation." Heidegger's *Destruktion* (which, before Derrida attached such significance to the term, he translates here as "a deconstruction, a de-structuration, the shaking that is necessary to bring out the structures, the strata, the system of deposits" [*QBH* 9])—this deconstruction "does not mean annihilation, annulment, rejection," or even "critique or contestation or refutation." Even if Hegel was already a critic of refutation, there is still a difference between Heidegger's *Destruktion* and Hegel's *Aufhebung* of refutation, but they are distinguished "by a nothing, a slight trembling of meaning" (*QBH* 9). Already there, for Derrida: the relation of critique is from the outset determined by the "problem of language." To Hegel's discourse, Heidegger "adds no proposition." Instead, "Heidegger's thought" must be considered "in its movement" (*QBH* 11).

So instead of a refutation or the correction of an error, Derrida writes in *Of Spirit* that what is at stake seems to be "neither thematic nor athematic." The "modality" of *Geist*, writes Derrida, "requires another category" (*OS* 19/6). With that in mind, let's take a closer look at Derrida's "critical" relation to Heidegger as evidenced by the four "guiding threads."

Of Spirit's four foci or guiding threads "[emanate] from four areas of hesitation and disquiet in [Derrida's] current reading of Heidegger" ("ORH" 171). They are: (1) the "privilege of the question" in Heidegger's thought, and Derrida's attempt to articulate an *affirmation* that would "[belong] to the beyond and to the possibility of any question, to the unquestionable itself in any question" (*OS* 24/9); (2) the identification of a "desire for rigorous non-contamination" in the idea that the "essence of technology is not technological" and Derrida's attempt to recognize instead the "fatal necessity of a contamination"; (3) the question of animality (and the determinations of man and life) in Heidegger and Derrida's attempt to show the inadequacy of Heidegger's thesis that the animal is "poor in world" [*Weltarm*]; and (4) the question of *epochality* and Derrida's suspicion of a "hidden teleology" in Heidegger's thought (*OS* 29/12).

That Derrida raises these points "a little provocatively" (he knows that Heidegger was no teleological thinker and that "still too teleological" is akin to "still too metaphysical") already shows that Derrida is not engaged in simply pointing out contradictions in Heidegger's work. I start with two general comments on how (not) to read these "critical" questions that Derrida poses to Heidegger.

First, to the extent that Derrida identifies themes that are systematically underrepresented or repressed—avoided—in Heidegger's work (animality, *Geist*, gender, body, sexual difference, politics), Derrida's writings can be seen as *emancipatory* with respect to these underrepresented themes. But as the question of feminism in *Spurs* already showed: everything depends on how the role of opposition and reversal within this emancipation is understood. The point is that the rehabilitation of these themes cannot only or simply be effectuated by means of a simple remembrance or (re-)presentation of what was repressed. Instead, it requires a thinking of the very forgetfulness of their forgetting; of what kind of law guides their avoidance. In raising the questions of animality, sexual difference, race, politics, it cannot be a matter of simply making present what was absent, thematizing what has been avoided, but it must be a matter of the limits of thematization; of simultaneously showing the necessity of a certain withdrawal or of what resists the possibility of presentation as such. What holds for all these underrepresented themes is that accounting for them would have to incorporate the respects in which they all—in their own way and to a certain extent—defy thematization as such. For Derrida, emancipation needs to be more than a simple overturning because Western, male, anthropocentric (and, ultimately: "carno-phallogocentric" ["EW" 280]) rationality *is* the metaphysics *of presence*.

Second, speaking in a general way about the four guiding threads, it is possible to read them oppositionally. If one were to do so, then that would mean that to the privilege of the question Derrida would oppose an affirmation; to the desire for non-contamination Derrida would oppose the "fatal necessity of a contamination," and so on. This oppositional model is consistent with at least one stratum of Derrida's discourse.

Such a reading is especially tempting when one goes by Derrida's remarks at the 1986 Essex Colloquium on "Reading Heidegger" as David Farrell Krell transcribed them in "On Reading Heidegger: An Outline of Remarks to the Essex Colloquium."[8] In the discussion, the first questions, posed by Paul Crowther, concern the latter's "shock" at the difference between Derrida's writings and his "verbally presented text." He describes listening to Derrida that day as "easy" and notes his "everyday style"; he states that Derrida has "talked in a very open way" and even that he "thought for a long time that [he] was listening to an Oxford analytic philosopher" ("ORH" 173).

I think that the difference in tone, the "everyday style" that Crowther notices, is in fact not very everyday at all, but that it is the seemingly everyday reflection of an essentially oppositional, thetic discourse. In response to Crowther's questions, Derrida states that instead of, or rather implicit in, an "everyday" style was a "tacit formalization" to which his oral discourse corresponded: "[. . .] the paradox is that this very easy and straightforward speech is at the same time very formalized, that is, implies many hidden complicities." The formalization in question was one by which Derrida attempted to "open discussion": "I think that the written texts

[. . .] usually are more difficult to question, more protective, strategically more clever, or 'rused,' and this limits discussion" ("ORH" 175).

The difference between Derrida's oral presentation and his texts therefore is a difference in strategy. I believe what Crowther noticed was the oppositionality of a discourse in terms of theses, positions, and oppositions, which came across as easy, everyday, open, and analytic. If Derrida's texts are "more strategically clever," then this must mean that there are good reasons why one cannot just oppose affirmation to the question, contamination to non-contamination, difference to animality, dissemination to gathering, and so on.

Of course, *Of Spirit* is itself the very written text that is strategically more clever than what was presented orally at the Essex colloquium. To indicate how that strategy is related to the limits of opposition and responsibility, I turn to *Of Spirit*'s sections V–VI, where the problem of the relation between avoidance and opposition is dealt with most explicitly.

IRREDUCIBLE COMPLICITY AND THE DESIRE FOR NON-CONTAMINATION

Of the various and ambiguous senses of *Geist* found throughout Heidegger's work (from implicitly avoiding the term, to the explicit call to avoid it, to its blatant use, back to avoiding it), sections V and VI of *Of Spirit* discuss the stage of the explicit use of *Geist* and *geistig* in the rectorial address. According to Derrida, the address is a "celebration" of *Geist*, an "exaltation of the spiritual." This is the exaltation of *Geist* as that which binds, gathers, or unites a people [*Volk*] as well as that to which the people aspire (the "highest") or what makes up their destiny and history [*geistig-geschichtlich ist Dasein*]. For Derrida, that makes this explicit exaltation of the spiritual a matter of *response* and *responsibility*—taking up the rectorate is a matter of *responding* to the call of the spiritual as well as of assuming responsibility *for* it. This responsibility is not unambiguous. In this exaltation of the spiritual, Heidegger *assumes* responsibility in the face of or before the spiritual, but, according to Derrida, "[this] responsibility is nonetheless exercised according to a strategy. Tortuous, at least double, the strategy can always hold an extra surprise in reserve for whoever thinks he controls it" (OS 63/38–39).

According to what "double strategy" does Heidegger here assume responsibility? On the one hand, *Geist* is the heading under which

Heidegger appealed to the unity, determination, destiny of the German people and the university before and in name of which he would assume responsibility in his rectorate. It was the attempt to elevate himself above the appeal to "obscure forces—forces which would not be spiritual, but natural, biological, racial." The problem with such elevation is that it "fatally [turns] back against its "subject'": "Because one cannot demarcate oneself from biologism, from naturalism, from racism in its genetic form, one cannot be opposed to them except by reinscribing spirit in an oppositional determination" (OS 63/39). The problem therefore is that the liberation from biologism, naturalism, racism, and so forth necessarily involves resisting oppositionality as such, from which one cannot simply detach oneself.

Because this inability to simply exceed is so crucial to Derrida's position, I give two other examples. In "Envoi," Derrida makes the point with respect to "representation." He casts doubt over what he sees "today," namely that "many people set their thinking *against* representation. In a more or less articulated or rigorous way, this thinking gives in facilely to an evaluation: representation is bad." The limits of representation cannot be shown by positing something else (by delineating or determining) or oneself (through a critique) over *against* it:

> [. . .] to determine language as representation is not the effect of an accidental prejudice, a theoretical fault or a manner of thinking, a limit or closure among others, a form of representation, precisely, that came about one day and that we could get rid of by a decision when the time comes. ("E" 102)

A second example: in the 1989 interview by Jean-Luc Nancy called "'Eating Well,' or the Calculation of the Subject" [*"Il faut bien manger" ou le calcul du sujet*], Derrida makes the point with respect to subjectivity. The premise of the interview is the question "Who comes after the subject?" But in the first few pages, Derrida is primarily concerned with resisting the form of that question, especially all the presuppositions behind the idea that "the subject" is or could somehow be left behind. One feels a mounting irritation in the questions of Nancy—surely Derrida would have to grant that *"something has happened*, there is a history both of the thinking of the subject and of its deconstruction" ("EW" 264). But, according to Derrida, the very question "Who comes after the subject?" still "echoes" a "discourse of opinion" that "one must begin by critiquing or deconstructing." This "doxa" is ruled by an oppositional "slogan" ("after the subject"), the effect of which "consists in saying: all these philosophers think they have put the subject behind them . . ." ("EW" 257).

In "Envoi," Derrida stresses that the opposition to representation is unable to "assign, in the final analysis, the place and the necessity of the evaluation" (i.e.: the negative evaluation of mere opposition). One cannot simply negate representation, because "the authority of representation constrains us, imposes itself on our thought through a whole dense, enigmatic, and heavily stratified history." Here the form of the problem becomes distinctly Heideggerian:

> [The authority of representation] programs us, precedes us, and predisposes us too much for us to make a mere object of it, a representation, an object of representation confronting us, set before us like a theme. It is even rather difficult to pose a systematic and historical question on the topic (a question of the type: "What is the system and the history of representation?"), given that our concepts of system and of history are essentially marked by the structure and the closure of representation. ("E" 103)

I have shown the structural resemblance between this kind of problem, the opening of *Being and Time*, the *Contributions*' problem of questioning machination on the other, and *Of Grammatology*'s diagnosis of logocentrism. Not only the concepts of system and of history, but the very form of the question "what is . . . ?" is itself already "constrained" by the "authority of representation." Derrida has already hinted at this earlier in the text in connection with the "Socratic question": "what is representation *itself and in general*?" "Socrates would never have been able to ask this kind of question about the word 'representation,'" according to Derrida, "for essential reasons" ("E" 101).

So it is a matter of explicating the structure of the "program" that we are inextricably "in," the "constraint" of which is "very strong." Even in the course of Derrida's most vehement critique of Heidegger, still the form of that problem is Heideggerian:

> [. . .] it reigns over the majority of discourses which, today and for a long time to come, state their opposition to racism, to totalitarianism, to nazism, to fascism, etc., and do this in

the name of spirit, and even of the freedom of (the) spirit, in the name of an axiomatic—for example, that of democracy or "human rights"—which, directly or not, comes back to this metaphysics of *subjectity*. All the pitfalls of the strategy of establishing demarcations belong to this program, whatever place one occupies in it. *The only choice is the choice between the terrifying contaminations it assigns. Even if all forms of complicity are not equivalent, they are irreducible* [My italics, JdJ]. The question of knowing which is the least grave of these forms of complicity is always there—its urgency and its seriousness could not be over-stressed—but it will never dissolve the irreducibility of this fact. This "fact" [*fait*], of course, is not simply a fact. First, and at least, because it is not yet done [*fait*], not altogether [*pas tout a fait*]: it calls more than ever, as for what in it remains to come after the disasters that have happened, for absolutely unprecedented responsibilities of "thought" and "action." This is what we should have to try to designate, if not to name, and begin to analyze here. (*OS* 65–66/40)

Surely, then, at this point, Derrida's critique of Heidegger is no longer very ambiguous? In one sense, this is very true: Derrida shows that Heidegger's use of *Geist* in the rectorial address amounts to nothing less than a "spiritualizing" of Nazism. It "capitalizes on the worst, that is on both evils at once: the sanctioning of Nazism, and the gesture that is still metaphysical" (*OS* 66/40). However, that spiritualization takes place by way of a mechanism or a "program" of complicity and reaffirmation that Derrida himself does not claim to be able to escape. The program itself consists in the very attempt to escape, the thought that one can exceed racism or biologism by elevating oneself above it to a position of reassuring legitimacy. This vehement critique of Heidegger can therefore least of all just be an opposition to Heidegger. Instead, it leads beyond the distinction between "Heideggerian" and "anti-Heideggerian" discourses:

If I analyze this "logic," and the aporias or limits, the presuppositions or the axiomatic decisions, above all the inversions and contaminations, in which we see it becoming entangled, this is rather in order to exhibit and then formalize the terrifying mechanisms of this program, all the double constraints which structure it. Is this unavoidable? Can one escape this program?

> No sign would suggest it, at least neither in "Heideggerian" discourses nor in "anti-Heideggerian" discourses. Can one transform this program? I do not know. In any case, it will not be avoided all at once and without reconnoitering it right down to its most tortuous ruses and most subtle resources. (OS 87–88/56)

The attempt to escape (oppose, transcend, go beyond, avoid) this terrifying mechanism by presenting a counter-thesis or (op)position to (or by trying to avoid) racism, naturalism, biologism, or any other kind of positivist reductionism reinforces it. Derrida distances himself from such a will to escape. He criticizes it under the heading of a "desire for purity" (the purity of the uncontaminated or rigorous distinction, the movement of metaphysics itself), and in Heidegger's works he calls it a "strategy of protection." What exceeds the positivism of such positions and marks their limit does not lie outside them and cannot truly be accomplished by a counter-position, however necessary the reversal may be. It can be shown how all of Derrida's main problems with Heidegger (the underrepresented themes of animality, sexual difference, technology, and so on) have this same structure.[9] Below I must limit my discussion of these to the "question of the question."

Reaffirmation, mere reversal, or what Derrida here calls "complicity" is *irreducible*. Derrida's question is how to formulate a *response* to this situation. The "fact" that not all forms of complicity are equivalent means that political deliberation takes on the form of a search for the "least grave" form of complicity. Such a response and such a decision will always be made in the name of something that will always risk becoming another oppositionally determined ideal or ideology. But what drives the deconstructive discourse that wants to take these constraints into account cannot be reduced to any such determinate (op)position. Instead, acting in response to this irreducibility, the attempt to take it into account from the start, must according to Derrida be a *commitment* (Derrida sometimes speaks of a promise), an *ability to respond* (a *response-ability*) that is "unprecedented" because it is not tied to any determined "axiomatic." It is this that calls for "absolutely unprecedented responsibilities," responsibilities that are *affirmative* (OS 66/40).

"Absolutely unprecedented"—if I emphasize irreducible complicity, then what are we to make of such revolutionary rhetoric? Is Derrida now, in spite of all his precautions and against the grain of his entire discourse, advocating for an absolute break with metaphysical (ethical) discourses of responsibility? How does such a responsibility and the concept of the other to which it responds relate to the impossibility of a clean break with metaphysics? And if this leads to the thought of an *affirmation*, if "deconstruction is affirmative," then does that not contradict what I have written about Derrida's indirectness, his structural hesitation and ambiguity?

UNPRECEDENTED RESPONSIBILITIES AND AFFIRMATION "BEFORE" THE QUESTION

It is from a meditation on the role of the question in Heidegger's work that Derrida arrives at the thought of affirmation. According to Derrida, "the point of departure in the existential analytic is legitimated first of all and only from the possibility, experience, structure, and regulated modifications of the *Fragen*." It is the "experience of the question" that makes Dasein into the exemplary entity to be questioned at the beginning of *Being and Time*. Derrida adds to this Heidegger's claim at the end of *Die Frage nach der Technik* that questioning is "the piety of thinking" [*denn das Fragen ist die Frommigkeit des Denkens*]. Derrida asks whether perhaps this privilege of the question itself "remained protected" in Heidegger (*OS* 25/9).

But if we were to wonder whether the privilege of the question perhaps itself remains unquestioned, then we will see that what is perhaps repressed, forgotten, avoided, or "protected" in this unquestioned privilege is hardly rehabilitated by *questioning* this privilege. The performative difficulty moves Derrida to concede that this matter may no longer even belong to the realm of "problematicity": "How, without confirming it a priori and circularly, can we *question* this inscription in the structure of the *Fragen* from which Dasein will have received, along with its privilege [*Vorrang*], its first, minimal, and most secure determination?" (*OS* 24/18).

What Derrida is after in this line of questioning the question is "a certain thinking of consent, of commitment in the form of a reply, of a responsible acquiescence, of agreement or confidence [*Zusage*], a sort of word given in return. Before any question and to make possible the question itself" [*Avant toute question et pour rendre possible la question même*] (*OS* 56/33). The key to understanding this lies in the interpretation of this "before" and "making possible" of the question. How does one get "before" the question if the question is already reaffirmed *in questioning it*? And what could "make it possible"?

Instead of seeing in this contortion a "self-contradiction" that would be grounds for refutation, Derrida interprets this structure as a symptom. This means that Derrida interprets the question of the question in terms of an a priori, always, already, having-had-to-have-subscribed-to. Such a subscription, confirmation, or acquiescence, with the future-perfect temporal structure of what one must always already have done, or what must always already have taken place, is what he calls *affirmation*.

In the main text of *Of Spirit*, Derrida only hints at this affirmation. He discusses the matter in a lengthy and already heavily commented-on footnote to the phrase "before any question" (OS 147n/129n).[10] The footnote is dedicated to Françoise Dastur, who brought Heidegger's idea of *Zusage* to Derrida's attention. Its importance lies in the fact that the *Zusage* seemed to displace the "privilege of the question" from a point *within* Heidegger's work, whereas Derrida had maintained that this privilege itself remained unquestioned throughout his writings.

The key to understanding the affirmation lies in how to interpret the "before." Insofar as the privilege of the question is only affirmed in questioning it, it is in a certain sense paradoxically unquestionable. What makes Derrida speak of "before the question" is that the privilege of the question is at a certain point "no longer a question." He clarifies:

> Not that it withdraws from the infinite legitimacy of questioning, but it tips over into the memory of a language, of an experience of language "older" than it, always anterior and presupposed, old enough never to have been present in an "experience" or a "speech act"—in the usual sense of these words. This moment—which is not a moment—is *marked* in Heidegger's text. (OS 147n/129n)

What is "older," "more original," "before"; différance as "older than" the ontological difference; contamination "more original" than non-contamination; affirmation "before" the question (one could add: deconstruction as "more than" critical; aiming at a "higher" responsibility, there are countless other such marks of this moment that structurally belongs to the logic of deconstruction). In all of these instances a certain hierarchy is articulated between the more original and the derived. This is where deconstruction is itself "still too metaphysical." As I have shown in chapter 1, deconstruction ruins the very hierarchy it proposes. "Older" and "before" are not titles of answers or solutions but of irreconcilabilities, because the thought of what is "older" or "makes possible" language undoes the possibility of a "condition of possibility," and so undoes itself. The very impossibility of "questioning" the privilege of the question (of getting beyond, behind, or before the question) shows an affirmation beyond, behind, or before the question. Here is how Derrida reconstructs this problem in the language of Heidegger:

> [. . .] at the moment at which we pose the ultimate question, i.e. when we interrogate (*Anfragen*) the possibility of any question, i.e. language, we must be already in the element of language. [. . .] Language is already there, in advance (*im voraus*) at the moment at which any question can arise about it. In this it exceeds the question. This advance is, before any contract, a sort of promise of originary alliance to which we must have in some sense already acquiesced, already said yes, given a pledge, whatever may be the negativity or problematicity of the discourse which may follow. This promise, this reply which is produced a priori in the form of acquiescence, this commitment of language towards language, this giving of language by language and to language is what Heidegger at this point regularly names *Zusage*. And it is in the name of this *Zusage* that he again puts in question, if one can still call it this, the ultimate authority, the supposed last instance of the questioning attitude. [. . .] (OS 147n/129–30n)

With the "before" of the "before any question," Derrida thus names an *irreducible* "before." This before is said to be always anterior and presupposed, "old enough *never to have been* present." Here is the future perfect: whatever the form or even the negativity of the discourse that may come: we will always already have said yes. The promise [*Zusage*] or pledge of this "yes" is therefore "sometimes wordless." It is "a sort of pre-originary pledge which precedes any other engagement in language or action." Derrida is explicit on the aporetic character of this "preceding": "But the fact that it precedes language does not mean that it is foreign to it. The gage engages *in* language and so always in a language" (OS 148n/130n, my italics, JdJ).

Different models of what we are to conclude from this present themselves.

The first would be that *Being and Time* departs from the privilege of the question as Dasein's own most secure determination and does not proceed to question this privilege itself. This is done only later when the thought of *Zusage* is introduced. The later Heidegger thus essentially breaks with the younger Heidegger: "[. . .] it has to be admitted that the thought of an affirmation anterior to any question and more proper to thought than any question must have an unlimited incidence [. . .] on the *quasi*-totality of Heidegger's previous path of thought" (OS 149n/131n).

But this model cannot hold. Not only because Derrida himself already points to aspects of *Being and Time* that echo the thought of the *Zusage*,[11] but because this model can only hold if the "before" was not inherently problematic or did not undo itself in its very explication. As if the thinking of the *Zusage* goes further or deeper than the thinking of the question, rather than denoting the very impossibility of going deeper in such a way, the affirmation of the question by questioning it, which is as much the unquestionability of the question.[12]

So Derrida explicitly rejects the possibility that the *Zusage* would provide a "retrospective upheaval" of Heidegger's work and come to "dictate a new order." That "now everything has to be begun again, taking as the point of departure the en-gage [*l'en-gage*] of the *Zusage* so as to construct a quite different discourse": "[. . .] without believing that we can henceforth not take account of this profound upheaval, we cannot take seriously the imperative of such a recommencement." Instead of recommencing, Derrida would propose an "other strategy," an other "stratigraphy" (OS 150n/132).

The difference between recommencement and a "different strategy," between retracing one's steps, moving differently into the same direction, and moving into an other direction altogether, is the difference between the "before" as a principle, condition, or a priori that would set everything in a new light, or the before as the very impossibility of such a principle that cannot yield a "new" discourse, but serves to disrupt or displace the old one, or to change one's relation to it.

To understand the relation between affirmation and indirectness, the short exchange between Geoffrey Bennington and Derrida at the Essex colloquium is helpful. Derrida stresses that the "yes" does not stand in opposition to a "no." The kind of affirmation meant here is "implied" even in "the most negative discourse" (in that sense, "it is not really a 'yes.' 'Yes' is a [. . .] linguistic translation of what I call affirmation"). This also means that "this yes is not a value, not an affirmation of a value, not an ethical stance" ("ORH" 176). Secondly, what this means is that it cannot be a matter of choosing "yes" as if one chooses "between yes and no" or takes up a position. For that reason, Bennington asks whether

Derrida's affirmation "might simply be a necessity." Derrida agrees to the extent that this is not the necessity of a "rule" or of a "law." Instead of the generality of law, this Necessity (which Derrida for this reason marks with a capital N) is said to be "singular," as it is not based on a rule or principle but with a "singular experience, with Ἀναρχη"; a necessity of the order of "the other which I can't escape" ("ORH 177").

That this affirmation does not involve "choice" is because Derrida's purpose in exploring this "yes" must be read in the context of developing a concept of responsibility that is no longer tied to autonomy. This is very clear in "Eating Well." Responsibility then means the ability to respond "before any question": "[. . .] that 'yes, yes' that answers before even being able to formulate a question, that is responsible without autonomy, before and in view of all possible autonomy of the who-subject" ("EW" 261). In this way, the "relation to the 'yes' or to the *Zusage* presupposed in every question" should lead to "a new (post-deconstructive) determination of the responsibility of the 'subject'" ("EW" 268). The word "subject" is in parentheses here because it is "problematic." Not so much because it is "inadequate" (insofar as that means that there might be other, adequate concepts), but precisely because "there neither can nor should be any concept adequate to what we call responsibility. Responsibility carries within it, and must do so, an essential excessiveness" ("EW" 272). Excess with respect to what? The subject, according to Derrida, is "also a principle of calculability," and "there is no responsibility, no ethico-political decision, that must not pass through the proofs of the incalculable or the undecidable" ("EW" 273).

This means that however "affirmative" deconstruction is, this affirmation is neither positive (in terms of a doctrine, principle, or program) nor negative (destructive). There is no tension in principle between the affirmation of which Derrida states that it "motivates deconstruction" and that is "unconditional, imperative and immediate" ("EW" 286) and its structural indirectness. This tension would only be there if affirmation meant something "positive." Instead, the affirmation is a matter of acquiescing to a "Necessity" that is not of the order of law, of responding in a way that is excessive and as such to "the other."[13]

THE UNDECONSTRUCTIBLE AND THE VULNERABILITY OF JUSTICE

With my claim that alterity is not reducible to externality, my proposal for a deconstructive ethics of complicity, and my thesis that this ethics can be understood from the perspective of indirectness rather than from a more Levinasian framework, I do not object to the term "other" per se, but to a specific interpretation of it.[14] This concerns the other as in some way external, but also the other as justification for the responsibility of deconstruction. One important objection that could be made to my argument is that, in *Force of Law*, Derrida introduced the notion of an "undeconstructible" justice, which therefore seems to exceed the deconstructible, exceed therefore the economy of complicity and contamination. In other words, the notion of the undeconstructible seems to be beyond or outside the movement of deconstruction. To fully address this important objection, one would have to provide a thorough reading of *Force of Law*, which must be saved for another occasion because it would require incorporating an entirely new register of concepts into this study, such as those of force, singularity, decision, and gift. But I am not the only one to have argued in this direction,[15] and I believe that my argument holds up in the face of the undeconstructible. I would like to sketch the outlines here of what a response to this objection would look like.

First of all, from its very first words and throughout *Force of Law*, the text presents the problem of justice as indissociable from the problem of language: it opens with a performative complication that shows the notion of a "direct" address (which Derrida is asked to give and is giving) to be essentially related to the content of said address: rectitudo and right. His argument is that deconstruction was always (about) justice, only perhaps not in *intentio recta*, but "obliquely." The indirect movement of deconstruction is what constitutes justice. The law of resemblance that I discussed in chapter 3 returns: Derrida distinguishes deconstruction as justice from "the sort of pessimistic, relativistic and empiricist skepticism" ("FL" 239), but only by showing a "mystical" moment that it seems to share with these discourses; this is the skeptical "moment of suspense" or "period of *epokhē*" ("FL" 248) through which the possibility of irresponsibility is "structurally present to the exercise of deconstruction" ("FL" 248). And yet, simultaneously, it is a "madness" that is "invincible to all skepticism" ("FL" 254).

What seems to fulfill the role of an externality is the "mystical foundation" of authority that Derrida, however, intends "to reinterpret and retrieve from its most conventional and most conventionalist reading" ("FL" 239). For Derrida's take on this mystical limit is "rather Wittgensteinian" in the sense that it is an *internal* limit:

> Discourse here meets its limit—*in itself, in its very performative power*. It is what I propose to call here the *mystical*. There is here a silence *walled up in* the violent structure of the founding act; *walled up, walled in* because this silence *is not exterior* to language. ("FL" 242, emphases added, JdJ)

At that point, Derrida introduces the distinction between deconstructible law and undeconstructible justice. But it is immediately clear that the very indirectness reserved for the movement of deconstruction itself ("if such a thing exists," etc.) forms the framework with which to understand this justice. In fact, and most emphatically: "*deconstruction is justice*" ("FL" 243, italicized in the original, JdJ). The undeconstructible cannot be an externality. It may not be deconstructible, but it is also not absolute in the sense of being outside, severed from, or beyond the *movement* of deconstruction—it is presented as nothing other than this very movement. Soon after Derrida's claim that deconstruction is justice, he comes back—very directly this time—to the theme of indirectness: "Why does deconstruction have the reputation, justified or not, of treating things *obliquely*, indirectly, in indirect style, with so many 'quotation marks,' and while always asking whether things arrive at the indicated address?" ("FL" 244). Derrida's answer is that this is because deconstruction is the negotiation of the aforementioned "mystical" internal limit, which he now calls an "experience of the aporia" or an "experience of the impossible." Derrida is clear that this is a hyperbolic impossibility and not simply an undecidability in the sense of an "oscillation" between two "decisions" ("FL" 252). It is the impossibility *within* each decision, which "deconstructs *from within* all assurance of presence, all certainty or all alleged criteriology assuring us of the justice of a decision" ("FL" 253, my italics, JdJ). I believe this thought to be in line with my proposal for an ethics of complicity, which sets itself apart from all desire for purity and non-contamination. That justice is undeconstructible does not mean it is absolute or external, and also not that it is pure or uncontaminated. Its structure is identical to that of the university without condition discussed in chapter 3: no existing reality (which for Derrida always means no *presence*) can correspond to it ("FL" 253). That also means that it cannot be thought as a (single) subsisting thing. It is, famously, also not an ideal, or an "idea in the Kantian sense," because it presents no type of "horizon" or "horizon of expectation" ("FL" 256) that would be able to compete with other such horizons of the same type—a competition that Derrida does not take himself to be engaged in ("FL" 254). Justice has no "messianic content."

It is not that justice is at odds with transcendence in all its possible senses; my claim against externality was never a claim against alterity. It is that transcendence is never pure or un-aporetic.[16] There is what Derrida calls a "messianic form" (sharply distinguished from all messianic content) that Derrida relates to the promise (which is related to the "perhaps" discussed in chapter 8), to singularity and indeed to the other. There is an openness to the future, which must structure the deconstructive commitment. But the promise cannot be experienced if what is promised is somehow already given, whether as an idea or an ideal, as a foreseeable future, or as a "horizon of expectation." What is left as undeconstructible seems to be nothing more than this structure or form of anticipation as such. It does not provide assurances. If Derrida states that the "idea of justice" (his quotation marks) is "owed to the other," then this points to the mystical limit, which was an *internal* limit: according to Derrida, deconstruction "cannot be motivated, [cannot] find its movement and its impulse [. . .] except in the demand for an increase or a supplement of justice, and so in the experience of an inadequation or an incalculable disproportion." It is in an experience of an inadequation that the demand for justice arises. For the distinction between justice and law can never be *pure:* "Everything would still be simple if this distinction between justice and law were a true distinction, an opposition the functioning of which was logically regulated and masterable" ("FL" 250). That justice is not an uncontaminated purity is especially clear when Derrida shows the risk that this could serve as an "alibi for staying out of juridico-political battles." Derrida writes: "Abandoned to itself [note that this is the same language Derrida uses to speak of the "conclusions" of his texts, JdJ], the incalculable and giving idea of justice is always very close to the bad, even the worst, for it can always be reappropriated by the most perverse calculation." But, crucially, Derrida "never held against calculation that condescending reticence of 'Heideggerian' haughtiness" ("EW" 287): "[One] must calculate" ("*De facto* and *de jure*"), which for Derrida means negotiating "the relation between the calculable and the incalculable, and negotiate without a rule that would not have to be reinvented there where we are 'thrown'" ("FL" 257).

The ethics of deconstruction is an ethics of complicity, which does not mean there is no promise, other, or singularity, but it means that this other cannot be a subsisting presence, single, opposite, external, pure, uncontaminated, idea, ideal, or reassurance. In other words: it cannot be an "escape." What is undeconstructible is the movement of deconstruction itself. Its motivation is not external to it, but its movement is a "performative force" that cannot claim theoretical legitimacy or *justesse*, and that never shies away from its own complicity and the recognition of its own "performative violence" ("FL" 271).

That is why this irreducible complicity is the point at which "the greatest force and the greatest weakness strangely exchange places" ("FL" 235). What Derrida attempts is to find a formulation for the responsibility that is neither dependent on a general rule, theory, position, or program, nor on any specific pre-given special interest, particular concern, contingent goal, or desire. There is an undeniably Platonic element here. But the excess of Derrida's "good beyond being" is not of the order of the behind or the before. It is not the responsibility of a deeper lying principle or ultimate insight. It exceeds both defense and justification as well as deniability, because it can only be affirmed in the questioning of the question; at work as an unavoidable avoidance. In this most positive of characteristics of deconstruction and in the clearest formulation of what makes it completely different from a "destructive" discourse, there is no contradiction with that discourse's indirectness. Instead, this responsibility is what motivates that very indirectness; a responsibility that Derrida takes up precisely *in and through* the indirect movement of showing of his writing.

CONCLUSION

I have shown in this chapter how, on the one hand, Derrida criticizes Heidegger for having avoided certain themes (gender, politics, race, animality, the body). At times, Derrida construes a certain Heidegger in such a way that he can play Heidegger out against himself in order to then define deconstruction in opposition to Heidegger's hermeneutics. The strategy is deliberate, but Derrida can be more or less transparent about this total movement at different times.[17] And this is no less true for Derrida's ambiguous relation to Hegel and "Hegelianism." Derrida admits: "here I do not have an answer" (*N* 26). On the other hand (like in *Spurs*' "question of woman"), this situation cannot simply be reversed by making present what was in Heidegger underrepresented. In several ways, Derrida stresses that the problems in Heidegger cannot be amended by reversing them. Instead, he argues that "complicity is irreducible." This holds equally for the critical relation to Heidegger. Through this unavoidability of avoidance, and especially in the affirmation of the "privilege of the question" in the attempt to question it, Derrida tries to illustrate the constraints within which a new concept of responsibility takes shape. The critical relation to Heidegger now becomes one in which Heidegger is reaffirmed in the attempt to exceed him. That affirmation is an unavoidability and an unconditionality that exceeds both the generality of the rule and any particular principle, ethics, standpoint, or interest.

What I wanted to stress here is how, at this point, where deconstruction is at its most positive, and where Derrida's writings differ most from a negative or destructive discourse—that this positivity does not contradict, but rather finds its expression in, Derrida's indirectness. It is the intellectual responsibility one takes, one's *commitment* or *engagement* in language, in questioning, deciding, distinguishing, that extends beyond the following of any rule or the endorsement of a theory or program. In that sense it is, for Derrida, always already "before." But what is *structurally* before therefore also will never in fact take place; we will not be able to think it in terms of a taking-place.

With that, Derrida points to an affirmation that is not so much before or outside as it is everywhere implicit *in* our engagement with language. Derrida does not say implicit. He is too much of a Heideggerian and therefore temporalizes this affirmation: it is what must always already have *taken place*. I must always already have said yes, in a "'past' that has never been present" (*MP* 22/21). This commitment or engagement is undeconstructible, but that is never reassuring. What this ethics of complicity is most vigilant against is that the notions of the undeconstructible or of the other are used as a justification in order to fashion that "remoralization of deconstruction" that leads to a self-congratulatory "community of complacent deconstructionists, reassured and reconciled with the world in ethical certainty, good conscience, satisfaction of service rendered, and the consciousness of duty accomplished" ("P" 15). There certainly is a promise and therewith a "relation to the other" at work in deconstruction, but that can never function as a reassurance and can never safeguard itself against the "reintroduction of the worst." In enacting deconstruction's responsibility, one is never "off the hook," never not complicit, and always engaged in a "bet." Before or "in" our every engagement with language, this affirmative responsibility is what Derrida's indirectness is an expression of. The entanglements of performativity are what necessitate his indirectness. This affirmative responsibility is what motivates it.

AFTERWORD

Philosophical Indirections

I have provided a reading of Derrida, Hegel, and Heidegger that accounts for why they fundamentally understand their philosophical projects in terms of a development, movement, or pathway instead of in terms of its conclusions or results. My question was what necessitates this "indirectness," as I have called it. I have tried to show that the writings of Hegel, Heidegger, and Derrida exceed the positivity of a position, what can be contained in the content of a proposition or determined through opposition. They are, *mutatis mutandis*, attempts to explicate the limits of that very (op-)positionality—respectively: the determinations of the understanding or of reflection (Hegel); representation (Heidegger); metaphysics (Derrida)—with regard to which no simple point of externality is possible. The absence of such a point of externality results in an irreducible entanglement of "method and object." I write this in full awareness that many readers of Derrida would already object to such terms. My main point is to go against precisely such straightforward nonacceptance of the discourse that would be deemed "too classical" or "too metaphysical." This entanglement means that the discourse is inextricably bound to the very oppositionality it attempts to exceed. That necessitates a certain kind of reflexivity or performativity of the investigation: that there are limits to the direct, thetic, or positional discourse cannot itself be simply posited but is enacted indirectly through a certain movement of showing.

Insofar as this book has therefore been about indirectness, the aforementioned reflexivity indicates that "indirectness" does not name a particular subject that I would have been able to demarcate. It is not a phenomenon that would have its own "field," of which this text would then be the complete description. Indirectness is not restricted to the texts of Derrida, Hegel, and Heidegger (or, for that matter, to those of Nietzsche or of the skeptics), nor are their writings exhaustively characterized by that term. What I have tried to do with the term indirect is to name a focal point with which to make sense of what these authors have written and especially of the way in which they have written it, and to argue that you can't understand the former without taking the latter into account. I have done this because the failure to recognize the indirect character of philosophical texts is the biggest obstacle in interpreting their significance and value. The failure to take it into account risks naively reintroducing a form of rationality—even if that rationality is in a certain sense unavoidable—that the texts themselves performatively exceed.

There are a few questions that I need to explicitly return to at this point. Before specifying some of the ideas to which I intended my work to provide a counter-thrust, I first indicate why, if I have been successful, my own exposition will not have displayed the implicit or explicit self-complication that has been my theme.

Because the question will be asked: what about my own perspective? What about my "entanglement of method and object"? What about my own reflexivity or performativity in representing, thematizing, making explicit, in the conventional form of a book-length treatise, this theme of indirectness, of what does not let itself be represented or thematized, of what is essentially implicit?

There is a more facile and a more principled response to this question. The facile one is that I have set out to do nothing more than to provide a commentary, and to provide a way of reading that goes against certain ideas about how to interpret the work of Hegel, Heidegger, and Derrida. Specifically, views that seemed to me too oppositional, too much focused on the determination of their philosophical positions, and too reductive of the ambiguity and self-contradiction that their exposition seeks to recognize and preserve instead of overcome. There is no reason why that reading could not be explicated unequivocally. In the conclusions to each of my chapters, I have attempted to be as clear and unequivocal as possible on my positions and theses in this regard.

The more principled answer is—and this is where the virtue comes in of being able to compare, side by side, approaches as different as Hegel's, Heidegger's, and Derrida's—that an awareness of the performative complexity of philosophical texts does not in itself necessitate a specific style. There is no single "right way" to go about this, and one of my main points has been not to confuse the explication of the limits of understanding, reflection, (op)positionality, or metaphysics with an *opposition* to them. It is not a matter of *doing away* with representation or opposition, nor with the traditional form of an academic treatise. At issue is precisely an "inner excess," or how *in* what presents itself as proposition, representation or claim, something more, less, or other than what is "posited" in them is taking place. That does not in principle prescribe or exclude any specific scientific or literary form. I have attempted to show systematically how the dynamic and force of the texts under discussion is not reducible to the content of their conclusions. That means that I have attempted throughout not to close them off by providing a definitive interpretation from an external point of view. I say more about this later. First, I make clear what I think are the interpretations that lacked the necessary focus on the indirect character of the texts I discussed.

INDIRECTNESS AND THE QUESTION OF CRITIQUE

First, I've tried to provide a counter-thrust to the idea that Derrida is engaged in a movement "towards the outside." In a very general way, one can say that the concept of the "(wholly) Other" has often been taken to be too much of a deconstructive point of anchorage, rather than as being itself thoroughly aporetic. Now, on the one hand, one could object here that, surely, Derrida's thought of irreducible contamination or complicity is quite well-known in commentary. "There is no sense in doing without metaphysics in order to shake metaphysics"—is that not one of the best-known Derridean adages? And yet. The very same commentaries often ascribe to Derrida a "new" (not-simply-metaphysical) *account of the nature of language* (as arche-writing, trace, or différance); understand Derrida's critical question of "alterity" or of the "other," or his attempt to "write otherwise" as the attempt to find a new or other language; and understand deconstruction in opposition to dialectics and hermeneutics. After all, does Derrida not consistently talk of breaking or cutting through, broaching [*entamer*] the order of metaphysics?

I have argued against this view. The movement of Derrida's writings cannot be reduced to the kinds of counter-positions with respect to metaphysics that one finds within them. Instead, he sought to chart the very structure of "irreducible complicity" by which counter-positions are metaphysically reasserted or reinscribed, which can only be done in a writing that does not itself "provide assurances." It was not a matter of finding a way of writing that would *not* be complicit, that would *avoid* these complicities. His structurally open question was rather how one accounts for those unavoidable constraints *in* writing. What kind of writing could or would do so? What this has consequences for above all is the initial question that prompted my investigation into Derrida: how to critically engage with a writing that seems to "avoid the ground on which it could find support"? This brings us to the question of critique.

The question of a critique of Derrida seems to be saturated by the very oppositionality that his texts are out to exceed. Initially, it revolved around his "empiricism" (lack of justification) and his "skepticism" (his self-refuting relativism or his performative self-contradiction). Here the accounts on both sides are problematic: as necessary as it was to defend Derrida against the reduction of his writings to a skepticism or a relativism, those who stood up in his defense have often too easily yielded to the explicit position that deconstruction simply "is not" skepticism (or empiricism, relativism, critique, a method, negative theology, etc.). I have shown at length that, when the question of critique is not a polemic of defense and refutation, then Derrida's relation to empiricism, skepticism, and critique becomes fascinating: it is an oppositional entanglement; its explicit denials nonetheless structured by a "law of resemblance." The most interesting part is not so much Derrida's distinction from a simple relativism, empiricism, or skepticism, but this resemblance that binds deconstruction to these figures structurally, without however being identical to them (a difference therefore described by Derrida as "in a certain sense, nothing"). Derrida is structurally vulnerable to the accusation of skepticism because his only "defense" lies in the movement of his texts, in what they bring out or *show* rather than what they posit or result in.[1]

That makes Derrida's indirectness both his strength and his weakness: on the one hand, the force of his texts is not that of the justified position. I strongly resist the tendencies in commentary to nonetheless provide Derrida with one. On the other hand, clearly, to take that vulnerability as grounds for refutation would be to negate the very indirectness that makes up the essence and value of Derrida's writing.

Does that mean that no critique of Derrida is possible, that his "undecidability" elevates him above criticism (which would in itself, we should not forget, be a valid criticism)? Certainly not. But it means that a true critique of Derrida's work (if it wants to find its mark) must take his indirectness into account. I have shown in different ways where Derrida's work can and must be criticized. As generous a reader as Derrida is, his readings are reductive in their own way. The specific structure of logocentrism or of metaphysics (of the specific type of conceptual demarcation, hierarchy, presence, and above all oppositionality) is always there, and it is not without its own limitations and its own blind spot. Sometimes so much so that, to bring out the aporetic nature of a distinction, Derrida must at times first introduce into his reading the type of binarity or oppositionality that he in fact hopes to exceed.[2] But the critique of Derrida's "style" must take into account what that style is an expression of. Derrida's concern with showing and preserving ambiguity and contradiction is with opening the texts he reads. Indirectness is not only vulnerability, nor simply negative, because Derrida wrests the texts from the polemics of positions. This is his main virtue. I have shown how texts like "Tympan," *Spurs*, and *Of Spirit* are exemplary cases in point. Derrida's enactment opens a reading that is suspended between unequivocal positions, which is also *what* the text states: just like Nietzsche's, the movement of Derrida's text is suspended in the openness of the "perhaps."

NECESSITY AND MOTIVATION: PERFORMATIVITY AND RESPONSIBILITY

I have tried to show at length the impossibilities and inextricabilities that guide the performativity and style of Derrida's writing, and its irreducibility to the positivity of a position. The more *positive* sense of that indirectness (not merely its "irreducibility to . . ."), which distinguishes it from a merely negative discourse, is what I have only been able to touch on briefly in my final chapter. What necessitates a certain indirectness can be found in the complexities and constraints of performativity, the impossibility to "oppose opposition," and the need to "write otherwise." But what motivates Derrida's indirectness, the attempt to maintain this vulnerability, is a resolve or commitment to what he takes to be the greatest philosophical or intellectual *responsibility*. Here indirectness becomes a normative or ethical imperative.

Derrida conceives this responsibility, which he calls affirmative, as the ability to respond to the "call of the other." It designates the form of engagement in, or commitment to, language that is not dependent on or reducible to any specific theory, axiom, program, goal, or principle. Nor can that affirmation, for that very reason, be questioned or doubted (like a theory can, or an axiom, proposition, hypothesis, or anything that can be posited). "Responsibility" is Derrida's term for this commitment to what we do when we are "in" language, when we interrogate, postulate, justify, question, criticize, decide. This commitment is affirmative because it "precedes" both every *specific* questioning or program as well as any *general* rule or law. But it precedes it without coming "before" it: it is Derrida's attempt to identify the responsibility that we take on and implicitly assume *in* our every engagement in language. One cannot help but think of Plato here: that what drives us ultimately (in doing philosophy, in thinking, in life), what makes up our concern, our goal, our motivation—the "good *itself*"—exceeds both the generality of the rule and the specificity of a determined special interest, program, or goal.

This means that, on the one hand, this responsibility is essentially related to an excess: "[. . .] there neither can nor should be any concept adequate to what we call responsibility. Responsibility carries within it, and must do so, an essential excessiveness" ("EW" 278). It is an *unconditional* responsibility, and it is a responsibility for the "other" because it is the affirmation of the very commitment that cannot be tied to a specific interest or program, or to something one would be able simply to do in any voluntaristic sense (hence a responsibility "without autonomy" ["EW" 261]). Because of this excess, the descriptions of the movement of deconstruction are all inherently paradoxical and self-contradictory (deconstruction is an "experience of the impossible"; every decision must "go through the undecidable"; and so on). This holds no less for the reflective categories that Hegel is forced to use in his attempt to exceed reflection ("identity of identity and non-identity") or for Heidegger's descriptions of his thinking of a path that is created *in* following it, or of a saying that is itself the "to be said." For Derrida, this unconditional responsibility therefore can be neither defended nor doubted. This makes it as strong as it is weak, and the last thing such an "insight" into unconditional responsibility should do is lead to a "remoralization of deconstruction." That is, lead to:

> the constitution of a consensual euphoria or, worse, a community of complacent deconstructionists, reassured and reconciled with the world in ethical certainty, good conscience, satisfaction of service rendered, and the consciousness of duty accomplished (or, more heroically still, yet to be accomplished). ("P" 15)

Derrida is emphatic on this point: he "prefers" giving "ammunition to the officials of anti-deconstruction" to this consensual euphoria. Against this remoralization or this reintroduction of ethical purity into deconstruction, I have argued for a Derridean *ethics of complicity*. Even if this ethics, this commitment, or this responsibility function in the name of justice, it cannot claim for itself the theoretical or juridical legitimacy of the fixed or unmovable point, the assurance or certainty with which it would be able to *safeguard* itself from skepticism.[3] Hegel, Nietzsche, Heidegger, and Derrida each in his own way tried to show the excess of the very understanding, oppositionality, and representation that he employed in showing it. This is the structural vulnerability of the indirect discourse—the exposition of which must be a self-complication. This means that at this point—but I believe this can be extrapolated to a general rule—*skepticism is always possible*. It is not "refutable." This is so because its irreducible virtue is to show the limitations of any given position. This is why, aside from defining himself against skepticism, Derrida acknowledged it as a "moment of attention to difference," and why Hegel acknowledged it as a "moment of truth." The only antidote to the type of reductive skepticism that merely posits its negative results as absolute is movement.

THE PHILOSOPHICAL TRADITION

The idea that alterity is not simply externality has consequences for how Derrida's relation to traditional metaphysics is understood. For Derrida's thinking has often been equated with the opposition to metaphysics (against dialectics, the hermeneutical circle, full meaning, phenomenology, (self-)presence, etc.) that is at best only a part of that movement. That is why, rather than understanding Derrida's writings as emancipatory with respect to metaphysics, one could paradoxically call Derrida an emancipator from that very emancipation—from that wish to rid or free oneself (once and for all, even) from traditional, logocentric metaphysics. What his writings resist above all is the *naive* breakthrough, the *perceived* externality, the outside that only amounts to a reversal and thus to nothing more than the same. I have done this by pointing to notions such as "inextricability," "differential contamination," and irreducible complicity. It is the awareness of this risk that also permeates the various reversals of Nietzsche's text, Hegel's critique of everything that is posited as wholly foreign to the movement of the concept,[4] and Heidegger's critiques of transcendence and of *Erlebnis*: the domesticated mystery that presents itself as interesting and question worthy but is in fact—as the mere opposite of machination—machination in disguise. What Heidegger's critiques of *Erlebnis* and transcendence show well is that what drives this thinking is an *urgency* with respect to questioning *us, here, now*—who or what we are or what we are inextricably bound up with or are "in." What is misleading about "transcendence" is that it suggests that the mystery is elsewhere, that the focus should be on the *jenseits*. The figure of transcendence risks functioning as a reassurance with respect to everything on *this side* of the limit. Thus it feeds Heidegger's "plight of the lack of a sense of plight."—"*Here* is the rose, dance *here,*" wrote Hegel.[5]

I have tried to show how the interpretation of Derrida as participating in a movement "towards the outside" creates a false opposition in two ways: (1) it does not take into account that Derrida's own relation to Hegel and Heidegger is inherently ambiguous and does not have the form of a counter-position; and (2) it does not take Hegel's and Heidegger's *own* indirectness into account. It does not take into account the extent to which the titles of dialectics, hermeneutics, or phenomenology themselves never simply designated "mere metaphysics," but that they are forms of *movement*, and therefore might be more aligned with Derrida's intentions than appearances might suggest.

At this point there is certainly more work to do. I have shown the *Contributions'* radical performativity to be exemplary of Heidegger's indirectness. We have barely begun to grasp the radicality of this "middle period" work, the "beyng-historical" works that succeeded it, and the notebooks that accompany them.

But the opposition between Hegel and Derrida was always bigger than the one between Derrida and Heidegger, and perhaps the biggest task lies in the interpretation of Hegel's indirectness. I have only skimmed the surface by reading some of Hegel's earlier works as explications of what is essentially implicit. I am convinced that this way of reading can and must be pursued into the *Science of Logic* and later works.[6] Certainly, the sections on method in "The Absolute Idea" give plenty of material with which to show the movement of the system as explication of the essentially implicit.

By reading all three as thinkers of movement, and by in all three cases arguing against the "outside," all the weight of explanation and interpretation falls on the meaning of "in." This is what I have tried to show in my discussion of Hegel's movement *of* or *in* the determinations; in the relation of Heidegger's early "being-in" to his later "movement of showing" *in* the propositions; the truth of beyng as it is concealed, sheltered *in* beings; poietic saying not as an other language, but as *attunement* to the call of beyng *in* the "everyday words and namings"; and in Derrida's deconstruction "from the inside." It is common to all these senses of "in" that they cannot be reduced to "containment" within a "totality." Such a reading could initiate a perhaps different kind of hermeneutics, or at least different from the restricted, polemical sense that Derrida sometimes gives to the term: as a project that only aims to "fill in the breach" toward "full meaning."

But such a program of reading that focuses on the essentially implicit does not reduce the differences between these thinkers. Instead, it brings differences between them into focus that are perhaps more subtle than those that can be articulated in terms of the exclusive disjunction of philosophical positions ("différance" *or* "difference," "absolute idealism" *or* "fundamental ontology," etc.), but that nevertheless fundamentally determine the sense of their respective philosophical projects, according to the different senses of what it means to be "in." Heidegger's quest for a "philosophical saying" cannot be opposed to Derrida's as the melancholic attempt to "get it right" that Derrida's differential thought would have left behind. And yet the specific form of Heidegger's poietic language, the particular blend of phenomenological language and Hölderlinian poetics, is undeniably imbued with a categorically different style or mood than Derrida's. But those are not differences of position. They are—to use Derrida's words—differences of "scenography," of "style of thinking, of philosophizing" ("ORH" 180). The more salient differences, however, were always those between Hegel on the one hand and Heidegger and Derrida on the other. The essence of the divergence lies in Heidegger's transformation (specifically: his *narrowing*) of the concept of *objectivity*. Though implied by my account, a sufficient meditation on this transformation will have to be undertaken elsewhere. For Hegel, the essentially implicit pertains to logical determinations, meaning that there can be (to put it in a language that Heidegger and Derrida could never use) different *forms of* objectivity: and these different forms structure the object and can thus themselves only be shown, investigated, and criticized through a dialectical development, and not themselves be "objectified," which would reduce philosophy to one way of knowing, instead of the tracing of the development of the different possible ways of knowing. But for Heidegger the essentially implicit takes on the form of what one is "always already in," such that it cannot be put "before" oneself as a describable object [*Gegen-stand*]. In Heidegger, Hegel's investigation of the *different forms* of objectivity is narrowed down to objectivity "as such," as it develops from mere *Vorhandenheit* in *Being and Time* to *Gegenstehenlassen* and *Anwesen*. Now "being-in" is no longer the inextricability of Hegelian immanence. The excess of movement with respect to the proposition is now a "hiddenness" or "concealment" rather than a "one-sidedness." It is still a matter of an irreducible inextricability, but of a very different form. Instead of counter-positing, a fruitful critique of Hegel, Heidegger, or Derrida would aim at such an explication of the different character of the kinds of showing at hand.

What I hope to have made clear is that although there is no safeguard against skepticism, the excess of the essentially implicit with respect to what can be represented or "contained" within propositions does not have to lead to a skepticism about language in the sense of a focus on what *cannot* be said: the ineffable, unsayable, unknowable. Such a focus unavoidably entails a fixed position on the limits of language that goes against itself. The focus on the implicit achieves the opposite: even given the limitations of the propositional form, of representation, and of oppositional determination, it is *in and through* them that we can and in fact do say more, less, or something else than what is merely "contained" in those determinations. Therefore, the insight into these limits does not lead to a negative or skeptical view on language as inadequate or as failing, but rather to a *productive* view on propositions and claims such that they might carry or co-implicate more than the content that is "contained" in them. But if this is the case, then such an indirect approach would put in question the presumed "directness" of philosophical "positions," and it would enable a different way to read the classical philosophical texts: one that takes Derrida's lessons on board without having to play these texts out against themselves, as Derrida himself not infrequently does. Perhaps there is even more movement to be found in the seemingly unequivocal, in the allegedly traditional, in the supposedly metaphysical. The history of metaphysics need not be constrained by Derrida's diagnosis of all-pervasive oppositional hierarchy, nor does what *does* exceed that hierarchy need to be deconstructively extracted *against* the "declared intentions" of the text.

In "conclusions" such as these, it is customary to look ahead to "future research." I have only been able to present the outlines of what an ethics of complicity would look like. What a future hermeneutics of the implicit could do, what I have attempted in reading Derrida, Hegel, and Heidegger here, is to start by looking back at those traditional texts that have too often been opposed to our times, to have them "break absolutely with constituted normality," to identify in them what exceeds the apparent positivity of their positions, and to treat them as resources for a showing that does not let itself be posited. There is still much work to do in reading philosophy beyond the textual positivism of this type. One very interesting question is what the character of philosophical language or writing could or should be "after Derrida." But, as I have indicated, the focus on the implicit does not prescribe (nor exclude) a specific scientific or literary form. Does the "plurality of styles" then mean that anything is possible? But isn't the "monstrosity" of Derrida's *avenir* defined in its opposition to the *mere possibility* of *la future*? Nothing essential is *impossible* anymore, lamented Heidegger. The source of Kierkegaard's entire "indirect" authorship was geared toward exposing the infinity or impossibility of what was taken to be a mere possibility or a realizable task. There is nothing to escape, and the excess is not elsewhere. What I have tried to argue throughout is that vigilance is perhaps most required where we risk getting too carried away by the prospect of "future possibilities" or by the thought of some *other* life.

NOTES

INTRODUCTION

1. G. W. F. Hegel, *Outlines of the Philosophy of Right*, trans. T. M. Knox, ed. Stephen Houlgate (Oxford: Oxford University Press, 2008), 4ff.

2. Martin Heidegger, *What Is Called Thinking?*, trans. J. Glenn Gray (New York: Harper and Row, 1968), 77.

3. Theodor W. Adorno, "The Essay as Form," trans. Bob Hullot-Kentor and Frederic Will, *New German Critique*, no. 32 (Spring–Summer 1984): 166.

4. Michel Foucault, *The Archeology of Knowledge* (New York: Pantheon, 1972), 205.

5. Though of the three philosophers that I consider here, Derrida is the only one to have explicitly developed such a concept of responsibility, one can also recognize it, for instance, in Hegel's fulminations against formalism in philosophy, or in Heidegger's attacks on, e.g., *Weltanschauungsphilosophie* or other forms of thought—attacks that are fundamentally about the task of philosophy and about philosophical responsibility.

6. I choose the word "indirect" not without reservations (see n. 7). What I have in mind is Kierkegaard's use of the term. On the one hand, for Kierkegaard, the term indirect applies both to Christ's necessarily indirect manifestation in the "form of unrecognizability": the God-man is a "sign," but a sign of a "contradiction." See Søren Kierkegaard, *Practice in Christianity*, trans. and ed. Howard V. Hong and Edna H. Hong (Princeton: Princeton University Press, 1991), esp. 124ff. But, more specifically, I think of the indirect character of Kierkegaard's *own* writings. I choose the term indirect primarily because, for Kierkegaard, it signifies the performative or reflexive necessity to adapt the style of his writings to his central problem. That central problem, for him, was the state of confusion about Christianity within the "Christendom" of his day. The confusion lies in the idea that one can "be" a Christian; that this would be a realizable or simply possible task, instead of being involved in a ceaseless becoming, or even in what is "humanly speaking" an impossibility. But that means that Kierkegaard

cannot in turn be the one who describes, posits, or presents the true essence of Christianity. It exceeds scientific or objective description because its decisive moment is "subjective" in the sense that Kierkegaard gives to the term: peculiar to one's singular existence. Moreover, the very confusion consists in the idea that the truth of Christianity could be handed down (in the form of a program, of guidelines or rules, in a treatise or a sermon). Instead, Kierkegaard's plurality of styles (most visible in his various pseudonyms) aims at indirectly tempting the reader to enter into a relation with him/herself (more precisely: into "becoming a self"). In a fragment in which he describes his own authorship as the expression of an "armed neutrality," he writes: "Therefore, to present in every way—dialectical, pathos-filled (in the various forms of pathos), psychological, modernized by continual reference to modern Christendom and to the fallacies of a science and scholarship—the ideal picture [*Billede*] of being a Christian: that was and is the task" (Søren Kierkegaard, *The Point of View*, trans. and ed. Howard V. Hong and Edna H. Hong [Princeton: Princeton University Press, 1998], 131). For Kierkegaard, this means that his "aesthetic productivity" is necessarily a "deception," albeit one that must be understood "in a special sense": "But a deception, that is indeed something rather ugly. To that I would answer: Do not be deceived by the word *deception*. One can deceive a person out of what is true, and—to recall old Socrates—one can deceive a person into what is true" (Søren Kierkegaard, *The Point of View*, 53). Hegel, Heidegger, and Derrida do not conceive of their productivity in terms of deceit. But it is indirect to the extent that what is at stake in their writings necessarily exceeds the positivity of a "position," and therefore demands a change in the way the investigation proceeds (in its style, its language, its concepts, its linearity, its method).

7. In "Envois," in *The Post Card*, Derrida writes of an "incorrigible indirection," a "*non-simplicity*," and an "*indirectness*" that "promise [. . .] an inexhaustible reserve for speculation," but adding, importantly, that "this reserve does not consist of substantial riches, but rather of additional turns, supplementary angles, differential ruses as far as the eye can see" (*PC* 280). And in "Passions: An Oblique Offering," in a meditation on how the concept of responsibility must exceed "the pro-positional form" and that "we *should not above all* approach in a direct, frontal *projective*, that is, thetic or thematic way," he stresses especially that it is not a matter of simply opposing an oblique approach to this direct one. "On reflection," he writes there, "the oblique does not seem to me to offer the best figure for all the moves that I have tried to describe in that way." For like the "in-" of "indirect," the oblique cannot help but receive its meaning through an oppositional negation of the straight line. That is: with recourse to the very oppositionality it purports to exceed: "The oblique remains the choice of a strategy that is still crude, obliged to ward off what is most urgent, a geometric calculus for diverting as quickly as possible both the frontal approach and the

straight line: presumed to be the shortest path from one point to another. Even in its rhetorical form and in the figure of figure that is called *oratio obliqua*, this displacement still appears too direct, linear, economic, in complicity with the diagonal arc" ("P" 13).

8. Leonard Lawlor, "Translator's Introduction" to *Voice and Phenomenon: Introduction to the Problem of the Sign in Husserl's Phenomenology*, by Jacques Derrida (Evanston: Northwestern University Press, 2011), xii.

9. My present concern is not to negate emancipation as such, but to question the extent to which a certain model or interpretation of emancipation is compatible with Derrida's work. In many places, Derrida associates the term emancipation with freedom and self-determination (for example, at Jacques Derrida, *The Beast and the Sovereign, Vol. I.*, ed. Geoffrey Bennington [Chicago: University of Chicago Press, 2009], 301). Those concepts are part of an Enlightenment-legacy that Derrida often confesses to believe in (e.g.: "nothing seems to me less outdated than the classical emancipatory ideal," "FL" 258). Though of course this belief is never without reservation. Compare, for instance: "In the first place, everything that may have heralded a philosophy of Enlightenment or inherited something from it (not only rationalism, which is not necessarily associated with it, but a progressive, teleological, humanistic, and critical rationalism) indeed struggles against a 'return of the worst,' which both education and an awareness of the past are always supposed to be able to prevent. Although this Enlightenment struggle often takes the form of deterrence and denial, one cannot help but take part in it and reaffirm this philosophy of emancipation. As for myself, I believe in its future, and I have never found myself in agreement with proclamations about the end of the great discourses of emancipation or revolution. But their affirmation itself attests to the possibility of what it is opposed to: the return of the worst, an uneducable repetition-compulsion in the death drive and radical evil, a history without progression, a history without history, etc" (*N* 106).

10. One very clear articulation of this suspicion can be found in *Positions*: "There *is not* a transgression, if one understands by that a pure and simple landing into a beyond of metaphysics, at a point which also would be, let us not forget, first of all a point of language or writing. Now, even in aggressions or transgressions, we are consorting with a code to which metaphysics is tied irreducibly, such that every transgressive gesture reencloses us—precisely by giving us a hold on the closure of metaphysics within this closure. But, by means of the work done on one side and the other of the limit the field inside is modified, and a transgression is produced that consequently is nowhere present as a *fait accompli*. One is never installed within transgression, *one never lives elsewhere* [my emphasis, JdJ]. Transgression implies that the limit is always at work. Now, the 'thought-that-means-nothing,' the thought that exceeds meaning and meaning-as-hearing-oneself-speak by interrogating them—this thought, announced in grammatology,

is given precisely as the thought for which there is no sure opposition between outside and inside. At the conclusion of a certain work, even the concepts of excess or of transgression can become suspect. This is why it has never been a question of opposing a graphocentrism to a logocentrism [. . .]" (*Pos* 21/12).

11. Here again, it is not a matter of making this apparently unequivocal thesis into an unequivocal position. I am aware that "externality" has itself been used very fruitfully and productively precisely in approaching the very concerns Derrida addresses under the heading of "alterity." I am thinking here especially of the work of Blanchot or Bataille. My point is not to refute this, but to stress that if this concept has been effective, it was not by designating a realm beyond a determinable border. It would, in other words, have to have been an externality that is somehow "within," and that would already get the deconstruction of that concept under way. There is nothing that excludes in principle the efficacy of the "external" as a deconstructive quasi-concept, as I believe Blanchot uses it. But this still means distinguishing the "external" as a "quasi-transcendental" from its colloquial oppositional meaning, and also recognizing that even if one successfully does so, there is still nothing to protect this quasi-transcendental externality from being, in the words of Derrida, "one day [. . .] superseded, lending itself if not to its own replacement, at least to enmeshing itself in a chain that in truth it never will have governed." According to Derrida, it not only "may well," but it "must" one day do so (*MP* 7/7).

12. *Of Grammatology* is filled with such remarks. See also, for instance: what "exceeds this closure *is nothing*" (G 405/286).

13. See: *BT* §12ff.

14. The term "reflection" has, in the literature on Derrida, no doubt been made most famous by Rodolphe Gasché in his 1986 *The Tain of the Mirror: Derrida and the Philosophy of Reflection* (Cambridge and London: Harvard University Press, 1986). But reflection has a multitude of senses and connotations (especially in the context of Hegel's philosophy), for which the image of the mirror can be misleading. For Hegel, philosophy is distinguished from all other sciences by not having the luxury of being able to define beforehand either its method or its object, because both need to be justified within the investigation itself. This necessitates an *immanent self*-development in which object and method are inextricably entangled and themselves undergo continual development. Hegel's "performativity" lies in this structurally reflexive character of the investigation. But the difficulty with Hegel's idea of a "reflection-in-itself" is that this very idea is *itself* not exempt from reflecting back on itself. That is to say: one must distinguish at least the following different senses of "reflection" for Hegel: there is the reflection "in itself" as it is a *part of* Hegel's very method; then there is the reflection as it is an *object for* that method; and then there is the very kind of philosophy ("phiolosophy of reflection") that Hegel's reflection-in-itself was

supposed to *overcome*. Where Gasché claims that Derrida's works are ultimately irreducible to the philosophy of reflection (after all is said and done, Derrida, according to Gasché, works on the "tain" of that mirror), I emphasize that, to a certain extent, it is precisely the reflexive character of indirectness that constitutes a shared concern for Hegel, Heidegger, and Derrida.

15. Derrida criticized the concept of performativity for good reasons, and its use in interpreting Hegel and Heidegger amounts to an anachronism. Though it introduces a valuable dimension of language irreducible to the content of conclusions—J. L. Austin, after all, distinguished the performative from the constative in his *How to Do Things with Words* (Oxford: Clarendon Press, 1962)—its meaning is still rooted in a distinction between theory and practice that I show to be problematic (even if Derrida sometimes formulates his indirectness in terms of "acts" or "practices" of writing, the meaning of which will have to be explained). In contemporary continental philosophy, the concept of performativity has a host of different meanings. I take it up in the sense in which, for example, David Wood uses it, who identifies under the heading of "performative reflexivity" the problems that he initially identified as the "paradoxes of reflection" and the "question of style" and of "strategy." See chapter 8 ("Performative Reflexivity") in his *Philosophy at the Limit* (London: Unwin Hyman, 1990), 132ff.; the "paradoxes of reflection" and the "question of strategy" in his *The Deconstruction of Time*, 2nd ed. (Evanston: Northwestern University Press, 2001), 279ff., and "The Performative Imperative: Reflections on Heidegger's *Contributions to Philosophy (From Eventuation)*," in his *Thinking After Heidegger* (Cambridge/Malden: Polity, 2002), 153. For Derrida's engagement with speech act theory, see "Signature Event Context," in *Margins of Philosophy* (Chicago: University of Chicago Press, 1982) and the subsequent polemic with John Searle in *Limited Inc* (Evanston: Northwestern University Press, 1988). Of course, since Austin "performativity" has acquired many other senses. For a good discussion of the term with respect to Derrida's work, see Joseph Hillis-Miller, "Derrida's Special Theory of Performativity," in *For Derrida* (New York: Fordham University Press, 2009), 133–73; and Michael Naas's response in "Pray Tell: Derrida's Performative Justice," in *The End of the World and Other Teachable Moments* (New York: Fordham University Press, 2014), 104–24.

16. There is an especially intimate link between the performative or reflexive entanglement under investigation here, and the tradition of self-reflection or self-consciousness. But this is so only up to a point. Though some feel that Derrida's warning that deconstruction does not belong to philosophy's eternal self-interrogation precisely elevates Derrida above that tradition, I show that all the authors I deal with in this book stress that there is no simply given self "upon" which the philosophical discourse would or could then reflect: for Hegel the self is nothing other than the unfolding or the movement *of* the philosophical exposition; Heidegger stresses that a true meditation on the self makes it

fundamentally enigmatic; and who "we" are is one of Derrida's most frequently repeated structurally open questions ("critique of self, but critique of whom exactly? To whom should the reflexive be returned?" ["P" 13]).

17. See Daniela Vallega-Neu, *Heidegger's Contributions to Philosophy: An Introduction* (Bloomington: Indiana University Press, 2003), 3. See also her *Heidegger's Poietic Writings: From Contributions to Philosophy to The Event* (Bloomington: Indiana University Press, 2018) and her "Poietic Saying," in *A Companion to Heidegger's Contributions to Philosophy*, ed. Charles E. Scott et al. (Bloomington: Indiana University Press, 2001), 66–80. For Heidegger's interpretation of ποίησις as bringing-forth, see "The Question Concerning Technology," in *The Question Concerning Technology and Other Essays*, trans. and introd. William Lovitt (New York and London: Garland, 1977), 10ff.

18. If there is anything that the detractors of continental philosophy protest to, it is generally the lack of rigor of logical argumentation or of formalizable procedures. In other words, the continental/analytic debate, as well as the polemics surrounding "postmodernity," center around method and its relation to responsibility. With what procedures does one philosophize responsibly? The infamous affair surrounding Derrida's Cambridge honorary degree provides a case in point. The main concerns of the signatories of the open letter in the *Times* protesting the award were that Derrida's work "does not meet accepted standards of clarity and rigor"; that he employs a "written style that defies comprehension"; and that it "stretches the normal forms of academic scholarship beyond recognition" (Barry Smith et al., "Derrida Degree: A Question of Honour," *Times* [London], Saturday, May 9, 1992). The signatories of that letter have misunderstood everything about Derrida's writing and about what I call indirectness. And yet, ironically, the reasons they cite do in fact correspond to what is at least an important and certainly consistent part of Derrida's writings, even the part for which he is most lauded by his admirers, to wit: to challenge accepted standards of supposed clarity and rigor; to defy what in an unquestioned manner counts as comprehensible; to challenge (sometimes by making unrecognizable) the supposedly "normal" forms of academic scholarship. In this way, paradoxically, the very thing that attracts Derrida's admirers is what he is vilified for by his critics. With this book, I aim to make understandable why three of the most prototypically "continental" authors hold that—to put it in Heidegger's terms—philosophy demands "a conceptuality of its own" and that it fundamentally "[belongs] to the broader horizon of an endeavor whose exposition requires other forms" (*PR* vii/1). This demand follows from the refusal to accept certain prevalent kinds of logic as the self-evident basis for all philosophical procedures.

19. A good example of such a defense, and one of the first of its kind, is Christopher Norris's 1982 *Deconstruction: Theory and Practice*, as well as his subsequent attempts to distinguish Derrida's work from "postmodernism" and "relativism," for instance in his *What's Wrong with Postmodernism: Critical Theory and*

the *Ends of Philosophy* (Baltimore: Johns Hopkins University Press, 1990) or his *Against Relativism: Philosophy of Science, Deconstruction and Critical Theory* (Oxford: Blackwell, 1997). In a more recent example, though it is a very different interpretation, there is still a trace of such a defense in Leonard Lawlor's claim that "Derrida's thought is motivated by the desire for truth." Lawlor explicitly states that the "original motivation" for his *Derrida and Husserl: The Basic Problem of Phenomenology* (Bloomington: Indiana University Press, 2002) was to "defend the Derridean faith" (Lawlor, *Derrida and Husserl*, 1).

20. The landscape of Hegel commentary has changed significantly in the past twenty years, with a marked increase in interpreters attentive to the importance of negativity, finitude, or limits in Hegel's philosophy; and its relation to contemporary concerns. Some of these are rooted in the classic French tradition of "existentialist" interpretations of Hegel. Perhaps there is no better way to begin to read Hegel than by approaching him, as does Jean Hyppolite, through the lens of the following paradox: that he is a thinker of finitude as well as an exorcist of transcendence. The existentialist interpretation of Hegel as it is found for instance with Kojève, Merleau-Ponty, and Hyppolite emphasizes finitude because it is fundamentally a humanist interpretation: "finitude" signifies the finitude of man. It aims for a secular reading of Hegel that emphasizes man's work, his mortality, or the struggle for recognition as the negativity that drives the movement. See Maurice Merleau-Ponty, "Hegel's Existentialism," in *Sense and Non-Sense*, trans. and Preface Hubert L. Dreyfus and Patricia Allen Dreyfus (Evanston: Northwestern University Press, 1964), 63–70; Alexandre Kojève, *Introduction to the Reading of Hegel*, ed. Allan Bloom, trans. James H. Nichols Jr. (Ithaca and London: Cornell University Press, 1980); and by Jean Hyppolite his seminal *Genesis and Structure of Hegel's Phenomenology of Spirit* (Evanston: Northwestern University Press, 1974), and especially *Logic and Existence* (Albany: State University of New York Press, 1997). More recently, there is a growing number of attempts to distinguish Hegel from the cliché-image of absolute idealism, and to show his relevance for contemporary concerns, by focusing on negativity, contradiction, and finitude. In part, this comes in the wake of French philosophers such as Jean-Luc Nancy or Catherine Malabou: Jean-Luc Nancy, *The Speculative Remark (One of Hegel's Bon Mots)*, trans. Céline Surprenant (Stanford: Stanford University Press, 2002); Jean-Luc Nancy, *Hegel: The Restlessness of the Negative*, trans. Jason Smith and Steven Miller (Minneapolis and London: University of Minnesota Press, 2002); Catherine Malabou, *The Future of Hegel: Plasticity, Temporality and Dialectic*, trans. Lisabeth During (London: Routledge, 2005). Also see Karin de Boer, *On Hegel: The Sway of the Negative* (Basingstoke: Palgrave Macmillan, 2010). An account of negativity as a "productive force," and even as "originary," can be found in Andrew Hass's *Hegel and the Art of Negation: Negativity, Creativity and Contemporary Thought* (London: I.B. Tauris, 2013). Hass shows convincingly with reference to three major texts by Derrida on Hegel ("From Restricted to General Economy:

A Hegelianism without Reserve," "The Pit and the Pyramid," and *Glas*) that the two are closer than Derrida at times thinks, in an account that is in line with my argument, stressing that "to look at Hegel directly requires indirection" (Hass, *Hegel and the Art of Negation*, 92). Rebecca Comay presents a thoroughly original Hegel in her *Mourning Sickness: Hegel and the French Revolution* (Stanford: Stanford University Press, 2010). And in Rebecca Comay and Frank Ruda, *The Dash—The Other Side of Absolute Knowing* (Cambridge and London: MIT Press, 2018), they show that it is precisely Hegel's most absolutist aspirations that address key contemporary concerns. Two works that stress Hegel's affinity with concerns in the contemporary French tradition are Simon Lumsden's *Self-Consciousness and the Critique of the Subject: Hegel, Heidegger and the Post-structuralists* (New York: Columbia University Press, 2014) and Johannes-Georg Schülein's *Metaphysik und ihre Kritik bei Hegel und Derrida* (Hamburg: Felix Meiner Verlag, 2016). A different expression of the recent trend is the focus on tragedy, showing how Hegel's philosophy is a resource for thinking fundamentally irreconcilable contradictions of reality, such as Theodore George's *Tragedies of Spirit: Tracing Finitude in Hegel's Phenomenology* (Albany: State University of New York Press, 2006), David Farrell Krell's *The Tragic Absolute: German Idealism and the Languishing of God* (Bloomington: Indiana University Press, 2005), and Christoph Menke's *Tragödie Im Sittlichen. Gerechtigkeit Und Freiheit Nach Hegel* (Frankfurt am Main: Suhrkamp, 1996). Also working from this perspective of Hegelian negativity as transformative is Katrin Pahl's wonderful *Tropes of Transport: Hegel and Emotion* (Evanston: Northwestern University Press, 2012). Finally, there is a recent focus in the literature tying negativity and contradiction to the concepts of life and finitude, based in a slightly different (broadly: more German) tradition. See for instance Brady Bowman's *Hegel and the Metaphysics of Absolute Negativity* (Cambridge: Cambridge University Press, 2013); Susan Songsuk Hahn's *Contradiction in Motion: Hegel's Organic Conception of Life and Value* (Ithaca: Cornell University Press, 2007), and Annette Sell's *Der Lebendige Begriff. Leben Und Logik Bei G.W.F. Hegel* (Freiburg: Verlag Karl Alber, 2013).

21. Jean Hyppolite, *Logic and Existence*, trans. Leonard Lawlor and Amit Sen (Albany: State University New York Press, 1997), 11.

22. The other six "beyng-historical" works are *Besinnung* (GA66), *Metaphysik und Nihilismus* (GA67), *Die Geschichte des Seyns* (GA69), *Über den Anfang* (GA70), *Das Ereignis* (GA71), and the forthcoming *Die Stege des Anfangs* (GA72).

23. I already mentioned the work of Vallega-Neu, for whom the *Contributions* effectuate a "transformation of language" such that "what the language of *Contributions* says is found in the performative motion, that is, in the occurrence of thinking and language, and not in something that this occurrence would present objectively" in Vallega-Neu, *Heidegger's Contributions to Philosophy: An Introduction*, 3. In the excellent collection *Heidegger and Language*, Jeffrey Powell emphasizes that "the entire text of *Contributions* is sandwiched between the concern for language" in Jeffrey Powell, ed., editor's introduction to *Heidegger and Language* (Blooming-

ton: Indiana University Press, 2013), 6. And Krzysztof Ziarek writes that "from *Contributions to Philosophy* onward," "more than presenting insights *about* language, this mode of writing enacts the event of language [. . .] in order to demonstrate how undergoing an experience with language remains irreducible to assertions or theories" in Krzysztof Ziarek, *Language After Heidegger* (Bloomington: Indiana University Press, 2013), 3.

CHAPTER 1

1. For an excellent discussion of the circumstances surrounding the preparation and publication of *Of Grammatology*, see Benoît Peeters, *Derrida: A Biography* (Cambridge and Malden: Polity, 2013), 155ff.

2. Jacques Derrida, *A Taste for the Secret* (Oxford: Blackwell, 2001), 29.

3. There are many examples. "Structure, Sign and Play in the Discourse of the Human Sciences" opens with the introduction and subsequent use of an unacceptable concept: "Perhaps something has occurred in the history of the concept of structure that could be called an 'event,' if this loaded word did not entail a meaning which it is precisely the function of structural—or structuralist—thought to reduce or to suspect. Let us speak of an 'event,' nevertheless, and let us use quotation marks to serve as a precaution" (*WD* 409/351). "Violence and Metaphysics" explicates the reflexive problem in terms of the philosophical questioning of philosophy (philosophy of philosophy, the questioning of questioning). *Voice and Phenomenon* revolves entirely around the still metaphysical character of phenomenology's overcoming of metaphysics. And one could also think of "Signature Event Context," as it opens with the question of the communicability of the sense of the word "communication."

4. David Wood recognizes the centrality of this question for Derrida's writings when he indicates that the central category of the first few pages of "Différance" is *repartons* ("let us move on"). David Wood, "Following Derrida," in *Time after Time* (Bloomington: Indiana University Press, 2007), 148.

5. "I think the form of the systematic, encyclopedic or circular book is impossible; and in *Of Grammatology* I start off by saying: that's it, no more books." Jacques Derrida, *A Taste for the Secret* (Oxford: Blackwell, 2001), 81.

6. Derrida, *A Taste for the Secret*, 29.

7. This also shows itself in why it is preliminarily left undecided how the second part *supplements* the first: because that part itself treats *of* the "supplement." Part two is said to aim at a "new logic of the supplement," which Derrida calls "a logic of incompleteness." Later, Derrida will defend his choice for the "example" of Rousseau on the grounds that it "tells us in a text what a text is" (G 233/163).

8. Heidegger calls it the "impotence of the sciences." See Martin Heidegger, "Science and Reflection," in *The Question Concerning Technology and Other Essays*, trans. and introd. William Lovitt (New York and London: Garland, 1977), 176.

9. Derrida shows this in countless of his earlier writings. As early as "Structure, Sign and Play," Derrida writes that "the metaphysics of presence is shaken with the help of the concept of *sign*" (*WD* 412/354). In *Voice and Phenomenon*, the sign is called a "privileged example." There it serves to expose the reflexive complication by which the phenomenological critique of metaphysics is seen as an "interior moment" of the "security metaphysics provides" (*VP* 4/4). Geoffrey Bennington also convincingly argues that "Derrida's thought is not essentially a philosophy of language" ("Derridabase," in *Jacques Derrida*, trans. Geoffrey Bennington [Chicago and London: University of Chicago Press, 1993], 50). He emphasizes a similar point very succinctly in Geoffrey Bennington, "Embarrassing Ourselves," *Los Angeles Review of Books*, March 20, 2016, https://lareviewofbooks.org/article/embarrassing-ourselves/.

10. Derrida argues that De Saussure himself already draws that conclusion, at least implicitly, for instance when he describes phonology as being "only an auxiliary discipline" (*G* 78/53).

11. Though Derrida himself uses this term often, he indicates that, strictly speaking, the term is inadequate: "Philosophy is, within writing, nothing but this movement of writing as effacement of the signifier and the desire of presence restored, of being, signified in its brilliance and its glory. The evolution and properly philosophic economy of writing go therefore in the direction of the effacing of the signifier, whether it take the form of forgetting or repression. Whether opposed or associated, these two last concepts are equally inadequate. At any rate, forgetfulness, if one understands it as the effacement of the power of retention by finitude, is the very possibility of repression. And repression, that without which dissimulation would have no meaning. The concept of repression is thus, at least as much as that of forgetting, the product of a philosophy (of meaning)" (*G* 405/286).

12. I think of the modes of despair that Kierkegaard has Anti-Climacus present from the perspective of finitude and infinitude. Though the despair of finitude is a lack of infinity, and the despair of infinity is a lack of finitude, it is emphatically not a matter of finding a compromise or "balance" between them. Instead, what Kierkegaard calls the "task" of "becoming a self" would rather have to consist in "an infinite moving away from itself in the infinitizing of the self, and an infinite coming back to itself in the finitizing process" (Kierkegaard, *The Sickness Unto Death: A Christian Psychological Exposition for Upbuilding and Awakening*, trans. and ed. Howard V. Hong and Edna H. Hong [Princeton: Princeton University Press, 1980, 29–30]). Kierkegaard explicitly writes that this is, "humanly speaking, utterly impossible" (38). There are parallels between the impossibility of this task and the task of deconstruction as an "experience of the impossible" that "does not provide assurances," as Derrida discusses it in "Force of Law." There Derrida stresses that undecidability is not an "oscillation" between two "decisions." I discuss this text and this impossibility in chapter 9.

CHAPTER 2

1. See introduction, n. 16. It may be objected here that Derrida very clearly states that his work cannot be reduced to a mere moment in philosophy's perpetual self-questioning. I agree with this, only to add that the "(non)place" from which Derrida works, arises in an attempt to question that very self-questioning, which for Derrida constitutes an undecidable (im)possibility. I return to the problem of the "privilege of the question" at length in chapter 9.

2. The background for the use of the concept of "logos" is the way Heidegger picks up the concept in *Being and Time*. There, the concepts with which logos is elucidated correspond to those already encountered here: determination through (de-)limitation (distinction and relation), essence and the "as such," and truth. Λόγος is a notoriously undefinable or untranslatable concept spanning a semantic range which includes, but is not limited to, "word," "sentence," "expression," "judgment," "thought," "reason," "ground (ratio)," "relation," "rationality," "logic," or "science." For Heidegger, the concept features, on the one hand, as an element of the title of his own "method" in *Being and Time*: phenomenology. On the other hand, it features as a decisive concept *within* it: *Being and Time* sets out to show a very specific determination of λόγος to have dominated the understanding of being [*Seinsverständnis*] in the history of Western metaphysics. This double situation of Heidegger's work with respect to the concept of λόγος—as both part of the investigation as well as object for it—already quite precisely expresses what Derrida calls the "ambiguity of the Heideggerian situation with respect to the metaphysics of presence and logocentrism": "It is at once contained within it and transgresses it. But it is impossible to separate the two" (G 36/22). I discuss this situation at length in Part III.

3. Where Derrida is stopped in his tracks by the complication of a "question of essence," he suspends that question. In doing so, he is able to "move on" from "unacceptable" distinctions. He writes that he will "not venture up to that perilous necessity" that would attempt to answer or address these questions directly, but will instead, "provisionally," "take shelter" in more "empirical" knowledge (G 109/74ff.).

4. Jacques Derrida, "Otobiographies," trans. Avital Ronell, in *The Ear of the Other: Otobiography, Transference, Translation*, ed. Christie McDonald, trans. Peggy Kamuf (New York: Schocken Books, 1985), 13.

5. The importance of this should not be underestimated. With this, Derrida has inspired many to identify "binary oppositions" or "binary thinking"—that is to say: as such and in general. The limitations of this approach are most evident when comparing Derrida with Hegel. Ironically, the philosopher viewed as the oppositional thinker par excellence is hardly ever interested in opposition*ality*, but is more concerned with showing how the content of a *specific, given* opposition engenders a new one. Derrida's generalization of opposition*ality* is for Hegel likely

an abstraction, or a reduction of the specific content of given oppositions to a generalized schema. It is in fact closer to Nietzsche's idea that the "grounding faith of metaphysicians is *the faith in the opposition of values*." Friedrich Nietzsche, *Beyond Good and Evil/On the Genealogy of Morality*, trans. Adrian Del Caro (Stanford: Stanford University Press, 2014), 6. I return to this quote in detail at the end of chapter 8.

6. Jacques Derrida, "Letter to a Japanese Friend," in *Derrida and Différance*, ed. David Wood and Robert Bernasconi (Evanston: Northwestern University Press, 1988), 4.

7. Kierkegaard and Heidegger are the main sources of this distinction. Here is how Derrida explains it in the film *Derrida*, directed by Kirby Dick and Amy Ziering Kofman: "In general, I try to distinguish between what one calls the future and "l'avenir." The future is that which—tomorrow, later, next century—will be. There's a future that is predictable, programmed, scheduled, foreseeable. But there is a future, l'avenir (to come), which refers to someone who comes whose arrival is totally unexpected. For me, that is the real future. That which is totally unpredictable. The Other who comes without my being able to anticipate their arrival. So if there is a real future beyond this other known future, it's this other unknown future, it's l'avenir [the "to-come"], in that it's the coming of the Other when I'm completely unable to foresee their arrival." *Derrida: Screenplay and Essays on the Film*, ed. Kirby Dick and Amy Ziering Kofman (Manchester: Manchester University Press, 2005), 53.

8. See also: "Monsters cannot be announced. One cannot say: 'here are our monsters,' without immediately turning the monsters into pets." Jacques Derrida, "Some Statements and Truisms about Neologisms, Newisms, Postisms, Parasitisms, and Other Small Seismisms," in *The States of Theory*, ed. David Carroll (New York: Columbia University Press, 1989), 80.

9. Derrida makes the same point in "Structure, Sign and Play": "[. . .] the metaphysics of presence is shaken with the help of the concept of sign. But [. . .] as soon as one seeks to demonstrate in this way that there is no transcendental or privileged signified and that the domain or play of signification henceforth has no limit, one must reject even the concept and word "sign" itself—which is precisely what cannot be done. [. . .] And what we are saying here about the sign can be extended to all the concepts and all the sentences of metaphysics" (*WD* 412/354). Derrida invokes the concept of the future to point to the closedness or the limitations of metaphysics itself, that is, the "greatest totality" or closure as such. The concept of the future figures similarly in *Aporias: Dying—Awaiting (One another) at the "Limits of Truth,"* trans. Thomas Dutoit (Stanford: Stanford University Press, 1993), fulfilling a function similar to the one indicated above. Conceived in that work in terms of the structure of the figure of death ("the future to come"), the future marks the aporetic "limit," which seems to allow no "passage," a limit not conceivable as an outer border that would leave a space beyond it.

10. The distinction between the "closure" and the "end" of metaphysics has been well commented on. Simon Critchley has convincingly made it the focal point of his reading in his *The Ethics of Deconstruction* (Edinburgh: Edinburgh University Press, 2014), esp. 20ff. But even if we grant that the closure of metaphysics does not necessarily signify its end, this still begs the question of how to interpret the occurrence of terms such as "epoch," "history," and "future" within it. If, as Derrida writes, it is not a matter of "moving on to something else," then the question remains: how to make sense of the quasi-revolutionary rhetoric, the aplomb with which Derrida announces his program (e.g., the "signs of liberation" of the signifier that, *only now*, show themselves "all over the world," etc.; G 14/4)?

CHAPTER 3

1. Marian Hobson makes the point in "Deconstruction, Empiricism, and the Postal Services," *French Studies* 36, no. 3 (1982): 290–314.

2. See for instance Derrida in "The Original Discussion of 'Différance' (1968)," in *Derrida and Différance*, ed. David Wood and Robert Bernasconi (Evanston: Northwestern University Press, 1988), and also LI 137 and WD 224/190.

3. Joshua Kates gives an overview of the central role skepticism plays in what he calls the "'first wave' of Derrida critics" in Joshua Kates, *Fielding Derrida: Philosophy, Literary Criticism, History, and the Work of Deconstruction* (New York: Fordham University Press, 2008), 11–25. These are primarily interpretations from the Anglophone world and from the field of literary theory. The concept is much less prominent in commentary from the same period working from a more philosophical background, as it is found for instance in the works from that period by Gasché, Sallis, Silverman, and Wood. For a discussion of Derrida himself concerning what he calls the "Americanization" of his work in its early reception, "most notably in the domain of literary theory and literature departments," see Derrida, "Deconstructions: The Im-Possible," in *French Theory in America*, ed. Sylvère Lotringer and Sande Cohen (London and New York: Routledge, 2001), 13–32. In a gesture that is central to my argument, Derrida there strictly distinguishes deconstruction from a "method" that creates "possibilities."

4. Joshua Kates's account (*Fielding Derrida*, 11–25) is a good example. I am completely on board with his intentions to the extent that he emphasizes the need to transcend polemics in the debate surrounding the "parallelism" between deconstruction and skepticism. Yet his account seems to come to a standstill at the diagnosis that both sides get something right. The "developmental account" of Derrida's development he proposes in order to answer these questions does not seem to return to the point.

5. Some typical examples include Christopher Norris, for whom the "point of departure" of deconstruction lies in the "radically metaphorical" character

of language; the "bottomless relativity of meaning," from which he concludes that "thought is deluded in its search for a truth beyond the mazy detours of language," in *Deconstruction: Theory and Practice*, 3rd ed. (London and New York: Routledge, 2002), 57. In a later edition of his influential work, Norris himself will admit that his formulations have contributed to an image of deconstruction as "[elevating] rhetoric above reason, "literature" above "philosophy," and stylistic play above the serious business of thinking constructively about issues in the realms of epistemology, ethics, and socio-political critique" (*Deconstruction: Theory and Practice*, 137–38). Concerning the possibility of certainty in interpretation and of securing meaning, it is especially Derrida's use of the term "play" [jeu] that conjures up skeptical connotations, such as in "[the] free play, or undecidability within every system of communication, the endless displacement of meaning—[which] releases us from believing that the individual can ever completely grasp the meaning of language" (S. J. Wilmore, "Scepticism and Deconstruction," *Man and World* 20, no. 4 (1987): 442–43); or, in the words of Christopher Butler: "[. . .] if there is no stopping-place we literally never arrive at a certain interpretation" in "Deconstruction and Scepticism," in *Interpretation, Deconstruction and Ideology* (Oxford: Clarendon Press, 1984), 62.

6. Jürgen Habermas, *The Philosophical Discourse of Modernity: Twelve Lectures*, trans. Frederick G. Lawrence (Cambridge, MA: MIT Press, 1987), 161–84.

7. Wolfgang W. Fuchs, "Post-Modernism Is Not a Scepticism," *Man and World* 22, no. 4 (1989): 398.

8. Anthony J. Cascardi, "Skepticism and Deconstruction," *Philosophy and Literature* 8, no. 1 (1984): 4.

9. Derrida in "The Original Discussion of 'Différance' (1968)," in *Derrida and Différance*, ed. David Wood and Robert Bernasconi (Evanston: Northwestern University Press, 1988), 93.

10. In spite of the staggering fact that even the "axial proposition" of *Of Grammatology* [il n'y a pas de hors-texte] has been interpreted as a claim that there "does not exist" a "(real) world" "outside of" the text. This is so far removed from Derrida's intentions that I only refer here to the work, for instance, of Simon Critchley (*The Ethics of Deconstruction*, 25ff.) or Christopher Norris (Norris, *Derrida*, 147ff.) to refute that view.

11. Sextus Empiricus, *Outlines of Skepticism*, ed. J. Annas and J. Barnes (Cambridge: Cambridge University Press, 2005), I: I, 4. I use the conventional notation to refer to Sextus's text (book: chapter, line number).

12. Sextus, I: VIII, 16ff.

13. Sextus, I: XII, 29.

14. Sextus, I: XX, 192, 193.

15. Fuchs gives a host of examples ("Post-Modernism Is Not a Scepticism," 393–402).

16. Several others have shown this to be a fruitful contrast. Particularly Ewa Ziarek in the first part of her *The Rhetoric of Failure: Deconstruction of Skepticism, Reinvention of Modernism* (Albany: State University of New York Press, 1996) and Simon Critchley throughout his *The Ethics of Deconstruction*.

17. "Skepticism is the *refutable*, but it returns." Emmanuel Levinas, *Otherwise than Being or Beyond Essence*, trans. Alphonso Lingis (Dordrecht: Kluwer Academic Publishers, 1991), 168.

18. Levinas, *Otherwise than Being or Beyond Essence*, 168ff.

19. In other words: how to think the other of being [*Penser l'autrement qu'être*], a project that does not merely coincidentally have the structure of a performative self-contradiction. The project is interpreted extensively by Derrida in *Violence and Metaphysics*.

20. Levinas, *Otherwise than Being or Beyond Essence*, 168ff.

21. Cascardi, "Skepticism and Deconstruction," 1.

22. Stanley Cavell, "What is the Scandal of Skepticism?," in *Philosophy the Day After Tomorrow* (Cambridge/London: Harvard University Press, 2005), 132–54.

23. Stanley Cavell, *The Claim of Reason* (Oxford: Oxford University Press, 1979), 241.

24. Ewa Ziarek, *The Rhetoric of Failure*, 3. Her account of the "affirmative address to the other" is developed at 103ff. I return to this notion of affirmation at the end of this book.

25. A good place to start for such an overview is *Conceptions of Critique in Modern and Contemporary Philosophy*, ed. Karin de Boer and Ruth Sonderegger (Basingstoke: Palgrave Macmillan, 2012).

26. Rodolphe Gasché, *The Honor of Thinking* (Stanford: Stanford University Press, 2007), 21.

27. Derrida, as quoted in Gasché, *The Honor of Thinking*, 21.

28. Derrida, as quoted in Gasché, *The Honor of Thinking*, 21–22.

29. Gasché, *The Honor of Thinking*, 21.

30. Gasché, *The Honor of Thinking*, 22.

31. Martin Heidegger, *What Is a Thing?*, trans. W. B. Barton Jr. and Vera Deutsch (South Bend, IN: Gateway Editions, 1967), 119–21.

32. Gasché, *The Honor of Thinking*, 22.

33. This vulnerability can be seen as a Nietzschean legacy. In *Beyond Good and Evil* (in the section that investigates the "prejudices of the philosophers"—could they be elaborated *philosophically*?), in positing the question "what in us exactly strives 'toward truth'?" [*was in uns will eigentlich "zur Wahrheit'?*], Nietzsche, too, recognizes that this results in the reflexive complication of a question of the question, or, as he puts it, "a rendez-vous of question and question mark" [*ein Stelldichein [. . .] von Fragen und Fragezeichen*]. Such a question involves, he famously states, a "risk," and "perhaps there is none greater" [*ein Wagnis; und*

vielleicht giebt es kein grösseres] in the sense that such an investigation can above all not afford *itself* sure footing, because it attempts to put in question the very *value* of sure footing. Friedrich Nietzsche, *Beyond Good and Evil/On the Genealogy of Morality*, trans. Adrian Del Caro (Stanford: Stanford University Press, 2014), 4ff.

34. The "essential" risk, or the risk that is no mere accident but rather structurally inscribed, is a recurrent theme for Derrida. In "Signature Event Context," Derrida argues that the risk to "fail" in conveying its "intended meaning" is structurally inscribed in the mark, as its condition of possibility (*MP* 367/309ff.).

35. See Simon Critchley, *The Ethics of Deconstruction*, 8 and especially 159ff: "Therefore, if one were to try to refute deconstruction by arguing that it employs logocentric language, one would always leave the door open for the return of deconstruction. The Derridean skeptical ghost would always return to haunt a logocentric Macbeth" (*The Ethics of Deconstruction*, 160).

CHAPTER 4

1. Immanuel Kant, *Critique of Practical Reason* (Cambridge: Cambridge University Press, 2015), 4ff. To the extent that reason "gives itself" objective reality, there is already here, implicit in Kant, a "movement of the concept."

2. Hegel writes: "This spiritual movement, which in its simplicity gives itself its determinateness, and in this determinateness gives itself its self-equality—this movement, which is thus the immanent development of the concept, is the absolute method of the concept, the absolute method of cognition and at the same time the immanent soul of the content.—On this self-constructing path alone, I say, is philosophy capable of being objective, demonstrative science" (*SL* 17/10).

3. In the case of "life," the relevant background is the Kantian idea of a "moral life," which is characterized by the opposition between the necessity of the moral law or of freedom on the one hand, and the course of nature on the other. This opposition would have to be sublated into the "intuition" of a "moral life." This is most clear in Hegel's 1802/03 *System of Ethical Life* [*System der Sittlichkeit*].

4. Walter Jaeschke's 1978 article on the subject is a classic, tracing the various meanings of the concept throughout Hegel's work, and especially chronicling the way in which at any given stage of Hegel's thinking the concept of "reflection" resists straightforward conceptualization: Walter Jaeschke, "Äußerliche Reflexion und immanente Reflexion: Eine Skizze der systematischen Geschichte des Reflexionsbegriffs in Hegels Logik-Entwürfen," *Hegel-Studien* 13 (1978): 85–117.

5. The same holds for *Entzweyung* ("bifurcation"), which is another name for the dynamic of reflection. As Jaeschke indicates in his *Hegel Handbuch. Leben—Werk—Wirkung* (Stuttgart and Weimar: Verlag J. B. Metzler, 2003), Hegel speaks of "relative" and "absolute" *Entzweyung*, where the first designates *Entzweyung* pre-

cisely *as the appearance of* the absolute and the latter is, in Jaeschke's terminology, a concept belonging to the "philosophy of culture" (Jaeschke, *Hegel Handbuch*, 114).

6. On top of that, there is the prominence of the concept of reflection in connection with Hegel's relation to Derrida through the ground-breaking work of Rodolphe Gasché, whose 1986 *The Tain of the Mirror* still sets the standard. Gasché's intentions are primarily to draw a line that starts with Descartes and ends with Hegel, and to position Derrida with respect to that tradition. This means that it is his primary interest to study how Hegelian "absolute" reflection is in fact a critique of (Cartesian/Kantian, transcendental, philosophical) reflection, or how Hegel's transition to "absolute" reflection in fact constitutes the "self-destruction" of reflection. Gasché has quite a specific view of Hegelian reflection. He characterizes the specificity of Hegelian speculative reflection in terms of its "mirroring function" (Gasché, *The Tain of the Mirror*, 45) in order to position Derrida with respect to it: on the "tain" of that mirror. In Part I, I have already indicated the risks of fashioning for Derrida such an irreducibly singular place with respect to the philosophical tradition. Here I would only like to point out that there is nothing yet in the concept of Hegelian speculative reflection that occasions or necessitates understanding it in terms of the image or representation of a mirror.

7. Jaeschke, *Hegel Handbuch*, 99 (translation mine, JdJ).

8. H. F. Fulda, "Über den Ursprung der Hegelschen Dialektik," in *Aquinas. Rivista internazionale di filosofia* 24 (1981): 368–405.

9. Dieter Henrich, *Hegel im Kontext* (Frankfurt: Suhrkamp, 1971), 36. Cited by Jaeschke in *Hegel Handbuch*, 99. Translation and emphasis mine, JdJ.

10. A more elaborate account of Hegel's relation to Kant, as I describe it in this section, can be found in Johan de Jong, "Hegel's Appropriation of Kant's Theoretical Philosophy in the Jena Period," in *The Bloomsbury Companion to Kant*, ed. Gary Banham, Dennis Schulting, and Nigel Hems (London and New York: Bloomsbury, 2012), 294–97.

11. I have chosen to exhibit the form of Hegel's critique by looking at his response to Kant, but there are numerous places in Hegel's oeuvre where his conception of non-oppositional critique can be found. A good place to start in the early works is the introduction to the *Kritische Journal der Philosophie* that Hegel co-edited with Schelling titled "On the Essence of Philosophical Criticism Generally, and Its Relationship to the Present State of Philosophy," in *Between Kant and Hegel: Texts in the Development of Post-Kantian Idealism*, trans. H. S. Harris, ed. George di Giovanni and H. S. Harris (Indianapolis: Hackett, 2000), 275–91. It is uncertain to what extent this text is written by Hegel or Schelling, but it is clear that the bulk of the text is in line with Hegel's thought at the time. There, Hegel and/or Schelling sharply distinguish criticism from "repudiation" by "two subjectivities in opposition" (276) as well as from the kind of "partisan polemic" that "wants to maintain a one-sided point of view as valid against others that are

likewise one-sided" (285). That it cannot be a matter of opposing oppositionality is clear from the fact that Hegel/Schelling write that "even the true philosophy cannot protect itself from the outward look of polemic against unphilosophy." But the unavoidable semblance of partisanship does not make philosophical criticism identical to it: if one confesses to be a party, one is "null and void for the true philosophy" (286). More famous examples of Hegel's resistance to refutation as a model for philosophical critique can be found in his *Lectures on the History of Philosophy*. Derrida discusses this in his *Heidegger: The Question of Being and History*, ed. Thomas Dutoit, with the assistance of Marguerite Derrida, trans. Geoffrey Bennington (Chicago: University of Chicago Press, 2016), 2ff.

12. G. W. F. Hegel, *Faith and Knowledge*, trans. and ed. Walter Cerf and H. S. Harris (Albany: State University of New York Press, 1977), 69. Translation mine, JdJ, of "Glauben und Wissen oder die Reflexionsphilosophie der Subjektivität in der Vollständigkeit ihrer Formen als Kantische, Jacobische und Fichtesche Philosophie" (*Werke in zwanzig Bänden*, Theorie-Werkausgabe, Band 2, Frankfurt am Main: Suhrkamp, 1970), 304.

13. This necessity conforms to the "presuppositionlessness" that Stephen Houlgate rightly identifies as being essential for Hegel: that no distinction can be accepted *prior* to the investigation. See Stephen Houlgate, *The Opening of Hegel's Logic: From Being to Infinity* (West Lafayette: Purdue University Press, 2006), 29ff.

14. Barbara Johnson translates "Hors livre: préfaces" as "Outwork, prefacing," in *Dissemination* (London/New York: Continuum, 2004). Because Derrida's notion of *exergue* is also translated as "outwork," and given the difficulties of finding a satisfactory English translation, I refer to the text under the French title throughout.

15. "This essay begins with general reflections about the need, presupposition, basic principles, etc. of philosophy. It is a fault in them that they are general reflections, but they are occasioned by the fact that presupposition, principles, and such like forms still adorn the entrance to philosophy with their cobwebs. So, up to a point it is still necessary to deal with them until the day comes when from beginning to end it is philosophy itself whose voice will be heard" ("Diff" 13/83).

16. Gasché, *The Tain of the Mirror*, 35ff.

17. I take the expression from Ewa Ziarek's *The Rhetoric of Failure: Deconstruction of Skepticism, Reinvention of Modernism* (Albany: State University of New York Press, 1996).

18. In the skepticism-article, it allows Hegel to identify what explains skepticism's recurrence in spite of its "refutation": because all "true philosophy" [*ächte Philosophie*] contains this "negative side," it will always be possible to extract this side from philosophy, to abstract from its positive side, and to treat it as absolute. This is for Hegel the process by which the different modifications of skepticism have come about, modifications that are sometimes still close to truth (Sextus) and sometimes completely removed from it (e.g., Schulze himself, skepticism that maintains that there is only subjective but no objective certainty, reference to the

"facts of consciousness"). This is what the Aufhebung of skepticism consists in: it is "negated" insofar as it is recognized as a "moment," a "side" of truth.

19. In Plato's *Republic*, when Socrates is confronted with Thrasymachus's view on justice (that it is better to be unjust), he considers what it would take to persuade him of the opposite: "If we oppose him with a speech parallel to his speech enumerating in turn the many good things that come from being just, and he replies, and then we do, we will have to count and measure the good things mentioned on each side, and we will need a jury to decide the case. But if, on the other hand, we investigate the question, as we have been doing, by seeking agreement with each other, we ourselves can be both jury and advocates at once" (348a7).

20. This is not "mere" appearance behind which a deeper reality is found. It is not that what merely appears to be in contradiction is in fact not in contradiction. It is rather that contradictories are, precisely, related contradictorily. That means that opposition and contradiction are not "mere" appearance of the absolute, but its very expression. Shoving oppositions aside in order to catch sight of the absolute "behind" them would be like the most naive conception of the "things in themselves," as Hegel describes it in his early skepticism-article: as if they were "rocks under snow" [*wie einen Felsen unter Schnee*] ("Skept" 220/318, translation amended, JdJ).

21. Hegel calls the path toward science already itself actual science in the introduction. See: "Because of this necessity, the way to Science is itself already Science, and hence, in virtue of its content, is the Science of the experience of consciousness" (*PH* 79/56).

22. See the chapter on "Presuppositionless Thinking," in Stephen Houlgate, *The Opening of Hegel's Logic: From Being to Infinity* (West Lafayette: Purdue University Press, 2006), 29ff. Specifically, "Does Hegel Have a Method?," 32ff.

23. The phrase is Stephen Houlgate's as he puts it in his discussion of the *Science of Logic* (Houlgate, *The Opening of Hegel's Logic*, 94).

24. There is another problem of an unavoidable self-violation in the philosophical expression. I believe, however, that it is clear from the text that Hegel views this problem as harmless to the integrity of the possibility of dialectical exposition, even though he calls it a "difficulty." Because it is the kind of problem that Derrida would no doubt focus his attention on, I feel I should include it here as a note. The difficulty concerns the risk that the speculative and ratiocinative senses of propositions are mixed up. And because Hegel already indicated that the speculative proposition has the external form of an ordinary proposition, as well as the fact that "the dialectical movement likewise has propositions for its parts and elements," Hegel is aware that this risk therefore seems to recur indefinitely, that is: that there is no possibility of safeguarding the philosophical investigation against that risk a priori. This seems therefore to be a problem not merely of the correct interpretation of the philosophical exposition, but of philosophical expo-

sition as such [*scheint daher immer zurückzukehren, und eine Schwierigkeit der Sache selbst zu sein*] (*PH* 61/40). But Hegel seems to dismiss this problem outright by pointing out that it belongs to a logic to which the dialectic cannot be reduced. It belongs to a conception of philosophical "proof" that is not that of dialectical self-unfolding. He compares it to the idea in "ordinary proofs" that the grounds that they presuppose themselves require a ground, and so forth ad infinitum. This belongs, says Hegel, to a merely "external cognition" that is fundamentally different from dialectical movement, because the latter is self-movement. Hegel's explanation is far from clear: "This form of justification and stating conditions [*des Begründens und Bedingens*] belongs to that method of proof which differs from the dialectical movement, and belongs therefore to external cognition. As regards the dialectical movement itself, its element is the pure concept; it thus has a content which is, in itself, subject through and through. Thus no content occurs which functions as an underlying subject, nor receives its meaning as a predicate; the proposition is, immediately, a merely empty form" (*PH* 62/40, translation amended, JdJ). Questions of the Derridean type will arise here: what enables Hegel to so decisively dismiss this skeptical risk? What Hegel seems to say here is that the subject that is the content of speculation is to be distinguished from a subject-as-ground or "foundational" subject [*zum Grunde liegendes Subjekt*]; the supposedly "solid basis" to which predicates are appended. Hegel takes the problem a bit further when considering the proper name. The name as such (that is, abstracting from its content and focusing only on its form [*der Name als Name*]) would indicate the "pure subject," that is: the empty "one" devoid of the concept [*das leere begrifflose Eins*]. Therefore, Hegel states: "For this reason it may be expedient, e.g., to avoid the name 'God,' since this word is not immediately also a concept, but rather the proper name, the fixed point of rest of the underlying subject; whereas, on the other hand, e.g. 'being' or 'the one,' 'singularity,' 'the subject,' etc. themselves immediately designate concepts" (*PH* 62/40, translation amended, JdJ). The risk of the name is to not convey movement, to not convey the concept in the word or to fixate. What the "proper name" [*der eigentliche Name*] does is express the solid or fixed being-at-rest of the underlying subject. So also here there is the risk of interpreting the speculative predicate "after the form of the proposition instead of as concept and essence" [*das spekulative Prädikat nach der Form des Satzes, nicht als Begriff und Wesen zu fassen*] (*PH* 61/41). Hegel however states that this is a risk that can either be "increased or diminished through the very way in which philosophy is expounded." But it is unclear how. He does not pursue the matter further. He simply indicates that the exposition should "preserve the dialectical form" and admit of nothing "except insofar as it is comprehended and is the concept" (*PH* 61/41). This is what Malabou picks up in her *The Future of Hegel: Plasticity, Temporality and Dialectic*, trans. Lisabeth During (London: Routledge, 2005) (hereafter *Future*). If "plasticity" means movement, then there are interesting parallels between her work and my present argument.

Consider what she does with Aufhebung: Hegelian dialectic cannot be a fixed scheme (*Future* 197) because what is presumed fixed (the very Aufhebung itself) is not fixed at all—the very Aufhebung is "plastic," it evolves: "The Aufhebung evolves, as a term, within the same process which it regulates and measures. [. . .] What must be demonstrated is the fact that Hegel does indeed restore the essential dialectical performativity of the aufheben and Aufhebung, that he in effect 'sublates' aufheben into aufheben, Aufhebung into Aufhebung" (*Future* 200). In that direction, the matter could be taken further. A different Derridean question could then arise: if the risk of conflating speculative proposition and propositional form is ineradicable, if there is no way to guarantee (because that would itself be a "fixation") the expression of the speculative movement—then is the very possibility of philosophical articulation not already compromised? Compromised from the beginning or even before the beginning (always already), compromised by this risk that is an essential risk?—But that question is no longer a Hegelian question. It not only did not, in fact, arise for Hegel, but it could not arise for him because that question presupposes an alteration the meaning of key terms. The operative are the temporalization of the "always already" as it belongs to twentieth-century phenomenology. Compare Derrida's temporalized interpretation of the "already": "Already (*déjà*), such is the name for what has been effaced or subtracted beforehand, but which has nevertheless left behind a mark, a signature which is retracted in that very thing from which it is withdrawn" (*Sp* 39). Such a temporalized conception of the always already can then lead to the question of the impossibility of philosophical signification (articulation, exposition) as such. An articulation that would "already" be compromised or complicated, already never be "pure." This is the difference between Hegel's question of how and with what philosophy or science must begin, and the Heideggerian/Derridean question of if it is even possible for science or philosophy to begin, or whether the very beginning is "already" complicated. It is also the point at which it becomes more understandable why Gasché would read in Hegel's critique of reflection the diagnosis of a "failure" of reflection.

CHAPTER 5

1. I think of the essays collected, for instance, in *Hegel and Language*, ed. Jere O'Neil Surber (Albany: State University of New York Press, 2006). Also Jim Vernon, *Hegel's Philosophy Language* (London: Continuum, 2007); Kathleen Dow Magnus, *Hegel and the Symbolic Mediation of Spirit* (Albany: State University of New York Press, 2001). A little less recent are the attempts to relate Hegel and Derrida through a discussion of the sign or language, for instance by Deborah Chaffin in "Hegel, Derrida, and the Sign," in *Derrida and Deconstruction*, ed. Hugh J. Silverman (London and New York: Routledge, 1989), 77–91. A good article that

is critical of Derrida's reading of Hegel is Wendell Kisner's "Erinnerung, Retrait, Absolute Reflection," *The Owl of Minerva* 26, no. 2 (1995): 171–86.

2. At the 1966 Baltimore seminar where Derrida read his "Structure, Sign and Play," Hyppolite delivered a lecture with the title "The Structure of Philosophic Language According to the 'Preface' to Hegel's *Phenomenology of the Mind*." It is transcribed in *The Structuralist Controversy: The Languages of Criticism and the Sciences of Man*, ed. Richard Macksey and Eugenio Donato (Baltimore and London: Johns Hopkins University Press, 1970), 157–85 (hereafter "SPL"). In that lecture, Hyppolite argues for Hegel as a thinker of finitude, but from a different perspective than I have done so far. Hyppolite argues that "Hegel's greatest moment is the point of oscillation between the architecture of the *Logic* and the common consciousness of the *Phenomenology*" ("SPL" 168). Because this "Absolute Difference" between the philosophical and the ordinary is maintained in oscillation, Hyppolite locates the "rhythm of philosophical discourse" in the "attenuation" of philosophical discourse by the "sense of finitude which accompanies it" ("SPL" 168). On the one hand (and in line with my present concerns), Hegelian finitude, so conceived, results in an emphasis on the performative character of philosophical exposition: "[. . .] for Hegel, true philosophic thought is thought in which knowledge is not an instrument exterior to the thing that is known; it is the thing known which speaks and which expresses itself" ("SPL" 166). Also, cf.: that in philosophical discourse "the search for the 'speaker' is simultaneous with the treatment of the object spoken of" ("SPL" 168) and that "Hegel's whole effort in the 'Preface' is to show that if there is a philosophic discourse it is one which does not make a distinction between the self of knowledge and the self of the object" ("SPL" 166). On the other hand, however, if reflection-in-itself is conceived as "language," then for Hyppolite this means that Hegelian philosophy consists in "[exorcizing] the phantom of an ineffable." Also in line with my reading is his emphasis, in the opening of *Logic and Existence* (hereafter *LE*), that "Absolute knowledge means the in principle elimination [. . .] of a transcendence essentially irreducible to our knowledge" (*LE* 3). Where we differ is that in Hyppolite's interpretation of "human language" as "the very medium of the dialectic" ("being [says] itself in man and man [becomes] universal consciousness of being through language" [*LE* 6]), his conception of "human" language is meant to counter what he sees as two specific misconceptions in the interpretation of Hegel: (1) a "religious" interpretation of Hegel in which the "universal consciousness of being" is a form of divine understanding (in line with more "right-Hegelian" views); and its correlate: (2) an "absolutist" interpretation of Hegel in which man "becomes God" instead of an affirmation of finitude. The counter-thrust to these two views is what makes up the "existentialist" or "humanist" interpretation of Hegel. The finitude of man or of humanity is not conceived as a this-side with respect to an absolute that would be "beyond." Instead, it is only *in* (finite) "human language" that "being says itself": "[. . .] this discourse that the philosopher forges about being, how-

ever, is as well the very discourse of being across the philosopher." And: "[. . .] it cannot be said that [Hegel] put himself in the place of God, for he well knew that when he was searching for the universal articulations of thought it was still as one concrete philosopher that he was carrying on the quest" ("SPL" 168–69). In short: it is "human experience" that is "the revelation of the identity of being and knowledge." This approach is not without its problems. Hyppolite himself recognizes that Hegel cannot simply be a humanist (see *LE* 20ff.). Though Hyppolite rightly emphasizes the performative or reflexive character of the exposition, this identification of Hegelian movement restricts it to *sense*, which complicates acknowledging the role of the essentially implicit. At this point of language, where Derrida and Hegel could have been closest, the reading of Hegelian philosophy as "language" makes Hegel into the philosopher who exorcises everything that would fall outside the movement of "sense." That is where the break between Derrida and Hegel begins, where Derrida's initial "originary dialectic" becomes the explicit opposition to Hegel's reappropriation of alterity. For an account of Hyppolite's influence on Derrida's early development, see Leonard Lawlor's *Derrida and Husserl: The Basic Problem of Phenomenology* (Indiana University Press: 2002), esp. 89ff.

3. Jean Hyppolite, *Logic and Existence*, 4.

4. It has been a deliberate choice not to make the theme of "presence" into a focal point of my investigation. The relevant differences (between Derridean metaphysics of presence, Hegelian presence of spirit to itself, or Heidegger's withdrawal of/in all presence) cannot be adequately understood in terms of different positions concerning the "theme" of presence. One cannot simply oppose Hegel's *bei-sich-sein im Anderen* to the Derridean undecidability of the (im)possibility of presence, as both try to think the movement of "identity" as it exceeds the content of any specific given determination or proposition. This does not mean that I am out to blur or even reduce all the differences between Hegel and Derrida. Rather, I want to show that (1) a certain oppositional scheme is insufficient to think those differences; that (2) there is, however, a certain unavoidability to oppositionality in thinking such "differences"; and that (3) even though they go about it differently, this simultaneous unavoidability and insufficiency is precisely *a theme for* Hegel, Heidegger, and Derrida.

5. Marian Hobson, Translator's Note to *The Problem of Genesis in Husserl's Philosophy* (Chicago and London: University of Chicago Press, 2003), viii.

6. Hobson, Translator's Note to *The Problem of Genesis*, ix.

7. Derrida, *The Problem of Genesis*, xv–xvi.

8. Hegel is largely absent from *Voice and Phenomenon* and *Of Grammatology*. In the latter, Hegel is presented as "the last philosopher of the book and the first thinker of writing" (G 41/26), and his *Encyclopedia* is presented as one of the three "landmarks" of logocentrism along with the work of Rousseau and Plato's *Phaedrus* (G 145–46/97). Though that suggests that Hegel occupies an important

position within logocentrism, the supporting analysis that surrounds these claims is very limited, and one needs to look elsewhere to find out what is at stake.

9. The answer is that, ultimately, there is no such legality. This also means that "one will never prove *philosophically*" that (a) deconstruction is necessary. There is no "legitimacy," and ultimately Derrida's texts must "authorize themselves." Such auto-authorization, which is in fact a lack of authorization, Derrida calls a "*limitrophic* violence" (*MP* xxi/xxv). He asks: "With what is one to *authorize oneself*, in the last analysis, if not once more with philosophy"? Like in *Of Grammatology*, he suggests that it is precisely a matter of putting in question the very "value of authority" and of "critique" (*MP* xviii/xxii).

10. We have seen that "exteriority and alterity are concepts which by themselves have never surprised philosophical discourse." The question is: "[. . .] can one puncture the tympanum of a philosopher and still be heard by him?" It is in this context that we find the second reference to Hegel: "How to put one's hands on the tympanum and how the tympanum could escape from the hands of the philosopher in order to make of phallogocentrism an impression that he no longer recognizes, in which he no longer rediscovers himself, of which he could become conscious only afterward and without being able to say to himself, again turning on his own hinge: I will have anticipated it, with absolute knowledge" (*MP* xiii/xxv). Not only does everything, in the Hegel of "Tympan," ultimately revert back to positivity, but "absolute knowledge" means that everything "will have been anticipated." "Tympan" introduces, therefore, and is itself in its very carrying out, the embodiment of a strategy of surprise.

11. Here is also the Hegelian point that Derrida misses: it is clear that there is absolutely nothing between illogicality and the mirage, on the one hand, and the "infallibility of calculations" on the other. In such a way, because there is no room for a unity in which difference would be *affirmed*, Derrida in his deconstruction of metaphysical oppositionality (inadvertently or not) ends up helping that oppositionality out a little bit by opposing only to mirage and illogicalness the evidence of infallibility. See also Afterword, n. 2.

12. An early version of this section was published in Dutch as "Hoe keert men zich (niet) tegen de tegenstelling? Hegel als Derrida's punt van vertrek." *De uil van Minerva* 28, no. 1 (2015): 26–45.

13. For an excellent account of Derrida's ambiguity with respect to Hegel in *Glas*, see Johannes-Georg Schülein's *Metaphysik und ihre Kritik bei Hegel und Derrida* (Hamburg: Felix Meiner Verlag, 2016), 298ff.

CHAPTER 6

1. For one of the few accounts that does pick up on this continuity from *Being and Time* to the *Contributions*, see Friedrich-Wilhelm von Herrmann's excel-

lent "Way and Method: Hermeneutic Phenomenology in Thinking the History of Being," in *Critical Heidegger*, ed. Christopher Macann (London and New York: Routledge, 1996), 171–90.

2. The preliminary character of the relation to an explicit conception of being itself follows from the "average understanding of Being" [*durchschnittlichen Seinsverständnis*], which will not be transformed into an explicit conception but will rather be shown to belong "*ultimately* [. . .] *to the essential constitution of Dasein itself* [*am Ende zur Wesensverfassung des Daseins selbst*]" (*BT* 7/7). To show that the relation to any explicit conception of being is essentially preliminary is thus a key component of the project. It is clear that such a thesis could not be the conclusion to some logical deduction.

3. This phenomenological moment—along with an eidetic reduction of sorts, namely that "Not arbitrary and accidental structures but essential ones are to be demonstrated in this everydayness" (*BT* 16–17/16)—is also present in Husserl, and concerns phenomenology as a movement against or away from "constructed" conceptions, abstract concepts or ideas, and toward the "things themselves." However, the specific way in which Heidegger unpacks that idea is not Husserlian: Heidegger aims at showing the phenomenally *more original* character of the relatively derivative objectivity, rationality, and explicit conceptions of being as they are current throughout Western metaphysics (as he gathers them under the concept of *logos*). In Husserl's work we find no such *hierarchical* conception of more and less original or derivative phenomena. This tells us something specific about Heidegger's own project: to uncover the essential structures [*Existenzialien*] that are more original than *Dasein*'s explicit conceptions (of itself and of being) as they have been conditioned both by the world in which he always already finds himself and by the history of Western metaphysics that conditions that world. It is because of this attempt to reach a more original level of analysis that a phenomenology of *Dasein* can imply a destruction of the history of Western metaphysics. This destruction aims at uncovering the "original experiences" out of which the concepts of metaphysics were born. It is thus not the nostalgic attempt to "go back" to the explicit conceptions of a certain time or to do away with the history of metaphysics. Heidegger stresses that the function of the destruction is "positive" to the extent that it is meant to reawaken the sense of the concepts of metaphysics such as it has been lost precisely by the influence of that very history and of the "world" on *Dasein*'s conceptions (he describes the latter influence as being "ontologically reflected back upon the interpretation of Dasein" [*BT* 16/16]). This also explains why Heidegger himself, when he introduces the concepts of phenomenology and hermeneutics in his sections on method, attempts to refer to their original Greek sense.

4. Edmund Husserl's "principle of all principles": "Enough now of absurd theories. No conceivable theory can make us err with respect to the *principle of all principles: that every originarily giving intuition* is *a legitimizing source of cognition*,

that *everything* that *gives itself* to us *originarily in 'intuition'* (so to speak in its 'corporeal' actuality) *is to be taken simply as it gives itself*, but also *only within the limits in which it so gives itself*." Edmund Husserl, *Ideas Pertaining to a Pure Phenomenology and to a Phenomenological Philosophy. First Book: General Introduction to a Pure Phenomenology*, trans. F. Kersten (The Hague: Martinus Nijhoff, 1983), 44. Translation amended, JdJ.

5. The hermeneutical moment forms a break with Husserl to the extent that it designates the way in which phenomenological explication always finds itself in an implicit self-complication. In the words of Derrida: it is always "ordered around its own blind spot" [*qu'elles s'ordonnent autour de leur propre tache aveugle*] (*G* 234/164). Rather than simply overcome this as a methodological obstacle, *Being and Time* sets out to show this very blind spot to be in fact essential to the being of *Dasein*. This is most explicit when Heidegger finally discusses the essentially circular "hermeneutical situation" of the question of being.

6. Both moments of Heidegger's method (phenomenology and hermeneutics) thus express a specific kind of relation between what is implicit and what is explicated. Phenomenology explicates what the matter is as it shows itself, but a phenomenology of *Dasein*'s everydayness has the added hermeneutical difficulty of having to articulate this "by itself." It is precisely for this reason that the various modes or degrees of understanding (from implicit to explicit) form the "equiprimordial" structures of "being-in as such": attunement [*Befindlichkeit*], understanding [*Verstehen*], and discourse [*Rede*]. They are themselves the phenomenally more original phenomena underlying the derivative (and traditionally metaphysical) modes of logic, assertion, and explicit language.

7. Heidegger makes the point explicitly: "The question of the potentiality-of-being-whole of Dasein has now completely cast off the character which we initially pointed out when we treated it as if it were just a theoretical, methodological question of the analytic of Dasein, arising from the attempt to have the whole of Dasein completely 'given.' The question of the wholeness of Dasein, initially discussed only with regard to ontological method, has its justification, but only because the ground for that justification goes back to an ontic possibility of Dasein" (*BT* 309/296).

8. This is the relevant passage: "Everydayness is, after all, precisely the being 'between' birth and death. And if existence determines the being of Dasein, and if its essence is coconstituted by potentiality-of-being, then, as long as Dasein exists, it must always, as such a potentiality, *not yet be* something? A being whose essence is made up of existence essentially opposes itself to the possibility of being comprehended as a whole being. Not only has the hermeneutical situation given us no assurance of 'having' the whole being up to now; it is even questionable whether the whole being is attainable at all, and whether a primordial, ontological interpretation of Dasein must not get stranded—on the kind of being of the thematic being itself" (*BT* 233/223).

9. Heidegger interrogates the sense of that phrase through a series of questions to which at first answers are given in the terms that traditionally make up the analysis of truth. Thus: what is the sense of "correspondence"? It is a *relation*. What is the relation? Is it a subject-object relation, or a relation belonging to "knowledge"? Is it the relation between the "real," psychological judgement and the "ideal" object of that judgement? Is the relation a relation of knowledge to "representations" [*Vorstellungen*]? Heidegger attempts to show that all such determinations presuppose a "relation" that remains ambiguous. When Heidegger states that the judgement stands in a relation to the thing itself in these terms: "Making statements is a being toward the existent thing itself [*Das Aussagen ist ein Sein zum seienden Ding selbst*]" (BT 218/209), then one can call this being-toward a "relation" only if that does not mean the extrinsic bringing-together of what was initially foreign to each other. The problem with the distinctions between real and ideal, representation and represented, subject and object, is that they already or still presuppose what is to be elucidated in the analysis: the "thing itself" is already one pole, the "representation" another, and "truth" would be their "correspendence." Heidegger tries to show, however, that the true judgement is actually a *revealing* of the "thing-itself." Only *on the basis* of such "revealing" can there be an "epistemological problem" (how to bring subject and object together).

10. Heidegger is somewhat ambiguous when it comes to the relation between truth as *adequatio* and unconcealment: at times he states that unconcealment underlies or is presupposed in correspondence, though in the quote mentioned he states that truth "*is not at all* of the structure of" a "comparison" of representations or (mental) contents or the correspondence between subject and object. I take this to mean that *in essence* truth does not have the form of a "relation," but rather as unconcealment, and the (epistemological) problems of such relations (of correspondence) are only possible on the basis of a phenomenally prior (always already) unconcealment. This is in line with Heidegger's comments on the relation between this definition of truth and the tradition: "[. . .] Truth, understood as an agreement, has its origin in disclosedness by way of a definite modification" (BT 223/214). This is also why Heidegger states that truth as unconcealment is itself only possible on the basis of being-in-the-world. He calls that phenomenon the *foundation* of the original phenomenon of truth [*grundverfassung des Daseins*]. I have stressed something similar to the extent that I have chosen being-in as the phenomenon guiding all of Heidegger's meditations. Now some will argue that it is at this point that a decisive break between the early and the later Heidegger occurs: the later Heidegger no longer thinks that the phenomenon of truth is founded on the essential structure of *Dasein*. For example, Gert-Jan van der Heiden writes that it is on this point that Heidegger will "change his mind"; Gert-Jan van der Heiden, *The Truth (and Untruth) of Language: Heidegger, Ricoeur, and Derrida on Disclosure and Displacement* (Pittsburgh: Duquesne University Press, 2010), 27. In an important sense, this is certainly true: in *On the Way*

to Language, Heidegger no longer understands the assertion and the asserted out of a primordial understanding [*Verstehen*]. On the other hand, *Verstehen* is itself a *Grundbefindlichkeit* of being-in. What makes Van der Heiden's book excellent is that it takes being-in as its key to unlocking the irreducible duality of language ("disclosure" and "displacement," or, concerning Heidegger specifically: disclosure and concealment). Van der Heiden himself traces the path from *Being and Time*'s (un)concealment to the "twofold concealment" in the Parmenides-lectures and already shows an essential communication between Heidegger's early and later work. That is the path I wish to follow in showing how *Being and Time*'s being-in prepares the way for the gradual intensification of the performative question: what kind of language would be able to explicate what is essentially concealed?

11. Kierkegaard, *The Sickness unto Death*, 25. This is to a large extent what guides the necessities of "indirect communication" and the need to "deceive" one's reader "into the truth"—in other words: Kierkegaard's need for a "new" and "different" language. The connection between, on the one hand, Heidegger's plight of the lack of plight that constitutes the abandonment by being and, on the other, Kierkegaard's concealment of despair in happiness is affirmed in section 53 of the *Contributions*, where Heidegger indicates what Kierkegaard would call the "dialectical" character of plight or distress. There Heidegger attempts to show how plight denotes the opposite of what it is vulgarly understood to be, namely the interruption of happiness or well-being.

12. In another formulation, Heidegger indicates this under the heading of the "silent passing by of the last god" [*die Stille des Vorbeiganges des letzten Gottes*]. The plight consists in the fact that the last God passes us by "in silence"; the pervasiveness of machination makes it so that we have become unable to decide as to our remoteness from or nearness to the gods. According to Heidegger, "Nearness to the last god is reticence, which must be set into work and word in the style of restraint" [*Die Nähe zum letzten Gott ist die Verschweigung. Diese muß im Stil der Verhaltenheit ins Werk und Wort gesetzt werden*] (CP 12/12).

13. Heidegger distinguishes three forms of transcendence: ontic, ontological, and fundamental-ontological. The vulgar transcendence of the Christian God as *a being* that would be *above all beings*, Heidegger calls "ontic." At times it seems that Heidegger short-sightedly equates the Christian God with this crassest of conceptions of transcendence. But the value of his analysis lies in identifying such a crass or vulgar conception of transcendence and distinguishing it from other forms. Heidegger primarily identifies "ontological" transcendence with reference to Plato's κοινόν (that which is shared or that which beings have "in common," in which they "partake"—μέθεξις—but which is itself irreducible to a being) and to the *general* with reference to the genera—γένη—of Aristotle's categories. Heidegger's problem with this transcendence is that it leaves unclarified the *relation* of beings to what transcends, thereby focusing only negatively on the *fact*

of the distinction of the transcendent from beings. Third, Heidegger mentions the "fundamental-ontological" transcendence of *Dasein* in *Being and Time*, which is to say *Dasein*'s existence, its "standing out" in the "open realm of beings." Here ontological transcendence regains its "original" sense according to Heidegger, insofar as it is understood as understanding of being [*Seinsverständnis*] (I have argued how *Seinsverständnis* already implies transcendence or what I have called what is or remains "essentially implicit"). Here the problem with transcendence as the problem of the determinable *diesseits* resurfaces: "Because Da-sein as Da-*sein* originally endures the open realm of concealment, we cannot in the strict sense speak of a transcendence of Da-sein; in the sphere of this determination, the representation of 'transcendence' in *every* sense must *disappear*" (*CP* 217/170).

14. I indicated that, aside from the Nietzsche who remains complicit with metaphysics because he understands his project as an *inversion* of Platonism, there is another Nietzsche who plays an equally important part. Heidegger writes: "On the other hand, Nietzsche was the first to recognize the key position of Plato and the bearing of Platonism on the history of the West (ascent of nihilism). More precisely, he had an *intimation* of the key position of Plato; for Plato's position between pre-Platonic and post-Platonic philosophy becomes visible only if the pre-Platonic is grasped out of itself in a primordial way and not, as in Nietzsche, interpreted Platonically. Nietzsche remained mired in this interpretation because he did not recognize the guiding question as such and did not carry out the transition to the basic question. Yet Nietzsche did (and this for the moment has greater weight) track down Platonism in its most covert forms: Christianity" (*CP* 219/171). *For what reason* does Heidegger not only see in Nietzsche a reaffirmation of metaphysics but also a questioning out of an other beginning? It is not because of Nietzsche's extravagance, because of his difference from or irreducibility to metaphysics; his supposed operating "outside" it. It is because Nietzsche inaugurated a true thinking *of* metaphysics insofar as he was able to identify the "key position" that Platonism takes up in it. Nietzsche overcame metaphysics not in his *moving away* from it, but in his questioning *of* it. Only to the extent that this does not lead to a new "representation" of metaphysics must metaphysics be "left to itself." For this reason, Heidegger states a little later that creating a "readiness for the leap into Da-sein" implies facing "the unavoidable task of initiating an overcoming of Platonism *through a more original knowledge of its essence*" (*CP* 219–20/172). The task of overcoming metaphysics as the task of a more original meditation on its own essence—this is how metaphysics is overcome "out of its ground." It is therefore necessary that there should be two Nietzsches present in the *Contributions*, as it is necessary in Derrida's works. That ambiguity is no "inconsistency."

15. Kierkegaard, *The Sickness unto Death*, specifically the "Despair to Will to Be Oneself: Defiance," 67ff.

CHAPTER 7

1. See also: "Yet the way of this inventive thinking of beyng does not already have a fixed and plotted course on a map of the land" (*CP* 86/69).

2. Heidegger uses the terms *Seinsverlassenheit* and *Seinsvergessenheit* almost exclusively throughout the *Contributions*, except for a few instances where he speaks of *Seynsverlassenheit* or *Seynsvergessenheit* (cf. sections 50, 55, 56, 136, and 249). The significance of that difference is not entirely clear.

3. See for example the title of section 32: "A decisive gaze *after* the carrying out of the resonating and the interplay."

4. Heidegger makes this point in section 51 in a surprising turn of phrase: "In this age, nothing essential—supposing this determination still makes sense—is any longer impossible or inaccessible" [*In diesem Zeitalter ist nichts Wesentliches—falls diese Bestimmung überhaupt noch einen Sinn hat—mehr unmöglich und unzugänglich*] (*CP* 108/86). One would expect Heidegger to say that in machination nothing essential is "possible" anymore. Instead, he states that there is no longer anything essential that is *impossible*. This is significant insofar as it makes clear that the wish for "other possibilities" beyond machination would still be an expression of machination.

5. Daniela Vallega-Neu coined this term, and everything she points out with it goes in the direction of the necessity of performativity in the face of the problem of entanglement that I attempt to raise in this book. I therefore do not argue against the distinction between representation and the poietic, but only point out that such a distinction itself risks falling prey to itself, placing the poietic over against the representational. Vallega-Neu herself does everything to counter such connotations, for example in her article "Poietic Saying," in *Companion to Heidegger's Contributions to Philosophy*, ed. Charles E. Scott (Bloomington: Indiana University Press, 2001), 66–80.

6. In §4 of the *Contributions*, Heidegger begins by giving a central place to the *question*, as what is at the heart of the turning that is to be prepared. He contrasts his sense of the question to a pejorative view, in which an open question signifies a mere lack of knowledge; a state of not-yet-knowing that one would want to rid oneself of: "[. . .] an empty, obstinate attachment to the uncertain, undecided, and undecidable." To this Heidegger contrasts, in terminology that is staggeringly Derridean: "[. . .] in questioning resides the tempestuous advance that says 'yes' to what has not been mastered and the broadening out into ponderable, yet unexplored, realms. What reigns here is a self surpassing into something above ourselves. To question is to be liberated for what, while remaining concealed, is compelling [*im Fragen ist der treibende Ansturm des Ja zum Unbewaltigten, die Weitung in das noch unausgewogene Zuerwagende. Hier waltet das Übersichhinausfahren in das uns Überhohende. Fragen ist die Befreiung zum verborgen Zwingenden*] (*CP* 10/10). Insofar as the "critique of subjectivity," the transformation of man into Da-sein, cannot

be *effectuated by man*, an affirmation of what cannot be mastered must take place. This transformation is a "self-surpassing" into something "above ourselves," which we now know not to understand oppositionally. It is in this context that Heidegger refers to *Being and Time*: "The question of 'meaning' [*Sinn*], i.e., according to the elucidations in *Being and Time* [. . .], the question of the grounding of a projected domain, or, in short, the question of the *truth of beyng*, is and remains *my* question and is my *unique* question, for at issue in it is indeed what is *most unique* [*und ist meine* einzige, *denn sie gilt ja dem* Einzigsten]. In the age that is *completely questionless* about everything, it is enough to begin by asking *the* question of all questions" (*CP* 11/11). The context in which Heidegger draws out this parallel between his works is that of *plight*. The question is necessary in an age of questionlessness. This basic setup is also present in the opening of *Being and Time* as the forgetfulness of being [*Seinsvergessenheit*]. Heidegger already in *Being and Time* indicates that it cannot be a simple matter of undoing a specific tradition that has made us forgetful, as if one could be simply *liberated from* forgetfulness, or substitute remembrance (ἀνάμνησις) for it. Instead, it leads to the recognition of a *concealment of being* that is *essential and irreducible*.

7. The texts are *Gelassenheit* (GA16) and *Zur Erörterung der Gelassenheit. Aus einem Feldweggespräch über das Denken* (in GA13), translated as Martin Heidegger, *Discourse On Thinking*, trans. John M. Anderson and E. Hans Freund. New York: Harper & Row, 1966. For the way in which "letting" in *Gelassenheit* relates to the "essentially implicit," see Kees Jan Brons, "Gelassenheit: Oorspronkelijk denken en beschrijven," in *De reikwijdte van het geduld. Wijsgerige en theologische opstellen. Aangeboden aan Auke de Jong bij zijn afscheid als hoogleraar* (Zoetermeer: Boekencentrum, 1999), 50–64.

8. This is also the background for the focus on *das (Nichtende) Nichts* in texts from the same period, notably *What is Metaphysics?* and *On the Essence of Ground* from 1929.

9. Though the poet fulfills a huge role in the meditations on the renewed relation to language necessary to think inceptually, Heidegger also continually distinguishes the thinker and the poet. Helpful in this regard may be his reflections on what, superficially speaking, undeniably seems to be the 1941 poem, titled *Winke* ("Intimations"), which is found in *Aus der Erfahrung des Denkens: 1910–1976* (GA13, 2nd ed., Frankfurt am Main: Vittorio Klostermann, 2002, 23–34). Here Heidegger adds the following qualification to his words: "The 'Intimations' [*Winke*] are not poems. Neither are they a 'philosophy' in verse and rhyme. The 'Intimations' are the words of a thinking, that partly uses these expressions, but is not fulfilled in them. This thinking finds no clue in beings, for it thinks beyng. This thinking finds no examples in thoughts, because thoughts think what is [*das Seiende*]. The saying of thinking is, in contrast to the poetic word, imageless [*bildlos*]. And where there seems to be an image, it is neither what is poeticized in a poem [*das Gedichtete einer Dichtung*] nor the intuitability of a

'sense' [*das Anschauliche eines »Sinnes«*], but only the sheet anchor of a hazarded yet unsuccessful imagelessness [*sondern nur der Notanker der gewagten, aber nicht geglückten Bildlosigkeit*]" (Heidegger, *Aus der Erfahrung des Denkens*, 33). Heidegger distinguishes thinking from both the poetic and the philosophical. According to Heidegger, what distinguishes thinking from poetry is the latter's dependence on images. For an excellent discussion of the "imageless" character of thinking, see Daniela Vallega-Neu, "Heidegger's Imageless Saying of the Event," in *Continental Philosophy Review* 47, no. 3/4 (2014): 1–19; and Krzysztof Ziarek. "Image-Less Thinking: The Time-Space for Imagination in Heidegger," in *International Yearbook for Hermeneutics 14*, ed. Günter Figal (Tübingen: Mohr Siebeck, 2015), 145–62.

10. See §36 of the *Contributions*: "to say the language of beings as the language of beyng" [*die Sprache des Seienden als Sprache des Seyns sagen*] (CP 78/62).

11. Vallega-Neu, *Heidegger's Contributions to Philosophy: An Introduction*, 61.

12. See Plato's *Theaetetus* 155d and Aristotle, *Metaphysics* 982b12.

13. See, for example CP sections 7, 9, 123, 129, 131, 146, 168, 221, 239, 248, and 254.

14. See: "that the withdrawal might not appear superficially as mere nullity but might reign as bestowal" [*damit der Entzug nicht vordergründlich als ein bloß Nichtiges erscheine, sondern als die Schenkung walte*] (CP 293/231). Also, for the link between intimation, gift or bestowal, concealment, withdrawal, and silence, see: "How is even the smallest space supposed to be acquired here for the presentiment that refusal is the first and highest gift of beyng, indeed its primordially essential occurrence itself? Refusal eventuates as the withdrawal that incorporates into the stillness in which truth, in accord with its essence, comes anew to the decision as to whether it can be grounded as the clearing for self-concealment" [*Dies Sichverbergen ist das Entbergen der Verweigerung, das Zugehorenlassen in das Befremdliche eines anderen Anfangs*] (CP 241/190).

15. It is because the inceptual thinking-saying preserves a certain failure-to-say that it remains essentially an *attempt* [*Versuch*]: "Nevertheless, here already the thoughtful speaking of a philosophy within the other beginning must be attempted, in the manner of a preliminary exercise" [*wie in einer Vorübung*] (CP 4/6). This is also reflected in the importance of the *Zwischen* of transitional thinking; it remains "in between."

16. Martin Heidegger, *The Event*, trans. Richard Rojcewicz (Bloomington and Indianapolis: Indiana University Press, 2013), xxiv.

CHAPTER 8

1. A very valuable resource in tracing all the layers of meaning involved is Ger Groot's superb Dutch translation and extensive introduction and annotation of the text in *Sporen. De stijlen van Nietzsche* (Amsterdam: SUN, 2005).

2. Derrida points the reader to the "element of style"—the hyphen—by which Nietzsche here introduces the pause before the distance, to graphically keep his "distance from distance" (*Sp* 47).

3. The literature is vast and impossible to summarize here. For a general introduction, see Nancy Holland, ed., *Feminist Interpretations of Jacques Derrida* (University Park: Pennsylvania State University Press, 2010); and Ellen K. Feder, Mary C. Rawlinson, and Emily Zakin, eds., *Derrida and Feminism: Recasting the Question of Woman* (New York and London: Routledge, 1997). The best starting point for a critical discussion is Kelly Oliver, *Womanizing Nietzsche: Philosophy's Relation to the Feminine* (New York: Routledge, 1995).

4. Derrida is out to show how the surface of Nietzsche's antifeminism operates within a "feminine operation" and that this operation cannot rid itself of that surface. Reversal and opposition are key here. Nietzsche derides the feminism of his time (and Derrida seems to follow him in this with an eye to 1970s feminism) to the extent that it aims at performing an opposition or a reversal of male rationality or dominance as it is complicit with logocentrism or the history of the determination of truth as *logos* (phallogocentrism). In that way, Derrida can write that "in truth the feminist women against whom Nietzsche multiplies his sarcasm are men" (*Sp* 65, translation amended, JdJ). The "feminine operation" cannot be an opposition to a male operation. Nietzsche's antifeminism is essentially an opposition to opposition, whereby its movement exceeds the simple "anti-" and shows itself as the "suspension" of opposition, or as *undecidability* (the "dangerous perhaps"). Derrida plays out this problematic in part with the help of what Derrida calls the "syntax" of "castration": "Feminism too seeks to castrate. It wants a castrated woman. Gone the style" (*Sp* 65). For a good discussion of these passages, see Suzanne Gearhart, "The Remnants of Philosophy: Psychoanalysis After *Glas*," in *Hegel After Derrida*, ed. Stuart Barnett (London and New York: Routledge, 1998), 147–70. For the differences in connotation of "castration" in Lacan and Freud, see Derrida's "Le facteur de la vérité," in *The Post Card: From Socrates to Freud and Beyond*, trans. Alan Bass (Chicago: University of Chicago Press, 1987), 411–96.

5. Much of Nietzsche's passages on women revolve around the opposition of depth and surface, superficiality or shallowness—an opposition that is deconstructed along similar lines as the one between reality and appearance. One famous example is aphorism 27 from *Twilight of the Idols:* "Women are considered profound. Why? Because no one fathoms their depths. Women aren't even shallow." Derrida discusses the passage at *Sp* 85.

6. Mainly: that the existential analytic was already organized around propriation through what Derrida calls the "opposition" of *Eigentlichkeit* and *Uneigentlichkeit*.

7. Friedrich Nietzsche, *Beyond Good and Evil / On the Genealogy of Morality*, trans. Adrian Del Caro (Stanford: Stanford University Press, 2014), 6–7.

8. The disappearing act doesn't end here. In the text that follows, which is littered with "*peut-êtres*," she sometimes translates it as "perhaps" but often simply omits the word, such as in translating the following triplet of "perhapses": "Nietzsche n'a *peut-être* rien voulu dire ou bien il a *peut-être* voulu dire peu de chose, ou n'importe quoi, ou encore fait semblant de vouloir dire quelque chose. Cette phrase n'est *peut-être* pas de Nietzsche [. . .]" (my italics, JdJ), as "What if Nietzsche himself meant to say nothing, or at least not much of anything, or anything whatever? Then again, what if Nietzsche was only pretending to say something? In fact, it is even possible that it is not Nietzsche's sentence [. . .]" (*Sp* 125–27).

9. The analyses of "perhaps" in Derrida's work are far too numerous to list here, but for one specific instance in which Derrida analyzes the importance of the perhaps with regard to Nietzsche, see Jacques Derrida, *The Politics of Friendship*, trans. George Collins (London and New York: Verso, 2005), especially 28ff.

CHAPTER 9

1. For the relation between *Of Spirit* and the *Geschlecht* series, as well as a number of excellent interpretive essays, see David Wood, ed., *Of Derrida, Heidegger, and Spirit* (Evanston: Northwestern University Press, 1993).

2. For a detailed discussion of the events at the time of the so-called "Heidegger Affair," see Benoît Peeters, *Derrida: A Biography* (Cambridge and Malden: Polity, 2013), 379ff. Derrida did in fact quickly respond to Farías's work in the interviews "Heidegger, the Philosophers' Hell" and "Comment donner raison? 'How to Concede, with Reasons?'" Both have been published in *Points . . . , Interviews, 1974–1994*, trans. Peggy Kamuf et al., ed. Elisabeth Weber (Stanford: Stanford University Press, 1995), 181–95.

3. Martin Heidegger, "Die Selbstbehauptung der deutschen Universität (1933)," in *Reden und andere Zeugnisse eines Lebensweges 1910–1976* (GA16, Frankfurt am Main: Vittorio Klostermann, 2000), 107–17.

4. Martin Heidegger, "Martin Heidegger im Gespräch (17. September 1969)," in *Reden und andere Zeugnisse eines Lebensweges 1910–1976* (GA16, Frankfurt am Main: Vittorio Klostermann, 2000), 709. Translation mine, JdJ.

5. "A reflection that presses in this direction does not turn itself against logic but occupies itself with making a sufficient determination of the λόγος." Martin Heidegger, "Kant's Thesis about Being," in *Pathmarks*, ed. William McNeill (Cambridge: Cambridge University Press, 1998), 362.

6. "First of all, I must say that I am not against technology. I have never spoken against technology, nor against the so-called demonic nature of technology. Instead, I attempt to understand the essence of technology [*Zunächst ist zu sagen, dass ich nicht gegen die Technik bin. Ich habe nie gegen die Technik gesprochen, auch nicht*

über das so genannte Dämonische der Technik, sondern ich versuche: das Wesen der Technik zu verstehen]." Martin Heidegger, "Martin Heidegger im Gespräch (17. September 1969)," in *Reden und andere Zeugnisse eines Lebensweges 1910–1976* (GA16, Frankfurt am Main: Vittorio Klostermann, 2000), 706. Translation mine, JdJ.

7. Jacques Derrida, *Heidegger: The Question of Being and History*, trans. Geoffrey Bennington (Chicago: University of Chicago Press, 2016).

8. "On Reading Heidegger: An Outline of Remarks to the Essex Colloquium," *Research in Phenomenology* 17, no. 1 (1987): 171–85.

9. The second "guiding thread" of *Of Spirit* is the question of technology. Derrida states that the "exemplary statement" that "the essence of technology is nothing technological" "remains, at least in one of its aspects, traditionally philosophical." How so? Because it is a strategy of protection. What does it protect? It serves a "desire for rigorous non-contamination," namely that the "thought of the essence," the "possibility of thought that questions," remains "protected from any original or essential contamination by technology." This thought of an irreducible *contamination* is in line with the thinking of an irreducible *complicity*: "yet can anything in language and in thought be sheltered absolutely from technicity? In the very will to protect oneself from 'x' one is more exposed to the danger of reproducing 'x' than when one tries to think contamination" ("ORH" 172). Derrida's reading of Heidegger is reductive here. That the essence of technology cannot be exhaustively determined by technological means does not necessarily imply the desire for a rigorous dissociation of thinking and technology. Heidegger's equally frequent injunctions that he is "not against technology" already put him on the path of a certain contamination (and this structure takes on many forms in Heidegger's work: the essence of science cannot be thought scientifically; the essence of *logos* cannot be determined logically). The relation of thinking to technology may well be compared to the relation of thinking to representational language: it is not dissociated from it, but rather a different way of being attuned *to* it. Heideggerian "thinking" is precisely the thinking of the essence *of* science, *of* technology, *of* logic. Thinking comes in when we need a "sufficient determination" *of* λόγος (Heidegger, *Pathmarks*, 362). See also chapter 9, n. 17. Derrida also finds a "strategy of protection" in Heidegger's thinking of beyng as withdrawal ("[. . .] the Heideggerian figure of Being's self-veiling, its withdrawal, reserve, reticence, holding-back, may well be a strategy of protection" ("ORH" 173). This thought, already found in "Envoi," means that the withdrawal from beings is to be regarded as safeguarding beyng from beings: a desire for the non-contamination of being and beings. For this reason, "contamination requires the thinking of a kind of différance that is not yet or no longer ontological difference" ("ORH" 173). But we know since the différance-essay that this "not yet or no longer" is aporetic: "'Older' than Being itself, such a différance has no name in our language [. . .] not [. . .] because we would have to seek it in another language [but] rather because there is no name for it at all, not even the name of essence or of being,

not even that of 'différance,' which is not a name, which is not a pure nominal unity [. . .]" (*MP* 28/27). In his discussion of animality, Derrida makes a structurally similar point: "[. . .] it is always a matter of marking an absolute limit between the living creature and the human *Dasein*, of taking a distance not only from all biologism and even all philosophy of life." How does one take such a distance? On the one hand, the "force and necessity" of Heidegger's analysis must be recognized, "without a doubt" and "right down to the details," the principle that "[breaks] with anthropomorphism, biologism and its political effects." On the other hand, these analyses "founder on essential difficulties" (*OS* 85–86/55). The contested thesis is the famous thesis from Heidegger's 1929/30 course on *The Fundamental Concepts of Metaphysics: World, Finitude, Solitude*, trans. William McNeill and Nicholas Walker (Bloomington: Indiana University Press, 1995), namely: that the stone is devoid of world [*weltlos*], the animal is poor in world [*weltarm*], and man is world-forming [*weltbildend*]. What distinguishes *weltbildend* from *weltarm* is that the animal has a world, but not "as such." Thinking the animal implies all the performative complications of thinking the limits of the "as such," or thinking the "as such" *as such*. The emancipation of the animal cannot be exhausted by turning "against" anthropocentrism, even if that may well be, to use a Derridean phrase, an indispensable phase. The same argument is made with reference to the avoidance of sexual difference in Heidegger's work in "*Geschlecht* I: Sexual Difference, Ontological Difference," in *Psyche: Inventions of the Other, Volume II*, ed. Peggy Kamuf and Elizabeth G. Rottenberg (Stanford: Stanford University Press, 2008), 7–26. On the one hand, there are certain essential reasons for it in order to avoid the kinds of dogmatic thought that would *ground* that difference anywhere in an "axiomatic," for example, through a biologism: "Sexual difference remains to be thought, from the moment one no longer pins one's hopes on a common *doxa* or a bio-anthropological science, both of which are sustained by a metaphysical pre-interpretation." In this sense, as an overcoming of biologism, naturalism, anthropology, and so forth, Heidegger's discourse is actually emancipatory. But on the other hand, according to Derrida, this can be done only by subordinating the question of sexual difference to a point that would supposedly exceed all of biologism, naturalism, anthropology, and so forth—the question of being: "But the price of that prudence? Is it not to distance sexuality from all originary structures? To deduce it? Or in any case derive it, and thus to confirm the most traditional philosophemes by repeating them with the force of new rigor?" (*Geschlecht I*, 22). Thus, the attempt to go beyond doxa in thinking sexual difference makes of that difference something derived, thereby reaffirming the "traditional philosopheme" in which sexual difference is reduced. The same is true of the central thread running through "Heidegger's Hand (*Geschlecht* II)," in *Psyche: Inventions of the Other, Volume II*, ed. Peggy Kamuf and Elizabeth G. Rottenberg (Stanford: Stanford University Press, 2008), 27–62, namely that logocentrism and phonocentrism nonetheless "dominate" in Heidegger's attempt to overcome them (through the different modalities of the hand, the distinction of man from animal, the assertion that the ape may have *Greiforgane*, but no hands or rather no *hand*, in the existential analytic's "redistribution" of the relations among *Dasein*, *Vorhandensein*, and *Zuhandensein* (*Geschlecht II*, 49).

10. The second half of *Of Derrida, Heidegger, and Spirit*, ed. David Wood (Evanston: Northwestern University Press, 1993) is largely devoted to the footnote, in essays by Geoffrey Bennington, Simon Critchley, Will McNeill, and John Sallis.

11. He mentions, among other things, *Rufsinn, Schuldigsein, Entschlossenheit* (*OS* 151n–52n/133n). I would add, as I have done above, that there are also possibilities of reading in the question itself Heidegger's attempt to explicate the relation to an irreducible "before." Because if we look closely to what Derrida's account of affirmation comes down to—that one cannot question language without already being in it—this seems to be in line with what I have presented as the opening of the problem of "already being-in" in the opening of *Being and Time*, and at least, as he admits toward the end of the footnote, with the thinking of *Ereignis* in the *Contributions*: "Thought about *Ereignis* takes its bearings from this acquiescence which responds—en-gages—to the address" (*OS* 154n/135).

12. In interpreting the "before," one might think back to the question of whether thinking is before/outside technology or a thinking *of* technology; whether essential or poetic language is before, outside, or beyond representational language; or whether it is a different attunement *to* it. In the same way, the pledge or promise "before" any question (and there is a certain unavoidability to using this "old name") is an affirmation *in* any question. Derrida temporalizes this structure in a typical fashion: instead of the affirmation "implicit in" every question, it "must always have already taken place before" any question.

13. One could imagine a link here between this singular Necessity and Heidegger's *Not-Sache*, the *Not der Notlosigkeit* that motivates and drives the *Contributions*.

14. In his *The Origins of Responsibility*, François Raffoul gives an excellent overview of different philosophical notions of responsibility and how Derrida's notion of an im-possible responsibility relates to them. Though he, too, stresses that Derridean ethics is an "openness to the other," he rightly explains that this is not to be conceived in a straightforwardly transcendent sense, but rather as an "experience of limits": "[this] transcendence happens *in* immanence, and does not constitute some theological beyond, nor even a teleological horizon. The im-possible does not await *at* the horizon, but pierces it in the urgency of its arrival" (François Raffoul, *The Origins of Responsibility* [Bloomington and Indianapolis: Indiana University Press, 2010], 301–2).

15. One of the few commentaries that I think is in line with my attempt here is Martin Hägglund's *Radical Atheism: Derrida and the Time of Life* (Stanford: Stanford University Press, 2008). Hägglund develops his argument in a very different style and context, namely that of time and religion. We differ insofar

as he seems less inclined to take on board the performative implications of the "account" of the "tracing of time" (that cannot, I think, strictly speaking, form a coherent account) as well as the "logic" of radical atheism that he seems to find consistent (11–12), and to which I would be tempted to oppose a performative logic of inconsistency of sorts. But where our arguments converge most is in his resistance to the Levinasian reading of the ethics of deconstruction; in his insistence that there can be no nonviolent relation to the other and no primary peace (77ff.); and in his political proposal of a "logic of *essential corruptibility*" (177).

16. On this point, compare the analysis of Walter Benjamin in the second part of *Force of Law*: "One 'touches' here without touching on this extraordinary paradox: the inaccessible transcendence of the law [loi], before which and prior to which 'man' stands fast, only appears infinitely transcendent and thus theological to the extent that, nearest to him, it depends only on him, on the performative act by which he institutes it: the law [loi] is transcendent, violent and nonviolent, because it depends only on who is before it (and so prior to it), on who produces it, founds it, authorizes it in an absolute performative whose presence always escapes him. The law [loi] is transcendent and theological, and so always to come, always promised, because it is immanent, finite, and thus already past. Every 'subject' is caught up in this aporetic structure in advance. Only the 'to-come' [avenir] will produce the intelligibility or the interpretability of this law [loi]" ("FL" 270).

17. A final example of this: in the discussion following Derrida's remarks at the Essex colloquium, John Sallis makes a point that I take to be very much in line with my reading. He suggests that "there may be a thread in Heidegger's work that is not entirely different from the kind of contamination that you are sketching" by pointing to "On the Essence of Truth." Just as I have tried to do in chapter 7, he points to Heidegger's reconception of *Wesen*, so that it "no longer comes to be determined in a way that simply excludes its opposite" ("ORH" 180). He points quite rightly to the role of *Unwesen* and ultimately of *Irre* in Heidegger's analysis of *Wesen*. Derrida is, however, clear in his response: what is happening there is not contamination. He places these thoughts in line with places where Heidegger writes that *Wahrheit ist Unwahrheit*, the fundamental characteristic of which is, according to Derrida, that it is only a "reversal": "[. . .] it is the *Un-*." It is "still too pure, too rigorously delimited" ("ORH" 180). Instead, Derrida attempts to find words that "introduce some instability which is not simply of the yes and no, of *Wesen* and *Unwesen*." I cite Derrida's response when Sallis once more maintains that it may precisely be in the notion of errancy that "a kind of necessary blurring of the distinction between Being and beings" takes place. I quote Derrida's response in full: "But, if I agree with you—and I do agree with you, to some extent—I still must ask: Why does this blurring of the distinction have no general effect on all of Heidegger's discourse? Because, when you say the essence of technology is not technical—and he makes such types of statements—then

you cannot blur the distinction. But if, in errancy, there is a situation in which this blurring occurs not by accident but unavoidably, this should have effects on the whole *corpus*, on the whole discourse. In that case you couldn't any longer draw such a rigorous distinction between the essence and that of which it is the essence. So, you can imagine the consequences of this contamination. Of course, I am not advocating the blurring of all distinctions! No, on the contrary. I am just asking the question. You have to take into account the *possibility* of the blurring of distinctions, even if you do not blur them. And then the whole rhetoric, the whole scenography changes; the whole style of discourse, all the procedures of demonstration, of affirmation, of drawing conclusions, are different. The style of thinking, of philosophizing, changes" ("ORH" 180). Of course the scenography did change for Heidegger. The *Contributions* and the subsequent manuscripts testify to Heidegger's far-reaching awareness of the consequences of these complications for the rhetoric, scenography, style of discourse, procedures of demonstration, of affirmation, of drawing conclusions, and so forth. But this is not the kind of change Derrida is looking for. And it is true that Heidegger's performative attempts at a philosophical saying, at the very least, express a very different mood than Derrida's textual interventions. On the other hand, in his response, Derrida is himself underestimating the performative complexities involved in distinguishing himself from "reversal" at the risk of positing a thought of contamination *against* and in distinction from the *Un-*. Contamination as non-*Un* or as *Un-Un*. This type of opposition is precisely the kind of performative complication with respect to which his texts are generally "strategically more clever." In this oral discussion, to use the language of *Spurs: perd le style*. In this case, Derrida is construing the Heidegger he is defining himself against, while neglecting to emphasize the inherently problematic character of the against-character of that gesture. Such a self-complication is what he usually accomplishes through his acts of writing. And it is not surprising that it is less evident in an oral discourse. The quality of Derrida's texts is often determined by the measure in which he succeeds to complicate what it is that he is doing at the very moment when he is doing it. See also Afterword, n. 2.

AFTERWORD

1. Although I hope to have shown that one misses the significance of philosophical skepticism if it is reduced to the status of a mere accusation. See for more on this my "Derrida, scepticisme en de waarde van hun zelfweerlegging," *Krisis* 2013, no. 2 (2013): 71–80.

2. Derrida's readings of Hegel and Heidegger are reductive, but one must be precise on this point. The problem is not so much (as I have shown in chapter 4) that Hegel's philosophy cannot be reduced to a dialectics of "reappropriation,"

or that Heidegger's thinking cannot be reduced to an "onto-hermeneutical" horizon. Because Derrida also affirms this: there are always several Hegels and several Heideggers at work in his texts. Rather, Derrida sometimes reintroduces into his readings something of the oppositionality or binarity that he is out to exceed. Derrida is at his best when he is completely transparent about this self-violation, flaunts it, and turns it around on itself in different ways. At other times, Derrida too can "lose the style." For instance, when Derrida, for all his concerns about the idea of a "single, linear, indivisible, oppositional limit," and about binary oppositions, describes his concept of responsibility as follows: "[. . .] there is no responsibility, no [. . .] decision, that must not pass through the [. . .] undecidable. *Otherwise everything would be reducible to* calculation [. . .]" ("EW" 273, my emphasis, JdJ). Without undecidability, *everything would be decidable*, program, calculation, etc. It seems that it is only through a rather crass distinction (if not a "single linear, indivisible, oppositional limit," a "binary opposition") between the calculable and the incalculable, the decidable and the undecidable that Derrida is able to propose this concept of responsibility. Is this incoherent? I have argued throughout that performative self-contradiction cannot be grounds for "refuting" a discourse that ostensibly attempts to maximize and affirm such a self-relation. And the fact that "opposition" is unavoidable but that not everything is reducible to it is itself one of Derrida's main concerns and best made points. My point is that Derrida's greatest virtue lies in a form of self-criticism through which he manages to complicate with the left hand everything that the right hand writes. But the measure in which he succeeds to performatively enact such self-complication differs from text to text.

3. And every *articulation* of it—and this holds no less for justice, responsibility, as well as all the neologisms with which Derrida and Heidegger have tried to indicate something essentially implicit or apparently beyond the grasp of our normal conceptuality—is inevitably *also* an oppositional determination. No doubt the explosive potential that Hegel must have associated with the term *Geist* is lost on us now, reinscribed as it has been in all the twentieth-century critiques of rationality. And Derrida himself has opened our eyes to the way in which Heidegger's use of that same concept falls back into what it wanted to exceed. No doubt *différance*, *trace*, and all the other terms will suffer the same fate, as Derrida already announces in 1968 in *La différance*.

4. Whether that is the Romantic "cult of the genius," mysticism, singular experience such as revelation, the absolute distinction of faith from reason, the thing in itself, or any external presupposition (principle, axiom, program) or predeterminations of method, object, or goal.

5. G. W. F. Hegel, *Outlines of the Philosophy of Right*, 15.

6. One good example of an attempt in this direction is Johannes-Georg Schülein's *Metaphysik und ihre Kritik bei Hegel und Derrida* (Hamburg: Felix Meiner Verlag, 2016), in which he convincingly argues, with respect to several key themes, the relation between Hegel and Derrida must exceed the oppositionality of the metaphysical/post-metaphysical distinction.

BIBLIOGRAPHY

Adorno, Theodor W. "The Essay as Form." Translated by Bob Hullot-Kentor and Frederic Will. *New German Critique*, no. 32 (Spring–Summer 1984): 151–71.
Aristotle. *The Complete Works of Aristotle: The Revised Oxford Translation*. Edited by Jonathan Barnes. Princeton: Princeton University Press, 1984.
Attridge, Derek. "Derrida and the Questioning of Literature." In *Acts of Literature*, edited by Derek Attridge, 1–29. London and New York: Routledge, 1992.
Baugh, Bruce. *French Hegel: From Surrealism to Postmodernism*. London and New York: Routledge, 2003.
Baum, Manfred. *Die Entstehung der Hegelschen Dialektik*. Bonn: Bouvier, 1986.
Bennington, Geoffrey. "Derridabase." In *Jacques Derrida*, edited by Geoffrey Bennington and Jacques Derrida. Translated by Geoffrey Bennington. Chicago and London: University of Chicago Press, 1993.
———. "Embarrassing Ourselves." *Los Angeles Review of Books*, March 20, 2016. https://lareviewofbooks.org/article/embarrassing-ourselves/.
Bernasconi, Robert. *The Question of Language in Heidegger's History of Being*. Atlantic Highlands: Humanities Press, 1985.
———. "Skepticism in the Face of Philosophy." In *Re-Reading Levinas*, edited by Robert Bernasconi and Simon Critchley, 149–61. Bloomington: Indiana University Press, 1991.
Boer, Karin de, and Ruth Sonderegger, eds. *Conceptions of Critique in Modern and Contemporary Philosophy*. Basingstoke: Palgrave Macmillan, 2012.
Boer, Karin de. "Différance as Negativity: The Hegelian Remains of Derrida's Philosophy." In *A Companion to Hegel*, edited by Stephen Houlgate and Michael Baur, 594–610. Oxford: Blackwell, 2010.
———. *On Hegel: The Sway of the Negative*. Basingstoke: Palgrave Macmillan, 2010.
Bowman, Brady, ed. *Darstellung und Erkenntnis: Beiträge zur Rolle nichtpropositionaler Erkenntnisformen in der deutschen Philosophie und Literatur nach Kant*. Paderborn: Mentis, 2007.
———. *Hegel and the Metaphysics of Absolute Negativity*. Cambridge: Cambridge University Press, 2013.

---. "Spinozist Pantheism and the Truth of 'Sense Certainty': What the Eleusinian Mysteries Tell Us about Hegel's Phenomenology." *Journal of the History of Philosophy* 50, no. 1 (2012): 85–110.
Bradley, Arthur. *Derrida's of Grammatology: A Philosophical Guide*. Bloomington: Indiana University Press, 2008.
---. "Thinking the Outside: Foucault, Derrida and Negative Theology." *Textual Practice* 16, no. 1 (2002): 57–74.
Brons, Kees Jan. "Gelassenheit: Oorspronkelijk denken en beschrijven." In *De reikwijdte van het geduld. Wijsgerige en theologische opstellen. Aangeboden aan Auke de Jong bij zijn afscheid als hoogleraar*, edited by Alle Hoekema, Victor Kal, and Hans de Vries, 50–64. Zoetermeer: Boekencentrum, 1999.
---. "Hegel en de theorie van de subjectiviteit." In *Metafysica op het scherp van de snede*, edited by J. D. J. Buve and Louk Fleischhacker, 188–212. Leeuwarden: Universitaire Pers Fryslân.
---. "Hegel, Husserl en Heidegger." In *Hegel actueel. Over de betekenis van het hegeliaanse denken voor wetenschap, religie en politiek in de XXIe eeuw*, edited by Jeroen Buve and Timo Slootweg, 323–45. Deventer: Deventer Universitaire Pers, 2008.
---. "De intimiteit van het denken." In *Subliem niemandsland. Opstellen over metafysica, intersubjectiviteit en transcendentie*, edited by W. F. C. M. Derkse, A. J. Leijen, and B. M. J. Nagel, 155–73. Best: Damon, 1996.
---. "Metafysica, taal en teken." In *Reflexiviteit en metafysica. Bijdragen aan het symposium ter gelegenheid van het afscheid van prof. J. A. H. Hollak*, edited by Louk Fleischhacker, 62–80. Delft: Eburon, 1987.
---. "Speculatief denken en metafysica." *Stoicheia* 5, no. 3 (1990): 27–43.
Bruzina, Ronald. *Edmund Husserl and Eugen Fink: Beginnings and Ends in Phenomenology, 1928–1938*. New Haven: Yale University Press, 2004.
Burnyeat, Myles F. "Protagoras and Self-Refutation in Later Greek Philosophy." *The Philosophical Review* 85, no. 1 (1976): 44–69.
Butler, Christopher. "Deconstruction and Scepticism." In *Interpretation, Deconstruction and Ideology*, 60–65. Oxford: Clarendon Press, 1984.
Caputo, John D. *The Prayers and Tears of Jacques Derrida: Religion without Religion*. Bloomington: Indiana University Press, 1997.
Cascardi, Anthony J. "Skepticism and Deconstruction." *Philosophy and Literature* 8, no. 1 (1984): 1–14.
Cavell, Stanley. *The Claim of Reason: Wittgenstein, Skepticism, Morality, and Tragedy*. Oxford: Oxford University Press, 1979.
---. *A Pitch of Philosophy*. Cambridge and London: Harvard University Press, 1994.
---. "What Is the Scandal of Skepticism?" In *Philosophy the Day After Tomorrow*, 132–54. Cambridge and London: Harvard University Press, 2005.

Chaffin, Deborah. "Hegel, Derrida, and the Sign." In *Derrida and Deconstruction*, edited by Hugh J. Silverman, 77–91. London and New York: Routledge, 1989.

Cobben, Paul G. "Das Verhältnis zwischen Brüder und Schwester: Derridas Deutung von Hegels Antigone." In *Kritik der postmodernen Vernunft: Über Derrida, Foucault und andere zeitgenössische Denker*, edited by Bernd Goebel and Fernando Suárez Müller, 147–76. Darmstadt: Wissenschaftliche Buchgesellschaft, 2007.

Comay, Rebecca. *Mourning Sickness: Hegel and the French Revolution*. Stanford: Stanford University Press, 2010.

Comay, Rebecca, and Frank Ruda. *The Dash—The Other Side of Absolute Knowing*. Cambridge and London: MIT Press, 2018.

Conant, James. "Varieties of Scepticism." In *Wittgenstein and Scepticism*, edited by Denis McManus, 97–136. London and New York: Routledge, 2004.

Cornell, Drucilla. *The Philosophy of the Limit*. London and New York: Routledge, 1992.

Coward, Harold, Toby Foshay, and Jacques Derrida, eds. *Derrida and Negative Theology*. Albany: State University of New York Press, 1992.

Critchley, Simon. "A Commentary upon Derrida's Reading of Hegel in Glas." In *Hegel After Derrida*, edited by Barnett, Stuart, 197–226. London and New York: Routledge, 1998.

———. *The Ethics of Deconstruction*. 3rd ed. Edinburgh: Edinburgh University Press, 2014.

Custer, Olivia. "Derrida: Echoes of the Forthcoming." In *Conceptions of Critique in Modern and Contemporary Philosophy*, edited by Karin de Boer and Ruth Sonderegger, 231–47. Basingstoke: Palgrave Macmillan, 2012.

Dahlstrom, Daniel O., ed. *Interpreting Heidegger: New Essays*. Cambridge: Cambridge University Press, 2011.

Dastur, Françoise. "Heidegger and Derrida: On Play and Difference." *Epoché: A Journal for the History of Philosophy* 3, no. 1/2 (1995): 1–23.

Davis, Bret W., ed. *Martin Heidegger: Key Concepts*. Durham: Acumen, 2010.

Derrida, Jacques. *Aporias: Dying—Awaiting (One another) at the "Limits of Truth"* [Apories: Mourir—s'attendre aux "limites de la vérite"]. Translated by Thomas Dutoit. Stanford: Stanford University Press, 1993.

———. "Deconstructions: The Im-Possible." In *French Theory in America*, edited by Sylvère Lotringer and Sande Cohen, 13–32. London and New York: Routledge, 2001.

———. *Dissemination* [La dissémination]. Translated by Barbara Johnson. London and New York: Continuum, 2004.

———. "Otobiographies," translated by Avital Ronell. In *The Ear of the Other: Otobiography, Transference, Translation*, edited by Christie McDonald, translated by Peggy Kamuf. New York: Schocken Books, 1985.

———. *Edmund Husserl's Origin of Geometry: An Introduction* [Introduction à "L'Origine de la géométrie" de Husserl]. Translated by John P. Leavey Jr. Lincoln: University of Nebraska Press, 1978.

———. "Force of Law: The 'Mystical Foundation of Authority.'" In *Acts of Religion*, edited by Gil Anidjar, 228–98. London and New York: Routledge, 2002.

———. *Glas*. Translated by John P. Leavey Jr. and Richard Rand. Lincoln: University of Nebraska Press, 1986.

———. *Heidegger: The Question of Being and History* [Heidegger: la question de l'Être et l'Histoire]. Edited by Thomas Dutoit. With the assistance of Marguerite Derrida. Translated by Geoffrey Bennington. Chicago: University of Chicago Press, 2016.

———. "How to Avoid Speaking: Denials." In *Derrida and Negative Theology* [Comment ne pas parler: Dénégations], translated by Ken Frieden, edited by Harold Coward and Toby Foshay, 73–142. Albany: State University of New York Press, 1992.

———. *Limited Inc*. Translated by Samuel Weber and Jeffrey Mehlman, edited by Gerald Graff. Evanston: Northwestern University Press, 1988.

———. *Margins of Philosophy* [Marges: de la philosophie]. Translated by Alan Bass. Chicago: University of Chicago Press, 1982.

———. *Monolingualism of the Other: Or, the Prosthesis of Origin* [La monolinguisme de l'autre: ou la prothèse d'origine]. Translated by Patrick Mensah. Stanford: Stanford University Press, 1998.

———. *Negotiations: Interventions and Interviews, 1971–2001*. Translated and edited by Elizabeth G. Rottenberg. Stanford: Stanford University Press, 2002.

———. *Of Grammatology* [De la grammatologie]. Translated by Gayatri Chakravorty Spivak. 2nd ed. Baltimore: Johns Hopkins University Press, 1997.

———. *Of Spirit: Heidegger and the Question* [De l'esprit: Heidegger et la question]. Translated by Geoffrey Bennington and Rachel Bowlby. Chicago: University of Chicago Press, 1991.

———. *On the Name* [Passions; Sauf le nom; Khôra]. Translated by David Wood, John P. Leavey Jr., and Ian McLeod, edited by Thomas Dutoit. Stanford: Stanford University Press, 1995.

———. "On Reading Heidegger: An Outline of Remarks to the Essex Colloquium." *Research in Phenomenology* 17, no. 1 (1987): 171–85.

———. "On Responsibility." *PLI—Warwick Journal of Philosophy* 6 (1997): 19–36.

———. *Points . . . , Interviews, 1974–1994* [Points de suspension, Entretiens]. Translated by Peggy Kamuf et al., edited by Elisabeth Weber. Stanford: Stanford University Press, 1995.

———. *Positions*. Translated by Alan Bass. Chicago: University of Chicago Press, 1981.

———. *The Politics of Friendship* [Politiques de l'amitié]. Translated by George Collins. London and New York: Verso, 2005.

———. *The Post Card: From Socrates to Freud and Beyond* [La carte postale. De Socrate à Freud et au-delà]. Translated by Alan Bass. Chicago: University of Chicago Press, 1987.

———. *Psyche: Inventions of the Other, Volume I* [Psyché: Inventions de l'autre], edited by Peggy Kamuf and Elizabeth G. Rottenberg. Stanford: Stanford University Press, 2007.

———. *Psyche: Inventions of the Other, Volume II* [Psyché: Inventions de l'autre], edited by Peggy Kamuf and Elizabeth G. Rottenberg. Stanford: Stanford University Press, 2008.

———. "Some Statements and Truisms about Neologisms, Newisms, Postisms, Parasitisms, and other Small Seismisms." In *The States of Theory*, edited by David Carroll, 63–94. New York: Columbia University Press, 1989.

———. *Speech and Phenomena, and Other Essays on Husserl's Theory of Signs*. Translated by David B. Allison. Evanston: Northwestern University Press, 1973.

———. *Sporen. De Stijlen van Nietzsche*. Ingeleid, geannoteerd en vertaald door Ger Groot. Amsterdam: SUN, 2005.

———. *Spurs: Nietzsche's Styles/Éperons: Les styles de Nietzsche*. Translated by Barbara Harlow. Chicago: University of Chicago Press, 1979.

———. "The Question of Style." In *Feminist Interpretations of Friedrich Nietzsche*. Translated by Ruben Berezdivin, edited by Kelly Oliver and Marilyn Pearsall, 50–66. University Park: Pennsylvania State University Press, 1998.

———. *The Problem of Genesis in Husserl's Philosophy* [Le problème de la genèse dans la philosophie de Husserl]. Translated by Marian Hobson. Chicago and London: University of Chicago Press, 2003.

———. *The Truth in Painting* [La vérité en peinture]. Translated by Geoff Bennington and Ian McLeod. Chicago: University of Chicago Press, 1987.

———. *Voice and Phenomenon: Introduction to the Problem of the Sign in Husserl's Phenomenology* [La voix et le phénomène]. Translated by Leonard Lawlor. Evanston: Northwestern University Press, 2011.

———. *Without Alibi*. Translated and edited by Peggy Kamuf. Stanford: Stanford University Press, 2002.

———. *Writing and Difference*. Translated by Alan Bass. Chicago: University of Chicago Press, 1978.

Derrida, Jacques, and Maurizio Ferraris. *A Taste for the Secret*. Translated by Giacomo Donis, edited by Giacomo Donis and David Webb. Oxford: Blackwell, 2001.

Descombes, Vincent. *Modern French Philosophy*. Translated by L. Scott-Fox and J. M. Harding. Cambridge: Cambridge University Press, 1980.

Dick, Kirby, and Amy Ziering Kofman, eds. *Derrida: Screenplay and Essays on the Film*. Manchester: Manchester University Press, 2005.

Dow Magnus, Kathleen. *Hegel and the Symbolic Mediation of Spirit*. Albany: State University of New York Press, 2001.

Dreyfus, Hubert L., and Mark A. Wrathall, eds. *A Companion to Heidegger*. Oxford: Blackwell, 2005.

Emad, Parvis, Friedrich-Wilhelm von Herrmann, Kenneth Maly et al., eds. *1989–2009: Twenty Years of Beiträge zur Philosophie (Vom Ereignis): The Impact and the Work Ahead*. Berlin: Duncker & Humblot, 2009.

Emad, Parvis. *On the Way to Heidegger's Contributions to Philosophy*. Madison: University of Wisconsin Press, 2007.

Feder, Ellen K., Mary C. Rawlinson, and Emily Zakin, eds. *Derrida and Feminism: Recasting the Question of Woman*. New York and London: Routledge, 1997.

Fink, Eugen. "Die phänomenologische Philosophie Edmund Husserls in der gegenwärtigen Kritik." *Kant-Studien* 38, no. 1–2 (1933): 319–83.

Forget, Philippe. "Das 'Gerede' vom performativen Widerspruch—Zu Habermas' Derrida-Kritik." *Allgemeine Zeitschrift für Philosophie* 16, no. 3 (1991): 47–57.

Foucault, Michel. *The Archeology of Knowledge* [L'archéologie du savoir]. Translated by A. M. Sheridan Smith. New York: Pantheon, 1972.

Früchtl, Josef. *Das unverschämte Ich. Eine Heldengeschichte der Moderne*. Frankfurt am Main: Suhrkamp, 2004.

Fuchs, Wolfgang W. "Post-Modernism Is Not a Scepticism." *Man and World* 22, no. 4 (1989): 393–402.

Fulda, Hans Friedrich. "Hegels Dialektik als Begriffsbewegung und Darstellungsweise." In *Seminar: Dialektik in der Philosophie Hegels*, edited by Rolf-Peter Horstmann, 124–74. Frankfurt am Main: Suhrkamp, 1978.

———. *Das Problem einer Einleitung in Hegels Wissenschaft der Logik*. 2nd ed. Frankfurt am Main: Vittorio Klostermann, 1975.

———. "Über den spekulativen Anfang." In *Subjektivität und Metaphysik. Festschrift für Wolfgang Cramer*, edited by Dieter Henrich, 109–27. Frankfurt am Main: Vittorio Klostermann, 1966.

———. "Über den Ursprung der Hegelschen Dialektik." *Aquinas. Rivista internazionale di filosofia* 24, no. 2/3 (1981): 368–89.

Fulda, Hans Friedrich, and Rolf-Peter Horstmann, eds. *Skeptizismus und spekulative Denken in der Philosophie Hegels*. Stuttgart: Klett-Cotta, 1996.

Fulda, Hans Friedrich, and Christian Krijnen, eds. *Systemphilosophie als Selbsterkenntnis: Hegel und der Neukantianismus*. Würzburg: Königshausen & Neumann, 2006.

Gadamer, Hans-Georg. "Hegels Dialektik des Selbstbewußtseins." In *Materialien zu Hegels "Phänomenologie des Geistes,"* edited by Hans Friedrich Fulda and Dieter Henrich, 217–42. Frankfurt am Main: Suhrkamp, 1973.

———. *Hegels Dialektik: Fünf hermeneutische Studien*. Tübingen: Mohr Siebeck, 1971.

———. "Die Idee der Hegelschen Logik." In *Hegels Dialektik: Sechs hermeneutische Studien*, 49–69. Tübingen: Mohr Siebeck, 1980.

Gadamer, Hans-Georg. *Hegels Dialektik: Fünf hermeneutische Studien*. Tübingen: Mohr Siebeck, 1971.

Gasché, Rodolphe. "'A Certain Walk to Follow': Derrida and the Question of Method." *Epoché: A Journal for the History of Philosophy* 18, no. 2 (2014): 525–50.

———. *The Honor of Thinking: Critique, Theory, Philosophy*. Stanford: Stanford University Press, 2007.

———. *Inventions of Difference: On Jacques Derrida*. Cambridge and London: Harvard University Press, 1994.

———. *The Tain of the Mirror: Derrida and the Philosophy of Reflection*. Cambridge and London: Harvard University Press, 1986.

Gearhart, Suzanne. "The Remnants of Philosophy: Psychoanalysis After *Glas*." In *Hegel After Derrida*, edited by Stuart Barnett, 147–70. London and New York: Routledge, 1998.

George, Theodore D. *Tragedies of Spirit: Tracing Finitude in Hegel's Phenomenology*. Albany: State University of New York Press, 2006.

Habermas, Jürgen. *The Philosophical Discourse of Modernity: Twelve Lectures*. Translated by Frederick G. Lawrence. Cambridge, MA: MIT Press, 1987.

Hägglund, Martin. *Radical Atheism: Derrida and the Time of Life*. Stanford: Stanford University Press, 2008.

Hahn, Songsuk Susan. *Contradiction in Motion: Hegel's Organic Conception of Life and Value*. Ithaca: Cornell University Press, 2007.

Hass, Andrew W. *Hegel and the Art of Negation: Negativity, Creativity and Contemporary Thought*. London: I.B. Tauris, 2013.

Hegel, G. W. F. *The Difference between Fichte's and Schelling's System of Philosophy* [Differenz des Fichte'schen und Schelling'schen Systems der Philosophie]. Translated by H. S. Harris and Walter Cerf. Albany: State University of New York Press, 1977.

———. *Faith and Knowledge* [Glauben und Wissen]. Translated by H. S. Harris and Walter Cerf. Albany: State University of New York Press, 1977.

———. *On Christianity: Early Theological Writings by Friedrich Hegel*. Translated by T. M. Knox and Richard Kroner. New York: Harper & Brothers, 1961.

———. "On the Essence of Philosophical Criticism Generally, and Its Relationship to the Present State of Philosophy" [Über das Wesen der philosophischen Kritik überhaupt und ihr Verhältnis zum gegenwärtigen Zustand der Philosophie insbesondere]. In *Between Kant and Hegel: Texts in the Development of Post-Kantian Idealism*. Translated by H. S. Harris, edited by George di Giovanni and H. S. Harris, 275–91. Indianapolis: Hackett, 2000.

———. "On the Relationship of Skepticism to Philosophy, Exposition of Its Different Modifications and Comparison of the Latest Form with the Ancient One" [Verhältnis des Skeptizismus zur Philosophie. Darstellung seiner verschiedenen Modifikationen und Vergleichung des neuesten mit dem alten]. In *Between Kant and Hegel: Texts in the Development of Post-Kantian Idealism*.

Translated by H. S. Harris, edited by George di Giovanni and H. S. Harris, 311–62. Indianapolis: Hackett Publishing Company, 2000.

———. *Outlines of the Philosophy of Right* [Grundlinien der Philosophie des Rechts]. Translated by T. M. Knox, edited by Stephen Houlgate. Oxford: Oxford University Press, 2008.

———. *Phenomenology of Spirit* [Phänomenologie des Geistes]. Translated by Arnold V. Miller. Oxford: Oxford University Press, 1977.

———. *The Science of Logic* [Wissenschaft der Logik]. Translated and edited by George di Giovanni. Cambridge: Cambridge University Press, 2010.

———. *Werke in zwanzig Bänden*. Theorie-Werkausgabe, Frankfurt am Main: Suhrkamp, 1970.

Heidegger, Martin. *Aus der Erfahrung des Denkens: 1910–1976* (GA 13). 2nd ed. Frankfurt am Main: Vittorio Klostermann, 2002.

———. *Being and Time* [Sein und Zeit]. Translated by Joan Stambaugh, edited by Dennis J. Schmidt. Albany: State University of New York Press, 2010.

———. *Contributions to Philosophy (of the Event)* [Beiträge zur Philosophie (Vom Ereignis)]. Translated by Richard Rojcewicz and Daniela Vallega-Neu. Bloomington: Indiana University Press, 2012.

———. *Country Path Conversations* [Feldweg-Gespräche (1944/45)]. Translated by Bret W. Davis. Bloomington: Indiana University Press, 2010.

———. *Discourse On Thinking* [Gelassenheit]. Translated by John M. Anderson and E. Hans Freund. New York: Harper & Row, 1966.

———. *The Event* [Das Ereignis]. Translated by Richard Rojcewicz. Bloomington and Indianapolis: Indiana University Press, 2013.

———. *The Fundamental Concepts of Metaphysics: World, Finitude, Solitude* [Die Grundbegriffe der Metaphysik. Welt—Endlichkeit—Einsamkeit]. Translated by William McNeill and Nicholas Walker. Bloomington: Indiana University Press, 1995.

———. *Gesamtausgabe*. Frankfurt am Main: Vittorio Klostermann, 1975–.

———. *An Introduction to Metaphysics* [Einführung in die Metaphysik]. Translated by Gregory Fried and Richard Polt. New Haven: Yale University Press, 2000.

———. *Mindfulness* [Besinnung]. Translated by Parvis Emad and Thomas Kalary. London: Athlone, 2006.

———. *Nietzsche Volumes I and II: The Will to Power as Art, The Eternal Recurrence of the Same*. Translated and edited by David Farrell Krell. New York: Harper Collins, 1991.

———. *Nietzsche Volumes III and IV: The Will to Power as Knowledge and as Metaphysics, Nihilism*. Edited by David Farell Krell. New York: Harper Collins, 1991.

———. *Off the Beaten Track* [Holzwege]. Edited by Julian Young and Kenneth Haynes. Cambridge: Cambridge University Press, 2002.

———. *On the Way to Language* [Unterwegs zur Sprache]. Translated by Peter D. Hertz. New York: Harper & Row, 1971.

———. *On Time and Being* [Zur Sache des Denkens]. Translated by Joan Stambaugh. New York: Harper & Row, 1972.

———. *Parmenides*. Translated by Andre Schuwer and Richard Rojcewicz. Bloomington: Indiana University Press, 1992.

———. *Pathmarks* [Wegmarken]. Edited by William McNeill. Cambridge: Cambridge University Press, 1998.

———. *Poetry, Language, Thought*. Translated by Albert Hofstadter. New York: Harper & Row, 1971.

———. *The Question Concerning Technology and Other Essays*. Translated and with an Introduction by William Lovitt. New York and London: Garland, 1977.

———. *Reden und andere Zeugnisse eines Lebensweges 1910–1976* (GA 16). Frankfurt am Main: Vittorio Klostermann, 2000.

———. *What Is a Thing?* [Die Frage nach dem Ding. Zu Kants Lehre von den transzendentalen Grundsätzen]. Translated by W. B. Barton Jr. and Vera Deutsch, with an analysis by Eugene T. Grendlin. South Bend, IN: Gateway Editions, 1967.

———. *What Is Called Thinking?* [Was heisst Denken?]. Translated by J. Glenn Gray. New York: Harper and Row, 1968.

Heiden, Gert-Jan van der. "The Poetic Experience of Language and the Task of Thinking: Derrida on Celan." *Philosophy Today* 53, no. 2 (2009): 115–25.

———. *The Truth (and Untruth) of Language: Heidegger, Ricoeur, and Derrida on Disclosure and Displacement*. Pittsburgh: Duquesne University Press, 2010.

Henrich, Dieter. "Anfang und Methode der Logik." In *Hegel im Kontext*, 73–94. Frankfurt am Main: Suhrkamp, 1971.

———. *Hegel im Kontext*. Frankfurt am Main: Suhrkamp, 1975.

———. "Hegels Logik der Reflexion. Neue Fassung." *Hegel-Studien* 18 (1978): 203–324.

Herrmann, Friedrich-Wilhelm von. *Wege ins Ereignis: Zu Heideggers "Beiträgen zur Philosophie."* Frankfurt am Main: Vittorio Klostermann, 1994.

———. "Way and Method: Hermeneutic Phenomenology in Thinking the History of Being." In *Critical Heidegger*, edited by Christopher Macann, 171–90. London and New York: Routledge, 1996.

Hiley, David R. "The Deep Challenge of Pyrrhonian Scepticism." *Journal of the History of Philosophy* 25, no. 2 (1987): 185–213.

Hillis-Miller, Joseph. *For Derrida*. New York: Fordham University Press, 2009.

Hobson, Marian. "Deconstruction, Empiricism, and the Postal Services." *French Studies* 36, no. 3 (1982): 290–314.

———. *Jacques Derrida: Opening Lines*. London and New York: Routledge, 1998.

Holland, Nancy J., ed. *Feminist Interpretations of Jacques Derrida*. University Park: Pennsylvania State University Press, 1997.

Houlgate, Stephen. "Hegel, Derrida, and Restricted Economy: The Case of Mechanical Memory." *Journal of the History of Philosophy* 34, no. 1 (2008): 79–93.

———. *An Introduction to Hegel: Freedom, Truth, and History*. Oxford: Blackwell, 2005.

———. "Essence, Reflexion, and Immediacy in Hegel's Science of Logic." In *A Companion to Hegel*, edited by Stephen Houlgate and Michael Baur, 139–58. Oxford: Blackwell, 2011.

———. *The Opening of Hegel's Logic: From Being to Infinity*. West Lafayette: Purdue University Press, 2006.

Houlgate, Stephen, and Michael Baur. *A Companion to Hegel*. Oxford: Blackwell, 2011.

Hyppolite, Jean. *Genesis and Structure of Hegel's Phenomenology of Spirit* [Genèse et structure de la Phénoménologie de l'esprit de Hegel]. Evanston: Northwestern University Press, 1974.

———. *Logic and Existence* [Logique et existence: Essai sur la Logique de Hegel]. Translated by Leonard Lawlor and Amit Sen. Albany: State University of New York Press, 1997.

———. *Studies on Marx and Hegel* [Études sur Marx et Hegel]. Translated by John O'Neil. New York: Harper & Row, 1969.

Husserl, Edmund. *Ideas Pertaining to a Pure Phenomenology and to a Phenomenological Philosophy. First Book: General Introduction to a Pure Phenomenology* [Ideen zu einer reinen Phänomenologie und phänomenologischen Philosophie. Erstes Buch: Allgemeine Einführung in die reine Phänomenologie]. Translated by F. Kersten. The Hague: Martinus Nijhoff, 1983.

Jaeschke, Walter. "Äußerliche Reflexion und immanente Reflexion: Eine Skizze der systematischen Geschichte des Reflexionsbegriffs in Hegels Logik-Entwürfen." *Hegel-Studien* 13 (1978): 85–117.

———. *Hegel Handbuch. Leben—Werk—Wirkung*. Stuttgart and Weimar: Verlag J. B. Metzler, 2003.

Jong, Johan de. "Derrida, scepticisme en de waarde van hun zelfweerlegging." *Krisis* 2013, no. 2 (2013): 71–80.

———. "Hegel's Appropriation of Kant's Theoretical Philosophy in the Jena Period." In *The Bloomsbury Companion to Kant*, edited by Gary Banham, Dennis Schulting, and Nigel Hems, 294–97. London and New York: Bloomsbury, 2012.

———. "Hoe keert men zich (niet) tegen de tegenstelling? Hegel als Derrida's punt van vertrek." *De uil van Minerva* 28, no. 1 (2015): 26–45.

Kant, Immanuel. *Critique of Practical Reason*. Translated and edited by Mary Gregor. With a revised introduction by Andrews Reath. Revised edition. Cambridge: Cambridge University Press, 2015.

———. *Critique of Pure Reason*. Translated and edited by Paul Guyer and Allen W. Wood. Cambridge: Cambridge University Press, 1998.

Kates, Joshua. *Essential History: Jacques Derrida and the Development of Deconstruction*. Evanston: Northwestern University Press, 2005.

———. *Fielding Derrida: Philosophy, Literary Criticism, History, and the Work of Deconstruction*. New York: Fordham University Press, 2008.

Kearney, Richard. *Debates in Continental Philosophy: Conversations with Contemporary Thinkers*. New York: Fordham University Press, 2004.
Kern, Andrea, and Christoph Menke, eds. *Philosophie der Dekonstruktion: Zum Verhältnis von Normativität und Praxis*. Frankfurt am Main: Suhrkamp, 2002.
Kierkegaard, Søren. *The Sickness Unto Death: A Christian Psychological Exposition for Upbuilding and Awakening* [Sygdommen til Døden: En christelig psychologisk Udvikling til Opbyggelse og Opvækkelse]. Translated and edited by Howard V. Hong and Edna H. Hong. Princeton: Princeton University Press, 1980.
———. *Practice in Christianity* [Indøvelse i Christendom]. Translated and edited by Howard V. Hong and Edna H. Hong. Princeton: Princeton University Press, 1991.
———. *The Point of View* [Synspunktet for min Forfatter-Virksomhed]. Translated and edited by Howard V. Hong and Edna H. Hong. Princeton: Princeton University Press, 1998.
Kisner, Wendell. "Erinnerung, Retrait, Absolute Reflection." *The Owl of Minerva* 26, no. 2 (1995): 171–86.
Kojève, Alexandre. *Introduction to the Reading of Hegel*. Edited by Allan Bloom, translated by James H. Nichols Jr. Ithaca and London: Cornell University Press, 1980.
Krell, David Farrell. "Marginalia to Geschlecht III: Derrida on Heidegger on Trakl." *CR: The New Centennial Review* 7, no. 2 (2007): 175–99.
———. *The Tragic Absolute: German Idealism and the Languishing of God*. Bloomington: Indiana University Press, 2005.
Krijnen, Christian. *Philosophie als System: Prinzipientheoretische Untersuchungen zum Systemgedanken bei Hegel, im Neukantianismus und in der Gegenwartsphilosophie*. Würzburg: Königshausen & Neumann, 2008.
L.-Waniek, Eva, and Erik M. Vogt, eds. *Derrida und Adorno: Zur Aktualität von Dekonstruktion und Frankfurter Schule*. Vienna: Turia + Kant, 2008.
Lau, Chong-Fuk. "Language and Metaphysics: The Dialectics of Hegel's Speculative Proposition." *Hegel and Language* (2006): 55–74.
Lawlor, Leonard. *Derrida and Husserl: The Basic Problem of Phenomenology*. Bloomington: Indiana University Press, 2002.
Leavey Jr., John P., Gregory L. Ulmer, and Jacques Derrida. *Glassary*. Lincoln: University of Nebraska Press, 1986.
Levinas, Emmanuel. *Otherwise than Being or Beyond Essence*. Translated by Alphonso Lingis. Dordrecht: Kluwer Academic Publishers, 1991.
———. "Wholly Otherwise." In *Re-Reading Levinas*, edited by Robert Bernasconi and Simon Critchley, 3–10. Bloomington: Indiana University Press, 1991.
Lindorfer, Bettina, and Jürgen Trabant. *Hegel, Zur Sprache: Beiträge Zur Geschichte Des Europäischen Sprachdenkens. Festschrift Für Jürgen Trabant Zum 60. Geburtstag*. Tübingen: Narr, 2002.
Llewelyn, John. *Beyond Metaphysics? The Hermeneutic Circle in Contemporary Continental Philosophy*. Cambridge: Cambridge University Press, 1985.

———. *Derrida on the Threshold of Sense*. Basingstoke: Palgrave Macmillan, 1986.
———. "A Point of Almost Absolute Proximity to Hegel." In *Deconstruction and Philosophy: The Texts of Jacques Derrida*, edited by John Sallis, 87–95. Chicago: University of Chicago Press, 1987.
Lumsden, Simon. "The Rise of the Non-Metaphysical Hegel." *Philosophy Compass* 3, no. 1 (2008): 51–65.
———. *Self-Consciousness and the Critique of the Subject: Hegel, Heidegger and the Post-structuralists*. New York: Columbia University Press, 2014.
Macksey, Richard, and Eugenio Donato, eds. *The Structuralist Controversy: The Languages of Criticism and the Sciences of Man*. Baltimore and London: Johns Hopkins University Press, 1970.
Malabou, Catherine. *The Future of Hegel: Plasticity, Temporality and Dialectic*. Translated by Lisabeth During. London: Routledge, 2005.
Maly, Kenneth. *Heidegger's Possibility: Language, Emergence—Saying Be-ing*. Toronto: University of Toronto Press, 2008.
Marcuse, Herbert. *Hegel's Ontology and the Theory of Historicity*. Translated by Seyla Benhabib. Cambridge, MA: MIT Press, 1989.
Marrati, Paola. *Genesis and Trace: Derrida Reading Husserl and Heidegger*. Stanford: Stanford University Press, 2005.
McKenna, William, and J. Claude Evans, eds. *Derrida and Phenomenology*. Dordrecht: Kluwer Academic Publishers, 1995.
Melville, Stephen W. *Philosophy Beside Itself: On Deconstruction and Modernism*. Minneapolis: University of Minnesota Press, 1986.
Menke, Christoph. *Tragödie im Sittlichen. Gerechtigkeit und Freiheit nach Hegel*. Frankfurt am Main: Suhrkamp, 1996.
Merleau-Ponty, Maurice. "Hegel's Existentialism." In *Sense and Non-Sense*, translated, with a Preface, by Hubert L. Dreyfus and Patricia Allen Dreyfus, 63–70. Evanston: Northwestern University Press, 1964.
Michelfelder, Diane P., and Richard E. Palmer. *Dialogue and Deconstruction: The Gadamer-Derrida Encounter*. Albany: State University of New York Press, 1989.
Mitchell, Andrew J. "The Coming of History: Heidegger and Nietzsche Against the Present." *Continental Philosophy Review* 46, no. 3 (2013): 395–411.
———. "The 'Letter on Humanism': Ek-Sistence, Being, and Language." In *The Bloomsbury Companion to Heidegger*, edited by François Raffoul and Eric S. Nelson, 237–42. London and New York: Bloomsbury, 2013.
———. "Contamination, Essence and Decomposition: Heidegger and Derrida." In *French Interpretations of Heidegger: An Exceptional Reception*, edited by David Pettigrew and François Raffoul, 131–50. Albany: State University of New York Press, 2008.
———. "Heidegger's Poetics of Relationality." In *Interpreting Heidegger: Critical Essays*, edited by Daniel O. Dahlstrom, 217–32. Cambridge: Cambridge University Press, 2011.

Naas, Michael. *The End of the World and Other Teachable Moments. Jacques Derrida's Final Seminar*. New York: Fordham University Press, 2014.

Nancy, Jean-Luc. *Hegel: The Restlessness of the Negative*. Translated by Jason Smith and Steven Miller. Minneapolis and London: University of Minnesota Press, 2002.

———. *The Speculative Remark (One of Hegel's Bon Mots)*. Translated by Céline Surprenant. Stanford: Stanford University Press, 2002.

Nietzsche, Friedrich. *Twilight of the Idols, Or, How to Philosophize with a Hammer* [Götzendämmerung]. Translated with an introduction and notes by Duncan Large. Oxford and New York: Oxford University Press, 1998.

———. *Beyond Good and Evil/On the Genealogy of Morality* [Jenseits von Gut und Böse/Zur Genealogie der Moral]. Translated, with an Afterword, by Adrian Del Caro. Stanford: Stanford University Press, 2014.

Neu, Daniela. *Die Notwendigkeit der Gründung im Zeitalter der Dekonstruktion*. Berlin: Duncker & Humblot, 1997.

Norris, Christopher. *Deconstruction: Theory and Practice*. 3rd ed. London and New York: Routledge, 2002.

———. *Derrida*. London: Fontana, 1987.

Nuzzo, Angelica. "The Language of Hegel's Speculative Philosophy." In *Hegel and Language*, edited by Jere O'Neil Surber, 75–91. Albany: State University of New York Press, 2006.

———. "Thinking Being: Method in Hegel's Logic of Being." In *A Companion to Hegel*, edited by Stephen Houlgate and Michael Baur, 111–38. Oxford: Blackwell, 2011.

Oliver, Kelly. *Womanizing Nietzsche: Philosophy's Relation to the "Feminine."* London and New York: Routledge, 1995.

Oliver, Kelly, and Marilyn Pearsall, eds. *Feminist Interpretations of Friedrich Nietzsche*. University Park: Pennsylvania State University Press, 1998.

O'Neil Surber, Jere, ed. *Hegel and Language*. Albany: State University of New York Press, 2006.

Pahl, Katrin. *Tropes of Transport: Hegel and Emotion*. Evanston: Northwestern University Press, 2012.

Plato. *The Republic*. Translated by C. D. C. Reeve. Indianapolis and Cambridge: Hackett Publishing Company, 2004.

———. *Theaetetus*. Translated by John McDowell. Oxford: Clarendon Press, 1973.

Peeters, Benoît. *Derrida: A Biography* [Derrida]. Cambridge and Malden: Polity, 2013.

Peperzak, Adriaan. "Presentation." In *Re-Reading Levinas*, edited by Robert Bernasconi and Simon Critchley, 51–66. Bloomington: Indiana University Press, 1991.

Pettigrew, David, and François Raffoul, eds. *French Interpretations of Heidegger: An Exceptional Reception*. Albany: State University of New York Press, 2008.

Pippin, Robert B. "Back to Hegel?" *Mediations* 26, no. 1–2 (2012).

---. *Hegel's Practical Philosophy: Rational Agency as Ethical Life*. Cambridge: Cambridge University Press, 2008.

---. *Hegel's Idealism: The Satisfactions of Self-Consciousness*. Cambridge: Cambridge University Press, 1989.

---. "Hegel's Logic of Essence." *Schelling-Studien* 1 (2013): 73–96.

---. "Negation in Hegel's Logik." In *Hegel—200 Jahre Wissenschaft der Logik*, edited by Anton Friedrich Koch, Friedrike Schick, Klaus Vieweg, and Claudia Wirsing. Hamburg: Meiner, forthcoming.

Polt, Richard. *The Emergency of Being: On Heidegger's Contributions to Philosophy*. Ithaca: Cornell University Press, 2006.

Powell, Jason. *Heidegger's Contributions to Philosophy: Life and the Last God*. London and New York: Continuum, 2007.

Powell, Jeffrey, ed. *Heidegger and Language*. Bloomington: Indiana University Press, 2013.

Priest, Graham. "Derrida and Self-Reference." *Australasian Journal of Philosophy* 72, no. 1 (1994): 103–11.

Raffoul, François. *Heidegger and the Subject*. Translated by David Pettigrew and Gregory Recco. Atlantic Highlands: Humanities Press, 1998.

---. *The Origins of Responsibility*. Bloomington and Indianapolis: Indiana University Press, 2010.

Raffoul, François, and Eric S. Nelson, eds. *The Bloomsbury Companion to Heidegger*. London and New York: Bloomsbury, 2013.

Rapaport, Herman. *Heidegger and Derrida: Reflections on Time and Language*. Lincoln: University of Nebraska Press, 1991.

Rorty, Richard. *Essays on Heidegger and Others: Philosophical Papers*. Vol. 2. Cambridge: Cambridge University Press, 1991.

---. "Philosophy as a Kind of Writing: An Essay on Derrida." In *Consequences of Pragmatism*, 90–109. Minneapolis: University of Minnesota Press, 1982.

Sallis, John. *Delimitations: Phenomenology and the End of Metaphysics*. Bloomington: Indiana University Press, 1995.

Saussure, Ferdinand de. *Course in General Linguistics*. Edited by Charles Bally and Albert Sechehaye with the collaboration of Albert Riedlinger. Translated and annotated by Roy Harris. Chicago and La Salle: Open Court, 1986.

Schwarz, Justus. "Die Denkform der Hegelschen Logik." *Kant-Studien* 50, no. 1–4 (1959): 37–76.

Sextus Empiricus. *Outlines of Skepticism*. Edited by J. Annas and J. Barnes. Cambridge: Cambridge University Press, 2005.

Schrift, Alan D. *Nietzsche's French Legacy: A Genealogy of Poststructuralism*. New York and London: Routledge, 1995.

Schülein, Johannes-Georg. *Metaphysik und ihre Kritik bei Hegel und Derrida*. Hamburg: Felix Meiner Verlag, 2016.

Scott, Charles E., Susan Schoenbohm, Daniela Vallega-Neu, and Alejandro Vallega, eds. *Companion to Heidegger's Contributions to Philosophy*. Bloomington: Indiana University Press, 2001.

Silverman, Hugh J. *Derrida and Deconstruction*. Vol. 2. London and New York: Routledge, 2004.

Silverman, Hugh J., and Don Ihde, eds. *Hermeneutics and Deconstruction*. Albany: State University of New York Press, 1985.

Smith, Barry, et al. "Derrida Degree: A Question of Honour." *Times* (London), Saturday, May 9, 1992.

Sussman, Henry. "Hegel, Glas, and the Broader Modernity." In *Hegel After Derrida*, edited by Barnett, Stuart, 260–92. London and New York: Routledge, 1998.

Vallega-Neu, Daniela. "At the Limit of Word and Thought: Reading Heidegger's Das Ereignis." In *International Yearbook for Hermeneutics. Focus: Reading*, edited by Günter Figal, 77–91. Tübingen: Mohr Siebeck, 2013.

———. "Ereignis." In *The Bloomsbury Companion to Heidegger*, edited by François Raffoul and Eric S. Nelson, 283–90. London and New York: Bloomsbury, 2013.

———. *Heidegger's Contributions to Philosophy: An Introduction*. Bloomington: Indiana University Press, 2003.

———. "Heidegger's Imageless Saying of the Event." *Continental Philosophy Review* 47, no. 3/4 (2014): 1–19.

———. *Heidegger's Poietic Writings: From Contributions to Philosophy to The Event*. Bloomington: Indiana University Press, 2018.

———. "Poietic Saying." In *A Companion to Heidegger's Contributions to Philosophy*, edited by Charles E. Scott et al., 66–80. Bloomington: Indiana University Press, 2001.

Vernon, Jim. *Hegel's Philosophy Language*. London: Continuum, 2007.

Wellmer, Albrecht. "On the Dialectic of Modernism and Postmodernism." *Praxis International* no. 4 (1985): 337–62.

Wilmore, S. J. "Scepticism and Deconstruction." *Man and World* 20, no. 4 (1987): 437–55.

Wood, David. *The Deconstruction of Time*. 2nd ed. Evanston: Northwestern University Press, 2001.

———, ed. *Derrida: A Critical Reader*. Oxford: Blackwell, 1992.

———, ed. *Of Derrida, Heidegger, and Spirit*. Evanston: Northwestern University Press, 1993.

———. *Philosophy at the Limit*. London: Unwin Hyman, 1990.

———. *The Step Back: Ethics and Politics After Deconstruction*. Albany: State University of New York Press, 2012.

———. *Thinking After Heidegger*. Cambridge and Malden: Polity, 2002.

———. *Time After Time*. Bloomington: Indiana University Press, 2007.

Wood, David, and Robert Bernasconi, eds. *Derrida and Différance*. Evanston: Northwestern University Press, 1988.
Zambrana, Rocío. "Hegel's Logic of Finitude." *Continental Philosophy Review* 45, no. 2 (2012): 213–33.
Ziarek, Ewa Płonowska. "The Rhetoric of Failure and Deconstruction." *Philosophy Today* 40, no. 1–4 (1996): 80–90.
———. *The Rhetoric of Failure: Deconstruction of Skepticism, Reinvention of Modernism*. Albany: State University of New York Press, 1996.
Ziarek, Krzysztof. "Image-Less Thinking: The Time-Space for Imagination in Heidegger." In *International Yearbook for Hermeneutics 14*. Edited by Günter Figal, 145–62. Tübingen: Mohr Siebeck, 2015.
———. *Language After Heidegger*. Bloomington: Indiana University Press, 2013.
———. "Noting Silence." *Critical Horizons* 11, no. 3 (2010): 359–77.
———. "Reticent Event: Letting Things Happen." *Textual Practice* 25, no. 2 (2011): 245–61.

INDEX

abandonment of/by being, 172, 187–88, 198, 200, 205, 212, 302n11
Abgrund. See abyss
absolute, 93, 103
  construing the, 89–90, 110
  language as, 13
abyss [*Abgrund*], 190, 195
accidental, 23, 25, 37, 131, 156, 249
acknowledging, 199
acquiescence, 253–55, 311. *See also* engagement; commitment
acts of writing. *See under* writing
actuality, pure, 111
Adorno, Theodor W., xx
affirmation, xxxiv, 61, 69, 75, 229, 242, 252, 254, 257, 262, 267–68
  and necessity or choice, 257
  anterior to any question, 256
age, 12, 40–44, 47, 53, 188, 191, 218, 304n4, 305n6. *See also* epoch
alterity, xxiii–xxv, xxviii–xxix, 32, 47–49, 55, 86, 127–30, 139, 144, 148
always already
  in Derrida, 6, 10–11, 21, 39, 102, 124, 144, 254–55, 262, 272
  in Heidegger, xxv, xxxi, 156–57, 160–62, 164, 167–68, 170, 177, 198

Americanization, 287n3
analytic philosophy, xxvi, 280n18
animality, xxxiii, 222, 246–48, 252, 261, 310n9
anticipation, 140–41, 145, 189–90, 260
antifeminism, 222–23, 226–27, 307n4
antinomies, 95, 98–99
antithesis, 93–96, 225
apophantic, 38
aporia, 49, 131, 251, 259, 267, 286n9
appearance, 67, 104, 108–9, 136, 166, 293n20. *See also under* being
apperception, 97
appropriation, event of. See *Ereignis*
Aquinas, Thomas, 159
arbitrariness, 20
arche-trace. *See under* trace
arche-writing. *See under* writing
argument, equal counter-, 107. *See also* skepticism
Aristotle, 15, 159, 213, 302n13, 306n12
assurance, 22, 30, 72, 78, 113, 236, 239, 259–62, 266, 269, 270, 284n12
ataraxia [ἀταραξια]. *See* tranquility
attempt, 189, 190, 306n15
attunement. *See under* disposition
Aufhebung. See sublation

autonomy, 17, 257, 268. *See also* responsibility
avenir. *See under* future
average everydayness, 164, 166, 168
avoidance, xxii, xxxiii, 233, 242, 244–45, 247–48, 261–62. *See also* unavoidable
axioms, 141–42

basic disposition. *See under* disposition
Bataille, Georges, 278n11
becoming, 103, 109–11
before the question. *See under* question
beginning, 101–2, 111. *See also* first beginning; other beginning
being
  and appearances, 67
  and beings, 160, 181
  and non-being, 103
  God is, 118
  history of being/beyng, 157, 206
  implicit character of, 159, 161
  prejudices about, 159–60
  reflection of, into itself, 124
  self-concealment of, 205
  understanding of, 161, 164, 303n13
  See also beyng; forgetfulness of being; ontological difference; question of being/beyng; truth; withdrawal
Being and Time, xxxii, 10, 38, 155–88, 194, 196, 198–208, 215–17, 234, 244–45, 250, 253, 255–56, 272, 285n2
being-in, xxv, xxxii, 10, 14, 58, 156–57, 162, 166–71, 183, 187, 198, 217, 234, 272
  distinction from being in, 167
being-in-the-world, 166–68, 301
Bennington, Geoffrey, 256, 284n9
Besinnung. *See* meditation; reflection

Bewahrung. *See* preservation; sheltering; truth
Bewegung. *See* movement
bet, 262
beyond. *See* borders; *jeneits/diesseits*; limits; transcendence
beyng
  and beings, simultaneity of, 196
  essential occurrence of, xxxi, 171, 189, 195–96, 201, 216
  -historical works, xxxi, 217, 234, 270, 282n22
  See also being; forgetfulness of being; ontological difference; question of being/beyng; truth; withdrawal
Beyond Good and Evil, 41, 224, 236, 286n5, 289n33
bifurcation, 96, 99–103, 109, 290n5
binary oppositions, xxiv, 35, 38, 139, 149, 150, 285n5, 313n2
biologism, 249, 251–52, 310n9
Blanchot, Maurice, 278n11
book, model of, 5, 8, 132, 140, 147, 283n4
borders, xxv, 5, 14, 34, 35, 39, 132, 140, 143–45, 175. *See also* boundary; *jenseits/diesseits*; limits; transcendence
boundary, xxiv, 35, 39, 141. *See also* borders; *jenseits/diesseits*; limits; transcendence
Butler, Christopher, 287n5

calculation, 137, 156, 211, 260, 298n11
Cambridge honorary degree, 280n18
care [*Sorge*], 168
Cascardi, Anthony J., 65
category (transcendental), 88
causa sui, 119
Cavell, Stanley, 68–69

certain way, in a. *See* in a certain way
choice, 30, 72, 211
circle
  as pejorative, 231
  hermeneutic, xxxii, 10, 231–35, 239–40, 269
  in Hegel, 111, 114
  in Heidegger, 162–63, 169, 215
  of metaphysics, 29, 32, 34, 38, 46, 81
  of skepticism, 65
  vicious, 38, 162
claims. *See under* proposition
closure, 33, 39, 42–44, 47, 53, 55, 139, 141, 150, 249–50, 286nn9–10
columns, 133
Comay, Rebecca, 282n20
commentary, 134, 264
commitment, xxxiii, xxxiv, 66, 252–53, 255, 260, 262, 267–69. *See also* engagement; language; *Zusage*
complicity
  ethics of, xxv, xxxiv, 49, 257–62, 269, 272
  irreducible, xxiv, xxxiii, 41, 48, 56, 58, 65, 74, 76, 225, 241–43, 248–53, 261, 265, 269, 309n9
  See also ethics
concealment, xxxi, 23, 40, 217–18, 234, 242, 272, 301n10
  clearing-concealing [*lichtende Verbergung*], 189
  in "On the Essence of Truth," 202–7
  in *Being and Time*, 157, 165, 171, 182, 303n13
  in *Contributions to Philosophy*, 185–86, 188, 191, 193, 215, 305n6, 306n14
  in Parmenides-lectures, 198–201
  hiddenness, 157, 166, 242, 272
  See also forgetfulness of being; preservation; sheltering; truth; withdrawal
concept
  in Derrida, 26, 36, 127
  in Hegel, 90, 97, 111, 112, 117, 119, 294n24
  movement of the, xix, 86–88, 141, 143, 146–47, 149, 270, 290n1
  transcendental vs. empirical, 88
  See also category
conceptual solidarity, xx, 10, 34, 41
conclusions. *See under* proposition
conditions of possibility, 10
conjuncture, 186–87
consciousness, 27, 37, 89, 97, 104. *See also* self-consciousness
contamination, 6, 21, 58, 258
  differential, 269
  fatal necessity of, 33, 246
  in Heidegger, 312n17
  irreducible, xxiv, xxv, 56, 60, 67, 74, 78, 247–48, 254, 265, 309n9
  originary, law of, 126
  See also under desire
continental philosophy, xxvi, 45, 279n18
  and analytic philosophy, xxvi, 279n18
contradiction, 99, 106
  as relation, 106
  necessity of, 105
  performative, 18, 30, 63, 66
  principle of, 107
  self-, xxviii, 62–71, 104–7, 115, 120, 227, 254, 264, 266
Contributions to Philosophy (Of the Event), xxvi, xxxi, 155–57, 171–220, 234, 279n15, 280n17, 282n23, 302n11, 304nn1–6, 306nn10–11, 313n17
counter, going to, xx, 173, 196
crisis, 19, 150–51

Critchley, Simon, 48, 69, 77, 287n10, 288n10, 289n16, 290n35
criterion, problem of, 108
criticism, xxii, xxix, 41, 58, 97, 266, 291n11
  anti-/hyper-, 74
  invulnerability to, 48
  self-, 314
  transcendental, 61–62, 72
critique, xx–xxii, xxvi–xxix, xxxiii–xxxiv, 6, 45, 51–52, 56, 66, 71–80, 87, 92
  deconstruction of, 75
  of critique, 73–74
  of Derrida, 66, 266, 313n2
  of Hegel by Derrida, 138, 148
  of Heidegger by Derrida, 228, 245
  of Kant by Hegel, 98
  philosophical, 72, 86, 292n11
  precritical, xx, 29, 51, 59–62
  See also critique; deconstructible; dialectics; ethics; hierarchy; justice; method; presence; skepticism
Critique of Practical Reason, 88
Critique of Pure Reason, 97
Crowther, Paul, 247–48

danger, of writing, 19. See also under writing
dangerous perhaps, 236–38, 240, 267, 307n4
Darstellung, 10, 86, 104–5, 107, 109, 124, 155. See also exposition; presentation
Dasein, 10, 158, 161–69, 177, 180, 183–84, 205, 208, 248, 253, 255
Da-sein, 173, 179, 182–83, 190, 194, 206–7, 218, 303nn13–14, 304n6
Dastur, Françoise, 254
death, 90, 112
decision, 27, 53, 72–75, 81, 174, 257–59, 268, 284n12, 306n14

deconstructible, 258–59
deconstruction, 26, 30, 37, 40, 42, 49, 81, 120, 245
  and alterity, xxv–xxvi
  and critique, xxvii, 71–80
  and empiricism, 52–61
  and indirectness, xx, xxii–xxiii, 3–13, 24–30, 266–67, 269
  and skepticism, 62–70
  anti-, 269
  ethics of, xxxiii–xxxiv, 69, 242, 260, 312n15
  is justice, 259
  logic of, 254
  of metaphysics, 14, 18, 23, 26, 30, 32, 37, 40, 42, 45–47, 49
  remoralization of, 79, 262, 268–69
  vulnerability of, xxix, 29, 52, 71, 76–81, 266–67, 269
delimitation, xxiv, 35, 29, 233. See also demarcation; determination; outlining
demarcation, xxviii, 32, 34–35, 48, 144, 232, 267. See also delimitation; determination; outlining
departure, point of, 58, 127–28, 140, 144, 149–50, 160, 166, 194
depth, 307n5
desire, 21, 24–25, 28, 37, 55, 77, 116, 230, 252
  for non-contamination, 242, 246–48, 254, 259, 309n9
  for purity, 55, 242–43, 252, 259–60, 269
despair, 284n12, 302n11, 303n15
destiny, 42, 215, 248–49
determination, 6, 13, 34–36, 38–39, 55, 58, 66, 74, 90–95, 110, 112, 128, 232, 249. See also delimitation; demarcation; indeterminacy; outlining

development
  Derrida's, 125–27, 243, 287n4
  Hegel's, 89
  Heidegger's, xxxi, 155, 180–81, 194, 199, 202, 217
  See also immanent self-development; movement
dialectics
  distinct from deconstruction, 127, 132, 140–41, 146, 149–51, 231–32, 239, 265, 269–70
  Hegelian, xxi, xxx, 87, 98
  originary, 114, 125
diesseits/jenseits. See jenseits/diesseits
différance, xxv, 17, 27–28, 36, 39, 44, 124, 133, 135–39, 205, 254, 265
"Différance" (essay), 135–39
difference, ontological. See under ontological
"Difference between Fichte's and Schelling's System of Philosophy, The," 85, 89, 91, 96, 100, 102, 105, 107, 128
diffidence [Scheu], 201, 213. See also withdrawal
direct, xxiii, xxvii, 3, 16, 52, 78, 79, 161, 181, 207, 233, 258, 263, 276n7, 282n20. See also indirect
dislocation, 9, 43
disobedience, 243
disposition
  attunement, xxxii, 195, 201, 204, 208–15, 218, 245, 271, 311n12
  basic, 182, 197–98, 209–10, 213, 216
  Stimmung, xxxii, 195, 204, 208–15
dissemination, 143–44, 149–50
Dissemination (book), 126, 135, 139–40, 149
distance, 224, 228, 233, 307n2
distinction, activity of 109
distress, 172, 188, 205, 302n11. See also plight

dogmatism, 114
double bind, 30, 44, 128
"Double Session, The," 144
dwelling, 114

Edmund Husserl's Origin of Geometry: An Introduction, 125
effacement, 6, 11–12, 21–22, 25, 284n11
  self-, 26, 142–43, 145–46, 151
  See also under limits
effects, of différance, 121, 136–37, 139
emancipation, xxiii, xxiv, xxxiv, 225–26, 234, 243, 246–47, 277n9, 310n9
  as Enlightenment legacy, 277n9
  critique of, 277n9
  from emancipation, 269
  from metaphysics, 269
empiricism, xxix, 51–65, 71, 78, 80, 87, 141–43, 148, 266
enactment, 143–44, 179, 207
Encyclopedia of the Philosophical Sciences in Basic Outline, 7, 104, 142
engagement, xxxiv, 255, 262, 267–68. See also commitment; language; Zusage
engendering. See under movement
entanglement
  Heidegger and Hegel, difference, xxxiii
  of avoiding with the question of being, 244
  of method and content, xxiii, xxv, xxxiv, 4, 6, 33, 39, 85, 87, 92, 124, 146, 199, 263
  of saying and what is to be said, 186–87, 193
  oppositional, 138, 266
  See also inextricability
Entzug. See withdrawal
Entzweiung. See bifurcation

epistēmē, xxviii, 18, 30, 31, 33, 42, 44.
    See also epoch
epistemology, 68
epoch, 11–15, 41–45, 49, 58, 61, 246,
    287n10. See also epistēmē; future;
    history
epochē [ἐποχη]. See suspension;
    skepticism
equivocality, xx, 14, 48, 135, 147, 224.
    See also indirect
erasure, 23, 26, 28–30, 33, 40, 43,
    61–62, 80, 135, 138–39, 147, 151
Ereignis, xxxii, 156, 176–77, 180, 182,
    184, 189–90, 192, 194–95, 203,
    205–6, 215–18, 231–35, 240,
    311n11
Erlebnis, 188, 208–12, 218, 270. See
    also experience
errancy [errance, Irre], 58, 186, 205–7,
    230, 234, 312n17. See also truth;
    wandering
Erschweigung. See silence: reticence
escape, 252, 261, 273
essence, 34–35, 37
    in Hegel, 91, 97, 106, 110, 114,
        118–19, 294n24
    in Heidegger, 167–68, 178, 186,
        195, 200–8, 211, 215, 246, 285n2,
        300n8, 303n14, 309n9, 312n17
    of language/writing, xxii, 15–17,
        19–21, 23, 27, 266
    question of, 31–35, 136, 250,
        285n3
    See also accidental; question
essentialism, 230
ethics, xxi, xxxiii, xxxiv, 61, 69, 164,
    222, 243, 262, 267, 268
    and deconstruction, 79, 242, 257–60
    and ontology, 69
    ethical stance, 243, 256
    ethical turn, xxxiii

    of complicity, xxxiv, 257, 259–61,
        269, 272
    See also complicity
Ethics (Spinoza), 106
event (of appropriation). See Ereignis
everydayness, 164, 166, 168
example, 4–6, 29, 53, 58, 283n7
excess, xxv, xxx, xxxiii, 43, 64, 120–21,
    147, 209–10, 212, 223, 225, 232
    and responsibility, 257, 261, 265,
        268
    See also overflowing
exergue, 4, 7–11, 34
existence, 37, 106, 143
    existential [Existenz] 167–68, 183
    See also standing out
existential analytic, 166–70, 180, 184,
    253, 307n6, 311n9
existentialism, xxx, 281n20
exorbitant, 53, 56, 207
expenditure, 137
experience
    and empiricism, 52
    and knowledge, 88
    of plight, 172 (see also plight)
    of the aporia, 259
    of the impossible, 27, 259, 268,
        284n12
    See also Erlebnis
exposition
    in Derrida, 5, 6, 269, 293n24
    in Hegel, 85–89, 92, 104–9, 113–
        14, 116, 119–20, 123–24, 143,
        146–47
    in Heidegger, 157, 161–63, 167,
        182–83, 185, 191, 199, 218
    indirect, xx, xxx, 264
    See also Darstellung; presentation
externality
    and alterity, xxiii, xxiv, xxv, xxviii,
        xxix, 12, 19–20, 32, 39, 49, 55

and ethics, 257, 259–60, 263, 269
and philosophy, 115, 121, 129–30, 139, 141–42, 146–47
fruitful uses of, 278n11

failure, xxxi
of language, xxxii, 156, 194
of the word, 195, 218
rhetoric of, 69, 104
falsity. *See under* truth
familiarity. *See under* knowledge
fascism, 250
feminine 'operation,' 222–26, 307n4
feminism, 222–23, 225–27, 230, 234, 246, 307n3–4. *See also* antifeminism
few and the rare, 189. *See also under* future
finitude, xxx, 30, 91, 96, 100, 102–3, 112, 114, 120, 124, 281n20
first beginning, 157, 171, 174, 178, 188–89, 213
fixation, xix, 96, 100, 102, 104, 106, 112, 114, 115, 293–95n24. *See also* rigid
fluid thoughts, 113
Force of Law: The "Mystical Foundation of Authority," 243, 258, 284n12, 312n16
forgetfulness of being, 159, 175, 187, 199–200, 205, 247, 284n11, 305n6. *See also* being; concealment; lethe; preservation; sheltering; truth; withdrawal
form and content, 105, 145, 147, 149
formalism, 112, 115–17, 142–43, 146, 149, 275n5. *See also* ratiocination
Foucault, Michel, xx
foundations, 104, 128, 142
fragment, 89, 99, 222, 229, 235, 238, 240

"Fragment of a System," 89, 90–94, 95, 114
Freud, Sigmund, 26, 37, 46, 47
Fuchs, Wolfgang W., 64
fugues, 186–87
Fulda, Hans Friedrich, 95
fundamental ontology, 138, 159, 164, 183, 188, 271
future, 43–44, 49, 56, 61, 174, 287n10
and justice, 260
avenir vs. future, 273, 286n7, 312n16
futural, 216
ones, 187–90 (*see also* few and the rare)
perfect, 140, 255
possibilities, 273
research, 272

Gasché, Rodolphe, xxv, 48, 57, 72–74, 104, 278n14, 291n6, 295n24
Geheimnis. See mystery
Geist, 89, 241–46, 248, 251
gender, xxxiii, 222, 246, 261
generation. *See under* movement
Geschlecht, 222, 240–42, 310n9
gesture and statement, xxvi, 15–20
gift [*Schenkung*], 214, 306n14
Glas, 96, 126, 135, 140
Glauben und Sein, 99
goal, 66, 111
God, 37, 275n6, 294n24, 302nn12–13
"is being," 118–19
is dead, 172
"is love," 116
last, 187, 302n12
man becomes, 296n2
ontological proof of, 98
See also religion
good beyond being, 261
grammatology, 8–10, 13, 18–19, 43–44, 53, 277n10

greatest totality, xxviii, 30, 33, 53, 286n9. *See also* logocentrism; totality
Groot, Ger, 306n1
grounding question [*Grundfrage*], the. *See under* question of being
Grundfrage. *See under* question of being
Grundstimmung. *See* disposition
guiding question, the [*Leitfrage*]. *See under* question of being

Habermas, Jürgen, 63
Hägglund, Martin, 311n15
Hass, Andrew, 281n20
Hegelianism, 87, 123, 126, 138, 140, 142, 175, 231, 261
Heiden, Gert-Jan van der, 301n10
Henrich, Dieter, 95
hermeneutic, xxi, 10, 155, 164–65, 231, 261, 265, 270–72
  circle, xxxii, 10, 231–35, 239–40, 269
  horizon, 234, 240
  onto-, 232, 239, 240
  situation, 10, 11, 166
hesitation, xxii, 23, 34, 67, 183, 214, 216, 246. *See also* trembling
heterogeneity, 225, 229–30, 234–35
hiddenness. *See under* concealment
hierarchy
  emancipation and transformation, 225, 228, 234, 235
  metaphysical, xxviii, 32, 34, 36–38, 40, 48, 272
  of deconstruction, 254
  of dispositions, 213
  transformation of, 228
  See also subordination
historicism, xxii, 63
history, 42, 49, 287n10
Hobson, Marian, 125, 287n1
Hölderlin, Friedrich, 172

"Hors livre, préfaces," 102, 121, 139–49
Houlgate, Stephen, 113, 119, 292n13, 293nn22–23
"'Humanism,' Letter on." *See* "Letter on 'Humanism'"
Husserl, Edmund, 19, 29–30, 47, 64, 125, 165, 299–300nn3–5
hypercriticism, 74. *See also* criticism
Hyppolite, Jean, xxx, 124, 281n20, 296n2

idealism, 97, 121
  absolute, 14, 86
  authentic or true, 97
identity, 101, 111–12
  logic of, 28, 36, 61
  of identity and non-identity, 90, 114, 268
illusion, 166, 229
immanence, xxv, xxvi, xxx, 14, 86, 100–4, 120–21, 141, 146, 157, 272
immanent self-development, 19, 100, 142, 278n14. *See also under* movement
immediacy, 17, 26, 111, 113, 124
implicit, xxv, xxvi, 20, 38, 46, 68
  complication, xxx, 7, 18, 31, 49, 157, 183, 300nn5–6
  essentially, 115, 120, 157, 161, 165, 198, 223, 264, 270–72, 297n2, 303n12, 305n7, 314n3
impossible. *See under* experience
in a certain way, xxiii, 13, 18, 55, 58–62, 67, 71, 80, 98, 141, 179
incalculable, 257, 260, 314n2
inceptual thinking, 186–87, 189, 192, 216, 306n15
incoherence, 23, 54, 174
incompetence of science. *See under* science

incompleteness
  logic of, 6–7, 283n7
  of *Being and Time*, 168, 169
indeterminacy, 11, 13, 29, 63–64, 67, 224, 236. *See also* determination
indirect, 263–73
  and ethics, 256–62, 267
  in Derrida, xx–xxiii, xxv–xxvii, xxix, xxxiii–xxxiv, 3–10, 12, 17, 23, 30, 32–33, 78–79
  in Derrida reading Hegel, 135, 147–48, 155
  in Derrida reading Heidegger, 222, 239, 242–43
  in Hegel, 105, 115
  in Heidegger, xxxii, 157, 164, 185
  in Kierkegaard, 275n6
  taking of byways, 186
  See also direct; equivocality; movement; oblique; oratio obliqua
ineffable, xxiii, xxiv, 139, 272, 296n2
inextricability, xxiv, xxv, 33, 48–49, 76, 156, 187, 192–93, 217, 269, 272. *See also* entanglement
infinity, 103, 112
inhabiting, 18, 58–59, 71
inside and outside, 6, 12–14, 20, 22, 24–25, 28, 30, 35, 38–39, 93, 120–21, 131, 271, 277n10
Inständigkeit. See standing in
instituted trace. *See under* trace
internal system, 19, 22, 24–25, 35
internalization, 14, 175
interplay [*Zuspiel*], 187–90
intimation, 182, 188, 195, 199, 213, 306n14
intuition, 19, 95, 97, 112, 290n3, 299n4
Irre. See errancy; truth; wandering

Jaeschke, Walter, 91, 93–95, 290nn4–5

jenseits/diesseits, xxiv, 103, 112, 121, 175, 270, 303n13. *See also* borders; boundary; limits; transcendence
joinings, 186–87
juncture, 186–87
justice, xxiii, xxvii, 77, 80–81, 243, 260, 269, 293n19
  and language, 258
  undeconstructible, 258–59
justification, xx, xxi, xxii, xxix, 30, 52–53, 57, 62, 79–81, 141, 243, 266
  ethical, 258, 261–62
  self-, 97, 100

Kant, Immanuel, 86, 88, 91–92, 96–99, 120, 187, 259, 290n1, 290n3, 291nn10–11
Kates, Joshua, 287nn3–4
Kehre, 156, 165, 171, 177, 179–80, 182, 184, 202, 206
  different meanings of, 180
Kierkegaard, Søren, 28, 37, 172, 179, 273, 275n6, 284n12, 286n7, 302n11
knowledge
  non-, 56, 60, 136
  not a knowledge at all, 33, 53–54, 58, 70
  of reason, 106
  philosophical, 105–6, 128, 183, 192
  positive and negative side of, 106
  vs. curiosity, 148
  vs. familiarity, 115–16
Kojève, Alexandre, xxx, 281n20
Krell, David Farrell, 209, 247
krinein, 72–73

language, xxiii
  and skepticism, 272, 288n5
  as writing, 19–23

language *(continued)*
  engagement/commitment in, 254–55, 262, 267–68, 311n11, 311n12
  in Hegel, 124, 295n1, 296n2
  in Heidegger, 155–58, 169–71, 179–84, 193–99, 202–10, 217–18, 282n23, 309n9
  metaphysical, 46, 136, 138
  problem of (Derrida), 11–13
  traditional view of (Derrida), 14–18
  See also absolute; entanglement; failure; justice; new language; nonsaying; poet; poietic saying; question; representation; saying and said (Levinas); silence; thinking-saying language; totality; unsaying; *Zusage*
law
  of contamination, 60, 78
  of resemblance, 60–62, 64, 80, 136, 138, 141, 258, 266
Lawlor, Leonard, xxiv
leap, 176, 187–90, 194, 218, 303n14
legibility, 24, 29–30, 44, 62, 139. *See also* misreading; reading
Leitfrage. *See under* question of being
lēthē [λήθη], 198–203. *See also* concealment; forgetting; preservation; sheltering; truth; withdrawal
"Letter on 'Humanism,'" 202–3, 205, 207, 215
letting, 199, 201
Levinas, Emmanuel, xxvi, xxxiii, 68–69
liberation, 30, 43, 61, 231, 249
life, 89, 101, 103–4, 112, 114
liminal, 143–44
limits, xxiii–xxv
  concept of, 127–28
  disdain of, 112
  effacement of, 6, 11–12, 21–22
  internal, 13–14, 30, 131–32, 258–60

  mastery of, 128
  See also concept; borders; boundary; *jenseits/diesseits*; limitrophic; liminal; metaphysics; philosophy; presentation; proposition; representation; transcendence; transformation
Limited Inc, 36, 64, 85
limitrophic, 132, 298n9
linguistics, 15, 18–19, 22, 196
liquification, 113
logic
  of all or nothing, 36
  of incompleteness, 6–7, 283n7
  oppositional, 36
  standpoint of, 215
  See also deconstruction; identity; logos; *Science of Logic*; silence; speculative; totality; transcendental
logocentric metaphysics, xxviii, 11, 30–50, 86–87, 120, 269
logocentrism, 53, 130, 172, 250, 267, 278n10, 285n2, 297n8, 307n4, 310n9
  meaning of, xxviii, 7, 13–14, 18, 24, 27, 30, 31–50
logos [λόγος]
  in Derrida, 7, 8, 16, 33, 54–55, 123, 130–31, 147, 307n4
  in Heidegger, 165–66, 170, 231, 245, 285n2, 299n3, 309n9
  in Hyppolite, 124
  different meanings of, 285n2

machination [*Machenschaft*], 156, 171–73, 179, 187–91, 198–99, 205, 210–13, 218, 250, 270, 304n4
madness, 130, 258
Malabou, Catherine, 294n24
Mallarmé, Stéphane, 144, 150
margin, 127, 131, 132, 143, 144, 148
Margins of Philosophy, 31, 46, 126–27

mark, 143–44, 223
marked, xxiii, 24, 31, 61–62, 135, 139, 144, 232, 239, 250, 254
mastery, 128, 179
materiality, 115
mathematics, 116, 145–46, 148
meditation [*Besinnung*], 192–93
Merleau-Ponty, Maurice, xxx, 281n20
metaphor, xix, 158, 287n5
metaphysics. *See* circle; deconstruction; emancipation; hierarchy; limits; logocentric metaphysics; logocentrism; Nietzsche; opposition; overcoming; presence; representation; reversal; totality; truth; *Violence and Metaphysics*
method, 201, 216, 227, 231
 and continental philosophy, xxvi, 280n18
 deconstruction as not a, 22–23, 77–78, 266, 287n3
 in Derrida, xx–xxiii, xxv, 3, 6–8, 10, 49, 52–54, 56, 58, 62, 78, 141
 in Hegel, xx–xxiii, xxv, 87, 91, 92, 112–13, 119, 142, 145, 148, 270, 278n14, 290n2, 294n24
 in Heidegger, xx–xxiii, xxv, xxxi, 38, 157, 160, 162–65, 169–70, 201, 216, 285n2, 298–99n1, 299n3, 300n6, 300n7
 in Nietzsche, 227, 231, 234
 of *Being and Time*, 164
 of present investigation, 264
 See also entanglement; "Question of Method"
misreading, 72, 78–79. *See also* legibility; reading
moment, 100, 104, 108, 110, 113–14
monstrosity, 43, 174, 273. *See also* future
mood, 195, 204, 209, 212–14, 271, 313n17. *See also* disposition

movement
 and justice, 259
 carrying out, 5, 10, 109, 111, 113, 142, 149, 202, 216
 chain, 141
 course, 185, 191
 development, xix, 45, 86, 99–100, 104, 109–11, 120, 170, 180, 194, 199, 202, 217, 234, 263, 271, 297n2
 engendering and generation, 89, 127
 going through, 28, 268
 march, 143, 144
 meaning of (Hegel), 94
 of concealment of origin, 40
 of difference effacing itself, 25
 of exteriorization, 24
 of showing, xix–xxvi, xxix, xxxi, xxxiv, 17, 22, 28, 30, 47–48, 59–60, 68, 71, 80, 87, 122, 151, 176, 181, 218, 242, 261, 263, 271
 origin of (Hegel), 87–89
 pathway, xix, xx, 51, 61, 110, 181, 182, 185, 191, 263
 passage, 55, 131, 286n9
 progression and proceeding, 6, 34, 86, 103, 108, 94, 146, 166, 185, 191, 277n9
 self-, 88, 100, 104, 111, 114, 117, 141, 146
 sequence of steps, 141, 207
 track, xix, xx, 28, 47, 51, 61–62, 80, 185
 unfolding, 6, 107
 unrest, 111
 vanish/disappear/pass over into, 89, 100, 118
 Weg, xix, 185, 191
mystery, 176, 191, 198, 201, 205–6, 210–11, 270
mystical, 258

name, 294n24
Nancy, Jean-Luc, 249
naturalism, 249, 252, 310n9
Nazism, 242, 250–51
necessity (and affirmation), 257
negation
  in Derrida, 229, 236, 244, 276n7
  in Heidegger, 73
  in Hegel, 92, 102–3, 281n20
  of all knowledge, 105
negative, 109, 276n7
  deconstruction as not, 61, 256–57, 262, 267
  discourse, xxiii, xxxiv, 26, 62, 169, 232
  dwelling with the, 114
  in Derrida, 13, 130, 132, 150, 244, 250
  in Hegel, 109–10, 113–19
  in Heidegger, 73, 197, 214
  interpretation, 27, 64
  monstrous power of, 113
  side of philosophy, 105–7, 292n18
  theology, 136, 266
negativity
  difference without, 124
  in Hegel, 91–92, 109–10, 114, 116, 281n20
  in Heidegger, 169
  pure, simple, 109
  reversion to positivity, xxx, 87, 120–22, 126–27, 132
neologisms, 25, 30, 155, 169, 314n3
new language, xxxii, 24, 155, 158, 181, 184, 193, 196–97, 218
Nietzsche, Friedrich
  and Heidegger, 172, 174, 178–79, 208
  and logocentric metaphysics, 22, 26, 36–37, 40–41, 45–47, 72, 286n5, 289n33
  and (plurality of) styles, xxxii–xxxiii, 221–40, 264, 267, 269, 306n1, 307nn2–7, 308n8

  and "Tympan," 129, 132–33
nihilism, xxii, xxviii, 52, 57, 63, 64, 172, 303n14
non-contamination. See contamination; desire
nonknowledge. See under knowledge
nonsaying, 208
non-truth. See under truth
Norris, Christopher, 287n5
nothing
  difference that is, 61, 80
  distinguished by, 246
  exceeding closure, 42, 278n12
  excess as, xxv, 273
  preface as, 143

object, 10, 12–13, 23, 33, 38, 86–88, 187, 204, 250, 271–72. See also method
objective validity, 88
objectivity, 88, 101, 169, 271–72
oblique, xxii, 78, 128, 135, 149, 234, 258–59, 276n7. See also indirect; oratio obliqua
obscure, 159
occult, 136
Of Grammatology, xix, xxvii, 3–35, 39, 43–44, 51–55, 58–59, 126, 131, 139, 146, 230–31, 250
Of Spirit: Heidegger and the Question, xxxiii, 221, 222, 240–48, 254, 267, 309n9
old name, retaining the, 24–25, 30, 60, 62, 139, 141, 148, 311n12
older than, 254
one-sided, xix, 78, 95, 108, 110, 120, 145, 291n11
"On the Essence of Truth," 201–3, 205, 207, 312n17
"On the Relationship of Skepticism to Philosophy, Exposition of its Different Modifications and Comparison of the Latest Form

with the Ancient One," 97–98, 105–7, 293n20
ontic, 163, 232, 300n7, 302n13
onto-hermeneutics, 232, 239, 240
ontological, 10, 28–29, 163, 169, 181, 231–33, 235
  difference, 160, 181, 196, 205, 254
  proof of the existence of God, 98
ontology, fundamental, 138, 159, 164, 183, 188, 271
opposition
  as not enough, 225
  classical, 26
  content or form of, 35
  excess of, 263
  fixed/rigid, 100, 104, 108
  highest, 98
  in Heidegger, 38
  of thought and being, 98
  of understanding and reason, 100
  of values, 236
  opposing opposition, 85, 94, 96, 100, 141, 225, 267
  political, 225, 243
  See also binary oppositions; entanglement; logic
oppositionality, xxii, xxiv–xxv, xxix, xxxiv, 32, 36, 60, 64, 85, 87, 96
oratio obliqua, 277n7. See also oblique
orb/orbit, 53, 56, 207
origin, 7, 8, 17, 19, 23, 26, 28, 35, 40, 47, 61, 95, 136, 139, 175
other beginning, 157, 171–74, 177–79, 187–88, 198, 208–9, 213, 303n14, 306n15
other, the, xxxiii
  and ethics, 258
  of philosophy, 129, 135
Otobiographies, 35
Outlines of Pyrrhonism, 66–67
outlining, 6, 12, 53. See also delimitation; demarcation; determination

outside and inside. See inside and outside
outside of reflection, 94
outside-text, xxv, 13, 127
overcoming, 33, 43, 45–49, 158, 173, 177–79, 184, 207, 244
  cessation of, 171
  of metaphysics, 39, 45–49, 173, 303n14
  of overcoming, 45–49, 176
  of philosophy, 128
  of Platonism, 303n14
  of reflection, 92, 98
  self-, 45–49
  See also transcendence
overflowing, 6, 11, 12, 19, 21, 27, 29, 47. See also excess

parcours. See under movement
Parmenides (Plato), 105–6
Parmenides-lectures (Heidegger), 197–99, 201, 205
parody, 225, 230
"Passions: An Oblique Offering," 79, 262, 268, 276n7, 279n16
passive, 170, 201
path(way). See under movement
performative force, 261
performativity, xxi, xxvi, xxix, xxxi, 75, 79, 86, 120, 169, 262, 263
  different meanings of, 279n15
  Hegel, 278n14
  Heidegger, xxxii
perhaps, 236–38, 240, 267, 307n4
phallogocentrism, 134, 224, 307n4
phenomenology, 138, 155, 164–65
Phenomenology of Spirit, 87, 100, 102, 108–19, 142, 146, 148
phenomenon, 165–66
philosophy
  beginning of, 101–2
  continental, xxvi, 45, 279n18
  definition of, 129

philosophy *(continued)*
    difference from sciences (Hegel), 86, 142, 278n14
    limits of, 128, 133–34
    need for/of, 101–4
    negative side of, 107
    non-, xxii, 46, 52, 54, 56
    object of, 10, 86
    other of, 129, 135
    scandal of, 69
    task of, xix, 100, 275n5
phonē, 16
phonetic writing, 7
phonocentric, 10, 16–17, 19, 23–25, 34, 43, 133
picture-thinking, 115. *See also* knowledge; representation
Plato, 19, 105, 108, 175, 199–200, 213, 261, 268, 293n19, 297n8, 302n13, 303n14, 306n12
Platonism, 174, 178, 226–28, 303n14
play, 21–22, 132, 288n5
plight, 172, 190, 205, 302n12, 305n6
    of the lack of a sense of plight, 172, 188, 270, 302n11
    See also distress
plurality of styles, xxxiii, 157, 222–23, 225–26, 228, 240
poet, 209
    distinction from thinker, 305n9
poietic saying, xxvi, xxxii, 180–82, 184, 196, 209, 271, 304n5
polemics, xxii, xxviii, xxix, 63, 267
    continental and analytic philosophy, 280n18
politics, xxxiii, 222, 246, 247, 261
positions. *See* binary oppositions; disposition; exposition; opposition; *Positions* (Derrida); proposition
Positions (book), 7, 9, 27, 126, 135, 144, 237, 277n10

postmodern, xxvi, xxx, 62, 130, 145, 148, 280nn18–19
poststructuralists, 130
Powell, Jeffrey, 282n23
precritical, xx, 29, 51, 59–62
predicates, 116
preface
    of *Of Grammatology*, 4–7
    of *Phenomenology of Spirit*, 105, 107–20
    status of, 139–51
presence, 17, 22, 23, 42, 61, 200, 233, 259–60, 267, 297n4
    and différance, 136–38, 141
    deconstruction of, 124
    desire for, 24–26, 284n11
    founding value of, 40–41
    metaphysics of, 33–34, 37–39, 64, 224, 247, 284n9, 286n9
    self-, 16, 23, 110, 144
presence-at-hand [*Vorhandenheit*], 38, 167, 169, 196, 211
presentation, xxi, xxiii, 3–4, 6, 9–10, 29, 37, 41, 105, 140
    complication of, 44
    Derrida on Heidegger, xxxiii
    Heidegger, 38
    mere, 37
    philosophical, limits of, 112
    See also Darstellung; exposition; unpresentable
preservation [*Bewahrung*], 87, 189, 200–1, 214. *See also* concealment; forgetfulness of being; sheltering; truth; withdrawal
presuppositionless, 102, 113, 292n13, 293n22
presuppositions, 102–3, 108
principles, 102, 128, 141–42
privilege
    of presence, 37, 40

Index   345

of the question, xxxiii, 242, 246–47,
    253–55, 262
Problem of Genesis in Husserl's
    Philosophy, The, 125
program, 251–52
progress, 211
progression. *See under* movement
proper name, 294n24
proposition, xix–xx, xxiii, xxvii, 5, 7,
    13, 14, 22, 59, 62, 87, 95, 263,
    265, 272
    claims, xix–xxii, xxiv, 4, 8, 14, 71,
        73, 94, 106
    conclusions, xix–xxiii, xxviii, 4, 21,
        51, 59, 61–62, 68, 70, 80
    destructive/hermetism of, 46
    in Heidegger, 169, 176–77, 181–83,
        195–96, 204, 206, 209–18, 246
    limits of (Derrida), 30, 86, 105, 177,
        182, 263
    mere, 28, 48
    results, 108, 111, 114, 142, 149
    speculative and of reason, 107, 115–
        22, 293n24
    statements, xx, xxvi, 12, 13, 15, 20,
        170, 309n9
propriation, 232, 233, 307n6. *See also*
    Ereignis
protest, xxxiv, 123, 130, 225, 243. *See*
    also resistance
psychoanalysis, 37, 41, 235
purity. *See under* desire
pyrrhonism, 66–70. *See also* skepticism

question, 31, 47, 131, 253–57
    and saying yes (Heidegger), 304n6
    authority of, 75
    before the, xxxiii, 253–57
    course of questioning, 186
    experience of the, 253
    Heidegger's unique, 305n6

of all questions, 305n6
of the question, 85, 252, 254,
    289n33
privilege of, xxxiii, 242, 246–47,
    253–55, 262
self-questioning, 49, 285n1
what is . . . ? / of essence, 31–35,
    136, 250, 285n3
See also affirmation; entanglement;
    question of being/beyng;
    unquestionable
question of being/beyng, xxxii, xxxiii,
    32, 34, 156, 159–64, 168–71, 180,
    183, 203, 232–34, 244, 305n6
    and sexual difference, 310n9
    grounding [*Grundfrage*] and guiding
        [*Leitfrage*], 99, 173, 175, 187, 198,
        208, 303n14
    no answer to, 162
"Question of Method," 11, 39, 52–53,
    55, 58
questionlessness, 187–88, 191, 210–11,
    218, 305n6
quotation marks, 73, 138, 224, 235,
    244–45, 259–60

race, xxxiii, 222, 242, 247, 261
racism, 249–52
Raffoul, François, 311n14
ratiocination, 116–19, 293n24. *See also*
    formalism
reading, 6, 29, 53, 71, 227, 229, 231,
    239. *See also* legibility; misreading
ready-to-hand [*Zuhandenheit*], 167, 169
reaffirmation, 74, 130, 175, 224–30,
    251–52, 303n14. *See also* reversal
reality, 17, 88, 293n20, 307n5
reappropriation, xxxi, 87, 127, 132,
    175
reason, 95–97, 99–110, 290n1
rectorial address (Heidegger), 245

recuperation of beings [*Wiederbringung des Seienden*], 182, 190, 193, 196, 209, 216. *See also* being; sheltering; preservation; truth
reflection, xix, xxi, xxv, xxvi, 86–87, 90, 91–97, 100, 103–4, 110, 120
   different meanings of, 278n14, 291n6
   meditation [*Besinnung*], 192–93
   tradition of, 48, 57
   See also self-reflection
reflexive complication, 7, 67, 284n9, 289n33
reflexivity, xxi, xxv, xxxiii, 86, 235, 263–64, 279n15
refusal. *See under* withdrawal
refutation, xxii, xxviii, xxix, 30, 65–66, 68, 77, 245–46, 254, 266, 269
   Hegel's critique of, 291n11, 292n18
   self-, xxviii, 63, 65, 80
relativism, xxii, xxviii, xxix, 13, 15, 22, 30, 52, 63–64, 66, 148, 235–36, 266
religion, 89, 112, 172, 311n15. *See also* God
remembrance, 199, 247, 305n6
remoralization, 79, 262, 268, 269
representation, xxiv–xxv, 16, 37, 116, 170, 175, 178–79, 181–83, 185–86, 192, 249
   and trace, 26
   and writing, 17
   authority of, 250
   critique of, 155
   Heidegger, 10, 38
   limit of, 213
   never possible, 192
   not against, 249
   of a representation, 17
   of language, 16
   of metaphysics, 178
   vs. poietic saying, 304n5

representational approximation [*vorstellende Angleichung*], 204
representational thinking, 115, 117
repression, 24, 25. *See also* forgetfulness of being; lēthē; psychoanalysis
   of writing, 24
repudiation. *See* refutation
resemblance, law of. *See* law of resemblance
reserve, 136–37
resistance, xxxiv, 13, 74, 75, 96. *See also* protest
resonating [*Anklang*], 170, 182, 187–89, 199
responsibility, xxi, xxvi, xxxiii, xxxiv, 49, 79, 80, 222, 242–43, 248–49, 253, 258, 261–62, 267–69, 314n2
   excessive, 257, 268
   higher, 254
   in Hegel and Heidegger, 275n5
   unconditional, 268
   without autonomy, 257
restraint, 182, 195, 198, 209, 213–16, 218. *See also* withdrawal
results. *See under* proposition
retain the old name. *See* old name
reticence [*Erschweigung, Verschweigung*]. *See under* silence
reversal
   and complicity, 246, 252, 312n17
   and strategy, 31, 40, 130, 136
   and transformation, 221–22, 225–30, 236, 239, 269, 307n4
   and transitional thinking, 173–75, 179, 182, 184
   necessary phase, 141, 148
   of metaphysics, 173, 175
   of the Hegelian philosophical task, 138
   See also reaffirmation
right word, the, 156, 181, 194

rigid, 110, 112, 114. *See also* fixation
risk
  essential/structural/inherent, 60, 70, 77–78, 290n34
  Nietzsche, 289n33
  of conflating speculative and ratiocinative propositions, 293n24
  of domestication, 129–30
  of reaffirmation, 192, 196, 224–25, 230, 240, 242, 252
  of transcendence, 176, 179
Rousseau, Jean-Jacques, 5, 7, 19, 53, 58, 283n7, 297n8
rupture, 47, 130, 133, 148, 239

said, and saying (Levinas), xxvi, 68
Sallis, John, 312n17
Saussure, Ferdinand de, 15–20, 26–27, 284n10
saying and said (Levinas), xxvi, 68
Schelling, Friedrich Wilhelm Joseph, 291n11
Schülein, Johannes-Georg, 298n13, 314n6
science
  incompetence of, xxvii, 4, 10, 18, 23, 29, 33, 65, 70
  Hegelian, 102, 104, 108–9, 113, 142, 149, 293n21
  of writing, 8–10, 43–44 (*see also* grammatology)
  scientificity of, 7–11, 21, 29, 31, 34, 39, 58
Science of Logic, 88–89, 91, 94, 102, 104, 113, 127, 142, 145–46, 270
"Self-Assertion of the German University, The," 245
self-complication, xx, xxx, 18, 49, 94, 115, 119, 127, 144–45, 157, 162, 269
  of *Being and Time*, 183
  of the present investigation, 264

self-consciousness, 97, 115, 124, 192, 279n16, 282n20. *See also* consciousness
self-contradiction, xxviii, 62–71, 104–7, 115, 120, 227, 254, 264, 266. *See also* contradiction
selfhood, 124, 192
self-positing, 109, 113
self-reflection, xxvi, 214, 192, 193, 279n16. *See also* reflection
self-relation, 111–12
selfsurpassing, 304n6. *See also* overcoming; transcendence
separation, 109
Sextus Empiricus, 66–67, 70, 292n18
sexual difference, 222–23, 232–33, 246–47, 252, 310n9
sheltering [*Bergung*], 182, 189–90, 201–2, 204, 206, 216. *See also* concealment; preservation; sheltering; truth; withdrawal
shock, 213–14
showing of itself by itself, 157, 166, 170, 183, 187
sichanderswerden, 109, 111, 124
sigetics, 197–98, 218. *See also* silence
sign, xxviii, 3, 9, 14, 15, 22–24, 33, 40, 44, 123, 131, 136
  arbitrariness of, 20
  destroying the concept of, 22
  of a sign, 21, 44, 139
signature, 35, 132
signifier and signified, 13, 15–17, 20–23, 25, 62, 131, 133, 233, 235
silence
  bearing, xxxii, 157, 182, 198–99, 206–9, 218, 302n12, 306n14
  logic of, 197, 218
  not exterior to language, 259
  reticence [*Erschweigung, Verschweigung*], xxxii, 157, 165,

silence: reticence *(continued)*
  182–83, 186, 189, 198–202, 209,
  216, 218, 260, 309n9
  See also withdrawal
simple, 191, 193, 201
simultaneity of beyng and beings. *See
  under* beyng
skepticism
  and deconstruction, xxix, 51, 52,
    55–57, 62–71, 77–78, 80, 258,
    266, 287nn3–4, 313n1
  and Hegel, 87, 104–7, 292n18
  as resource, 65
  no safeguard against, 269, 272
  not refutable, 269
  principle of, 107
  pyrrhonian, 67–70
  truth of, 69
solicit, 54–55
solidarity, conceptual, xx, 10, 34, 41
Sorge, 168
soul, 15, 17, 100, 112, 114, 290n2
speculation, principle of, 98
speculative
  exposition, 105, 107–8, 115, 118–19
  logic, 145
  philosophy, 91, 100, 113–14, 123
  proposition, 115–19
speech, 9, 14, 21, 25, 36, 133, 194
  straightforward and formalized, 247
speech act theory, 279n15
Spinoza, 106
spirit. See *Geist*; *Of Spirit: Heidegger
  and the Question*
Spurs: Nietzsche's Styles, xxxii, 221–40,
  246, 261, 267
standing in [*Inständigkeit*], 198, 208
standing out [*Existenz*], 303. *See also*
  existential
standpoint, xix, xx, 10, 91, 95, 99, 105
  ethical, 243
  neutral, 99, 100
  of *Being and Time*, 203

statements. *See under* proposition
Stimmung. See under disposition
strategy
  and responsibility, 243, 245, 248,
    251–52, 256, 261
  and writing, xxii, xxviii, 13–14, 18,
    22, 25, 27, 42, 44–45, 47, 62, 80,
    124–25, 134–36, 141
  double, 248
  Heidegger, 245
  in Nietzsche, 225, 227, 229, 235,
    237
  oblique, 276
  of protection, 309n9
  See also indirect; reversal;
    withdrawal
"Structure, Sign and Play in the
  Discourse of the Human
  Sciences," 46, 55
style
  difference between Heidegger's and
    Derrida's, 271, 312–13n17
  different meanings of, 223
  everyday, 247
  indirect, xxiii, 259, 264
  in Derrida, xxi, xxiii, xxv, xxviii, 5,
    55, 59, 127, 132, 135, 247, 259,
    280n18, 307n2, 307n4
  in Heidegger, xxv, xxxii, 156, 158,
    183, 185, 216, 302n12
  in Nietzsche, 221–31, 235, 239, 240
subject, 109, 116–17, 249
subjectivism, 97
subjectivity, 101, 109
sublation [*Aufhebung*], 96, 98–99, 101,
  106, 114, 118, 131–32, 138, 149–
  50, 174, 246, 293n18, 295n24
subordination, 18, 34, 37. *See also*
  hierarchy
substance, 37, 107, 109, 114, 116, 119,
  137
superficiality, 307
supplement, 126, 260, 283n7

supplementary complication, 36, 39
surprise, 52, 64, 86, 127–28, 132–35, 248
suspension
  of antitheses/oppositions, 96, 101, 114
  of judgment, 67–68, 96, 258
  of truth, 224–26, 231, 238, 267, 307n4
  See also skepticism; sublation
synthesis, 90, 93, 103
system, 106, 187
systematicity, 185

technology, 156, 172, 218, 245–46, 252, 308n6, 309n8, 311n12
teleology, 146–47, 241–42, 246
temporalization, 10, 295
text, 27, 29, 58–62, 121, 126, 235, 283n7
  philosophical, xx–xxi, 264, 272
textual
  intervention, xxxii, 143–45
  labor, 141
  maneuvers, xxxi, 123, 127, 130, 132, 138
theory, xxi, xxiii, xxvii, 4, 7–10, 13–14, 17–19, 22, 33, 36, 70, 279n15
thinking-saying language, 179, 189, 196–97, 306n15
third term, 97–99, 121, 149, 150
threshold, 143–44. *See also* limits
"Time and Being," xix, 176, 202–3, 206, 214–15, 217
totalitarianism, 250
totality
  and language, 5, 6, 11–14
  and metaphysics, 31–32, 34, 271, 286n9
  in Hegel, 96–97, 103, 110, 120
  logic of, 35
trace, xxv, 26, 29, 31, 40, 62, 126, 135, 138, 223
  arche-/originary, 4, 28, 61

instituted, 17, 25–26, 28, 36
  of the trace, 139
  thought of the, 44, 58
traditional, 42, 269–73
  determination of writing, 14–18
tragedy, 282n20
tranquility [ἀταραξια], 67, 70
transcendence
  and justice, 260
  fundamental-ontological, 302n13
  Heidegger's critique of, 270
  leap over, 176
  of Dasein, 169, 302n13
  of transcendence, 158, 175–78
  ontic, 302n13
  ontological, 302n13
  See also borders; boundary; *jenseits/ diesseits*; limits; overcoming; selfsurpassing; transgression
transcendental
  criticism, 61–62, 72
  in Hegel, 95, 99
  logic, 88
  quasi- and ultra-, 28–29, 51, 60–61, 278n11
  signified, 15, 21–22, 286n9
transformation
  and transitional thinking, 172–75, 179–80, 182–84, 190, 193, 203, 207
  of hierarchy, 40
  of the limit, 39
  political, 225–26, 228, 234, 243
transgression, 31, 44, 55, 95, 128, 277n10
transitional thinking, 156, 158, 171, 173, 177–78, 184, 306n15
trembling, xxii, 23, 28, 246. *See also* hesitation
truth
  and empiricism, 54–56
  and falsity, 114
  and first beginning, 188

truth *(continued)*
  as aletheia [ἀλήθεια], 165, 170, 199–200, 206
  as correctness/correspondence vs. (un)concealment, 164–65, 188, 199, 204, 212, 301nn9–10
  in *Being and Time*, 170
  is the whole, 110
  metaphysical determination of (Derrida), 16
  of being, xxxii, 231–33, 235
  of beyng, 157, 173, 175, 181–84, 186, 190, 193–207, 215–17, 271, 305n6
  of skepticism, 68–69
  of the understanding, 105
  origin of (Derrida), 7–9
  progressive unfolding of, 108
  untruth/non-truth of, 203, 205, 224
  vs. truths, xx
  See also concealment; errancy; preservation; sheltering; skepticism; suspension; withdrawal
turning. See *Kehre*
Twilight of the Idols, 228, 307n5
"Tympan," 94, 102, 123, 127–39, 240

unassertive, 182, 197–98, 201, 218, 239. *See also* withdrawal
unavoidable, 38, 40, 74, 90, 158, 186, 192, 207, 221, 224, 251, 261, 264, 266
unconditional, 49, 75–77, 257, 268
undecidability, xxii, 41, 49, 66, 131, 143, 237, 240, 259, 266, 284n12, 288n5, 307n4, 314n2
undeconstructible, 257–62
undercutting, xxii, xxvii, 5, 18, 23, 26, 75
understanding [*Verstand*], 85–103, 106, 109, 114, 116, 120

understanding of being [*Seinsverständnis*]. *See under* being
unfolding. *See under* movement
unity, xxii, 8, 42, 96–98, 105, 111, 115, 120, 298n11, 310n9
University Without Condition, The, 74–77, 249, 259
unpredictable, 43, 286n7. *See also* future
unpresentable, 43, 136, 139
unquestionable, 242, 246, 254
unsaying, 206. *See also* silence
unthinkable, 137
untruth, 203, 205, 224. *See also* truth
unveiling, 224, 231, 240
utopian, xxiv, 65

Vallega-Neu, Daniela, xxvi, 209, 212, 282n23, 304n5
vanity, 116
Verbergung. *See* sheltering
Verhaltenheit. *See* withdrawal
Vernunft. *See* reason
Verschweigung. *See under* silence: reticence
Verstand. *See* understanding
violence, 19, 132, 261
Violence and Metaphysics, 46–47, 54
voice, 16–17, 20, 23, 25, 27, 131, 133
Voice and Phenomenon, 40, 124, 125
vulnerability, xxix, 52, 56, 71, 76–77, 79, 80–81, 266–67, 269. *See also under* deconstruction

wandering, 19, 56, 58, 60, 78, 131, 141, 148, 186, 231. *See also* errancy; truth
way [*Weg*]. *See under* movement
weight, no, xxv, 44, 61
West, the/Western thought, 12, 15, 37, 53, 156, 188, 205, 226, 227, 303n14
What is a Thing?, 73

whole. *See* totality

Wilmore, S.J., 288n5

withdrawal, xxxii, 157, 165, 182, 198–202, 203, 205–6, 214–15, 217, 234, 247, 306n14
  as strategy of protection, 309n9
  refusal, 157
  restraint [*Verhaltenheit*], 182, 195, 198, 209, 213–18, 302n12
  unassertiveness, 182, 197–98, 201, 218, 239
  withholding, 214
  See also being; concealment; forgetfulness of being; preservation; sheltering; silence; truth

withholding. *See under* withdrawal

woman, 222–27, 229, 230–35, 240, 242, 261, 307nn3–4

wonder, 213, 253

Wood, David, 279n15, 283n4

words, 156, 193–98, 201, 202, 209, 210, 244, 271, 305n9, 312n17

world, 166–68, 208, 228. *See also* being-in-the-world

writing, 7
  acts of, 24, 27–28, 30, 144, 225
  arche-/generalized/originary, xxvii, 4, 17–25, 29–30, 33, 36, 44, 265
  debased/repressed/as threat, 7, 16, 17, 19, 24
  derivative/narrow, 17, 23
  exteriorization of, 20
  otherwise, xxviii, 49, 85, 127, 132, 135, 143, 265, 267
  phoneticization of, 7
  science of, 8–10, 43–44 (*see also* grammatology)
  traditional, 14–15, 18

yes, xx, 30, 75, 255–57, 262, 304n6

Zarathustra, 129, 134

Ziarek, Ewa Plonowska, 289n16, 289n24

Ziarek, Krzysztof, 283n23, 306n9

Zusage, 253–57. *See also* commitment; engagement

Zuspiel. *See* interplay

www.ingramcontent.com/pod-product-compliance
Lightning Source LLC
Chambersburg PA
CBHW030126240426
43672CB00005B/32